"Homework for Tuesday the 27th"

We will discuss Tone of essay 136

Lead Essay on

126 no body knows my name

READING
FOR MEANING

Renée
Roberts

READING
FOR MEANING

Halsey P. Taylor

California State Polytechnic University, Pomona

HARCOURT BRACE JOVANOVICH, INC.

New York   Chicago   San Francisco   Atlanta

To my wife, Sheila Flume Taylor

ISBN: 0-15-575634-6

Library of Congress Catalog Card Number: 74-28511

Printed in the United States of America

For Copyrights and Acknowledgments see pages 315-17.

preface

I have designed *Reading for Meaning* for the purpose of teaching college students to *approach questioningly* everything they read, whether the work is an essay in an anthology, a book on a reading list, an assigned or freely selected piece of imaginative literature, or simply an article found in a magazine in a doctor's office. I have paid particular attention, though, to the kinds of reading that students are likely to encounter frequently in college—non-fiction selections developing abstract ideas.

The book demonstrates ways readers can make use of the signals writers employ to direct attention to their ideas and to the development of these ideas in their works. It shows readers how to use a questioning approach in the reading of titles, opening sentences, and key sentences and phrases in the body of a work. Each reading selection in the book provides students with practice in following a writer's development of a thesis (or theme); students are taught to attend to organizational pattern, tone, inferences, and assumptions.

After first demonstrating that one can read even a single expository paragraph questioningly, I introduce Francis Robinson's SQ3R textbook study method in Chapter Two. Then, in later chapters, I demonstrate the ways in which this method can be adapted to the reading of increasingly difficult and subtly developed material.

Reading for Meaning asks students to express in their own words the questions and the stated and implied ideas they find in the selections; it also encourages them to express their reactions to those ideas and to the ways in which they are developed. In other words, students are urged to *think along with* writers. They are shown how to avoid confusing what the writer actually said with what they expected the writer to say. In the supplementary section at the end of each chapter, students will find sample responses that they can compare with their own.

The book, then, may be used by students who work independently, as they do in reading laboratories. But it can also serve as a textbook for group use; the different questions and answers that readers find in the selections will generate fruitful class discussions. In my own reading classes I have had students use the book in both these ways and I have also used it in the early weeks of my composition classes to prepare students for later reading in an essay anthology.

In closing, I wish to thank Deanne Milan of the City College of San Francisco and Glenn Knudsvig of the University of Michigan for their helpful reviews of the manuscript, and the members of a faculty-administration committee on sabbaticals at California Polytechnic for making possible a leave during which I completed this book. I also wish to thank Don Craig, a former colleague who contributed informal, constructive reactions to my work, and, finally, my wife, who served as a sounding board for my ideas throughout the project.

H.P.T.

contents

5 how to preview a non-fiction book   149

6 recognizing main ideas
and organizational patterns in non-fiction   193

7 reading beneath the lines- for tone, inferences, and assumptions   233

8 on reading imaginative literature   279

© 1974 United Feature Syndicate, Inc.

READING
FOR MEANING

how to
read a paragraph

If, as you picked this book up for the first time, you asked yourself, "Why should I read a book with a title like this anyway?" you may be well on your way to developing an important reading skill. And if you checked the table of contents and flipped through the pages to find out how the content of the book supports its title, you have already developed that skill significantly. But if it never occurred to you to do any of these things, don't be surprised.

Most readers do not acquire the skill of reading to answer questions. That is because they ignore some important signals writers use to indicate to the reader the questions they raise and direct his attention to the answers they provide. These signals include the obvious "markers" you probably noticed if you did skim this book for a minute or two—the main title, the titles of chapters, and subheadings. But they also include the more subtle signals that will be the concern of this chapter—*general sentences* stating the main idea of a unit of thought and sentences or phrases *implying* important ideas or points of view.

You may at first find it strange to be asked to regard a general statement or a group of words with a clear implication as a signal to ask a question. But a good way to discover that this method of reading does make sense is to try it out on small units of thought. For that reason, this chapter treats the skill of questioning reading as it applies to the reading of *paragraphs*, particularly the kinds you are most likely to come across in college materials.

FINDING QUESTION-SIGNALS AND MAIN IDEAS IN PARAGRAPHS

A paragraph in Loren Eiseley's *The Unexpected Universe*, for example, begins with this sentence:

> Ours is certainly the most time-conscious generation that has ever lived.

▶ WHAT QUESTION DO YOU THINK THE REST OF THAT PASSAGE WILL ANSWER?

Some questions you might have thought of include:

> *How* (or in what ways) is the statement true?
> *What* are the causes of this condition?
> *Why* does this condition exist?

If you had had the book in your hands so that you could read the paragraph in its context, you would probably have known that the question it answers is the first one. Here is the complete passage:

> Ours is certainly the most time-conscious generation that has ever lived. Our cameras, our television, our archaeological probings, our C^{14} datings, pollen counts, under-water researches, magnetometer readings have resurrected lost cities, placing them accurately in stratigraphic succession. Each Christmas season the art of ice age Lascaux is placed beside that of Rembrandt on our coffee tables. Views of Pompeii share honors with Chichén Itzá upon the television screen in the living room. We unearth obscure ancestral primates and, in the motion picture "2001," watch a struck fragment of bone fly into the air and become a spaceship drifting among the stars, thus telescoping in an instant the whole technological history of man. We expect the average onlooker to comprehend the symbolism; such a civilization, one must assume, should show a deep veneration for the past.
>
> (From *The Unexpected Universe* by Loren Eiseley)

This paragraph, you will notice, gives very specific information (names of people and places and references to specific events and kinds of objects). And all this information points out ways in which our civilization has become time-conscious; in other words, it supports the generalization with which the passage began. To say that a paragraph answers a question is another way of saying that it develops a *topic*, a fact you have probably known since you first wrote topic sentences and expanded them into paragraphs in the sixth or seventh grade.

Certainly the first sentence of the Eiseley passage is a topic sentence; a kind of sentence that often appears at the beginning of a paragraph. However, the first sentence of a paragraph may serve as a question-raising general sentence even when it is not, strictly speaking, a topic sentence.

Consider this one, for example:

> Our love had a somewhat different beginning from the usual love affair of young Communists.

▶ WHAT QUESTION DO YOU EXPECT A PARAGRAPH DEVELOPING FROM THIS BEGINNING TO ANSWER?

You might have expected it to comment on the usual relationship of Communist lovers and to demonstrate how the love of these two people was different. And you will find that it does. But notice what additional information the paragraph includes and observe what the topic turns out to be. Which sentence is the *topic sentence*—that is, either the most *general* one or the sentence that somehow states the *largest* or *most important* idea in the paragraph? (Underline it.)

> Our love had a somewhat different beginning from the usual love affair between young Communists. It was love from the first instant. That is to say, I knew I was a Communist, and she knew she wasn't, and we fell in love not because we saw things alike ideologically, but because we couldn't keep away from each other. At first I thought she found me attractive because of my reputation as a young writer. Other people, particularly women, thought so too. Having sensed that, she ignored, even underestimated, that side of me. At first I was angry, and then pleased—our relationship was developing unencumbered by any strains, uncomplicated and pure.
>
>   (From *Memoir of a Revolutionary* by Milovan Djilas)

Did you recognize the last sentence as the topic sentence? It stresses that the love these two shared was based on their strong personal attractions toward each other and not on anything else—neither on political concerns nor on her admiration of his writing. But the question that the first sentence raised was an

important one. Because you were probably wondering (even if almost unconsciously) what the usual Communist love relationship is like, you were ready for
Djilan's comment that he and his girlfriend experienced a genuine strong emotion. And although Djilan does not explicitly say that most Communists experience instead a kind of intellectual relationship based on shared ideological
interests, he certainly *implies* this idea as an important secondary point.

You will find some paragraphs in which even the main idea is implied rather
than directly stated. For example, the passage below from Ralph Nader's introduction to the book *The Consumer and Corporate Responsibility*, suggests a role
that consumers can play in encouraging Detroit manufacturers to produce better
automobiles. (You would know that he is discussing consumer responsibility for
bringing about improved production if you had read the paragraphs leading up
to this one.) The first sentence is not even a conventionally constructed sentence
(Nader's style is informal throughout), and for that reason it will probably raise
several questions for you rather than simply one. But they will be questions that
the writer wanted you to have in mind as you read the rest of the paragraph.
Use the space below the sentence to record any questions it suggests to you,
even those that you are not at all sure the writer will answer.

> Take for instance, a commonplace observation—the front
> bumper of an automobile.

▶

Now read the remainder of the paragraph to see which of your questions are
answered and to find the implied idea.

> Take, for instance, a commonplace observation—the front
> bumper of an automobile. Nearly everyday most people casually or
> unconsciously look at car bumpers. Their view usually stops there.
> A few moments of consumer education would open the following
> sequence: Bumpers are supposed to protect automobiles from
> minor property damage in minor collisions. For many years, how-
> ever, bumper design has been largely ornamental: bumpers have
> been recessed and of different heights for different models. Much
> needless property damage has resulted when cars bumped or
> crashed at two, three, five, or eight miles per hour. Such damage
> costs U.S. motorists over one billion dollars a year. Insurance
> premiums rise as a consequence. More replacement parts, such as
> fender sectors, grille segments, and headlights have to be produced.

More coal, steel, glass, plastic, and other raw materials must be used, and more electricity and fuel expended. Prices of these commodities mount. Pollution of the air and water increases. What consumers spend on bumper repair, they do not spend on other goods and services which they might otherwise have purchased, and so reduce their standard of living as they would have it. Why did the auto companies design such bumpers? It is obvious that they knew how to do better, judging from the models of some fifty years ago, if not from the last generation's advances in technology. Could it be that the companies profited by faulty design and covered their actions by promoting the aesthetics of egg-shell bumpers? Why not write and ask these companies? Why did the auto insurance companies take so long to expose the facts and criticize the auto industry? Why not write and ask insurance companies, government auto safety agencies, university research institutes, and other sources for facts and viewpoints? Why do auto companies now promise to build more protective bumpers in future vehicles? How did this process of change get underway?

(From *The Consumer and Corporate Responsibility*
by Ralph Nader)

▶ STATE BRIEFLY THE IDEA THAT IS IMPLIED THROUGHOUT THE PARA-
GRAPH AND INDICATE WHICH OF YOUR QUESTIONS IT ANSWERS:

You probably found that this paragraph takes you beyond an answer to your original question, which could have been: "What's wrong with bumpers?" or "Aren't the bumpers of my car all right?" The idea Nader implies here is that if people really observed the bumpers of today's automobiles and thought about how different they are from the car-protecting devices they are supposed to be, they would bombard Detroit with letters of protest that would eventually bring about change. The first sentence prepares the reader to accept this line of thought, but neither that sentence nor any other sentence in the paragraph states the main idea directly.

Even when a paragraph does have one sentence that makes a generalization, that topic sentence does not have to appear either at the beginning or at the end. But if it comes somewhere after the opening sentence, usually the first sentence will raise a question that in some way introduces it. That is true of the following paragraph from *On Aggression* by Konrad Lorenz. As you read this one, underline the topic sentence and notice the relationship between the idea it states and the question the first sentence raises. (Lorenz uses one technical term here—*pseudo-speciation*. It means simply the treatment of other members of one's own species—in this case, humankind—as if they were members of an entirely different species.) You may need to read the passage twice before you can be sure of the topic sentence.

It is perfectly right and legitimate that we should consider as "good" the manners which our parents have taught us, that we should hold sacred the social norms and rites handed down to us by the tradition of our culture. What we must guard against, with all the power of rational responsibility, is our natural inclination to regard the social rites and norms of other cultures as inferior. The dark side of pseudo-speciation is that it makes us consider the members of pseudo-species other than our own as not human, as many primitive tribes are demonstrably doing, in whose language the word for their own particular tribe is synonymous with "Man." From their viewpoint it is not, strictly speaking, cannibalism if they eat the fallen warriors of an enemy tribe. The moral of the natural history of pseudo-speciation is that we must learn to tolerate other cultures, to shed entirely our own cultural and national arrogance, and to realize that the social norms and rites of other cultures, to which their members keep faith as we do to our own, have the same right to be respected and to be regarded as sacred. Without the tolerance born of this realization, it is all too easy for one man to see the personification of all evil in the god of his neighbor, and the very inviolability of rites and social norms which constitutes their most important property can lead to the most terrible of all wars, to religious war—which is exactly what is threatening us today.

(From *On Aggression* by Konrad Lorenz)

▶ WHAT RELATIONSHIP DO YOU SEE BETWEEN THE FIRST SENTENCE AND THE TOPIC SENTENCE?

Did you see that the second sentence is the topic sentence? What it does is answer the question posed by the first sentence: Why should we possibly consider the manners our parents have taught us anything but "good"? And although you may not have said just that, you probably did see that the first sentence makes you wonder why he brings the subject up and the second sentence tells you exactly why.

At this point you may be wondering whether you are supposed to think that every time you begin reading a paragraph you should slow down enough to consciously ask yourself a question before you go on. The answer, of course, is No. Often you will find that the ideas of paragraphs flow together to answer a general question you have had in mind since before you began to read the work as a whole. And you may be nearly unconscious or completely unconscious of the question-answering function of individual paragraphs as you read them. Nevertheless, most paragraphs are structured so that they answer questions that are parts of a larger one. And sometimes in your reading you will find it helpful to pause at the beginning of a paragraph and ask yourself what specific question the first sentence suggests. Through the practice you are getting in this chapter, you are learning how to do this when you need to. But perhaps even more important, you are developing a questioning attitude that will make it possible for you to find meaning in paragraphs and in larger units of thought in much of your reading without any deliberate analysis at all.

PARAGRAPHS FOR PRACTICE

For each of the following paragraphs, (1) indicate the question the first sentence suggests to you; (2) state briefly in your own words the most important information the paragraph provides in answering that question; and (3) underline any topic sentences, that is, statements of the main idea. (That idea may be implied, as you have seen, or it may be stated in more than one topic sentence. If the idea is implied, make this clear in your summary.) The first sentence is not separated from the others, but it will probably be a good idea to fill in the space for "Question the first sentence suggests" before you read the rest of the paragraph. When you have given your answers, turn to the Chapter Supplement (pp. 12–14) for some comments to compare with yours.

1. With the coming of the V-2 to America a new chapter, or even a new volume, began for a fairly old science. This was the science which had more or less begun some three centuries ago when Monsieur Perier carried a barometer up a mountainside in France to see whether the air pressure would really drop. "Man," a famous biologist phrased it at a much later date, "is a creature which inhabits the bottom of the air ocean." True enough, but he should have added that Man, although he didn't actually dislike his environment, has always been possessed by the desire to leave the bottom of the air ocean, to get into the air ocean itself, and, if at all possible, above it, to see what space is like. The V-2 was Man's first chance to do this, even if, for a beginning, the rockets merely served as Man's messengers with their operators resigned to stay planet-bound at the bottom for a little while longer, until they were certain of the natural facts they would encounter higher up. To find out Man needed remote sensing organs—called instruments—which not only could be more sensitive than his natural organs but which also could detect and measure things like magnetism.

In addition to such organs, Man needed a mechanical messenger which would carry them to places where Man could not or would not yet go himself.

(From *Rockets, Missiles, and Men in Space* by Willy Ley)

▶   QUESTION THE FIRST SENTENCE SUGGESTS:

▶   SUMMARY OF PARAGRAPH:

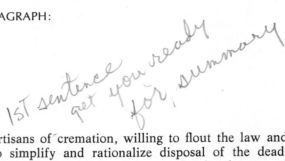

1st sentence get you ready for, summary

2. The early partisans of cremation, willing to flout the law and imprisonment to simplify and rationalize disposal of the dead, would whirl in their urns could they but see what has become of their favorite cause today in America. For cremation, like every other aspect of the disposal of the dead, has long since been taken over by the funeral industry, which prescribes the procedures to be followed and establishes its own regulations to which the customers must adhere. Therefore, he who seeks to avoid the purchase of a casket, embalming and the full treatment will not succeed by the mere fact of choosing cremation rather than burial. Also, he is much more likely to end up in an urn housed in a niche in an elaborate "Columbarium," complete with Perpetual Care, than to be scattered or privately buried in some favorite country spot.
(From *The American Way of Death* by Jessica Mitford)

▶   QUESTION THE FIRST SENTENCE SUGGESTS:

▶   SUMMARY OF PARAGRAPH:

3. All the objectively observable characteristics of the goose's behavior on losing its mate are roughly identical with those accompanying human grief. This applies particularly to the phenomena

observable in the sympathetic nervous system. John Bowlby, in his study of infant grief, has given an equally convincing and moving description of this primal grieving, and it is almost incredible how detailed are the analogies we find here in human beings and in birds. Just as in the human face, it is the neighborhood of the eyes that in geese bears the permanent marks of deep grief. The lowering of the tonus in the sympathicus causes the eye to sink back deeply in its socket and, at the same time, decreases the tension of the outer facial muscles supporting the eye region from below. Both factors contribute to the formation of a fold of loose skin below the eye which as early as in the ancient Greek mask of tragedy had become the conventionalized expression of grief. My dear old greylag Ada, several times a widow, was particularly easy to recognize because of the grief-marked expression of her eyes. A knowledgeable visitor who knew nothing about Ada's history standing beside at the lake suddenly pointed her out among many geese, saying, "That goose must have been through a lot!"

(From *On Aggression* by Konrad Lorenz)

▶ QUESTION THE FIRST SENTENCE SUGGESTS:

▶ SUMMARY OF PARAGRAPH:

4. Most of us were brought up to believe that talking is merely a tool which something deeper called "thinking" puts to work. Thinking, we have assumed, depends on laws of reason and logic common to all mankind. These laws are said to be implicit in the mental machinery of humans, whether they speak English or Choctaw. Languages, it follows, are simply parallel methods for expressing this universal logic. On this assumption it also follows that any logical idea can be translated unbroken, or even unbent, into any language. A few minutes in the glass palace of the United Nations in New York will quickly disabuse one of this quaint notion. Even such a common concept as "democracy" may not survive translation.

(From *Power of Words* by Stuart Chase)

▶ QUESTION THE FIRST SENTENCE SUGGESTS:

▶ SUMMARY OF PARAGRAPH:

5. Let us return to our hypothetical Mr. Miller, who has been introduced as a "Jew." To a person for whom these affective connotations are very much alive, and who habitually confuses what is inside his head with what is outside, Mr. Miller is a man "not to be trusted." If Mr. Miller succeeds in business, that "proves" that "Jews are smart;" if Mr. Johansen succeeds in business, it only proves that Mr. Johansen is smart. If Mr. Miller fails in business, it is alleged that he nevertheless has "money salted away somewhere." If Mr. Miller is strange or foreign in his habits, that "proves" that "Jews don't assimilate." If he is thoroughly American—i.e., indistinguishable from other natives—he is "trying to pass himself off as one of us." If Mr. Miller fails to give to charity, that is because "Jews are tight;" if he gives generously, he is "trying to buy his way into society." If Mr. Miller lives in the Jewish section of town, that is because "Jews are so clannish;" if he moves to a locality where there are no other Jews, that is because "they try to horn in everywhere." In short, Mr. Miller is automatically condemned, no matter who he is or what he does.

(From *Language in Thought and Action* by S. I. Hayakawa)

▶ QUESTION THE FIRST SENTENCE SUGGESTS:

▶ SUMMARY OF PARAGRAPH:

6. The task of confining the gypsy moth to the northeastern corner of the country has been accomplished by a variety of methods, and in the nearly one hundred years since its arrival on this continent the fear that it would invade the great hardwood forests of the southern Appalachians has not been justified. Thirteen parasites and predators were imported from abroad and successfully established in New England. The Agriculture Department itself has credited these importations with appreciably reducing the frequency and destructiveness of gypsy moth outbreaks. This natural control, plus quarantine measures and local spraying, achieved what the Department in 1955 described as "outstanding restriction of distribution and damage."

(From *Silent Spring* by Rachel Carson)

The question not the answer

▶ QUESTION THE FIRST SENTENCE SUGGESTS:

1sT n HsT

(my guess 1sT n 2nd) however I was influenced by the answer in the back of books

▶ SUMMARY OF PARAGRAPH:

7. One might surmise that in general publishing, given the fact that manuscripts are usually submitted in complete form and given, also, the presumption that an author (rather than an editor) has chosen a subject and has by himself brought it to fulfillment, there would be little need for the intervention of editors in the actual process of writing. But this is too simple a view of publishing—and of writing. Even the most accomplished writer may demand an intimate attention from his editor. Cyril Connolly, in speaking of Thomas Wolfe and his editor, Maxwell Perkins, found it "unnecessary to point out that American publishers are a dedicated group: they are loyal, generous and infinitely painstaking; they live for their authors and not for social climbing or the books they want to write themselves; they know how to be confessors, solicitors, auditors and witch doctors. . . ." Writing is the loneliest of professions, and the writer, like all artists, tends to exhaust his personal resources: in the dialogue between the writer and the reader there is an uneven exchange, for what enriches the one has depleted the other. (Alberto Moravia, in *Conjugal Love,* symbolizes the fears of a writer that he must preserve himself in order to

3rd

create; the hero denies himself his wife's bed.) If a writer must borrow assistance, or merely encouragement, then it would seem natural that he turn to an editor who can be expected to be not only sympathetic but also suitably knowledgeable. For the editor this is flattering but dangerous, for he must decide at what point assistance becomes interference.

(From *Now Barabbas* by William Jovanovich)

▶ QUESTION THE FIRST SENTENCE SUGGESTS:

▶ SUMMARY OF PARAGRAPH:

You may have some information in your summaries that was not included in the summaries in the supplement, and some of the points mentioned there may not have seemed important to you. The relative importance of each of the parts of the small body of information a paragraph contains is certainly a debatable point. But what is significant is the discovery you probably made that with a question in mind from the beginning, you could understand and remember more of the content of a short reading selection than you thought you could. The next chapter will show you how to apply this discovery to a more typical college reading project—an assigned chapter in a textbook.

CHAPTER SUPPLEMENT

I. Comments on "Paragraphs for Practice"

1. *Topic sentence:* The first sentence.

    Question: How has that old science changed?—or something to that effect. (Probably an important secondary question would be: What is that science?)

    Summary: The invention of the V-2 made possible later developments in rocketry that eventually led to the exploration of space. For this reason, it was an especially important event in the history of a science that began when man first learned how to measure the pressure of the earth's atmosphere. The science Ley refers to is, then, meteorology—the study of the earth's atmosphere —but his point is that V-2 helped man accomplish goals far beyond those of the early meteorologists; its development prepared him to explore what lies *beyond* the earth's atmosphere.

2. *Topic sentence:* The second sentence.

   Question: Why would the early crusaders for cremation be unhappy if they were alive today? (The second sentence answers this question quite directly.)

   Summary: People who request cremation will be supporting the mortuary business more than they may intend to because their families will find that they have to buy caskets, pay for embalming, and go through the same procedures that are required when the body is to be buried.

3. *Topic sentence:* The first sentence.

   Question: In what ways does a goose's expression of grief resemble that of a human being?

   Summary: When geese experience mate-loss they develop folds under their eyes that make them look much like grieving human beings.

4. *Topic sentence:* There is none; the idea is implied throughout the pargaraph.

   Question: Isn't talking simply a tool for thinking? If not, what is the relationship of language and thought?

   Summary: The point the author makes in this paragraph (and he makes it only indirectly) is that the thoughts of speakers of different languages differ, and for that reason some thoughts are not translatable. He first implies this idea in the second sentence when he says: "Thinking, we have assumed, depends on laws of reason and logic common to all mankind." His use of the word "assumed" implies that he is going to deny this proposition.

5. *Topic sentence:* The last one. (The reason the last sentence is a topic sentence is that all the details in the paragraph showing what would happen if Mr. Miller did this or that build up to the final and general statement: "Mr. Miller is automatically condemned. . . .")

   Question: This one is not as definite as the others, but your question might have been: Why was Mr. Miller introduced as a "Jew?" and certainly that question would start you thinking on the track the writer wants you to be on.

   Summary: Everything that Mr. Miller does is held against him because people find a way of making his actions fit their stereotype of "Jew."

6. *Topic sentence:* Probably the first sentence and the last one should both be considered topic sentences since each generalizes about the success of the program of confining the gypsy moth.

   Question: How has the gypsy moth been "confined"?

   Summary: Various enemies of the gypsy moth have been imported and "planted" in New England, its habitat so far. These natural enemies have kept its numbers down enough so that it has not been able to migrate to the south, where it could destroy valuable hardwood forests.

7. *Topic sentence:* The third sentence.

Question: What role does an editor play in the preparation of a manuscript?

Summary: The editor must decide how much help will really be constructive for a particular author and then give that amount of help.

how to
tackle a textbook

You have a reading style that is in some ways all your own. And you always will have, even after you have learned to adapt to complete works the paragraph-reading skill you learned in the last chapter. That is just as it should be, for reading—or at least "college" reading—is a much more complex matter than talking on the telephone or driving a car or writing a letter, and it is clear enough that people have individual ways of doing these things. Also, reading is usually a private activity. Except for the rare occasions when you read aloud, no one else will ever know much about what happens in your mind when you react to printed symbols. Surely, then, no one can tell you exactly what should be happening. All that a book like this one can do is point out approaches to college reading that have worked for other people (or for readers they have known) and then let you discover for yourself how useful these techniques are to you. In this book the "other people" are the author, his students, other teachers of reading and literature, and educational psychologists who have looked into the study-reading habits of college students.

It may be best to begin with what the psychologists have to say about *text-*

book study because this is the least personal sort of reading you will be asked to do in college. That is, it is the sort for which a set of recommended procedures is most likely to "work" for you in much the same way that it does for the next student. Then later chapters will consider ways you can combine some of these techniques with others (some of them quite "personal") as you continue to develop a flexible reading style that will be appropriate for the various kinds of reading you will be doing in the years ahead.

THE SQ3R TEXTBOOK STUDY METHOD

Textbook writers often design their books with a particular kind of reader-response in mind. At least that is the opinion of people who have carefully examined a wide variety of textbooks and analyzed the study practices of successful students. One of these investigators, an educational psychologist named Francis Robinson, developed a technique that he found to be particularly effective for the textbooks and the students of the early 1940s. Through the years since that time many students have attributed improved course work and reduced study time to learning the technique of "SQ3R"-ing a textbook chapter. Mastery of the SQ3R method may do as much for you.

In spite of its mysterious and mathematical-sounding label, the plan consists of five very simple (but not necessarily obvious) steps:

1. S—*Survey* the entire chapter to get an idea of its scope and direction. Instead of reading through any portion completely, check for signals the writer has provided to focus your attention on especially important ideas and information. These will probably include a few introductory sentences and *subheadings* and they may include a *chapter outline*, key words in *boldface print*, and a *summary* or *review* section.
2. Q—Ask a *question* that you expect the first section of the chapter to answer. (Use the first subheading as the source for your question; that is, turn it into a question.)
3. R—*Read* the first section, looking for an answer to your question.
4. R—*Recite* the various parts of the answer to the question. (Steps 2, 3, and 4 are then repeated on all sections of the chapter.)
5. R—*Review* the entire chapter, making certain that you understand how the various parts go together.

The method works best on texts that follow the design which Robinson found to be standard in 1942—and many of today's texts do use that form. In these books, chapters are divided into short, easily managed sections, each of which has a *subheading* clearly indicating the ground to be covered in that part. The last part of each chapter is a *summary* or *review* section. Throughout the chapter there are often *graphic aids* to help the reader understand and remember the *factual information* presented.

Take a look at the books on your shelf and see how many of them fit the above description. Some you could probably lay aside simply from a glance at the title. Books with titles like *Rudy's Red Wagon* and *A New Radical's Guide to Economic Reality* will probably not present "factual information" in neatly arranged segments, each with an appropriate subheading; and they will almost certainly not contain "summary" sections. Many of the books that are assigned in classes today are more informally written and more openly expressive of the writer's personality than were the textbooks of thirty years ago. But for some courses and for certain purposes the traditional format is still appropriate, and you will probably find books in your collection that follow it quite closely. If you happen to have a current chapter assignment in a text of this kind, try applying to it at least step one—*surveying* the chapter—as you understand it from the brief description on page 16. (This step should not take more than two or three minutes.) Then turn to Chapter Supplement I (p. 25) and survey in the same way the chapter from Kagan and Havemann's *Psychology: An Introduction*, a widely studied text that is used in the following sections to demonstrate the five steps in the SQ3R study plan.

Step One: Surveying (or Previewing)

As you surveyed either chapter, did you find yourself tempted to read through word for word from the beginning of the chapter instead of just quickly reading the introductory paragraph, noting the subheadings in the main part of the chapter, and skimming through the conclusion? If so, you are in good company, for many students—especially very conscientious ones—are uncomfortable doing anything else with words on the printed page. But that's not surveying—or previewing as Robinson might just as well have called it.

When you *survey* or *preview* a short non-fiction work, you check it over (or skim it) *before* reading it through to see where the title and other key parts are taking you. In surveying a textbook chapter, it is usually a good idea to look for at least a tentative, general *answer to the question implied by the title* (for example, what is the scope and what are the goals of psychology?), and for the *range* or *scope* of the chapter, the *points of emphasis*, an *underlying idea* (if there is one), and the *organizational pattern*—although you will not necessarily put it this formally to yourself. As Robinson points out, conventional textbooks are set up in a way that makes this kind of pre-reading easy; the subheadings and the summary section can be especially helpful.

Try surveying the chapter from *Psychology: An Introduction* again. (Through the rest of this step-by-step treatment of SQ3R you will be moving back and forth between Chapter Supplement I and the main part of the chapter.) Again, limit yourself to two or three minutes; concentrate on getting an overview of the chapter, not on learning specific details. This time be sure to make use of the study aids that are provided—the chapter outline on the first page, the three levels of subheadings in the body of the chapter, and the itemized summary at the end. (When a summary or review section is as long and as thorough as this one is, you probably will not need to read it all the way through when you survey; by skimming it you should be able to find a few words and phrases that will remind you of points you picked up earlier.)

In the space below, state your impression of the direction the chapter will take. (If the terms "range" or "scope," "points of emphasis," "organizational pattern," and "underlying idea" seem appropriate, try them out; otherwise simply use your own language to anticipate what will be in the chapter.) You will surely want to look for an answer to the question inspired by the title.

▶

After you have noted what you found in your survey, compare your observations with those in Chapter Supplement II (p. 58). You may not have found exactly the same clues in your previewing, and you probably did not state the approach of the chapter in exactly the same way. But the chances are good that you got enough out of that two minutes of "pre-reading" to make the next important step very easy for you.

Step Two: Questioning

The subheadings used liberally by most writers of textbooks can easily be converted into questions. Each section with a subheading usually represents a division of the chapter topic that the writer considers important enough to be treated separately. Therefore, Robinson suggests that after the student surveys the chapter, he should take up each section in turn, converting the subheading into a question and then reading to find the answer to that question. Steps two and three, then, are closely related.

To begin finding out how this second step works, try framing questions for the major subheadings of the Kagan-Havemann chapter; they are listed below. Many of these headings make clear that the question to be answered is simply: What is it? (or What are they?) But before you decide that the question a heading suggests is as general as this, quickly preview the section following it again to see if you can find any obvious clues (like italicized phrases and second- or third-level subheadings) indicating a more specific topic. Subheadings, like titles, should always be compared with other signals that follow them. After you have finished, check Chapter Supplement III (p. 58) for some questions to compare with yours.

▶ SUBHEADING   QUESTION

A Definition of Psychology

The History of Psychology

The Methods of Psychology

Applications of Psychology

Psychology and Social Problems

Step Three: Reading

For each of the textbooks you study from—or at least those that provide as many study aids as the Kagan Havemann chapter does—you will need to decide for yourself whether the sections you should use for step three are those following the major headings or those coming after subordinate headings. For the chapter you just previewed, it makes sense to regard the major divisions as units for study since there are many of them and since the subordinate sections cover relatively little ground. Try using step three with the section headed "Applications of Psychology" (p. 46). Put your question for this subheading (or one of the questions the Chapter Supplement suggests for it) in the space below and then read the section to find out to what extent and in what ways the question is answered.

▶

Was any information you expected to find not included here? If you asked a very general question (like "What are the applications of psychology?") you may have been expecting some points that are treated in the next section instead —for example, facts about the ways psychology can help you understand personal and social problems. But if you had in mind a question that covered only the ground indicated by the second-level subheadings (that is, one about the *methods* psychologists use to solve these problems) you were prepared for the writers' treatment of what psychologists call "applied psychology." And, whether you knew it or not, you were preparing yourself for an examination question such as: In what sense is psychology an applied science? (You may be surprised to find how often your subheading questions turn up in exams, although the wording of the test questions may be somewhat different from yours.)

Step Four: Recitation

In step four, you take a brief set of notes on the chapter section just completed, including both general and specific points. If that doesn't sound like "reciting" to you, you can call the procedure anything you like. The point is that you are encouraged not to worry about (or "recite") the specific information you think you will have to know for an examination until *after* you have read a chapter section through once. To check your memory, and above all to convince yourself that you *can* remember what you read *purposefully*, it is a good idea to begin these notes with your book closed. They should be as brief and to the point as possible. Many students waste time and energy taking lengthy notes without distinguishing between key points and relatively minor ones. (For example, did you ever start to buy a used textbook in which you found that four-fifths of the lines on every page were underlined?) One way to keep your notes short and pithy is to use phrases rather than complete sentences; a topic outline form with major and minor subheadings and with a main idea or thesis statement at the top (if you find one) can often be helpful.

For the section you just read, try taking notes that might prepare you for an exam in a psychology class. Use the purposely small space on the page below, but do not overlook important details. See what you can do with your book closed; that way you will be sure to use your own words. You will probably be surprised to find how much you recall. It is a good idea to try first to remember the divisions represented by the second-level subheadings. These can become the major (I, II, III) headings in an outline, and then you can fill in details under these headings as you remember them.

▶

When you check the text again to see if your notes are complete and accurate, you will of course want to add any important points you omitted. However, the more you practice reading "SQ3R" style, the more information you will probably remember before checking back to the text.

After you have finished putting down the ideas and the details you think are important, turn to Chapter Supplement IV (p. 59), where you will find an outline that pays particular attention to information the writers emphasize through their use of organizational signals (secondary subheadings and italicized words and phrases). After you have compared your notes with the outline, go back to the beginning of the sample chapter and study the other sections in turn, again taking brief notes in your own words. No models are provided in the supplement for these sections because you are encouraged to work out your own style of note-taking.

▶   A DEFINITION OF PSYCHOLOGY

▶   THE HISTORY OF PSYCHOLOGY

▶   THE METHODS OF PSYCHOLOGY

▶ PSYCHOLOGY AND SOCIAL PROBLEMS

Step Five: Reviewing

The last step, a quick review of the content of the entire chapter, is important for two reasons: it provides a final check on your memory, and it sharpens your understanding of the way the various pieces of information you have been acquiring fit together. Try reviewing the notes you have just taken. To test your recall, cover up parts of the notes or have someone ask you questions. A test of recall of your notes is a good way to prepare for chapter examinations. To be sure you have not only mastered the content of the chapter but also understood how the generalizations and details included relate to an underlying idea, you can think back to your survey. Does the information you have in your notes answer the question implied by the title? If not, what question, if any, is answered? Are you sure you can remember this information and present it as you will be asked to do in an exam? Then your SQ3R approach to a textbook chapter has been completed—with one exception, which is treated in the next part.

POINT OF VIEW IN TEXTBOOKS

The SQ3R method was designed to help students learn how to acquire information easily and quickly for the purpose of doing well on examinations. Certainly it is important for college students to acquire this skill. But it may have occurred to you that *information* often gets tangled up with opinion, or *point of view*. Although it is customary to talk about textbooks as if they were simply conveyors of "factual information," many textbooks clearly express the point of view of those who wrote them. That is, they do if you know what to look for.

Two points you can look for are the *kinds of information* a textbook writer gives about a subject and the *kinds of language* he uses to talk about that subject. Consider, for example, the section on the history of psychology in the chapter you just read. When you took notes on that section, were you aware that the paragraphs on extra-sensory perception, or ESP (pp. 32–33), presented a point of view? Read those paragraphs again and this time underline any words or phrases having negative connotations for you that are used to refer to the study of ESP. Also, comment in the space below on the information the writers give about ESP and the psychologists who are studying it. Would you expect to find the same points in a text by a psychologist who regards the study of ESP favorably?

▶

You might have underlined *rather mysterious means*; *possessor or creature of unproved forces*, and even *mainstream of psychological investigation* (because the implication is that the study of ESP lies outside it). Did you notice that the treatment of research in ESP minimizes its importance and stresses the small number of psychologists who are doing it? Perhaps you wondered how small the "minority" is and who some of these researchers are. How do you think an introductory text written by a psychologist actively engaged in ESP research would have treated the same topic?

The authors of *Psychology: An Introduction* make clear throughout the chapter that psychologists differ in their professional opinions and approaches; therefore, you should not have been very surprised to find the writers identifying themselves directly and openly with one group of psychologists on the issue of ESP. But you will discover that some textbook writers express points of view in much less direct ways. For instance, you might expect that a manual-type textbook—for example, a book on methods of gardening or a driver's training handbook—would be simply a list of rules or directions or procedures. But if the gardening text were written by someone who believed strongly in the exclusive use of organic fertilizer, wouldn't his attitude on this subject be apparent in his work? And some driver's training texts assume that the best way to learn is to begin with a car that has an automatic transmission. If your high school instructor followed such an approach, weren't you learning to drive under the influence of a point of view?

There is nothing sinister about all this. Textbook writers have as much right to hold points of view—and to express them in their work—as anyone else. But you should be aware of the necessity to read textbooks, like all other material, with a critical eye.

You will need to decide for yourself how to combine consideration of a textbook writer's point of view with your use of the SQ3R method. One way is to make a search for point of view a part of each of the five steps. For example, your question for the Kagan-Havemann chapter could become: What do these writers think is the legitimate scope and what do they believe are the proper goals of psychology? Then each of your subheading questions would also have something to do with the writers' opinions: What do they think are the most important events in the history of psychology? And so on. In studying any chapter, if you start questioning point of view directly, you will be looking for it as you read, review, and recite.

Another method would be to go through the SQ3R procedure as outlined earlier, but keep the question of point of view in the back of your mind. Then you could go back over the chapter to check your earlier impressions.

Blank spaces are provided below for you to write down your comments as you try SQ3R-ing one of your own textbooks with particular attention to recognizing the writer's point of view. It will be a good idea to choose a textbook on a subject other than psychology but one that makes use of many of the study aids you found in the textbook you just studied.

▶ STEP ONE: SURVEYING

▶ STEP TWO: QUESTIONING

▶ STEP THREE: READING

▶ STEP FOUR: RECITATION

▶ STEP FIVE: REVIEWING

You will find that your method of using SQ3R will vary at least slightly from textbook to textbook as you adjust not only to different ways of handling point of view but to different writing styles and variations in format. (Formal summary sections, for example, are not as common as they once were, even in basically "conventional" textbooks.) And you may have already discovered that books in different fields require different sorts of "reading" and "reciting." (If you used for the last project a book in one of the sciences or in a technical study, did you find that you needed more detailed notes than you took for the Kagan-Havemann chapter?) But the SQ3R method presented in this chapter provides at least a good starting point as you work out a college textbook study style that is effective for you. As later chapters will show, it also provides you with a framework for the development of other important reading skills.

CHAPTER SUPPLEMENTS

I. Chapter One, "The Scope and Goals of Psychology," from Psychology: An Introduction by Jerome Kagan and Ernest Havemann

Note: Throughout this chapter you will find references to figures that were in Psychology: An Introduction as it was originally published but that could not be reproduced here. These references should be ignored; they are not necessary for the purposes of the exercises in this chapter.

OUTLINE

A DEFINITION OF PSYCHOLOGY, 27

The Variety of Human Behavior/How Psychology Views Behavior/Some Other Influences on Behavior/The Goals of Psychology

THE HISTORY OF PSYCHOLOGY, 31

Wilhelm Wundt and His Laboratory/Francis Galton and Measurement/William James's "Science of Mental Life"/John Watson, Behaviorist/S-R Psychology and B. F. Skinner/Some New Schools of Psychology/Sigmund Freud and Psychoanalysis

CHAPTER 1
THE SCOPE AND GOALS
OF PSYCHOLOGY

Although the science of psychology is only about a century old, the word *psychology* has become one of the most popular in the English language. People often say they "use psychology" to get a job or a raise or to talk parents into a larger allowance. They talk about striking at the "psychological moment." When a friend starts behaving strangely, they say he has a "psychological problem." To judge by the number of times the word is used in everyday conversation, one might suppose that everybody who speaks English knows exactly what it means.

Yet, in actual fact, the science of psychology is quite different from what most people believe it to be, and often its findings are contrary to what people have generally taken for granted about human nature. Many people, for example, pride themselves on being "good psychologists" who can size up another man just by looking at him and can judge the other man's feelings by studying his facial expressions. Scientific investigation has proved that this is not easy at all. If you and your friends try to match the faces with the personalities of the people in Figure 1–1, you will probably find that none of you have much success. You will probably have the same trouble guessing the emotions that are being expressed in Figure 1–2.

By the time a student arrives at college he has usually been tested and retested in numerous ways—for intelligence, mechanical skill, mathematical ability, and various kinds of vocational aptitude. He has also seen many other tests in newspapers and magazines; he has been invited to score himself as an introvert or an extrovert, an optimist or a pessimist, a good marriage prospect or a bad one. Thus many students think of psychology as being first of all the source for tests of all kinds of human traits and abilities. This is partly true, for tests have been devised that are good predictors of school grades, musical performance, and ability to work efficiently as an accountant or an electronics engineer or a hospital nurse. But testing is only one small part of psychology. And many of the tests seen in newspapers and magazines have no scientific value at all; they are merely parlor games. A psychologist would want to know a lot more than can be revealed by a few true-false questions before he would attempt to assess your personality or try to predict how you might succeed at such a complicated human relationship as marriage.

Many people believe that psychology provides some magic answers that will enable them to solve their own personal problems, advise others, and indeed manipulate the behavior of others to their own advantage. Again this is partly true, for psychologists have learned a great deal about the human personality and methods of relieving personality problems; they also have come to understand many of the factors that influence behavior and how behavior can often be changed by varying these factors. But even the best-trained psychologists, after many years of study and experience, do not claim to perform any magic. A psychologist who tries to help a person solve his personality difficulties knows that it may take a long time even to understand the problems, much less do anything to relieve them. Moreover, as the book will make clear, human behavior springs from so many complicated sources that it is very difficult for a person to understand why he himself behaves as he does, much less to understand and influence the behavior of someone else.

A DEFINITION OF PSYCHOLOGY

Some students are so surprised by the content of an introductory psychology course that they have a hard time getting the "feel" of the subject; they keep looking for what they had expected to find and fail to appreciate what is actually there. If you approach the subject with an open mind and are prepared to enjoy being surprised, you will have a much easier and more rewarding time.

What then is psychology really like? As the poet Alexander Pope wrote, "The proper study of mankind is man"—and one way to start trying to define psychology would be as the science that studies man. But this is only a partial definition. Psychology also studies lower animals; it is interested in the behavior of all living creatures, which it designates by the scientific term *organisms*. Indeed comparative psychology, which is the study of organisms other than man in an effort to find comparisons with human behavior, is a flourishing branch of the science—partly because the psychologist can perform experiments with lower animals that it would be unethical to attempt with human beings (for example, the removal of parts of the brain to discover what role these brain structures play in behavior). Moreover, in the case of human beings, psychology is interested not only in behavior but also in patterns of brain activity such as thinking and feelings.

Perhaps the best possible definition of psychology is this: *Psychology is the science that systematically studies and attempts to explain observable behavior and its relationship to the unseen mental processes that go on inside the organism and to external events in the environment.*

The Variety of Human Behavior

The definition covers an almost breathtaking range of subject matter. To demonstrate the great variety of human behavior and mental processes—and at the same time to introduce some of the major topics covered in this book—let us examine how a college woman might have started this day, from the time she woke up until the time she arrived at her first class.

She wakens quickly at the sound of the alarm, turns off the clock, and turns on the light in her room. Looking out a window for signs of the weather, she notes that the sky is cloudy. For further information she turns on the radio. But she has just missed the weather report, so she dials the telephone number of a friend who is always up early. The friend says there is only a 15 percent chance of rain, and she decides to ignore it when she chooses her clothes for the day.

She eats breakfast, gathers her notebooks, and goes to her car. As she starts the engine she sees that the gas is low and makes a note to stop at a filling station. Backing out of the driveway, she waits for two children who are walking by, then for a mail truck. She stops for a traffic light, turns into the street she usually takes to school, finds it blocked off for repairs, and proceeds to an alternate route. The lot in which she usually parks is filled; so she goes to a different one. Since she does not know the quickest route to her classroom from this lot, she asks another student who is getting out of a car. The directions are complicated—turn left after a block, then right, then cut across a corner of the campus—but she has no trouble following them and is in her usual seat when the class starts. As her instructor begins his lecture, she listens to the words and takes notes. An observer would see nothing but the movement of her pen, yet obviously a great deal of mental processing is going on as she decides which of the words are the key ideas and translates them into her language.

And so the day begins. It is still very early in the morning of a more or less typical day in the life of a more or less typical student. Yet what a remarkable amount of activity has already occurred!

In this age of electronic computers it has become fashionable to admire the speed and precision of the computers and, conversely, to take a somewhat disparaging view of human capabilities. The computer can add and multiply faster than any human being; it can guide spaceships to the moon and to Mars. Why then should we not concede that the human being is a poor rival to the computer and rapidly becoming obsolete? Why should we bother studying the psychology of a human machine that is so overshadowed by the electronic machine?

The young woman, waking and going to school, gives us the answer. She demonstrates that the electronic machine, for all its brilliant accomplishments, does not as yet begin to approach the skill and versatility of the human machine.

Note all the very complicated "inputs" that our human machine has received in the course of the early morning: the sounds of the alarm clock, the radio, the telephone, the instructions on how to walk to the classroom, and the lecture; the sights of the sky, the traffic and traffic signals, and the blocked roadway. Note all the "data processing" she has done: making the decisions on what to wear, to take an alternate route to the campus, to park in an alternate lot. And note how many complicated actions she performed: dressing, eating, driving a car, asking directions, walking to the classroom, taking lecture notes. The more one studies it, the more one is forced to marvel at its intricate workings.

How Psychology Views Behavior

To the psychologist, the young woman's activities on this early morning fall into several categories that form prominent divisions of the subject matter of the science and of this book. For example, her movements while dressing and driving her car represented skills she did not have when she was born but instead acquired through learning; this important process and the rules it follows are the subject of Chapters 2, 3, and 4. Finding her usual route to the campus blocked presented her with a problem that she immediately surmounted by taking an alternate street—but though her decision seemed easy and indeed almost automatic, it actually required a great deal of complicated mental activity of the kind described in Chapter 5 ("Language, Thinking, and Problem Solving").

Her inputs of sounds and sights depended on her sense organs, in this case her ears and eyes, and the way they respond to the environment and send messages to her brain, as will be explained in Chapter 6 ("The Senses"). Out of the messages from her sense organs she organized meaningful patterns of what was happening in the world around her, as will be explained in Chapter 7 ("Perception"). Her sleeping and eating were responses to biological drives, representing a combination of physiological needs and brain activity, that demanded satisfaction; the drives and how they influence behavior are discussed in Chapter 10 ("Drives and Motives").

Some Other Influences on Behavior

Even if the topics mentioned up to now were the only forms of behavior and mental activity, psychology would constitute a rich field of study. But there is a good deal more, as can be seen if we compare this young woman with another woman in her class. Let us say that both student A and student B are the same age. They come from much the same kinds of families and went to the very same high school. On their College Boards, which are a kind of intelligence test that measures ability to succeed in college, they made about the same scores (see Figure 1–3).

Miss A.	BACKGROUND	Miss B.
18	Age	18
Excellent	Health	Excellent
None	Physical defects	None
Mechanic	Father	T.V. repairman
Nurse	Mother	Store clerk
San Pedro H.S.	High school	San Pedro H.S.
	COLLEGE BOARD SCORES	
542	Verbal	545
521	Math	519
	RECORD IN COLLEGE	
C's	Grades	A's and B's
Marriage	Ambition	Career
Few, but close	Friends	Many
Yes	Seeks advice?	No
Apologetic	Usual response to criticism	Angry

There the resemblance ends. Student A is content to get C's in her courses; her special ambition is to become a wife and mother; she likes to spend her spare time reading or in the quiet company of a few close friends; she often seeks advice; she seldom says an unkind word about anyone; if she is criticized, she tends to become flustered and to apologize. Student B, on the other hand, studies hard and usually makes A's and B's; her ambition is to be a lawyer; she is usually surrounded by friends; she shuns advice; she is frequently sarcastic and insulting; if she is criticized she strikes back.

These two young women have the same biological drives and have had very similar opportunities for learning; they have an approximately equal capacity for thinking and problem solving; their sense organs operate in much the same ways. Why, then, are they so different?

One reason is that human beings vary in the kinds of events that trigger emotions such as fear and anger and in the way they display their emotions, as will be explained in Chapter 9. Moreover, human behavior springs from a variety of motives. As will be discussed in Chapter 10, all of us as we grow up acquire through the learning process a number of motives or desires that we attempt to fulfill. The pattern of motives—among others, whether we lean more strongly to achievement or affiliation, to independence or dependence—can create innumerable individual differences. Emotions, motives, and many other factors go to make up different kinds of personality and cause some people to engage in what is called abnormal behavior (the subjects of Chapters 11 and 12).

The Goals of Psychology

Thus the scope of psychology is very wide indeed; the subject matter of the science covers all the *overt* or observable behavior that human beings and other organisms exhibit and also the *covert* or hidden mental processes that go on inside the organism and often affect overt behavior. *The goals of psychology,* it can now be added, *are to understand and predict behavior.*

To put this another way, the goal of psychology, as in every science, is to create satisfactory theories—in this case, statements of general principles that provide a plausible explanation for the phenomena of behavior and mental life observed in the past and that, if sufficiently accurate, will be borne out by future phenomena. In the field of learning in particular, as will be seen in the next three chapters, we already have some fairly powerful theories, derived from the evidence of the past, that enable us to predict when and how learning is most likely to take place.

THE HISTORY OF PSYCHOLOGY

Mankind's efforts to understand and to predict human behavior go back, presumably, to the very origins of the human race. We can assume from what is known about some of the primitive tribes that exist today in isolation from modern civilization that men have always been mystified by their dreams. A man goes to sleep and in his dreams seems to travel. He goes fishing on a distant river; he goes hunting on a distant plain; he meets his friends; he even meets and converses with people who are long since dead. When he wakes up, anyone can tell him that his body has not moved at all from his bed. What could be more natural than to suppose that the human body is also inhabited by a human soul, which can leave and reenter the body at will and survives after death? The ancient Greek philosophers were also fascinated by this apparent division of human existence into body and soul. And they speculated endlessly on the nature of the human mind, which they conceived to be a part of the soul, or perhaps the same thing. This was the age in which the science of mathematics was reaching great heights, and the Greek philosophers marveled that the human mind could create the world of mathematics—a world, though purely imaginary and theoretical, that was much more logical and "pure" than the real world of sleeping and eating and physical illness and death.

As for attempts to predict behavior, the Greeks had their oracles, notably the Delphic Oracle, who were supposed to bring them messages from the gods. Presumably all civilizations, and even the generations that preceded civilization, have had soothsayers, witch doctors, and wise men to whom they looked for guidance about the future. We still have them today, even in our modern scientific America. Almost every city has its fortune tellers, and the newspapers print columns in which astrologers predict what will happen to us today.

In recent years there seems to have been an increased popular interest among Americans, and especially young people, in such occult matters as astrology and fortune telling with tarot cards; and some students are attracted to the introductory psychology course because they expect it to deal with extrasensory perception, mental telepathy, and clairvoyant insights into the future. The student who has such expectations is likely to be disappointed.

True, some psychologists have made studies of extrasensory perception (or ESP for short), which means the ability to receive information about the environment through some rather mysterious means existing outside the channels of the known human senses of vision, hearing, taste, smell, and touch—for example, the ability to make better than chance judgments of how cards are arranged in a shuffled deck or to perform mental telepathy, which means the ability of one mind to perceive what is going on in another mind without any known means of communication, as if somehow one brain could send invisible signals to another. A few psychologists have decided on the basis of experiments that there is firm evidence that some people are gifted with ESP (1, 2).* However, the great majority of psychologists remain unconvinced and believe that the whole weight of scientific knowledge and everyday observation rules against any such possibilities. (If there were such a thing as ESP and it were actually possible to sense the arrangement of cards in a deck, then it would seem that the Nevada gambling houses would be consistent losers and would have to go out of business.) Though a minority claim to have found evidence supporting the existence of ESP, most psychologists believe that the evidence is at best highly controversial and the whole idea rather implausible.

*The numbers in parentheses, which will be found throughout the book, are keyed to references and source materials (concerning both text and illustrations) that are listed at the end of the volume.

Indeed what distinguishes the mainstream of psychological investigation from many previous attempts to understand and predict human behavior is that psychology refuses to regard man as the possessor or creature of unproved forces. Although a few of its practitioners may hold to the contrary, psychology does not believe that a man's life is affected by the position of the stars at the moment of his birth. Moreover, it does not seek divine revelations from some Delphic Oracle and is not content to describe man as some past philosopher, however brilliant, may have imagined him to be. It does not accept the adages of previous generations, no matter how common-sensical those adages may seem to be. (Many of the adages, as a matter of fact, are mutually contradictory. Is it true that "a bird in the hand is worth two in the bush," or do we do better to believe "nothing ventured, nothing gained"?)

Instead, the science of psychology is *empirical*—that is, it is based on controlled experiments and on observations made with the greatest possible precision and objectivity. This is the quality it shares with other natural sciences, such as physics and chemistry; this, indeed, is what makes it a science.

Wilhelm Wundt and his Laboratory

Like other sciences, psychology evolved slowly and was the result of many contributions by many men. The philosophers of the seventeenth and eighteenth centuries helped create the realistically inquiring attitude of mind that made the science possible. The physiologists of the nineteenth century did their part by making numerous discoveries about the human nervous system and the human brain. The year in which all these factors came together and psychology emerged as a science in its own right is usually put at 1879, when Wilhelm Wundt established the first psychology laboratory at Germany's University of Leipzig.

Wilhelm Wundt, shown at left, was a solemn, hard-working, and tireless man who devoted himself to scholarship from the time he was a boy until he died at the age of eighty-eight. A preacher's son, he first became a physician, but instead of practicing medicine he taught physiology. He soon lost interest in the physical aspects of human behavior, for he was much more concerned with consciousness. His laboratory was the first place in the world where a serious and organized attempt was made to analyze and explain human consciousness.

Wundt was the University of Leipzig's most popular lecturer; no classroom there was big enough to hold all the students who wanted to listen. And his laboratory attracted scholars from all over the world, including a number from the United States, who absorbed the notion of experimental psychology and returned to their homelands to introduce the work to others. Wundt and his followers belonged to what is known as the *structural* school of psychology, so named because its members concentrated on the structure or contents of conscious experience, such as sensations, images, and feelings. Their method was introspection, or inward examination of mental processes.

Compared with some of the modern experiments that will be discussed later in the chapter, Wundt's work may seem rather unexciting. For example, he was interested in the human reaction to the sounds of a metronome, and he and his students spent hours in the laboratory listening to the click of a metronome set at low speeds and high speeds, sometimes sounding only a few clicks at a time, sometimes sounding many. As they listened, they tried to analyze their conscious experiences. Wundt decided that listening to some kinds of clicks was more pleasant than listening to others. He noticed that he had a feeling of slight tension before each click and a feeling of relief afterward. He also concluded that a rapid series of beats made him conscious of excitement and that a slow series made him relaxed. Wundt and his students listened to the same kinds of clicks, then carefully reported their conscious experiences and compared notes. They may not have produced powerful laws about behavior, but they did establish a systematic method of study.

Francis Galton and Measurement

Wilhelm Wundt and his followers were interested mostly in discovering in what ways human beings are alike—in particular, whether they had the same kinds of conscious experiences in response to the same kinds of events, such as the clicks of a metronome. To this day, the sameness of human behavior is one of the chief interests of psychology; it still seeks laws governing the kinds of behavior that all people have in common.

Another of its modern interests, however, is the study of *individual differences,* a phrase you will find used time and again in this book and in any future psychology courses you may take. Psychology tries to learn, for example, why the young woman discussed earlier in this chapter is so different from the other woman in her class. No two human beings, not even identical twins, are exactly alike; they differ physically, and their behavior is different. Psychologists want to know why and how they got this way.

In this area the pioneer was Francis Galton, an Englishman whose most important work was done in the 1880's, shortly after Wilhelm Wundt's laboratory first opened its doors. By coincidence, Galton was also a physician by early training, but there the resemblance to Wundt ends—proof that even two of the founding fathers of the same science are likely to display enormous individual differences.

As can be seen on page 15, the two men were quite unlike in physical appearance. And where Wundt was solemn and studious, Galton was quick and restless. Before he began concentrating on the work that made him famous in psychology, he was at various times an inventor, world traveler, geographer, and meteorologist.

Galton began his psychological studies because of an interest in heredity. He made a study that showed that men who had achieved unusual success in life had sired a greater number of successful sons than less eminent fathers. He also discovered that when a tall man married a tall woman, their children were usually taller than average. This seemed to him to be another proof of the importance of heredity, although he was baffled by the fact that the children, though taller than average, were usually not so tall as the parents. From these studies and observations he moved on to attempt measurements of human size, strength, and abilities. He invented devices to test people's hearing, sense of smell, color vision, and ability to judge weights and used them on thousands of people. At one time he set up his equipment at an International Health Exhibition in London. So great was popular interest in the emerging science of psychology that people actually paid an entrance fee to visit his laboratory and contribute their measurements to his growing array of statistics.

No matter what Galton measured, he always found wide individual differences. Galton established the principle that all human traits vary over a wide range from small to large, weak to strong, slow to fast; this is true of height, weight, physical strength, and various kinds of abilities, including, as we now know, the ability to learn, which is commonly called intelligence. There can be no further doubt, after Galton's discoveries, that the men who drew up the Declaration of Independence were only partly right when they wrote, "All men are created equal." Men may be equal in the eyes of God or at the bar of justice, but in other respects they are not identical.

William James's "Science of Mental Life"

The most prominent of the early American psychologists was William James, whose photograph is shown at left. James was another man who studied medicine but never practiced. Like Galton, he possessed many talents and had a difficult time finding his true vocation. At one time he wanted to be an artist, then a chemist, and once he joined a zoological expedition to Brazil. In his late twenties he suffered a severe mental breakdown and went through a long period of depression in which he seriously thought of committing suicide. But he recovered—largely, he believed, through what he called "an achievement of the will"—and went on to become a Harvard professor and prolific writer on psychology and philosophy.

James firmly believed in experimentation, and there is some evidence that he established a laboratory of sorts at Harvard even before the more famous Wundt laboratory opened in Leipzig. But James himself never conducted any experiments; he was much more interested in observing the workings of his own mind and the behavior of other people in real-life situations. He differed from Wundt in that he took a much broader view of human consciousness; he was less interested in its structure or contents than in how it helps men adjust to their environments. He and his followers developed the *functional* school of psychology, so named because it emphasized the functions of mental processes, especially as related to behavior, rather than their structure.

A textbook written by James began with the words, "Psychology is the study of mental life." But the distinguishing feature of mental life, he felt, was that human beings constantly seek certain end results and must constantly choose among various means of achieving them. The study of the long-term and short-term goals men seek and the actions they take or abandon in pursuing these goals was the core of James' work. In one passage he wrote:

> I would . . . if I could, be both handsome and fat and well-dressed, and a great athlete, and make a million a year, be a wit, a *bon-vivant,* and a lady-killer, as well as a philosopher; a philanthropist, statesman, warrior, and African explorer, as well as a "tone-poet" and saint. But the thing is simply impossible. The millionaire's work would run counter to the saint's; the *bon-vivant* and the philanthropist would trip each other up; the philosopher and the lady-killer could not well keep house in the same tenement of clay. Such different characters may conceivably at the outset of life be possible to a man. But to make any of them actual, the rest must more or less be suppressed. . . . This is as strong an example as there is of . . . selective industry of the mind. (3)

James contributed some valuable observations on specific aspects of human experience, such as habits, emotions, religious feelings, and mental disturbances. But mostly he was interested in the broad pattern of human strivings—the cradle-to-grave progress of human beings as thinking organisms who adopt certain goals and ambitions, including spiritual ones, and struggle by various means to attain the goals or become reconciled to failure.

John Watson, Behaviorist

Was William James perhaps more a philosopher than a scientist? One American who thought so was John Watson, who about the year 1913 founded the movement known as *behaviorism.* He declared that "mental life" was something that cannot be seen or measured and thus cannot be studied scientifically. Instead of trying to examine any such vague thing as "mental life" or consciousness, he concluded, psychologists should concentrate on overt behavior —the kinds of actions that are plainly visible.

There was no room in Watson's theories for anything like

James's "achievement of the will." He believed that everything we do is predetermined by our past experiences; to him all human behavior was a series of events in which a *stimulus,* that is, an event in the environment, produces a *response,* that is, an observable muscular movement or some physiological reaction, such as increased heart rate or glandular secretion, that can also be observed and measured with the proper instruments. (For example, shining a bright light into the eye of a person or other organism is a stimulus that causes an immediate response in which the pupil of the eye contracts; a loud and unexpected noise is a stimulus that usually causes the response of muscular contraction or "jumping" and increased heart rate.) Watson believed that through *conditioning,* a type of learning that will be discussed in Chapter 2, almost any kind of stimulus could be made to produce almost any kind of response; indeed he once said that he could take any dozen babies at birth and, by conditioning them in various ways, turn them into anything he wished—doctor, lawyer, beggar, or thief.

Watson was inclined to doubt that there was any such thing as a human mind. He conceded that human beings had thoughts, but he believed that these were simply a form of talking to oneself, by making tiny movements of the vocal cords. He also conceded that people have what they call feelings, but he believed that these were only some form of conditioned glandular response to a stimulus in the environment.

Watson's theories burst upon the world at a time when many psychologists were dissatisfied with the progress of their science. The attempts to examine man's consciousness—his "mental life," to use the James terminology—had not been very fruitful; there was some question whether looking inward into the human mind was really scientific at all. The notion that it is better to examine and measure overt behavior than to try to study the invisible mind was very appealing, and for many years Watson was the most influential of American psychologists.

S-R Psychology and B. F. Skinner

One school of psychological thought that grew out of Watson's theories is known as *stimulus-response psychology,* or S-R psychology for short. The S-R psychologists emphasize study of the stimuli that produce behavioral responses, the rewards and punishments that help establish and maintain these responses, and the modification of behavior through changes in the patterns of rewards and punishments. The leader of the S-R school has been B. F. Skinner, who ranks as another of the most prominent American psychologists of the past half-century. Skinner has been chiefly interested in the learning process and has revised and expanded Watson's ideas into a theory of learning that continues to influence much psychological thinking. He has made many important contributions to our knowledge of how patterns of rewards and punishments

produce and modify connections between a stimulus and a response and thus help control the organism's behavior—often in the
most complex ways.

Some New Schools of Psychology

There is no doubt that Watson and his successors among the S-R
psychologists did a great deal to advance the science. They emphasized that psychology should be empirical and based as much
as possible on controlled experiments and measurements of behavior and that too much introspection (that is, examination of a
"mental life" that nobody but its possessor can observe in operation) can lead to chaos. But for many years Watson's insistence on
behaviorism put psychology into a straitjacket. There is a good
deal more to human life and behavior than a series of conditioned
responses or other responses following one after another in a pattern over which we have no control. Human beings are by no
means pieces of machinery that automatically perform in a certain
way every time a certain button is pushed. We do make choices,
as William James pointed out. We have complicated thoughts,
feelings, emotions, and attitudes that cannot possibly be explained
by a simple pushbutton theory.

All these aspects of "mental life," once ruled out of bounds
by the behaviorists, have now been drawn back into the field of
study and have led to the development of a number of new schools
of psychology.

One of the new schools is known as *cognitive psychology;* its
followers maintain that human behavior cannot be explained in
full by stimulus-response connections and indeed that the human
mind is not just a reflection of the stimuli that its possessor has
encountered; instead the mind actively processes the information
it receives into new forms and categories. The cognitive psychologists tend to think of the mind as a sort of "mental executive"
that actively makes comparisons and decisions. A simple example
sometimes cited is this: if you say a string of digits to another
person, such as 5, 9, 3, 2, 8, 6, then repeat the same string with one
digit missing, or 5, 9, 3, 8, 6, your listener will have no trouble
stating immediately that the missing number is 2. What has happened, as the cognitive psychologists interpret it, is that he is not
just making a specific response dictated by a specific stimulus but
instead has engaged in some sort of decision-making process that
scans the two strings of digits, compares them, and notes the difference. What is most important about human mental activity, the cognitive psychologists believe, is that it includes such comparisons
and understandings, as well as the discovery of meanings and the
use of knowledge to find new principles that aid in constructive
thinking and problem solving.

Perhaps the leading figure of the cognitive school is the Swiss
psychologist Jean Piaget, who has extensively investigated the

manner in which the mental skills of children develop as they grow older. Piaget's observations of the stage-by-stage process through which children become increasingly able to understand and think about new situations (pages 530–32) are among the outstanding psychological contributions of recent years.

Another new school with a quite different approach is called *humanistic psychology*; this school, as its name implies, is especially interested in the qualities that distinguish human beings from other animals. Among the leaders of humanistic psychology have been the American psychologists Carl Rogers, who invented the optimistic form of treatment of emotional disturbances called *client-centered therapy* (pages 415–16), and Abraham Maslow, who introduced the theory that human beings possess a motive called *self-actualization* (pages 356–57), which makes them strive to realize fully their potential for creativity, dignity, and self-worth.

Sigmund Freud and Psychoanalysis

Another movement that originated apart from psychology but has had a profound influence on psychological thinking is the school of *psychoanalysis* which was founded around the turn of the century by Sigmund Freud. Freud began his career in Vienna in the 1880's as a physician and neurologist. He became interested in psychological processes as the result of his experiences with patients who were suffering from hysteria—that is, from paralysis of the legs or arms that seemed to have no physical cause. His final theories represent a lifetime of observing and treating many kinds of neurotic patients and also of attempting to analyze his own personality.

Freud himself was rather neurotic in his youth, suffering from feelings of anxiety and deep depression. He retained some neurotic symptoms all his life, he was a compulsive smoker of as many as twenty cigars a day, was nervous about traveling, and was given to what were probably hypochondriacal complaints about poor digestion, constipation, and heart palpitation. However, he managed to overcome his early inclinations toward depression and lived a rich professional, family, and social life—an indication that in his case the physician had managed to heal himself, at least in large part.

One of Freud's great insights into the human personality was the discovery of how it is influenced by *unconscious processes*, especially motives of which we are unaware. At first his ideas were bitterly attacked; many people were repelled by his notion that man, far from being a rational animal, is largely at the mercy of his irrational unconscious thoughts. Many were shocked by his emphasis on the role of sexual motives (which were prominent among those that the society of that period preferred to deny) and particularly by his insistence that even young children have intense sexual desires. Over the years, however, the furor has died out. There is considerable controversy over the value of psychoanalytic methods in treating neurotic patients, but even those who criticize psychoanalysis as a form of therapy accept some of Freud's basic notions about personality and its formation. His theories will be discussed in detail on pages 404–08.

All the various strands of psychological thinking that have been described here are now being drawn together, and it appears likely that the science is entering its richest and most rewarding period—in which it will manage to combine all the best features of Wundt's structuralism, Galton's interest in individual differences and statistical methods, James's concern wih the functionalism of man's will and spiritual aspirations, Watson's warning that science must be kept empirical, the importance of learning as emphasized by the S-R psychologists, the cognitive psychologists' view of mental activity as a processing of information, the humanists' concern for man's dignity and worth, and Freud's insights into some of the more baffling aspects of human personality. Although followers of the various schools often disagree sharply with one another, all have made contributions that may someday be synthesized into general theories that will greatly expand man's knowledge of his behavior and his mental processes and suggest ways to alleviate emotional disturbances and better understand human nature.

THE METHODS OF PSYCHOLOGY

Each school of psychology has tended to emphasize one aspect of behavior or mental processes, and each has developed its own preferred methods for studying the phenomena in which it has been most interested. As has already been stated, the structuralists concentrated on introspective reports on the elements of consciousness, the functionalists on the relationship between introspective reports of consciousness and adjustment to the environment. The behaviorists and S-R psychologists have taken the more mechanical view that psychology is essentially a study of what the organism does, and that what the organism does can in turn be explained as a series of stimtilus-response connections.

In general, because human behavior and mental processes take such a wide variety of forms, psychology has had to adopt a number of different ways of studying them and is constantly seeking new ways. Among the most prominent methods of study now in use are the following.

The Experiment

The most powerful tool of psychology, as of all sciences, is the study method known as the *experiment*—in which the psychologist, usually in his laboratory, makes a careful and rigidly controlled examination of cause and effect. Just as the chemist can determine that combining hydrogen and oxygen will produce water, the psychologist can determine that certain conditions will result in certain measurable changes in the behavior of his subjects, either human or animal.

For example, one psychologist was interested in this question: If a person is suffering from anxiety—that is, if he is worried and fearful about what might be about to happen to him—is he more likely than usual to seek the company of other people? This is an important question because it concerns the effects of anxiety, which as will be seen in Chapter 9 is one of the most influential of human emotions, and also the operation of the affiliation motive, which will be discussed in detail in Chapter 10. In everyday terms, the question gets to the core of whether it is true, as is generally believed, that "misery loves company."

To answer the question, the psychologist devised an experiment in which women students at a university, when they arrived at his laboratory to take part in the study, found a frightening looking piece of apparatus and were told that it was designed to deliver severe electric shocks. After being thus made anxious about the nature of the experiment, they were told that they had their choice of waiting their turn alone or in the company of other subjects; and the experimenter carefully noted their decisions. It turned out that only 9 percent preferred to wait alone and fully 63 percent preferred company, while 28 percent said that company or lack of it made no difference to them.

The Independent and Dependent Variables. Every experiment is an attempt to discover relationships among certain conditions or events that can be changed or that result from changes; these are called *variables*. The experimenter sets up some of the conditions; he controls and manipulates them. Any condition controlled by the experimenter, because it is set up independently of anything the subject does or does not do, is called an *independent variable*. The change in the subject's behavior that results from a change in an independent variable is called the *dependent variable*. In the experiment with what the university women believed was a shock machine, the subjects' degree of anxiety was the *independent variable*. Their behavior in response to the independent variable—that is, their decision whether to wait alone or in company—was the *dependent variable*.

In most human situations, in and out of the laboratory, there are many variables. Ordinarily, however, the experimenter wants to study the effect of only one independent variable; therefore he tries to hold other variables constant. In his case, for example, he did not want his results to be confused by any differences between women and men (the sex variable); therefore he studied only female subjects. He was not interested in the effect of any age variable; therefore he chose subjects who were all of college age rather than a mixed group of adults, teenagers, and elementary school pupils. He manipulated only one independent variable, degree of anxiety, and measured its effect on one dependent variable, the tendency to prefer company.

The Control Group. As has been said, measurements of the dependent variable in this experiment showed 9 percent of subjects preferring to wait alone, 63 percent preferring company, and 28 percent in the "don't care" category. As you doubtless have already decided, however, these results are strangely unsatisfactory; it is impossible to figure out, from these figures alone, what if anything the experiment proves. The natural questions to ask are: What would have happened if the subjects had *not* been made anxious? What kind of preferences would they then have displayed toward waiting alone or in company?

To answer these questions, the psychologist used another important experimental tool known as a *control group.* He selected an approximately equal number of women students from the same university, asked them to report to the same laboratory, gave them the same choice of waiting alone or in company—but did not make them anxious. Instead of seeing and being told about a "shock machine," they were told that the experiment would not be at all unpleasant. Of these nonanxious subjects in the control group, it turned out, 7 percent preferred to wait alone, 33 percent preferred company, and 60 percent were in the "don't care" category. As you can see, this information about the control group enables us to interpret the results for the anxious women. The total design of the experiment included manipulation of an *independent variable* (anxiety) and measurement of the resulting changes in a *dependent variable* (preference for company, or what is called affiliative behavior), for both an *experimental group* (the subjects made anxious) and a *control group* (the nonanxious subjects). The results, which are presented in several forms in Figure 1–4, show clearly that at least under these particular experimental circumstances, college women suffering from anxiety are much more likely to display affiliative behavior than women who are free from anxiety (4).

Control groups are essential to many psychological experiments, and their selection demands considerable care. In dealing with human subjects, the ideal method would be to find many pairs of identical twins, who, as will be seen in Chapter 8, are as nearly alike as any two people can possibly be, and assign one member of each pair to the experimental group and the other to the control group. Since this is usually impossible, experimenters take many other precautions to ensure that their experimental and control groups are similar in all important respects. In most experiments on learning, for example, a psychologist would want to make sure that his experimental and control groups were approximately equal at least in average age and average number of grades or years of college completed—as well as, if at all possible, in average scores on intelligence tests and average grades obtained in their classes.

Single Blind and Double Blind. In many experiments, another precaution is necessary. For example, one way of studying the effect of marijuana on a person's ability to drive an automobile would be to recruit an experimental group who would receive the drug, then measure their performance on a test simulating driving performance. But obviously their performance might be affected by their knowledge of whether they had taken the drug and their expectations of what it might do to them. To avoid this possibility, it would be important to keep them from knowing whether they had received the drug; this could be done by giving half the subjects an injection of the drug and the other half an injection of a salt solution that would have no effect, without telling them which was which. This experimental method, in which subjects are prevented from knowing whether they belong to the experimental or the control group, is called the single blind technique.

Not even the single blind technique, however, would ensure valid results, for if the experimenter knew which of his subjects had or had not taken the drug, his judgment of their driving performance might be affected by this knowledge. To make the experiment foolproof, the drug or salt solution would have to be injected by a third party so that the experimenter himself would have no way of knowing which subjects had received which kind of injection. This method, in which neither the subject nor the experimenter knows who is in the experimental group and who is in the control group, is the *double blind technique.* It is particularly valuable in studying the effects of all kinds of drugs—for example, the adrenalin that has been used in studies of emotions (pages 311–12) and the various tranquilizers and antidepressants used in the treatment of emotional disturbances (page 424.) It is also used in other experiments where knowledge of the experimental conditions might affect the performance of the subjects or the judgment of the experimenter.

The Virtues of the Experiment. As developed and refined over the years, and with the checks provided by such methods as use of a control group and the double blind technique, the experiment is indeed psychology's most powerful tool. For one thing, an experiment can be repeated by another experimenter at another time and in another place, ruling out the possibility that the results were accidental or influenced by the first experimenter's personality or preconceived notions of what would happen. (In this connection, a word frequently found in psychological literature is *replicate*; to replicate an experiment is to perform it again in the same manner and obtain the same results.) When facts have been established by the experimental method and verified time and again by other experimenters, we can have great faith in their validity.

Naturalistic Observation

In many cases, unfortunately, experiments are impossible. This is true not only in psychology but in other sciences as well; astronomers cannot manipulate the planets and stars but can only watch their behavior. Psychologists work under a special handicap, however, because it would be highly unethical to perform many experiments that might result in important additions to our store of knowledge. For example, we cannot deliberately rear a group of children under conditions of brutal deprivation and punishment and then compare their behavior with a control group brought up under more humane conditions.

One thing the psychologist can do, however, is what the astronomer does—observe events pertinent to his science with extreme care and precision and with an open and unprejudiced mind. Thus some of our most valuable knowledge of the behavior of infants and how they develop has come from science-oriented observers who actually went into the homes where babies were growing up. Or sometimes young children have been brought into nurseries where they could be watched at play and in contact with other children, often by observers looking through a one-way mirror so that they could see the children without themselves being seen, as shown Figure 1–5. This is the study method known as *naturalistic observation*.

Unlike the experimenter, the investigator who is using the method of naturalistic observation does not manipulate the situation and cannot control all the variables. Indeed he tries to remain unseen, as behind the one-way mirror, or at least as inconspicuous as possible, lest his very presence affect the behavior that he is trying to study. His method has been especially useful in adding to our knowledge not only of children but also of animals and the people of other societies.

In a sense all human beings constantly use the technique of observation; everybody observes the behavior of other people and draws some conclusions from this behavior. If we note that a woman student dislikes speaking up in a classroom and blushes easily in social situations, we conclude that she is shy, and we treat her accordingly. (We may try to put her at her ease, or if we feel so inclined, we may enjoy embarrassing her and making her squirm.) Scientific observations are much more rigorously disciplined than those ordinarily made in everyday life. The observer sticks to the facts. He tries to describe behavior objectively and exactly, and he is loath to jump to conclusions about the motives behind it.

Tests

The pioneer work done by Francis Galton on tests of human abilities has already been mentioned. Since Galton's time, many more tests have been devised, measuring not only abilities but feelings, motives, attitudes, and opinions; and the tests have been tried on enough persons to determine exactly what they measure and how well. As will be seen in Chapter 14, a carefully designed test—which itself has been tested by repeated use and by analysis of the results—is a valuable tool for exploring human behavior and especially for comparing one human being with another.

Interviews

One of the best-known studies using the interview method was the work of Alfred Kinsey, who became interested in human sexual behavior when some of his students at Indiana University asked him for sexual advice. When he went to the university library for information, he found many books of opinion about sexual behavior but almost none that cast any light on what kind of sexual experiences men and women actually had in real life or how often. So Kinsey determined to find out, and the only possible way seemed to be to interview as many men and women as he could and ask them about their sexual feelings and experiences from childhood until the present time, as he is shown doing at the left. His well-known reports on male and female sexual behavior were the result.

Questionnaires

Closely related to the interview is the *questionnaire,* which is especially useful in gathering information quickly from large numbers of people. A questionnaire is a set of written questions that can be answered easily, usually by putting a checkmark in the appropriate place. In order to obtain accurate results, a questionnaire must be carefully worded. For example, an investigator interested in crime might want to know whether the inmates of a state penitentiary had fathers who tended to be very lenient or very strict. But if he simply asked, "Was your father very lenient toward you?" he might not get accurate answers. For one thing, many convicts would not know the meaning of the word *lenient.* For another, many people tend to answer *yes* to any question just to be agreeable. So he would probably put the question like this:

When you did something that your father did not like, did he
☐ always spank you?   ☐ tell you you were a bad
☐ sometimes spank you?   boy and let it go at that?
☐ bawl you out?   ☐ laugh and forget it?

Interviews and questionnaires are sometimes challenged by critics who think that the people who are asked the questions may not tell the truth. Kinsey's work, for example, has been attacked on the ground that nobody would be likely to be honest about his sexual behavior. But an investigator who is experienced in interviewing or in making up questionnaires and checkng them against the facts that he can obtain in other ways knows how to recognize people who are not telling the truth or who are exaggerating. Interviews and questionnaires do not always reveal the complete truth, but when carefully planned and executed, they can be extremely useful.

To summarize this section on the methods of psychological investigation, it should be pointed out again that human behavior is considerably more complex than the behavior of even the most remarkable computer ever invented. It is certainly much harder to study than is the behavior of two chemicals in a test tube or gas in a pressure chamber. Moreover, human beings cannot be manipulated the way the chemist can manipulate chemicals. If we want to find out whether very lenient or very harsh treatment by parents inclines a child toward being a criminal, we cannot deliberately indulge a thousand selected children and subject another thousand to brutal discipline. We have to study human behavior as best we can, by any humane method that seems scientifically promising.

APPLICATIONS OF PSYCHOLOGY

All our modern sciences were founded by men whose chief motive was simply to satisfy their own curiosity about the mysteries of the universe. The first physicists were curious about the nature of light and the behavior of falling objects, the first chemists about the nature of matter. These pioneers sought knowledge for the sake of knowledge; they were interested in *pure science;* they did not know or especially care whether their discoveries would ever serve any useful purpose.

Yet the discoveries of the pure scientists have of course been put to practical use, and in our modern world we are surrounded on all sides by *applied science.* The physicist's knowledge of electricity has been put to work in lighting and air conditioning the buildings in which we live and work. The automobile is also a product of applied physics, as are radios, television sets, and spaceships. Applied chemistry has produced medicines, plastics, and synthetic fabrics.

Psychology, too, is a pure science that has already had many practical applications, even though it is much younger than physics or chemistry. In today's world, many psychologists are busy studying the pure science; they are interested solely in increasing our knowledge of human behavior. Many other psychologists, however, are engaged in the practice of applied science and are using the knowledge we now have in many practical ways. This work has changed our world more than most people realize.

Clinical Psychology and Counseling

Clinical psychology is the diagnosis and treatment of behavior problems. *Counseling* is a closely related field that offers assistance to people who need temporary guidance on problems such as school difficulties, vocational choices, or marriage conflicts. More psychologists today specialize in these two fields than in any other branch of the science; the number has been variously estimated at somewhere between 39 percent (5) and 48 percent (6).

In diagnosing problems, clinical and counseling psychologists often use the kinds of tests of personality, abilities, vocational aptitudes, and interests that will be described in Chapter 14. In the treatment of behavior disorders, clinical psychologists use the method called *psychotherapy* (Chapter 12), which generally takes the form of getting the troubled person to talk about his fears and conflicts and perhaps, with the psychologist's help, to see them in a new and more constructive light. In general, clinical psychologists believe that mental and emotional disorders that have no obvious physical basis are the result of an unfortunate form of learning; it is the patient's prior experiences, the attitudes he has developed toward them, and the emotions they now arouse that account for his present troubles.

Many clinical psychologists practice *group therapy*, which is the treatment of a number of people at the same time—partly to save time and money and partly because groups often seem to be more helpful than individual therapy. One such method is the recently well-publicized *encounter group*, which will be discussed further in Chapter 12.

Psychology in Schools and Industry

Some clinical psychologists and counselors work in schools, where they not only attempt to diagnose the cause of students' problems but also consult with teachers and families in an attempt to change the conditions that have caused the problems. Others work in industrial firms, where it has been found that many employees fail at the job not because of lack of skill but because of bad personal relations with their fellow workers or bosses. In addition, psychology has found many other applications in the schools and in industry.

In the schools, psychology's best-known contribution has been its standardized tests. Intelligence tests offer a reasonably good prediction of how well a student can be expected to perform— although, as will be discussed in Chapter 14, they have certain weaknesses and are more successful in rating students from middle-income homes than students from low-income homes. Standardized achievement tests are a generally accurate measure of how well an individual student is progressing year by year in various skills, such as reading and arithmetic, or of how one school compares with others in the nation.

Psychology has also influenced teaching methods, the organization of the curriculum, and the preparation of textbooks and educational films. Indeed most of the principles of learning that will be discussed in Part 2 of this book can be applied to schoolwork. Some colleges have a special course in the applied psychology of learning designed to help students to do better in their classes.

In industry, psychologists have discovered many facts about worker fatigue, working hours, rest periods, and employee morale. They have also created many training devices that make it easier to learn particular skills and contributed to *human engineering,* which is the design of equipment and machinery that will be more efficient and easier to use because they fit the actual size, strength, and capabilities of the human beings who will use them.

Public Opinion Surveys

The Gallup Poll is one well-known example of the application of psychological techniques to the examination of public opinion, which has disclosed many previously unknown facts about how people feel about all kinds of public issues, including military expenditures, welfare programs, racial tensions, sexual behavior, birth control and abortion, marriage and divorce, and many others. Thanks to public opinion surveys, it is now possible to acquire much more information than ever before on what our society is really like and how opinion actually divides on important social issues.

Public opinion surveys depend for their accuracy on two techniques that will be discussed in Chapter 13. Careful *sampling,* that is, selecting a group of people who are representative of the entire population in regard to education, income, religion, place of residence, and political affiliation, makes it possible to determine the attitudes of the nation as a whole by surveying a relatively small number of people. *Statistical analysis* makes it possible to interpret the validity and significance of the results. Public opinion surveys have been used to predict election results and by businessmen to measure the reaction to various types of products and sales and advertising campaigns. Probably their greatest value, however, is the information they help provide on social problems—a topic that deserves discussion of its own.

PSYCHOLOGY AND SOCIAL PROBLEMS

As anyone who reads a newspaper or watches a television news program is well aware, hardly a day goes by without some important and often disquieting new development in the pattern of modern American society. The years since the end of the Second World War have produced rapid and sometimes bewildering social change. The population has grown swiftly and the cities have become more and more crowded; at the same time there has been an education boom that has given more and more young people high school and college degrees. Technology has sent men to the moon and produced an "affluent society" in which more people enjoy more material goods than ever before in history—yet it also has resulted in widespread pollution, concern about the ecology, numerous large pockets of poverty, and uncertainty about the ability of material prosperity to satisfy human yearnings. Issues of race relations and school integration are constantly in the news. The divorce rate has risen, and the women's liberation movement has raised some profound questions about the whole institution of marriage and the family and the relationships between men and women.

Of all the problems of modern society, perhaps the basic one is this: How, in this new world of rapid and tumultuous change, can man get along satisfactorily with himself and with his fellows? It is a question to which many psychologists have devoted themselves in many various ways. One must not expect too much of the science, of course—for the psychologist, as a human being, is just as baffled by the upheavals in his society as anyone else. However, the psychologist can at least investigate and analyze some of the facts; and factual information, rather than mere guess or prejudice, is the great need of the modern world.

It would be impossible to list all the social problems to which psychology has contributed insights. Some of them, however, deserve special mention here.

The "Generation Gap"

One of the most widely discussed and controversial problems of recent years has centered around what has come to be called the "generation gap." Because of differences in dress, life styles, and attitudes, many young people have decided that adults represent an "establishment" that they are prepared to reject or perhaps even tear down; many adults have decided that young people are self-indulgent, mindlessly rebellious, and dangerous to the American society.

This is a problem that public opinion polls and psychological analysis of trends in American society can at least put into perspective. The surveys show that there are indeed a number of sharp differences of opinion between many young people and many older people, on all kinds of topics ranging from military policies to issues of race and poverty and the nature of the college curriculum. But the evidence seems to indicate that these differences represent more of an "education gap" than a "generation gap." As a 1971 report of the Census Bureau made clear, there has been a tremendous boom in education in the United States. In a mere three decades beginning in 1940, the number of young Americans with college degrees almost tripled, going from 6 to 16 percent; the number with at least a year of college more than doubled, going from 13 to 31 percent; the number with high school diplomas rose from 38 to 75 percent (7).

These figures mean that today's young people, on the average, have had far more formal education than their parents. In fact nearly two-thirds of today's college students have fathers who never went to college. And many research studies have shown that people who have attended college tend to have different opinions from noncollege people on such questions as politics, sexual behavior, child-rearing practices, religion, and relations among ethnic and racial groups (8); they also tend to be more concerned about the general welfare of society than about their own personal advancement. In the opinion of some psychologists who have studied the so-called generation gap, today's young people often seem threatening to their elders in part because they have more education and have developed the kinds of attitudes that increased education generally fosters.

Surveys have also shown that the "gap," whatever its cause, is not nearly so large as some of the militant young people and more conservative adults often assume—or as even an objective observer might gather from some of the news events reported on television and in the newspapers. Careful psychological surveys made in 1965 and 1968 showed that only about 2 to 10 percent of all college students took active part in the various campus protests of those years, with the lower figure holding for such abstract issues as educational reform and the higher figure for more personal issues such as dormitory rules and standards of dress (9). A public opinion survey of Americans aged fifteen to twenty-one, made at the end of 1970, showed that 66 percent did not have trouble communicating with their parents, 73 percent agreed with their parents' values and ideals, and 84 percent were satisfied with the kind of education they had received up to that point (10). Quite clearly, the American youth movement, if thought of as a highly militant attack on the Establishment and its ideas, is not nearly so large as its own leaders and the adults who oppose it often believe. Moreover, a study of history and of current trends in other nations shows that differences between young people and their elders have existed many times before and exist today in many other parts of the world, including Mexico, France, Japan, and the Soviet Union.

Drugs

One thorny aspect of the "generation gap" has centered around the use of drugs, notably marijuana. Many adults are convinced that marijuana is a dangerous drug that leads to antisocial behavior and probably to addiction to even more dangerous drugs such as heroin. Indeed possession of marijuana is a crime throughout the United States and in many places is punishable by long prison sentences. Many young people, however, use marijuana despite the fact that it is illegal and consider it no more dangerous than alcohol. A large-scale survey of freshmen entering college in 1970 showed that 38 percent favored legalizing the use of marijuana—almost double the number who had favored legalization only two years earlier (11).

Research into the actual effects of marijuana poses some extremely difficult problems. Even if a psychologist set up a careful double blind experiment to inquire into its effect on automobile driving, as described on page 24, the results would have little real value. They would show only what happens when a known amount of the active chemical in marijuana is administered under laboratory conditions and the subject then tested on a machine that simulates the driving experience (see Figure 1–6). They would not necessarily predict what might happen when many different kinds of drivers, in many different kinds of automobiles under different road conditions, smoke varying quanties of marijuana (12). This is especially true because researchers have found that there are probably more than 100 different varieties of the marijuana plant, some of which may be 400 times as strong as others (13). Moreover, marijuana users often combine the drug with varying amounts of alcohol, thus further complicating the problem of studying its effects.

Thus all experimental evidence on marijuana has to be viewed with reservations. Insofar as can be judged from laboratory experiments, marijuana raises the pulse rate and causes reddening of the eyes and dryness of the mouth and throat; it does not produce any other marked physical effects. As for the psychological effects, laboratory subjects often report than they get feelings of happiness and elation, become more friendly for a time and then tend to withdraw, become less aggressive, have trouble concentrating, tend to get dizzy and feel as if they were dreaming, and eventually become sleepy. On a simulated test of driving skill they make more speedometer errors, as if they were not watching the speedometer as much as they normally would (14). Tests of ability to think through a series of logical steps have suggested that the drug reduces short-term memory (see pages 99–101) and the ability to make decisions rapidly (15). In one experiment a control group received marijuana from which the active ingredients had been removed, while other groups received various strengths of the drug. The subjects then were asked to start with a number such as 114, subtract 7, then add either 1, 2, or 3, and repeat the process until they reached another number, such as 54. The combined score for speed and accuracy was highest for the control group, which did about 50 percent better than subjects who had received a small dose of marijuana and more than 100 percent better than subjects who had received a large dose (16).

Studies of people who use the drug outside the laboratory have suggested that they probably have different reasons and obtain different kinds of reactions. One investigator, after interviewing a large group of college students and "street people" who were regular users, concluded that they fell into three categories: 1) "insight users," who believed the drug gave them an expanded awareness and made them more creative; 2) "social users," who took the drug mostly for enjoyment and a feeling of warmth and togetherness with their friends; and 3) "release users," who found that it lowered their inhibitions and gave them a feeling of escape from reality (17). This study may explain why there are so many conflicting reports about the kinds of effects that users experience.

Some observers have concluded that the regular use of marijuana produces long-term personality changes, notably loss of motivation, ambition, and judgment (18). Other observers, however, have concluded that it is less likely that the drug causes loss of motivation than that people who have low motivation to begin with are more inclined than others to use it heavily (19).

So far as is known, marijuana does not produce any physical dependence that makes its users crave the drug and suffer withdrawal symptoms in its absence, as do users of "hard" drugs such as heroin. However, it does seem to produce a psychological dependence. In Egypt, where marijuana can be obtained easily despite laws against it, a study of people who use it five to fifty times a month showed that two-thirds wanted to stop—yet continued because of its soothing and mood-elevating effects as well as the fact that they were used to smoking it in social situations (20). Whether the use of marijuana tends to lead to addiction to heroin is not known. Many heroin addicts began with marijuana (21)— but obviously only a small number of marijuana users go on to hard drugs (14).

As for statistics on the number of young people who use marijuana, the National Institute of Mental Health estimated in 1969 that between 2 and 4 percent of students in high schools and colleges across the nation used it regularly, between 5 and 10 percent used it socially on occasions when it was readily available, and between 13 and 26 percent had used it anywhere from one to ten times and then had given it up. This means that the total number of students who had ever used the drug ran between 20 and 40 percent, depending on the school (22). However, the statistics seem to change rapidly. A public opinion poll in early 1971 indicated that 42 percent of students in college at that time had tried marijuana at least once (23). There is some indication that marijuana use has some of the aspects of a fad—that it may become widespread on a particular campus for a time, then drop off (19).

There is no question at all about the extreme danger of "hard" drugs. Heroin is highly addictive, and anyone who thinks he can get away with trying it for a few times is likely to become dependent on it before he is ever aware that he is "hooked." The addict needs more and more of the drug as time goes on, not only to achieve the feeling the drug produces but also to avoid extremely painful withdrawal symptoms, and his habit may eventually cost as much as $125 a day—a fact that leads many addicts to turn to crime. Overdose frequently kills addicts; indeed in New York City heroin addiction is the leading cause of death among people between the ages of fifteen and thirty-five (24). As for the amphetamines, sometimes known as "pep pills," "meth," and "speed," these too are addictive in that users build up a tolerance and must use more and more to achieve the same effect. The "high" created by amphetamines, especially when injected into the blood stream, may be accompanied by severe feelings of anxiety and irrational thinking leading to violent behavior, followed by a depression in which the user becomes suicidal. The drug can cause psychological disturbances that make it impossible for the user to keep attending college or work at a job (25), and prolonged abuse of the drug has been found to produce brain damage (26).

The Population Explosion

Another serious social problem of recent years has been the population explosion that has occurred throughout the world, chiefly because improved sanitation methods and medical techniques have greatly increased the average life span. In the underdeveloped nations, population has been increasing so rapidly as to threaten to outstrip the food supply and to result in widespread starvation. In the United States, where a careful census is taken every ten years, total population increased from 76 million at the beginning of this century to 203.2 million at the time of the 1970 census. Moreover, there has been a vast migration of Americans from rural areas and small towns to big cities. In 1900, as is shown in Figure 1–7, more than half of all Americans lived in areas described as rural; by 1970, almost 75 percent of them lived in urban areas. The combination of population growth and the move to the cities has produced many new problems of crowding, housing, personal relationships, pollution of the environment, and violence and crime.

Although statistics on crime leave much to be desired—because many crimes are never reported and because different law enforcement agencies have different ways of tabulating those that are reported—there seems to be little doubt that crimes of all sorts have been increasing rather rapidly in he United States. And although crime and violence are certainly not confined to the cities, there appears to be something about the big-city environment that fosters them. In one experiment, for example, a psychologist arranged to have an automobile abandoned in the streets of New York City, with its license plates removed and the hood up. Within ten minutes, a respectable looking family composed of a father, mother, and young son emptied the trunk and glove compartment and removed the radiator and battery. Within three days the car was a pile of junk, stripped of all useful parts, its windows broken, and its body and fenders battered. The same psychologist similarly abandoned another automobile in the city of Palo Alto, California, which had a population of about 55,000 at the time. This car remained undamaged and unlooted for a full week; in fact one man who walked past it while rain was falling tried to protect it by lowering the hood (28).

Violence, Anonymity, and "Bystander Apathy." One factor that appears to encourage crime and violence is the anonymity of big-city life. In New York a person can walk for blocks without meeting anyone he knows; he is simply a face in the crowd. And there is experimental evidence that people are more likely to behave aggressively when their identities are not known than when they could be held responsible for their actions (29).

Along somewhat similar lines, psychologists have been interested in what has become known as "bystander apathy"—a term that grew out of a well-publicized 1964 incident in New York City in which a young woman named Kitty Genovese was murdered on the street one early morning in full view of thirty-eight neighbors who heard her cries and ran to their apartment windows. Although the assault went on for a half-hour and many of the spectators watched for the entire time, no one called the police or took any other action. When confronted with such a remarkable incident, any psychologist interested in social problems —indeed in the whole large field known as *social psychology* (the subject of Chapter 16)—naturally must ask, "Why?"

In one study inspired by the Genovese case, investigators rang doorbells, explained that they had mislaid the address of a friend in the neighborhood, and asked to use the phone. Half the investigators were men and half were women, and they went to homes in both a large city (middle-income housing developments in New York) and small towns. The results are shown in Figure 1–8. In both the big city and the small towns, the women investigators were admitted to more homes than the men—but both women and men investigators received much more help in the small towns than in the city (30). The psychologists who conducted the experiment believe that one explanation for the results is that big-city residents have a greater suspicion and fear of strangers.

Further light on bystander apathy comes from experiments that have explored the relationship between the number of people who witness an incident—such as a fire, a theft, or a call for help —and the likelihood that anyone will take any action. In a typical experiment of this kind, men students at a university who arrived at a psychology laboratory were asked to sit in a small waiting room until they could be interviewed. Some of the subjects waited alone, others in groups of three, and still others in groups of three that contained only one actual subject and two confederates of the experimenter. Soon smoke began to seep into the room through a ventilator in the wall; the smoke continued until someone took steps to report a fire, or if no one did, for six minutes. As is shown in Figure 1–9, most of the subjects who were alone took action to report the smoke, usually rather quickly. But when three subjects were waiting together, only 13 percent ever reported the smoke. Of the subjects who were sitting with two of the experimener's confederates—who were of course instructed to pay no attention to the smoke—only 10 percent took action.

Similar experiments also have shown that a person is much more likely to do something about an apparent emergency if he is the only witness, much more likely to display bystander apathy if he is only one of several or many witnesses, especially if the others seem indifferent to what is happening. The psychologist who designed the experiments believes that two factors may be at work: 1) the presence of others may relieve the individual of feelings of personal responsibility, and 2) any apparent indifference on the part of the others may cause him to downgrade the seriousness of the situation. At any rate, a person who needs help is hardly likely to find safety in numbers; the fewer people present the greater are his chances of getting assistance.

Apathy and the Big-City Rush. Another possible explanation for bystander apathy comes from an experiment in which the subjects were students at a theological seminary—and therefore men who might be expected to lend a helping hand to anyone in trouble. The subjects had volunteered to record a brief talk; when they arrived at the experimenter's office they received some printed material that was to be the basis of the talk, studied it, and then were directed to proceed to a recording studio in a nearby building. The route, as shown on a map each received, took them through an alley in which they passed a confederate of the experimenter who was lying in a doorway, coughing and groaning as if in pain. The question, of course, was how many of them would stop to assist the man in trouble—as did the subject shown in Figure 1–10.

In an attempt to study some of the factors that might influence the subjects, the experimenter gave half of them a discussion of job opportunities for seminary graduates to use as the basis for their talk; he gave the other half the story of the Good Samaritan, which, it seemed, might remind them of man's duty to help his fellow man. Moreover, the experimenter tried to measure whether they would be influenced by how much of a hurry they were in to reach the recording studio; he told some of them that they were early and should take their time, others that they were just about on schedule, and still others that they were late and should rush to the studio as fast as possible. In other words, the experimenter put a third of his subjects in what he termed a "low hurry" situation, a third in an "intermediate hurry," and another third in a "high hurry" situation.

Which subjects offered help to the man in pain and which did not? It turned out that it made no significant difference whether a subject had just read the Good Samaritan parable or the material on job opportunities. What did make a difference was how much of a hurry he was in. Of the "low hurry" subjects, 63 percent offered help; of the "intermediate hurry" subjects, 45 percent; and of the "high hurry" subjects, only 10 percent (32). The study would seem to indicate that bystander apathy is encouraged not only by the crowding in today's world but also by the rush of big-city life as contrasted with the more leisurely pace of smaller towns.

Some Conflicting Evidence on Bystander Apathy. Before leaving the subject of bystander apathy, it must be pointed out that not all experiments have produced uniform results. For example, in one study investigators pretended to collapse on the floor of a New York City subway car. In some cases they smelled of alcohol and carried a whisky bottle in a paper bag; it was logical for people riding in the car to assume that they were drunk. In other cases they showed no signs of having been drinking but instead carried a cane; it was logical to assume that their collapse was due to illness. Over a large number of trials, someone in the car went to the assistance of the "drunk" half the time, to the assistance of the "sick man" 95 percent of the time (33). In this experiment the by-standers"—actually by-sitters—may have been more inclined to help because they were in a face-to-face situation with the "victim" and in a confined space where they could not just ignore him and walk past. At any rate, the various experiments on bystander apathy indicate that it is a rather complex phenomenon that depends on many factors and takes varied forms under different circumstances.

Other Social Problems

There are many other social problems for which the findings of psychology have provided, if not the answers, at least some solid and objective information. Some of the information has already been put to work by our society. For example, research by clinical psychologists into the problem of abnormal behavior has helped bring about vast changes in the treatment of the mentally disturbed, who are no longer subjected to such barbarous practices as having holes bored into their skulls to let out evil spirits or being dosed with nauseating chemicals to purge them of their ailments. Disturbed children are no longer all classified alike and thrown together into institutions for the hopeless. Research has made it possible to distinguish among those who are mentally retarded for organic reasons or through faulty heredity, those who have been held back by bad environments, those who suffer from the psychosis called schizophrenia, and those who are delinquents; these various groups now receive different and often more successful treatment.

Research also has dispelled the old pessimistic notion that many people are destined from birth to be stupid or psychotic; it has shown that environment as well as heredity plays an important part in creating these problems. In particular, psychologists have learned the importance of the early years of childhood in establishing personality and have pointed the way toward more favorable methods of dealing with the child in the family, nursery schools, and day-care centers. They are investigating whether violence on TV can be harmful to children and have helped in the creation of shows that have a proven educational value. They also have provided valuable information about teaching in the schools, the problems of adolescents, sexual behavior and homosexuality, tensions in marriage, and the problems of divorce.

Summary

1. Psychology is the science that systematically studies and attempts to explain observable behavior and its relationship to the unseen mental processes that go on inside the organism and to external events in the environment.
2. The subject matter of psychology includes learning, thinking, problem solving, the senses, perception, emotions, motives, personality, and abnormal behavior.
3. The goals of psychology are to understand and predict behavior.
4. The science of psychology is empirical, which means that it is based on studies made with the greatest possible precision and objectivity.
5. Psychology began as a science when Wilhelm Wundt opened the first psychology laboratory in 1879.
6. Other important early psychologists were Francis Galton, who was interested in measuring individual differences; William James, who believed psychology to be "the science of mental life"; and John Watson, the founder of behaviorism.
7. Other important names in the history of psychology are B. F. Skinner, of the school of stimulus-response psychology; Jean Piaget, of the cognitive school; Carl Rogers and Abraham Maslow, of the humanistic school; and Sigmund Freud, the founder of psychoanalysis.
8. The methods of psychology include the experiment, naturalistic observation, tests, interviews, and questionnaires.
9. In an experiment, the experimenter controls the independent variable, which is set up independently of anything his subject does or does not do, and then studies the dependent variable, which is a change in the subject's behavior resulting from a change in the independent variable.
10. Although psychology is a pure science, interested in knowledge for the sake of knowledge, many of its findings have had a practical application in modern life. Examples of applied psychology include:
   a. Clinical and counseling psychology, or the diagnosis and treatment of behavior problems.
   b. The use of standardized tests and of the principles of learning.
   c. The use by industry of studies of the effects of fatigue, working hours, and employee morale; also of human engineering, which is the design of equipment and machinery

that fit the actual size, strength, and capabilities of the human beings who will use them.

d. Public opinion surveys.

11. Psychology has contributed insights into many social problems, including the generation gap, the use of drugs, and the results of the population explosion (including violence, crime, and "bystander apathy").

II. Surveying (Previewing) Chapter One of Psychology: An Introduction

Range, or Scope, of the Chapter: The title, of course, implies the question: What is the scope and what are the goals of psychology? The major subheadings indicate that the chapter will treat the past and present objectives of psychologists and the methods they have worked out to accomplish these objectives.

Underlying idea and points of emphasis: The chapter surveys the content of the introductory psychology course and previews the chapters that follow. It stresses that psychology is a newly developed science making use of empirical methods for the purpose of understanding and predicting human behavior (and in this way answers the title question).

Organizational Pattern: As the title and the introductory paragraphs under the major subheadings show, the purpose of the chapter is to correct any misunderstanding the reader may have about what psychologists do and what they do not do. And as the second- and third-level subheadings make clear, it does this by stressing throughout that psychology is indeed a science.

III. Questions for the Major Subheadings

SUBHEADING	QUESTION
A Definition of Psychology	What is psychology?
	or (probably a better question):
	What topics does psychology deal with?
The History of Psychology	What are the most important events in the history of psychology?
The Methods of Psychology	What methods do psychologists use to study the problems they are concerned with?
Applications of Psychology	In what ways can the "pure" science of psychology be applied to the study of people's problems?
	or:
	What specific methods do psychologists use to apply the principles of psychology to solutions to personal and social problems?
Psychology and Social Problems	How can psychological principles help us understand the problems of groups of people?

IV. Outline of section on "Applications of Psychology"

Main idea: In each of the sciences, one group of specialists is particularly concerned with the application of scientific principles to the solution of "practical" problems; in psychology, these people are called "applied psychologists."

I. Clinical psychologists and counselors
  A. Clinical psychologists diagnose and treat various kinds of behavior problems, using:
    1. tests
    2. psychotherapy
    3. group therapy
    4. encounter group therapy
  B. Counselors deal with school, vocational choice, and marriage problems
II. School and industrial psychologists
  A. School psychologists
    1. Consult with students, parents, and teachers concerning students' problems
    2. Administer standardized tests
      a. intelligence tests
      b. achievement tests
    3. Work with school personnel
      a. developing textbooks and other teaching aids
      b. improving curriculum
      c. providing information on study skills
  B. Industrial psychologists
    1. Study on-the-job problems
    2. Develop training devices
    3. Work out problems in "human engineering"—the design of suitable equipment and machinery

getting started in popular magazine articles 3

Not all the reading you do while in college will be textbook study. You will read fiction and non-fiction, short works and long ones, material that attempts to separate facts from point of view and material that does not. You will sometimes read works because they have been assigned or recommended and sometimes simply because you find them interesting. In all this reading you will find ways to use the skill you began learning in the last two chapters—that of looking for and interpreting the signals a writer plants in key places to make clear his purpose and his point of view. Perhaps the best way to begin extending this skill is to practice finding and interpreting these signals in articles in popular magazines. Then, in later chapters you will find it easy to apply this same skill to more diffi- cult articles, to non-fiction books, and even to works of fiction.

Your purpose in reading a magazine article is ordinarily simply to spend a few enjoyable minutes learning about something new or seeing how a writer develops an unusual idea. You do not expect to memorize information for an exam; therefore, you don't want summary sections and you usually do not need subheadings. And a title like "The Scope and Goals of Psychology" would probably turn you off completely. What you do want and expect is an attention-grabbing, direction-pointing title followed by some rather obvious clues within the article itself—words, phrases, and sentences that emphasize the writer's main point and relate subordinate ideas to that point. In most articles, that is exactly what you will find. However, learning to recognize internal signals or clues and relate them to the title quickly and easily may take a little practice.

TITLES AS SIGNALS

You may already be quite adept at interpreting magazine article titles. In fact, when you pick up magazines like those you find in a doctor's office, you probably decide whether or not to read articles (or parts of them) chiefly on the basis of what the titles promise. Although you certainly do not always analyze what you are doing, the chances are you select articles either because you are especially interested in acquiring factual *information* on the topic the title suggests, that is, in reading a *report* on the subject, or because a word or phrase in the title suggests a *point of view* that somehow intrigues you. Consider the following list of titles, for example. If you ran across these while browsing through magazines, which ones would you read only if you needed or wanted factual information on the subject? (Which ones imply that the article will answer quite directly the question *what* or *how?*) Put *report* beside these titles, skipping over for now the ones that interest you chiefly because the wording suggests a special way of looking at the subject.

1. "How to Grow Asparagus . . . from Seeds"
2. "The Nibbling Away of the West"
3. "Marketplace of the Unnecessary"
4. "Plants Have a Few Tricks, Too"
5. "The Dilemma of the Black Policeman"
6. "Should Chiropractors Be Paid with Your Tax Dollars?"
7. "Greening of Chicago"
8. "Mariner Ten Visits Littlest Planet"

You almost certainly noted "How to Grow Asparagus . . . from Seeds," you probably marked "Mariner Ten Visits Littlest Planet," and you may have included "Plants Have a Few Tricks, Too" (although "tricks" is a rather original word to use in referring to the behavior of plants). If you marked others, you have a strong appetite for facts. But think for a moment about what the other titles do that these titles (with the possible exception of "Tricks") do not do.

They all imply that the writer's point of view toward his subject will be explained in the article. "Should Chiropractors Be Paid with Your Tax Dollars?", with its direct appeal to the reader's pursestrings, is probably the most striking example. Would the writer have raised the question in the first place if his answer were to be anything but negative? And "Marketplace of the Unnecessary" plants in the reader's mind not only the question: What is the marketplace? but also: Why is what is sold there unnecessary?

Go through the list again, underlining words in the other titles that suggest that the writer will express a point of view—that is, that he will make a judgment about his subject and not simply provide information on it. Then turn to Chapter Supplement I (p. 76) and compare the answers given there with yours.

You are finding, then, that popular magazine article titles, like the titles of textbook chapters, suggest questions for which you can find the answers as you read. And, like those titles, they prepare you for supporting signals as you read on. But don't expect to find the subdivisions and subheadings that textbook writers usually provide. As the titles of articles indicate, the judgments article writers make or the bodies of information they treat are usually too narrow or too limited to be segmented that way.

What you will usually find is an introductory paragraph or a series of introductory paragraphs leading into the rest of the article in the same way that the opening sentence or opening sentences of each of the paragraphs you examined in Chapter One led into the rest of that paragraph. And within one or more of these introductory passages (especially in articles that make judgments) there will usually be a sentence that directly states the main idea of the article, answering the main question the title suggests. This kind of sentence is called a *thesis statement.*

The titles of magazine articles may suggest several questions to you because the language in these titles has usually been selected to attract your attention and to direct your thinking to topics you may have paid little attention to in the past. For this reason you may find that in addition to a thesis sentence that answers the main question there are several other "signal" sentences answering or in some way commenting on secondary questions the title brings to mind.

MATCHING TITLES WITH SIGNALS IN INTRODUCTORY PARAGRAPHS

The following section provides the opening paragraph or the first several paragraphs of most of the articles whose titles are listed on page 62. You are asked to match up titles with signal sentences, including statements of thesis. These sentences will usually answer either secondary or main questions suggested by the title, but some of them will ask additional questions or in some way qualify the questions the titles imply.

The articles are arranged more or less in the order of increasing complexity. The first one is worked out for you, and tips are provided for some of the others. However, you are encouraged to do your own thinking throughout.

In Chapter Supplement III, beginning on page 78, all these articles are presented in their complete form. You will have a chance, then, to read those that interest you particularly and to see how the writer develops his thesis or presents further information on his topic. (Your instructor may have other suggestions.)

1. "How to Grow Asparagus . . . from Seeds," by John McMahan (from *Natural Gardening*, February 1973)

Apparent purpose: To provide *information* that will make it possible for the reader to grow his own asparagus easily and successfully. (Note: There *could* be a point of view here. See, for example, the comments on manuals on page 23 of Chapter 2. It is probable, though, that an article with a "how to" title will have less of the writer's feelings and attitudes in it than most articles have.)

Possible title questions:
1. What procedures should one follow in planting and caring for asparagus?
2. Why start with seeds?
3. Why bother to plant asparagus in the first place?

Probable main question: Number 1.

Introductory paragraphs: The numbers in the margin indicate the paragraphs that answer or begin to answer the numbered questions above. In this passage, then, entire paragraphs serve as supportive signals.

Near the compost pile in one corner of our rhubarb patch is a little, straw-covered rectangle that pays its way ten times over with delicious asparagus in spring.

If you like asparagus, and have any ground at all, you should grow your own, too. It thrives anywhere north of Georgia, grows in all types of soil, doesn't cost much to start or maintain, and is easy to care for. A planting starts producing the second year and lasts fifteen to twenty years, or longer. Should you neglect it for any reason, it will produce anyhow, and keep on doing so for years.

(3)   Needless to say, there's no comparison between the succulent, tender spears you grow yourself and the dry, woody sticks in the supermarket.

(2)   My favorite approach to asparagus is to start it from seed. Then the cost of establishing a planting is unbelievably low. In fact, one ounce of seed, at a cost of eighty cents or so, will grow into enough for four people. For this amount, you can't buy one mess in the store, let alone have all you want for years and years.

(1)   To prepare for starting asparagus from seed, order an ounce of seed . . .

There is nothing difficult here. In fact, if you found this article in your own browsing, you would probably not be conscious of asking questions at all; and the direction of the opening paragraphs would be obvious without any formal analysis. Nevertheless, the writer has organized the article with the purpose of providing early answers to questions that his title suggests. Note that he works up to the main question by answering the secondary questions first. By the time you get to the sentence beginning with "To prepare for," you know that the rest of the article will be about methods. The writer expects you to go through the question and answer business without even thinking about it, and you probably would. (You may be intuitively aware that a "how to" article cannot really have a thesis statement and therefore you will not look for one.) The next example is a little trickier.

2. "The Nibbling Away of the West," by James Nathan Miller (from *The Reader's Digest*, December 1972)

Apparent purpose: To provide information that will convince the reader that the writer has a legitimate concern about something that is happening to "the West." "Nibbling" is a term that suggests a judgment. Compare: "Johnny, stop nibbling at your food" with "Johnny is eating his dinner."

Possible title questions:
1. Who is doing the nibbling?
2. Where does it occur? (What is meant by "The West?")
3. Does the writer mean the literal kind of nibbling—eating—or something else? (We do talk about nibbling away at jobs and other things besides food.)
4. Why is this "nibbling" a problem?
5. What can be done about it?

Probable main question: Either 4 or 5, or a combination of both. You expect the writer's *point of view* about the situation he discusses to come out in the article; whether he will pose a specific solution is uncertain at this point.

Introductory paragraphs: Underline phrases that answer each of the questions above and place in the margin the numbers of the questions being answered. In this article, in addition to these signal phrases there is a thesis sentence. What is it? Underline it and write "thesis" in the margin. Then compare your answers with those in Chapter Supplement II (p. 77).

> Last summer I stood at the edge of a 40-foot cliff that formed one bank of the San Simon River in southeast Arizona. Looking at the opposite cliff, 200 feet away across the bone-dry gorge, I found it almost impossible to believe that this 60-mile-long gash in the earth had been produced mainly by the nibbling and pawing of cattle. The story of how it was done is probably the country's most flagrant—and least recognized—example of the squandering of a national resource: the overgrazing of the West by cattle and sheep.
>
> The San Simon River runs through the middle of 1.2 million acres of public domain known as the Safford Grazing District, which is under the jurisdiction of the U.S. Bureau of Land Management (BLM). It is a Delaware-size patch of cactus and sagebrush that the agency rents out to 173 stockmen—one of 52 such districts in the 11 western states. Altogether, these districts total 177 million acres, an area slightly larger than Texas.

Perhaps you discovered how easy it is to follow the information the writer presents in paragraph two, once you have noted his thesis. You will find this is true of the information in the rest of the article as well.

3. "Marketplace of the Unnecessary," by Jack Smith (from *Westways*, October 1972)

Apparent purpose: To describe an unusual kind of shopping area, giving information but at the same time presenting the writer's perspective (See comments on page 00.)

Possible title questions:
1. Where is the marketplace?
2. What is sold there?
3. Why are the things that are sold "unnecessary"? (A reader who knew Smith's generally light-touch writing in his newspaper columns would probably ask: How serious is he here? Is he criticizing or just humorously commenting as he uses this word?)
4. What is so special or unusual about this marketplace?

▶ IF THE TITLE SUGGESTS ANY ADDITIONAL QUESTIONS TO YOU, ADD THEM HERE:

Probable main question: You really can't tell at this point. Questions 2, 3, and 4 all seem important.

Introductory paragraphs: Question 1 is answered in several different ways in these paragraphs. Underline the phrases that answer it and put 1 beside them. Questions 2 and 3 are not referred to at all here.

Question 4 is answered partially by a phrase that gives *factual information* about ways the place he is talking about differs from other markets and partially by a phrase that expresses Smith's *point of view* about the things that are sold there (without showing why they are "unnecessary"). Underline these phrases and identify them by marking in the margin "factual info." and "pt. of view." Then check Chapter Supplement II (p. 77) for comments.

Some years ago when I was interviewing Romain Gary, the French novelist and diplomat, he spoke of Los Angeles as one of the beautiful cities of the world. He had been posted here a few years earlier as French consul general and was back on a visit.

Why do Americans always say Los Angeles is such an ugly city?" he asked. "This is a great piece of conventional thinking. People like to hate something, and once they hate, they can't quit."

"Ventura Boulevard, for example, is supposed to be an ugly place. I adore driving through Ventura Boulevard. People look at me with incomprehension when I say that. I know all the shacks and cubicles are temporary. But meanwhile they are so full of wonderful things. . . ."

If Gary were to drive the length of Ventura Boulevard today

he would find that the shacks and cubicles are still there, most of of them; but if he were to stop and look inside, he might be pleased to find they are still "so full of wonderful things."

Ventura Boulevard, from Studio City to Woodland Hills, is a twelve-mile long marketplace. It was designed by the automobile. . . .

Remembering the title, you may be wondering how the things sold on Ventura Boulevard can be both "wonderful" and "unnecessary." If you look at one more sentence from the article, you will find an answer to this question, and you will also see how in introductory paragraphs a writer can open up new questions and yet bring the reader back to the title question.

. . . As Gary suggested, one shops by car, shopping here for a wig, there for a pound of mocha; driving on for a pizza, a steam bath, a game of miniature golf, a boa constrictor or a karate lesson; then turning around to shop the other side of the street for an antique rocker, a car wash, a poodle trim, a house plant or a water bed.

Try putting in your own words the idea you find Smith developing so far in the essay. Consider both what he finds unusual about this "marketplace" and how he feels about what he finds.

▶

Did you sense that Smith finds the whole scene a bit ridiculous—but pleasantly ridiculous? The words "wonderful" and "unnecessary" do go together then. The merchants of this marketplace sell all kinds of exotic things most people would never think of looking for, as the rest of the article bears out.

4. "Plants Have a Few Tricks, Too" (from *Natural History*, December 1972)

Apparent Purpose: To provide information about the "behavior" of plants.

Title questions: This time, list your own questions. In the comments following the introductory paragraphs, there are some questions that you can compare with yours. The exact wording of your questions is not important, however. What is important is that you use the clues the writer gives you in the title to begin thinking along with him.

▶

Probable main question:

▶

Introductory paragraphs: As you read, underline and number the answers to your questions as you come to them and underline and label any sentence that looks like a thesis statement, one which answers your main question in a general way.

   All creatures living in the wild are subject to attack by predators, and their survival as a species depends in large measure on their success in fending off such attacks. Animals have many obvious self-defense mechanisms. Some, for example, hide from enemies by merging into the landscape so that it is difficult to see them; others hide by deliberately popping into a hole or under a rock. Because of their speed, some creatures outrun potential predators, while others outlast them by superior stamina during a long pursuit. A cornered or alarmed animal can ward off an enemy by obnoxious odors, gestures, or noises, and in a pinch can stand and fight off an attacker. Even when faced with a microscopic invader, such as a bacterium, a fungus, or a foreign protein of any kind, many animals can react with a variety of defenses, including ingestion of the attacker by special mobile body cells or the formation of specific antibodies that couple with the invading protein or cell and render it harmless.
   Plants, by contrast, seem at first sight to be relatively defenseless against attack, but a closer look reveals that they do have some mechanisms for warding off other organisms. For the most part, they are incapable of sufficiently rapid motion to do damage to an animal, although the insect-trapping devices of the sundew and of Venus's-flytrap have been widely popularized. Upon mechanical stimulation the leaves of the sensitive plant will rapidly fold, which is said to protect the plant against foraging animals. . . .

  Did you anticipate the kind of information that the first paragraph gives—comment about the ways animals defend themselves against attackers? As the writer says in his thesis statement (first sentence, paragraph two), this information is included to provide contrast with the main topic. Many magazine article writers use this sort of beginning. Jack Smith did, for example, when he contrasted what most people say about Los Angeles with what the French consul and Smith think about it. In "Plants Have a Few Tricks, Too," however, the comparison is more extensive, as the last word in the title suggests that it will be.

Possible title questions, then, are:

1. What other forms of life have "tricks"?
2. Do plants act at all like animals?
3 What are these plant "tricks"?
4. How effective are they?

You may have thought of other questions or worded these differently. But as you have seen, the first paragraph does answer question 1 in some detail and the second one begins to answer question 2. You could expect either 3 or 4 to be the main question, and if you read the rest of the article (see pp. 91–93), you will find that it answers both specifically. (A straight informative article does not always answer a single large question, as does an article developing a point of view.)

5. "The Dilemma of the Black Policeman," by Alex Poinsett (from *Ebony*, May 1971)

Apparent purpose: As Chapter Supplement I suggests, the purpose of this article is not entirely clear from the title. (Titles are not always self-explanatory.) But you do know that the writer is concerned about a problem, and therefore his point of view will probably come out quite clearly early in the article.

Title questions: Because you probably remember that "dilemma" means a problem to which there is no clear solution, your first question about this title could well be:

1. What difficulty do black policemen have that is serious enough to deserve that description?

But if you had found the title in the Table of Contents of the magazine in which the article originally appeared, your eye would have been attracted by the following caption almost as soon as you began to think about the title:

"Lawmen Find Their Loyalty Torn Between Two Masters"
This comment partially answers question 1, but it also raises another question. List it below:

▶ 2.

The space on the following page is provided for additional questions that the title and secondary caption together may suggest to you. Include a possible *main question,* if you think of one.

▶

Introductory paragraphs: Again, you will probably find your questions answered directly in the beginning of the article. And by the time you have finished the fourth paragraph, you will not only know what the writer's main question is, but you will have been given a general answer to that question.

This article begins, as most of the others have, with specific information rather than with generalizations. The examples given in the first three paragraphs begin to answer the first two title questions. Put numbers in the margin when you find these questions being answered by examples.

> In a Chicago police garage, a black policeman removes his gunbelt and warns a white police officer, "I'm going to beat your brains out." The angry policeman is bent on punishing his colleague for hauling a black youth from a paddy wagon and clubbing him to the ground. But three other black officers stop the fight before it starts.
>
> In Atlanta a black patrolman bitterly complains before a news conference that he saw five white officers beat three black prisoners inside the police station.
>
> In San Francisco, a black officer reports: "We've been lucky that there hasn't been a real shootout." And a Detroit black policeman concludes: "It's bad out here, man, real bad. And if something isn't done soon by somebody, you'll see a lot more black officers pulling their guns on white officers."

The next paragraph starts out with a general statement, gives specific information to support it, and concludes with additional generalizations. Underline these general statements, put in the margins the numbers of the questions they answer, and write "thesis" beside the sentence you feel serves as a thesis statement. Also, underline the emotive or judgment-making words in each of these sentences.

> These glimpses into the violent world of the policeman hint at the rising hostility between black and white policemen in several major cities across the nation. Fist fights in locker rooms, racial slurs scrawled on police station walls, refusals to share patrol cars with colleagues of a different color—all are eruptions from an undercurrent of animosity that has been surfacing in recent years,

splitting police departments into racial camps. Last summer, for example, 20 blacks and 200 whites exchanged punches because a white girl danced with a black man at the annual Fraternal Order of Police picnic in Pittsburgh. And an Atlantic City convention of the black National Council of Police Societies resolved last summer that henceforth black policemen would try to prevent the killing of blacks by white policemen, even if it meant arresting them. These tension-filled responses speak to the rampant racism characterizing most police departments. It is racism in which, as social analyst W. H. Ferry angrily puts it, "the cop's trigger-finger is the gavel of justice in blacktown."

Now try stating the main question you expect the writer to answer as you think back to the title and caption that went with it, matching them with the other clues you have been given in the introductory portion of the article. Then state in your own words the answer he has begun to give.

▶ PROBABLE MAIN QUESTION:

▶ GENERAL ANSWER:

Compare your observations with those given in Chapter Supplement II, (p. 77).

You probably had no difficulty recognizing emotive language in "The Dilemma of the Black Policeman." Words like "racism" and "hostility" are more packed with feeling than the language used in the introductory paragraphs of any of the earlier articles. You will find some equally strong wording in "Should Chiropractors Be Paid with Your Tax Dollars?" Both writers use a combination of specific information and judgment-making expressions to accomplish their purpose: to attract readers to the positions they hold on current social issues. There is no reason for writers not to do this, but there is every reason for you as a reader to be aware when the technique is being used. Instead of being manipulated, you will then read critically; that is, you will read to see how effectively the evidence given supports the generalizations made.

6. "Should Chiropractors Be Paid with Your Tax Dollars?" by Albert Q. Maisel (from *Reader's Digest*, July 1971)

Apparent purpose: To convince the reader that he may be asked to give undeserved support to the chiropractic profession.

Title questions: The title asks what you can assume will be the main question;

and, as suggested earlier, you can expect that the writer's answer will be "No." (Note that he places the emotionally-loaded phrase "your tax dollars" at the end of the title, giving it a strongly negative emphasis.) What other questions do you expect him to answer along the way?

▶

Some possible questions are: What is a chiropractor? Who says they should be paid out of taxes? Are chiropractors paid by anyone other than their own clients? (The word "paid" is an odd one here; although it is a specific term, it has emotional undertones.) What is the issue here, anyway? What is the writer arguing against? Why is he as opposed to chiropractors as he appears to be?

Introductory paragraphs: As you read the first several paragraphs of this article, you may be surprised to find that it starts out to be a relatively factual, objective report. It may appear to be simply an historical account of the development of the chiropractic profession. However, remembering the negative tone of the title, you will want to watch for signals that show how the writer is interpreting the information he puts together. The signals are quite subtle this time. Rather than writing general sentences that sum up exactly what he is thinking about the subject, this writer simply works in *emotive* words or phrases. Many of these are expressions that would be given a sarcastic inflection if read aloud and for that reason have a negative *connotation*. The writer's negative attitude becomes increasingly obvious as you read on. Try putting a question mark in the margin when you first suspect a negative point of view, the abbreviation *"neg."* when you are reasonably certain, and an exclamation point when there is no question.

The battle lines are firmly drawn between the chiropractors and their foes. In lobbying for federal payment for their services, chiropractors argue that they are members of a recognized health profession, licensed by all states except Louisiana and Mississippi. As such, they contend that they should be granted the same status that Medicare has accorded to doctors of medicine and osteopathy.

Critics of chiropractic, including the American Medical Association, maintain that it is a form of quackery, and that those who practice it are no more entitled to recognition than snake-oil peddlers. Because chiropractors lack both the training and the background to diagnose or treat diseases, critics claim, underwriting their "services" would actually endanger the lives of countless Medicare patients by delaying accurate diagnosis of major ailments.

Given these diametrically opposed viewpoints, let us try to discover where the truth and the public interest lie.

The Palmer Method. Chiropractic owes its existence to a single man, David Daniel Palmer, a grocer-turned-"magnetic healer" who, in 1895, "cured" one patient of deafness, another of heart trouble, by manual adjustments of their vertebrae. On the basis of these two cases, Palmer concluded: "If diseases so dissimilar as deafness and heart trouble came from pressure on nerves," then "a subluxated [partly dislocated] vertebra is the cause of 95 percent of all diseases." Since then, chiropractors have adhered basically to Palmer's single-cause theory of disease and to his method of treating all illness by adjustments of the spine.

Today, the estimated 15,000 to 17,000 active chiropractors are divided into two, often bitterly contending, groups. Representing the so-called "straights" is the International Chiropractors Association, which regards any form of treatment other than spinal adjustment as a heretical deviation from the doctrines laid down by the founder. The "mixers," represented by the American Chiropractic Association, augment their spinal adjustments with nutritional supplements and with some forms of physiotherapy. Both groups, however, renounce the use of all forms of medication, vaccination, and surgery.

Schools for Salesmanship. After making his discovery, Palmer opened a chiropractic school to teach others how to adjust spines. The course ran for several months, and the only admission requirement was a $500 fee. His son, B. J. Palmer, put the school on its feet with advertising that effectively promoted a cheap way to acquire quickly both a good income and prestige. "Our school," he explained, "is on a business, not a professional, basis. We manufacture chiropractors."

Before comparing your analysis of the writer's signals with that given in Chapter Supplement II (p. 78), try writing a brief statement of the idea developed in this part of the article.

▶

Did you realize that Maisel traces the evolution of the occupation of chiropractor as a way of showing why he thinks that the federal government should not grant chiropractors the status of medical doctors? In a way, he is "signaling," through this introductory section, that the approach of the entire article will be historical, but that the history he presents will defend his basic position that chiropractors are not legitimate doctors. In the rest of the article, then, you could expect him to show that twentieth century chiropractors have some of the same limitations that he found in those who started the movement.

7. "The Greening of Chicago," by Carol Costello (from *Holiday,* January–February 1973)

Apparent purpose: See comments in Chapter Supplement I (p. 76).

Title question: There is one obvious question this time, although it could be put in a number of ways. How would you put it?

▶

Introductory paragraphs: "Greening," like other articles in this group, begins with information and comments that contrast with the principal point that the writer is building up to. Generalizations, however, are handled a bit differently here: There are more of them and they relate to one another in a different way. As you read the first several pargaraphs, put "con." in the margin when you think the writer is building up to a contrasting point and "gen." when he makes a general statement that seems to have something to do with his main idea. Don't worry about a thesis sentence yet.

Say "Chicago" to a European kid and he will mimic a machine gun and mutter knowingly, "Al Capone." Everybody knows about Chicago, Sandburg's "city of the big shoulders." It's the tough, heavy-handed Hog Butcher to the World, the vice-ridden Toddlin' Town, the gutsy City That Made Its River Run Backwards. It's the "city on the make" that keeps pulling itself up by sheer chutzpah and razzmatazz.

Chicagoans love to rail about their city's faults, but they can't leave until they see if Mayor Daley, Saul Bellow, and the Picasso sculpture in the Civic Center can get through another year together, "I should go to New York, but. . . ." They don't have to finish the sentence, whether they are sitting in a neighborhood bar or the Pump Room.

But a funny thing is happening in Chicago. It began, perhaps coincidentally, about the time the stockyards were torn down. While no one was looking, Chicago began slouching towards Consciousness III.

Consciousness III, according to Charles Reich's *The Greening of America,* dawned with the bell-bottomed Age of Aquarius. It is a joyful, iconoclastic celebration of self that eclipses the Consciousness I jungle of pioneer America, where it was every man for himself and only the hardy survived, and the stifling corporate meritocracy of Consciousness II.

In Chicago, Consciousness III means forgetting about the Second City syndrome, taking a look around, and doing new things with the old forms. Some people call it the Chicago Renaissance, but it's just the same old dynamics stalking new territory. Chicago is learning to enjoy itself. If "I will" can build skyscrapers, railroads, and steel mills, why not the finer things in life?

The first two paragraphs, as you probably discovered, present a stereotyped picture of the "old Chicago." All the details in these paragraphs contrast with the "new Chicago" that Carol Costello says is now emerging. Several general sentences in paragraphs 3, 4, and 5 sum up these new developments. They are arranged below in the order in which they appear in these paragraphs.

1. "But a funny thing is happening in Chicago."
2. "While no one was looking, Chicago began slouching toward Consciousness III."
3. "It [Consciousness III] is a joyful, iconoclastic celebration of self. . . ."
4. "Chicago is learning to enjoy itself."
5. "Why not the finer things in life?" (for Chicago)

All these sentences may be called *general* because all of them could apply to more than one kind of situation or object or event. However, some represent higher levels of generalization than others do. "But a funny thing is happening in Chicago," for example, could mean almost anything, depending on the point of view of the writer. Try arranging these sentences in the frame below, with the number of the most general statement at the top and those of the others listed in the order of decreasing level of generalization.

▶

    ———

    ———

    ———

    ———

    ———

Didn't you come up with something very much like what you started out with? With the exception of sentence 4, which is about at the same level as sentence 3, the statements become increasingly less general in the order in which they are presented in the article. Which of these sentences do you think states the thesis in the most specific terms in which it could be expressed? Put "thesis" beside that sentence. Have you found a general answer to your original question? Express it in a few of your own words in the space below:

▶

You could consider either sentence 4 or sentence 5 to be a thesis sentence— or possibly both together. There is no way of knowing yet for certain what kinds of "greening" the writer will be discussing, but these will surely include the arts ("the finer things") and they will probably include other forms of enjoyment. Your question and general answer could be something like the following:

In what sense is Chicago "greening"?

New developments in the arts and in entertainment (this would have to be a guess at this point) suggest that Chicago is losing some of its atmosphere of sombreness and business efficiency and that the people in Chicago are learning to enjoy themselves.

Of course, there is much more to reading any piece of prose, even a popular magazine article, than simply understanding the writer's point of view as it is presented or implied in the early paragraphs. However, you will find that the skill you have developed in this chapter (supplemented by speed reading skills you have probably been acquiring through other sources) will make it possible for you to read quickly and comprehendingly the kind of non-fiction that has been sampled here. In this kind of material, once you have discovered exactly what the writer is talking about, what his attitude is toward his subject, and what kind of language he is going to use to get across that attitude, you will probably have little difficulty following the development of his idea (although you may occasionally need to use a dictionary). Other kinds of writing will require additional techniques, but in learning these techniques you will be building on skills already learned in these first three chapters.

CHAPTER SUPPLEMENTS

I. "Point of View Words" in Article Titles

1. "Nibbling Away of the West"—The writer probably doesn't like what he sees happening to the West. How much he dislikes whatever it is he is talking about you can't tell until you read the article.
2. "Dilemma of the Black Policeman"—At first glance you may expect the article to be strictly informative. However, if you check "dilemma" in a dictionary, you will find that it is used to describe a situation in which a person has a choice between two courses of action—but they are equally undesirable. The writer's choice of the word indicates that he has some feelings about the problem—although of course you do not know what they are or what the problem is. He will certainly show the *sense* in which he finds the problem to be a dilemma.
3. "Greening of Chicago"—This one could easily fool you. You could expect it to be an informative account of the way some person or group is making Chicago greener through a tree-planting program. But if you know the book title *The Greening of America*, you may have sensed the word play here and correctly guessed that the article is about new ways of living and a new attitude toward life that the writer sees developing in Chicago. And writers rarely treat other people's attitudes without revealing their own. Therefore, you will

expect a point of view about what's happening in Chicago to come through here.

II. Signals in Opening Paragraphs

"Nibbling Away of the West":
1. <u>cattle</u>
2. <u>Southeast Arizona</u> (However, note that in the last line of paragraph one, the writer refers to the overgrazing of "the West"—a title word. You can't tell at this point whether he is going to talk about just this one portion of the West or about a wider territory, but the repetition of the title word implies the latter.)
3. <u>nibbling and pawing of cattle</u> (literal eating)
4. <u>Thesis statement:</u> "The story of how it was done is probably the country's most <u>flagrant</u>—and least recognized—example of the <u>squandering</u> of a national resource: the overgrazing of the West by cattle and <u>sheep</u>." (The words that are underlined are judgmental terms that make very clear how the writer feels about the problem he is reporting. At this point there is still no way of knowing whether he will suggest a specific solution to the problem.)

"Marketplace of the Unnecessary":
1. <u>Los Angeles</u> (second paragraph); more specifically, <u>Ventura Boulevard</u> (third and fourth paragraphs); and even more specifically, <u>Ventura Boulevard, from Studio City to Woodland Hills</u> (fifth paragraph)
4. The phrase that gives factual information about the unusualness of this shopping place is "a twelve-mile long marketplace." The one that provides Smith's point of view is "so full of wonderful things."

"Dilemma of the Black Policeman":
Paragraphs 1, 2, 3: These give examples of the problem—strife between black and white members of city police departments. They also imply that the two "masters" the black policemen serve are their employers (police department management) and their consciences (or their sense of brotherhood).

Paragraph 4: The first sentence is a general sentence; the key judgment-making phrases are "violent world" and "rising hostility." The last two sentences are also general and either of these (or the two together) could be considered thesis sentences. "Tension-filled," "rampant racism" and "racism" (repeated) are all judgment-making expressions. "Racism" is especially important, as it sums up the writer's point of view.

Main question and general answer: Did you sense by the time you had finished the fourth paragraph that the writer is really concerned with the *cause* of strife between racial groups in police departments? He is not simply going to describe the situation that exists; he is rather going to trace it to its roots. In the last two sentences (and earlier in phrases like "punishing his colleague for hauling a black youth from the paddy wagon") he makes quite clear where he thinks the responsibility lies: many white police officers have prejudice toward blacks. You can expect him to develop this point throughout the rest of the article.

"Should Chiropractors Be Paid with Your Tax Dollars?":
Signals in the opening paragraphs: The issue here, as Maisel tells us in the last sentence of the first paragraph, is whether Medicare should be used to pay chiropractors' fees for Medicare beneficiaries. And his answer, of course, is a strong negative.

A key emotive term is "quackery" (in the second line of the second paragraph), a term that provides a strong hint of his point of view (a "negative—?" signal). Although Maisel uses the word here to show the position of the "critics of chiropractic," as the article progresses it becomes increasingly clear that he, too, regards chiropractic as "quackery." Not only does he allow the reader to associate chiropractors with "snake-oil peddlers" (paragraph two, line four), but he refers to the founder of chiropractic as a "magnetic healer" who "cured" a patient of deafness (paragraph four, line three). Note how sarcasm is accomplished by the use of quotation marks around "cured" and around "services" (line six, paragraph two). Aren't these "neg." signals?

The last two quoted paragraphs expand on the quackery idea. In the first of these, the International Chiropractors Association, the "straights," is compared with religious organizations (paragraph five, line five). ("Heretical" and doctrines" are usually used in reference to religious groups.) And, in the last paragraph, the original chiropractic school is made to sound like a business operation. Certainly the implication is that chiropractors are not professional medical practictioners. As the usual definition of a "quack" is a "pretender to medical knowledge or skill" it seems clear that Maisel's purpose here is to show that chiropractors should not be given federal support because they are "pretenders" rather than legitimate doctors. It would be appropriate to put "!" anywhere in this paragraph (and you may have found "!" signals even earlier).

III. Articles for Study

HOW TO GROW ASPARAGUS...
FROM SEEDS

by John McMahan
from Natural Gardening, *February 1973*

Near the compost pile in one corner of our rhubarb patch is a little, straw-covered rectangle that pays its way ten times over with delicious asparagus in spring.

If you like asparagus, and have any ground at all, you should grow your own, too. It thrives anywhere north of Georgia, grows in all types of soil, doesn't cost much to start or maintain, and is easy to care for. A planting starts producing the second year and last fifteen to twenty years, or longer. Should you neglect it for any reason, it will produce anyhow, and keep on doing so for years.

Needless to say, there's no comparison between the succulent, tender spears you grow yourself and the dry, woody sticks in the supermarket.

My favorite approach to asparagus is to start it from seed. Then the cost of establishing a planting is unbelievably low. In fact, one ounce of seed, at a cost of eighty cents or so, will grow into enough for four people. For this amount, you can't buy one mess in the store, let alone have all you want for years and years.

To prepare for starting asparagus from seed, order an ounce of seed ('Mary Washington' is an excellent variety), and choose a spot on your property measuring about 20 feet by 10 feet—or its equivalent (enough for 80 feet of row).

As early in the spring as possible, plow, spade, or till the plot, and work it down. Then, lay out four rows, 2½ feet apart, and sow the asparagus seed evenly in them. Cover the seed carefully with ½ inch of fine soil.

The seed will sprout and grow slowly, giving rise to tiny spears followed by the characteristic fern-like plants of summer in miniature. Cultivate and hoe them during the summer to kill weeds and to keep the soil loose and crumbly. If you don't have time to give them perfect care, don't worry because they will tolerate a little neglect.

When winter comes, you should do three things if you want the greatest returns for the least work.

First, mulch the patch to stop weed growth the following summer. For mulching material, you can use straw, sawdust, pine needles, wood chips, etc. Use whatever's cheap and available where you live.

Apply the mulch heavily between rows (6 inches or more for straw, 2 to 3 for heavier materials), very lightly over the row itself. Mulch will retard sprouting a week or so in the spring, but this slight drawback is over-balanced by a longer harvest period, a larger overall crop and no weeding chores.

Second, apply fertilizer sometime in the late winter. Be sure to do this before new growth starts. If you use commercial fertilizer, scatter about 15 pounds of 10-10-10 or something similar. Organic fertilizers are even better, either with or in place of the commercial mixtures. Some common ones are compost, bonemeal, rock phosphate, potash rock, greenstand, cottonseed meal, soybean meal, dried blood, and various manures. You may apply the organic materials more freely than you do the others because they aren't likely to "burn" new growth.

Finally, a few weeks before new growth is expected, cut off all the past summer's top growth. A power mower or swinging scythe works well at this job. By doing it, you'll get the old tops out of the way and down on the ground where they'll decompose sooner. The reason for waiting until late winter is to give any nutrients in the stalks time to move down to the roots.

From this point on, the asparagus will take care of itself, except for the yearly mowing of old growth and an occasional round of re-fertilizing and re-mulching. Even if you were to neglect the planting completely now, it would still produce for many years.

Some people advise digging the year-old roots and re-setting them farther apart, a practice which greatly enlarges your planting but also sets it back in production. In my experience it's been just as satisfactory (and much easier) to leave the plants where they are and let them do what they will. If you choose to re-set, wait and apply fertilizer and mulch to the re-set plantation.

Watching for asparagus to sprout in the spring quickly becomes a yearly pleasure. Harvest begins with the first sprout and continues steadily until hot weather. And, even later in the summer, you can usually pick a mess after a good shower.

For the first two months in spring, you can harvest all the shoots if you want to. In fact, close harvesting of early spears will stimulate further sprouting. After that, for the good of the plants, it's wise to let some grow on to maturity.

Of course you can't harvest anything the year you plant the seeds because the shoots are too tiny. The second year they'll still be small, and you need to use some restraint. But the third you can let your appetite be your guide.

The harvest seems to improve with each passing year. And you can expect a harvest every spring because stopping the sprouting of asparagus would be like stopping spring itself.

The only disease of note is asparagus rust. Avoid it by planting a resistant variety like 'Mary Washington'. If you do this, you won't even know the disease exists.

Asparagus beetles eat the shoots and lay eggs on them which look like black specks. Cucumber beetles occasionally join the banquet, too. Fortunately, if you like asparagus young and tender, you'll harvest 95 per cent of the crop before the beetles can get to it.

So, don't panic if you see these handsome beetles in the asparagus patch. Just restrict them to their five per cent by beating them to the harvest; and if it makes you feel better, give them the heel of your boot whenever you can.

THE NIBBLING AWAY OF THE WEST

by James Nathan Miller
from The Reader's Digest, *December 1972*

Last summer I stood at the edge of a 40-foot cliff that formed one bank of the San Simon River in southeast Arizona. Looking at the opposite cliff, 200 feet away across the bone-dry gorge, I found it almost impossible to believe that this 60-mile-long gash in the earth had been produced mainly by the nibbling and pawing of cattle. The story of how it was done is probably the country's most flagrant—and least recognized—example of the squandering of a national resource: the overgrazing of the West by cattle and sheep.

The San Simon River runs through the middle of 1.2 million acres of public domain known as the Safford Grazing District, which is under the jurisdiction of the U.S. Bureau of Land Management (BLM). It is a Delaware-size patch of cactus and sagebrush that the agency rents out to 173 stockmen—one of 52 such districts in the 11 western states. Altogether, these districts total 177 million acres, an area slightly larger than Texas.

To understand how the Safford District got into its present shape, start with the sight that greeted immigrants in the 1870s as they rode into the valley of the San Simon. It was "a promised land," wrote an early settler: from end to end, a thick, waving sea of perennial grass and wild flowers so tall that they brushed the settlers' stirrups. Antelope abounded, and down the valley's middle tumbled a clear stream lined with cottonwoods, alive with birds and small game.

The grass that made all this possible was what's called "climax vegetation." Over the centuries, its roots and foliage had woven themselves into such a dense mat that no other plant could penetrate the mass. Sagebrush and cactus had been forced up into the hills, leaving the grass the land's final possessor and protector.

Pocket Grand Canyon. By the 1880s the valley floor was filled with 50,000 head of grazing cattle, consuming 1000 tons of grass a day, and within a dozen years the entire valley had been nibbled as bald as a billiard table. Then the grass—its roots compressed and torn by the pounding herd, its blades unable to form seeds— began to sicken and die. Into the bare patches, down from the hills, crept the scraggly sagebrush and cactus.

The stream was killed just as rapidly. First, the hoofs of watering cattle cut away at the cottonwood roots; the the trees sickened, the water turned to mud, the fish died, the birds and animals disappeared. Finally, the massive summer thunderstorms, no longer swallowed up by the great sponge of grass, came-rushing downhill to slice pocket-size Grand Canyons through the unprotected earth. By 1900 the once-verdant valley had become a desolate wasteland, and by 1934 it—along with tens of millions of acres of similar western rangeland—was in such pitiful condition that the government stepped in to stop the damage.

But today, after four decades of government management, these lands are still being heavily overgrazed. In the San Simon valley the damage is worse this year than almost ever before, because the BLM has allowed grazing-as-usual despite a two-year drought that has virtually wiped the remaining grass off a large part of the Southwest. Many pastures are 90-percent bare earth, their soil pouring into western rivers at almost a ton per acre each year. "When it rains here," says Safford District manager William Earp, "the range melts away like sugar."

But there's still enough topsoil to grow plenty of grass. If the BLM would just reduce the grazing to the point where the remaining scattered clumps could produce seed, in five years or so the valley would start to green up again, and in perhaps 15 or 20 years most of it would be just as it was the old days.

"Let Them Graze." Why doesn't the Bureau restrict grazing? In Washington, Harrison J. Loesch, Assistant Secretary of the Interior in charge of the BLM, gave me the answer. If he could, he admitted, "I'd be inclined to pull every head of cattle off the range in Arizona until the drought is over." But he can't. "Every time you lower a man's grazing a bit, you get a squawk. So you have to do it gradually or get into a big Congressional hassle."

That's the crux of the matter: the political power of the livestock industry. Back in the Safford District, a BLM range manager explained, "Whenever we try to cut the number of cows, a rancher will write to his Congressman, and pretty soon word comes down from headquarters: Let them graze."

Nationally, the damage is on a scale all its own—the country's "biggest source of resource deterioration and environmental degradation," in the words of an internal BLM memorandum. The BLM admits it is improving only 14 percent of its huge domain. The rest—150 million acres, or a thousand times the strip-mined area of the United States—is either deteriorating or in a static condition. Each year half a billion tons of topsoil are washed away from the public lands—more mud than is discharged by the Colorado and Mississippi rivers combined.

Wildlife, too, is taking a terrible beating as domestic livestock trample its habitat and gobble its forage. In hundreds of critical winter feeding grounds, deer, elk and other species, driven down from the mountains by the heavy snow, stalk the public cow pastures like scavengers. According to the BLM's own figures, 37 percent of its wildlife habitat is in "unsatisfactory" condition. But experts within the agency put the actual figure closer to 50 percent.

The BLM is not alone. For all these conditions the U.S. Forest Service (USFS)—which manages 105 million grazing acres of its own—must share the blame.

Belly-Deep in Flowers. Yet the fact is that the overwhelming majority of these man-made deserts can be made to bloom again. On a two-square-mile meadow called Mule Park, in Colorado's Gunnison National Forest, I saw a dramatic example of how it's done.

In the 1940s, Mule Park was a sea of dirt pounded bare by 500 head of cattle. Then, in 1950, the Forest Service forced the local rancher to cut his herd to 291 animals, built fences and water holes to distribute the cows over a wide area, allowing the fields to reseed themselves. The cows were scientifically rotated from pasture to pasture, giving the grass plenty of time for vigorous root-and-seed-producing growth between grazings. In certain fields the cattle were admitted just long enough to brush the seeds off the plants and trample them into the ground. It worked so well that in 1963 the rancher was allowed to increase the herd to 490 head—

just ten under the original number. Today the cows in Mule Park graze belly-deep in a sea of wild flowers and perenial grasses.

The catch: only ten percent of the BLM's land (and a claimed 50 percent of USFS land) is under such management plans, in which the ranchers share costs with the government in building fences and digging wells. For although many progressive ranchers are deeply concerned about the land's deterioration, the great majority fight anything smacking of even temporary reduction in grazing.

But it's important to keep two facts in mind. First, these people are not "robber barons." While plenty of millionaire cattlemen use the public lands, for every one of these there are dozens of small, marginal, hard-working ranchers trying to support their families on a hundred head of cattle or so. Second, though most of the range they have ruined is publicly owned, they did nothing illegal in ruining it. For, until 1934, there were no laws covering this land. The BLM's domain is "the land nobody wanted"—neither homesteaders, nor miners nor loggers—and there has always been the basic assumption in the West that the ranchers, who arrived first on this range and whose livelihoods depend on it, have special rights to it.

Rabbits in the Cabbage Patch. Indeed, this is the very assumption that underlies the law governing the public domain today. It's not a "conservation act" or a "land-reclamation act": it's the Taylor *Grazing* Act of 1934, whose purpose is "to stop injury to the public grazing lands . . . and to stabilize the livestock industry." Written for and by ranchers, it gives them almost complete control over the BLM. For instance:

In each grazing district set up under the act, there is a 5- to 12-man "advisory" board to help government range managers set policy. Except for one so-called "wildlife representative," the act says, the board members must be "local stockmen recommended by the users of the range." Thus, in the words of range ecologist William Meiners (who last year quit the BLM in disgust), "The rabbits have been put in charge of the cabbage patch."

As a result, every meaningful BLM attempt to cut grazing has been beaten back. In 1945, when the U.S. Grazing Service (predecessor of the BLM) tried to enforce significant reductions, Congress slashed its budget, fired its director, and a year later abolished it and created the BLM. Today this agency, administering an area 85 percent as large as the entire United States east of the Mississippi, has a budget of only $120 million—about what the Corps of Engineers spends on a medium-sized dam. Since 1946 it has lowered grazing only half a percent a year. At this rate, says Congressman John Saylor (R., Pa.), it will take 180 years to reduce it to proper levels.

The Irreplaceable. Here are three basic changes that could help put an end to overgrazing:

• Make the BLM and the USFS issue environmental statements on the effects of present grazing on public lands, as required
by the 1969 National Environmental Policy Act. Today, most people looking at an overgrazed area think it is "beautiful desert
country." An environmental statement—if honestly written—
would wake them up to the devastation they are really seeing.

• Change the Taylor Act to require the BLM to consider *all*
uses of the land—watershed protection, wildlife, scenic values,
recreation—instead of just the stability of the livestock industry.
(The USFS already has such a mandate; all *it* needs is more public
pressure to offset rancher pressure.)

• Give the BLM money to build more fences and water holes
for its rotation plans, and to hire the biologists and ecologists it
needs to broaden the plans beyond livestock.

One final, and vitally important, question: How seriously
would a grazing cut affect U.S. livestock production? Nationally,
the industry would hardly notice it; only three percent of its forage
comes from public lands. But locally—especially in the Southwest
—reductions would hit many small family operations hard. In
these cases (involving perhaps 20,000 families), Congress should
certainly provide relief. One suggestion is to give the affected
ranchers first priority on the range-improvements jobs.

In almost all the districts affected, grazing would be reduced,
not abolished. Moreover, most reductions would be temporary.
All experts agree that once the land is cured—in three or four
years in some areas, 10 or 20 in others—it will support approximately double the present numbers of livestock *and* wildlife.

But far more important than increasing the animals is saving
the land. For the land is the one irreplaceable ingredient; when it
is gone—and it certainly is going—that's all there is. Indeed, on a
strictly cost-benefit basis, there is perhaps no better investment the
country could make than the relatively few million dollars it would
cost to stop the massive nibbling away, trampling down and running off of the western landscape.

MARKETPLACE OF THE UNNECESSARY

by Jack Smith
from Westways, *October 1972*

Some years ago when I was interviewing Romain Gary, the French
novelist and diplomat, he spoke of Los Angeles as one of the beautiful cities of the world. He had been posted here a few years
earlier as French counsul general, and was back on a visit.

"Why do Americans always say Los Angeles is such an ugly
city?" he asked. "This is a great piece of conventional thinking.
People like to hate something, and once they hate they can't quit.

"Ventura Boulevard, for example, is supposed to be an ugly

place. I adore driving through Ventura Boulevard. People look at me with incomprehension when I say that. I know all the shacks and cubicles are temporary. They will be replaced with something beautiful. But meanwhile they are so full of wonderful things. . . ."

If Gary were to drive the length of Ventura Boulevard today he would find that the shacks and cubicles are still there, most of them; but if he were to stop and look inside, he might be pleased to find they are still "so full of wonderful things."

Ventura Boulevard, from Studio City to Woodland Hills, is a twelve-mile-long marketplace. It was designed by the automobile. As Gary suggested, one shops by car, stopping here for a wig, there for a pound of mocha; driving on for a pizza, a steam bath, a game of miniature golf, a boa constrictor or a karate lesson; then turning around to shop the other side of the street for an antique rocker, a car wash, a poodle trim, a house plant or a water bed.

The boulevard is the world's longest village street. Though it contains five distinct town centers—Studio City, Sherman Oaks, Encino, Tarzana and Woodland Hills—it has an overall character of intimacy and individuality. It is almost quaint. Small old frame cottages still survive, though they may be painted psychedelic colors and serve as funky stores. There are oak trees older than any of the buildings, and parkways that have kept the storefronts out for blocks.

The shops have names that reflect the proprietor's whim and fancy. Some are delightful, some clever, some merely cute. A shopper is very likely to be greeted in a shop by the proprietor himself, and if it isn't a busy Saturday, offered a conversation and perhaps a cup of coffee.

I invite the reader to enter a few shops with me. We don't have to buy anything, you know.

Basically Butterflies is at 11352 Ventura. *Butterflies, insects, collecting equipment,* says a sign in the window. The window is full of moths and butterflies, gorgeous and dazzling, some as large as a man's hand. They are not live, but impaled on pins or otherwise fixed as decorations or collector's specimens.

There was a girl at the counter, barefooted, in jeans and a loose sweater. I asked her how expensive a butterfly might be.

"Well, here's one," she said, showing me a very large specimen with wings of black and blue, "that costs $140. It's a *bird wing*, from New Guinea. It's really rare."

I was fascinated by a display of great beetles, so large and complex of structure that they looked like models for some early man-made flying machine. They were formidable, with their weird faces, not to say forbidding.

"Aren't they *creepy!*" said the girl.

It was exactly the kind of nonprofessional, low-key approach that makes the boulevard so amiable.

The Main Street is at 11326. The store looks like a cottage, painted yellow, with bay and dormer windows. From the name, I expected its wares to be early Americana, but they turned out to be mostly imported gourmet cooking utensils—pans for quiche lorraine, omelet skillets, knives and chopping blocks and grinders.

"Can I offer you some coffee while you browse?"

It was the proprietor, a young man with red hair. He brought me a cup of coffee. "The bar opens at twelve," he said.

"The bar?"

"Cocktails, for our customers."

I asked him why the name Main Street, for a store of such thoroughly Gallic flavor.

"We started out in Redondo," he said, "and we had things like that, Americana; but we found out what people wanted to buy were our utensils. When we came up here, I was afraid this country French decor was too elegant, might scare people away. So I said, well, we're on the main street of the Valley—let's keep the name."

The Casa de Pets is at 11814. Exotic animals. Casa is a name much favored by boulevard entrepreneurs, however inappropriate. There is a Cadillac dealer called Casa de Cadillac, a dry cleaning place called Casa de Cleaning, and even a car wash called Casa de Cascade, not to mention numerous *Casa de* cafes, some of them no more Mexican or Spanish in cuisine than Fat Jack's Hot Dogs or Saul's Delicatessen.

"I am Dr. Borondy," said a man in the Casa de Pets. He spoke with an accent, eastern European, I guessed, and said he was a veterinarian and zoologist as well as a merchant of exotic animals.

"What kind of animals do you have?" I asked.

"I handle everything," he said.

He led me into the holding rooms. There was a musky odor but the place was clean and cool.

"What's that?" I asked, looking into a pool at a seven-foot lizard.

"It is a monitor," I thought he said. "It is coming from Asia."

We looked at pythons and a boa, an Indian clawless otter, an African long-eared desert hedgehog, and an Australian bush-tailed phalanger. Dr. Borondy even took me into his little office and showed me a scorpion in a jar and a tarantula in a margarine box, both quite alive.

"I have a cockatoo," the doctor said, "who walks on the high wire and roller skates."

"How much is he?" I asked.

"He is $3,500."

It was higher than I wished to go for a cockatoo.

"Of course," said Dr. Borondy as I moved toward the exit, "I also handle elephants."

Next to food stands and cafes, there seem to be more antique shops than anything else on the boulevard. Their names suggest that they deal more in "junque" than real antiques, more in nostalgia than in art:

Treasures & Trash . . . Scavengers Paradise . . . No Name Second Hand Shop . . . The Nickelodeon . . . The Very Thing . . . Up Your Attic . . . Pick-a-Dilly . . . Yesterday House . . . The Cobweb Palace . . .

There was a young man behind the small counter in the Nice and Easy, working on a piece of costume jewelry. His things were from the recent American past. He had an oak icebox for $85 and a square oak table for $150.

"People are going back to the real grain, natural look," he told me. "It's this ecology thing, I guess. They like to see the wood. There was a woman in here the other day, ninety years old, she must have been. She bought an old oak table. Said she had a brand new dining set, but it was too frail-looking, she was afraid it would fall apart.

"I always liked old things. I love to buy old things. This is my first store. People come in, I want them to like everything. I feel uncomfortable and then they'll say, 'I like your store,' and it makes my day."

The Plant Shop is at 11370. It is one of the new growth of shops reflecting the sudden craze for house plants. Like the cafes and the antique shops, the little plant shops vie with each other for catchy names . . . The Green Madness . . . The Muddy Wheel . . . The Knot Garden (plants, macrame, beads) . . . The Plant Orphanage . . . This Sensual Earth. . . .

Someone said "Hello" when I entered The Plant Shop. There was a girl at the counter but I saw she had a parrot on her shoulder. I wasn't sure whether the girl or the parrot had spoken.

"Did someone say hello?" I asked.

"It was Winston," said the girl. "He's a neat parrot."

She showed me around the shop. "All of a sudden," she said, "everybody's turned on to house plants. In New York, you know, they have to *buy dirt.* Can you imagine?

"That's a fiddle leaf fica," she said, looking at a plant that was taller than I was. "Then we have these little miniatures like this. They're very rare."

"Winston looks wet," I said.

"Oh, yes. I water him when I water the plants. He likes it."

The A to Z Research Factory is painted red, white and blue. *Consultants, Self-Indulgence Technologists. Groups. Awakening Sensitivity.*

There was a mirror on the door. *We reflect yourself.* The door was locked. I read a card tacked on beside the pushbutton. *Push button to ring. Then release button. Wait for Answer. State your name and your appointment. If no answer, Thank You.*

I rang and waited. There was no answer. I rang several times more and then walked on, full of unawakened sensitivity.

Out in Tarzana a man was up on a ladder hanging a sign

above a large store. He finished the bottom line first. *Pedlar*. Then he hung *Party* above it. Party Pedlar.

It was a store that sells things for parties. There were stuffed animals bigger than life and greeting cards as big as pup tents. The decor was orange and pink.

"We're not really open yet," said a woman who turned out to be Molly Sakowski. She was opening the store with her husband Sid. "But people have been coming in all day. They can't wait. It's so much fun."

The Sakowskis had run a party store in Granada Hills but it was damaged in the earthquake and they gave it up. The same thing had happened, I found out later, to Dee and Paul Cook, who had moved to 13832½ Ventura. Their antique shop had been in Newhall.

"The earthquake broke everything," said Mrs. Cook. "We had to start all over again on nothing. The rents are reasonable here. It's a wild little street, really.

"Where we got our name, people are always finding something in here and saying, 'My grandmother had one of those—I'll never forget it.' So we called it Grannie's Unforgettables.

"The first two weeks we were very busy. People here are curious. They're very aware about the boulevard. When one place goes out, they're ready and waiting for the next one to open. Even without a sign up, we had tons of business.

"But you can't get rich. People come here, expect to make their first million. Next thing you know, they close up. You can survive, but you can't make a million."

The narrow shop was jammed with things. Most had the look of the 1920s and '30s. It was the sort of stuff that seems to come out of attics and garages as bottomless as the magic pitcher.

The boutiques (we used to call them shops, but now they are called boutiques, which means shops) also bear names that sound as if they were inspired by champagne . . . The Gibson Girl . . . Smashing Seconds . . . Mrs. Robinson's . . . The Grandmother's Giftique . . . The Male Image . . . The Tender Wrap . . . Jon's Drawer, material things . . . Funky Threads for Kids. . . .

The Hidery is a custom leather shop at 13551½. *From the Suave to the Barbaric for Adults and Children.* It reeks of the rich, good, slightly pungent smell of leather. Claire Silver-Eagle is the proprietor. You can see her craftsmen at work at a table in the rear, making leather shirts and jackets, vests and bags for the custom trade and wholesale.

"This boulevard used to have empty shops all over," said Ms. Silver-Eagle. "It wasn't very interesting. There were very few craft shops. It was dull as Main Street in some little hick town in the Midwest. Now there are more and more boutiques that sell crafted things, offbeat things, funky things."

"How long," I asked, "has the leather fad been going on?"

"How long?" said Ms. Silver-Eagle, raising an eyebrow. "Why, several hundred years, at least."

The cuisine of the boulevard is cosmopolitan, heavy on the pasta, delicatessen and hamburger. There are a few old established places with excellent reputations, such as the Tail o' the Cock, the Moskva Cliff, the Sportsmen's Lodge. There are more small French and Italian restaurants than anywhere outside of Rome or Paris, for one street, at least . . . Graniere . . . Travaglini's . . . Chez Gregoire . . . Fiore d'Italia.

The trend seems to be toward the franchise houses. There's a McDonald's or a Denny's every few blocks, it seems, like milestones. But in between the big restaurants and the franchise places there are a hundred holes in the wall that give the boulevard its character. There are brash little joints like the Tokyo Chef, which pushes teriyaki burgers; clean little delis like Al Bucker's, redolent of bagels and pastrami; and savory joints like The Weiner Factory.

The Weiner Factory is said to be frequented by two or three celebrities, the chief one being Burt Prelutzky. But its main allure is in its Polish sausages and its graffiti. I entered the factory under the big sign saying, *We have sold over 4 hamburgers this year.*

"What can we do for you?" said a man behind an apron and a good Polish mustache.

"I just wanted to look at the walls."

"You going to steal our graffiti?"

"It's copyrighted?" I asked.

"I never thought of that. Help yourself."

It looked to me as if they had painted out some of the old graffiti and started all over again. "Nixon sleeps with the lights on" sounded familiar, though, and so did "The world is coming to an end—stock up now on bumper stickers."

There is a small art gallery with a sign, *For Sale—Worst Art on the Boulevard*. It is the one sign in the place, I believe, that is absolutely correct.

But the boulevard is not without culture of a higher form. I found a class of about fifteen women practicing at the Anna Cheselka School of Ballet. They were in tights and leotards of various colors, and were themselves of assorted height and conformation. A recorder was playing suitable music and the women were doing their pirouettes and arabesques in front of a mirror that ran the full length of the room.

A man was watching from the small lobby. It was strewn with wraps and street shoes. The man was Mme. Cheselka's husband.

"We teach ballet from A to Z," he told me.

I wondered who the women were.

"Some are the mothers of children in the beginner's class," he said. "Some used to be professional dancers. They feel it's in their bones to continue. Some are just ladies who want . . . to do something for themselves."

I asked about the discarded garments in the lobby.

"Oh, we have dressing rooms. But some of the ladies don't take the time. They're very busy, you know. They're already dressed for the class so they just slip out of their pants and shoes in here and then they pull them on again and away they go."

Marlow's bookstore is at 18718, in Tarzana. I thought I recognized the proprietor, because of his beard, but it turned out I was thinking of the previous proprietor, who also had a beard.

"I've only been here since February," said the new man. He was very soft-spoken and his beard was trim. "I wasn't a bookman when we bought the business, my wife and I. I'm an aerodynamicist. I got caught in the —." He smiled and shrugged.

I wondered how an aerodynamicist had happened to pick a bookstore as a refuge.

"We'd been interested in a boat charter business in Hawaii. But that fell through. So we were looking in the paper, under boat charter, and my wife said, 'What's the next thing after that?' I looked down at the next ad and it said 'Bookstore.' It was for this place."

"Your name's Marlow?" I asked.

"Oh, no. I'm Jim Boyd. We kept the old name. Marlow's a good name for a bookstore, don't you think? It's the same name of the poet, without the *e* of course."

There may be a wispy and ephemeral quality about many of the enterprises on the boulevard. Everything needed to sustain civilization can be found in the great shopping centers in the Valley north of the street. But the boulevard is a marketplace of the unnecessary, and as the architect Robert Alexander once told me, the unnecessary is what we human beings need.

Meanwhile, the boulevard isn't going to blow away. The big banks have moved in, giving the street a sporadic skyline and holding it down with large concrete buildings and tons of money.

Whether these new structures are the beautiful buildings of Romain Gary's vision must be judged by the beholder. And it may be that when the boulevard is all beautiful to see, it will no longer be full of wonderful things.

I don't believe there is another street in the world where you can buy a butterfly, learn to tap dance, get a free personality analysis, order an elephant, learn to swim, play miniature golf, eat escargots and teriyaki burgers, and buy books from an aerodynamicist.

There is a little shop on the boulevard called The Serendipity. It is a name that might well apply to the whole street. Ventura Boulevard is the kind of place where you can go shopping for one thing and end up buying something you had no idea existed.

I was driving down the boulevard in this frame of mind, heading home, when I saw a sign that said,

Typewriters . . . Adders.

It didn't surprise me in the least. I had already seen stranger things. I'd gone nearly a block farther before it struck me that adders meant machines, not reptiles.

Then again I could be wrong.

PLANTS HAVE A FEW TRICKS, TOO

by Arthur W. Galston

From Natural History, *December 1972*

All creatures living in the wild are subject to attack by predators, and their survival as a species depends in large measure on their success in fending off such attacks. Animals have many obvious self-defense mechanisms. Some, for example, hide from enemies by merging into the landscape so that it is difficult to see them; others hide by deliberately popping into a hole or under a rock. Because of their speed, some creatures outrun potential predators, while others outlast them by superior stamina during a long pursuit. A cornered or alarmed animal can ward off an enemy by obnoxious odors, gestures, or noises, and in a pinch can stand and fight off an attacker. Even when faced with a microscopic invader, such as a bacterium, a fungus, or a foreign protein of any kind, many animals can react with a variety of defenses, including ingestion of the attacker by special mobile body cells or the formation of specific antibodies that couple with the invading protein or cell and render it harmless.

Plants, by contrast, seem at first sight to be relatively defenseless against attack, but a closer look reveals that they do have some mechanisms for warding off other organisms. For the most part, they are incapable of sufficiently rapid motion to do damage to an animal, although the insect-trapping devices of the sundew and of Venus's-flytrap have been widely popularized. Upon mechanical stimulation the leaves of the sensitive plant will rapidly fold, which is said to protect the plant against foraging animals. Thus, botanical humor has it that a goat entering a patch of wild *Mimosa pudica* would starve to death, because the plant's sudden folding of its leaves after jostling would make it seem unavailable for foraging. I personally doubt whether such an obvious ploy would deter an omnivorous goat.

Another kind of movement results from the tactile sensitivity and coiling growth of tendrils and other climbing organs; this permits some vines to grow over trees and, as in the case of the strangler fig, to completely kill the more upright host. The tree can do nothing to escape the ever tightening clutches of its unwanted epiphyte.

Most successful plant defenses are exerted against insects and microbes. It is well known, for example, that among closely related varieties or species of plants, some are eaten by insects while others are not, and that some are susceptible to a disease while others are not. In such cases the differences between the related plants are often a clue to their defense mechanisms. Protection may be rather mechanical; some leaves are very leathery in texture and are covered on both surfaces by a waxy cuticle or a thick, cushiony tuft of matted hairs. Such structural modifications of the leaf's surface repel some insect predators much as thorns repel some animals.

Other defense mechanisms are more chemical. For example, many wild plants contain bitter-tasting chemicals like alkaloids, tannins, or simple phenols, whose value to the plant is not well defined. Because of a general belief that everything in a wild creature must have some function (or else it would have been selected against and eliminated during the course of evolution), it has been suggested that these materials may discourage insects and large animals from eating the plant. Similarly, pungent, volatile materials like those of the onion and mustard are said to repel some insects at a distance, before they even get to the plant.

In some instances plant pathologists have been able to draw correlations between a plant's content of certain chemical components, such as the phenols, and its resistance to fungal diseases. Phenols are, after all, well-known germicidal materials; the carbolic acid so easily smelled in hospital corridors is phenol itself. If effective against external microbes, why not against internal ones as well?

But there are some difficulties with this theory. Why don't the phenols kill the plant itself? The answer may be that the phenols, tannins, and other germicidal materials of plants are found in vacuoles, separated from the living part of the cell by a membrane through which they cannot pass. They do not, therefore, act to repel or kill an invader unless the cell is first attacked in such a way as to break the membrane down and "liberate" the previously restricted phenol. The invader thus triggers the release of a counterweapon hidden in a storage vault in the cell.

In recent years, a more active defense against microbial invaders has been shown to exist in some plants. When they are invaded by filamentous fungi, these plants respond by making a germicidal compound that they did not contain before the invasion. These substances are called phytoalexins, from the Greek *phyton*, "plant," and *alexin*, a warding-off substance. Unlike antibodies, they tend not to be specific with regard to fungal toxicity, and are restricted to a zone immediately surrounding the infected area. Thus, they are of no use in providing systemic immunity.

One phytoalexin, a complex phenol called pisatin, has been isolated from pea pods inoculated with the pathogenic fungus *Ascochyta* or the nonpathogenic fungus *Monilinia*. In general, pea varieties resistant to the pathogenic organism form more pisatin than nonresistant varieties, a picture consistent with a functional role for pisatin in disease resistance. Some especially virulent invaders have the ability to break down the pisatin that is formed by the plant, which may account for their virulence. Plant and invader appear to deliver thrust and counterthrust in the chemical battle for survival.

Tissues invaded by filamentous fungi also seem to form large quantities of certain oxidative enzymes, like peroxidase. When peroxidase acts on phenols, it converts them to "free radicals," especially active forms of these compounds that may be the actual toxic material acting against the fungi. Thus, the active defense mechanism of the plant may involve not only the formation of a potential chemical toxin but also of the catalytic "fuse" that activates it.

There is much interest in these recent findings among plant geneticists, for the production of new agriculturally important and disease-resistant crops may be linked to phytoalexin production and activation. If successful, such an approach might even lessen our dependence on troublesome, externally applied pesticides.

THE DILEMMA
OF THE BLACK POLICEMAN

by Alex Poinsett

from Ebony, *May 1971*

In a Chicago police garage, a black policeman removes his gunbelt and warns a white police officer: "I'm going to beat your brains out." The angry policeman is bent on punishing his colleague for hauling a black youth from a paddy wagon and clubbing him to the ground. But three other black officers stop the fight before it starts.

In Atlanta, a black patrolman bitterly complains before a news conference that he saw five white officers beat three black prisoners inside the police station.

In San Francisco, a black officer reports: "We've been lucky that there hasn't been a real shootout." And a Detroit black policeman concludes: "It's bad out here, man, real bad. And if something isn't done soon by somebody, you'll see a lot more black officers pulling their guns on white officers."

These glimpses into the violent world of the policeman hint at the rising hostility between black and white policemen in several major cities across the nation. Fist fights in locker rooms, racial slurs scrawled on police station walls, refusals to share patrol cars with colleagues of a different color—all are eruptions from an undercurrent of animosity that has been surfacing in recent years, splitting police departments into racial camps. Last summer, for example, 20 blacks and 200 whites exchanged punches because a white girl danced with a black man at the annual Fraternal Order of Police picnic in Pittsburgh. And an Atlantic City convention of the black National Council of Police Societies resolved last summer that henceforth black policemen would try to prevent the killing of blacks by white policemen, even if it meant arresting them. These tension-filled responses speak to the rampant racism characterizing most police departments. It is racism in which, as social analyst W. H. Ferry angrily puts it, "the cop's trigger-finger is the gavel of justice in blacktown."

Predictably, then, Alabama's Gov. George Wallace is a hero to many white policemen because of his persistent attacks against the rights of black people. He has been publicly supported by John Harrington, president of the Fraternal Order of Police, the largest police organization in America, with more than 90,000 members and affiliates in more than 900 communities. Further uncovering police conservatism, a University of California study reveals that in Philadelphia, membership in the John Birch Society was permitted by the Police Department even though "it is officially discouraged for being inconsistent with the police service." At the same time, however, the department searched for active Black Muslims among its black officers—"to get rid of them." Meanwhile, a 1966, National Crime Commission study of Boston, Chicago and Washington found that 79 per cent of white policemen in black precincts were prejudiced against blacks. Forty-five per cent were classified as "extreme anti-Negro." Two years later the National Advisory Commission on Civil Disorders (the Kerner Commission) noted that blacks consider the police as essentially "occupation forces" and not "community protectors." In fact, many of the urban rebellions of the 1960s studied by the commission were sparked by police violence, according to John J. Grimes, a New York policeman for seven years and now a Harvard University law student who has authored a masters thesis on the subject. Grimes observes that the police officer "stands not only for civic order as defined in formal laws and regulations, but also for 'white supremacy' and the whole set of social customs associated with this concept."

Into this mine field lightly steps the black policeman, at once subject to all the explosive tensions and conflicts arising from police work on the one hand and from his blackness on the other. It is a crazy, zig-zag gauntlet he runs, a gauntlet lined on one side with police, on the other with members of the black community. To the police he must be a defender of the established order, but his blackness makes his white colleagues suspect and distrust him. To the black community he "Toms" to an establishment that is insensitive to black needs and thus he is accused of perpetuating the suffering of blacks. As a black man he may have a genuine commitment to the black community. But as a "black in blue" he may pass a fellow black on the street who has no knowledge of his commitment and be ridiculed with "Oink! Oink!" As a policeman, he is obliged to keep the peace, for example, at street demonstrations and riots. As a black man he may be sympathetic with his friends and family on the other side of the barrier. Yet his position, the close scrutiny of white cops and the provocative behavior that sometimes emerges in demonstrations may force him to club and beat those demonstrating for causes with which he essentially agrees. If he is a totally loyal servant of the system which oppresses his people, he may find himself "overreacting" against them in a desperate, almost compulsive effort to prove his objectivity, his professionalism. Indeed, in a less public setting, he may even find himself earning his "brownie points" by accumulating a record of abuse of his own people. Or he may inflict a different sort of pain on the black community by serving as a police spy, infiltrator and informer.

In moments of soul-searching, the black policeman may defend his police service largely on the grounds that it is one of the best paying jobs available to him, one that provides security for his family. For generally it is discrimination and segregation limiting his job opportunities on the outside that makes police work attractive to him, rather than any positive characteristics in police work itself. Yet when he gets inside, the black policeman finds that nothing really has changed, that racial discrimination also goes along with his badge. It was not written down anywhere, but in Washington everyone knew a black cop did not join the elite motorcycle units or ride in comfortable squad cars. In Los Angeles, he risked veiled racial slurs when he took his family to the Police Academy swimming pool. And in the South, he often could not arrest or testify against white persons.

In short, the black policeman has been trapped in a cruel series of binds, much like blacks in the larger society. If he "goes along with the program," he tacitly shares the "ethical" norms of conduct, belief and valuation of the police world as defined by the white majority. And he is rewarded by being considered a "good Negro policeman." If, on the other hand, he vigorously resists the role of a "dirty worker" for white society, in the eyes of his fellow officers he is at the very least open to the charge of ambiguous loyalties.

To penetrate this web of contradictions, to reconcile the dilemmas arising from their multiple obligations, perhaps even to preserve their sanity, increasing numbers of black policemen have been banding together to form associations—black caucuses in police departments—whose first commitment is to the black community. Like 26-year-old San Francisco patrolman Palmer Jackson, they are declaring: "We're black men first, and then we are police officers." Black pride is a magnet for many of them. Wearing Afro haircuts that burst symbolically from the limiting confines of their police caps, they greet each other as "brother." Some of them live in the slum communities they are assigned to patrol, identifying with their neighbors, keeping up a drumroll of protest about the inequities of law enforcement and the brutality of white officers toward blacks.

"What the black policeman is beginning to get away from is that old thing of being a 'Tom,'" explains Patrolman Renault Robinson, executive director of the Afro-American Patrolmen's League in Chicago. "Before, we've always been the good mercenary in a colonial situation. Now we're saying we're black men first and policemen second."

Similarly, San Francisco's three-year-old, all-black Officers for Justice has declared:

> We will no longer permit ourselves to be relegated
> to the role of brutal pawns in a chess game, affect-
> ing the communities in which we serve. We are
> husbands, fathers, brothers, neighbors and members
> of the black community. Donning the blue uniform
> has not changed this. On the contrary, it has sharp-
> ened our perception of our responsibilities as black
> males in a society seemingly unresponsive to the
> needs of black people. We see our role as the role
> of a protector of this community, and this is the role
> we intend to fulfill.

Translating such resolve into action, Los Angeles' Oscar Joel Bryant Assn., named after a black policeman killed on duty, succeeded in forcing the transfer of a captain and a community relations officer whom it demonstrated to be insensitive to the needs of Venice, a Los Angeles district populated largely by blacks, Chicanos and hippies.

"I'm tired of hearing where black children are beaten by white cops; where black women are insulted by white cops. We're going to knock 'em up, knock 'em down, break 'em in, and treat them just as they treat us," declares patrolman Leonard Weir, president of New York's Society of Afro-American Policemen.

A Black Muslim who is dead serious about his mission, Weir sparked the formation of the Society in 1964. Five years later the organization was charted as the National Society of Afro-American Policemen, Inc., with affiliated chapters in Michigan, New Jersey and Pennsylvania. In 1968, Weir journeyed to Chicago at Renault Robinson's request to help form the League there. Today, the Chicago group claims 1,000 members, nearly half the blacks on the city's 12,678-man police force. Meanwhile, the Guardians, once only a social organization of black patrolmen, but now increasingly militant, has chapters in many cities. In New York, for example, they count 75 per cent of the 2,400 black cops on a force of 31,700. All of these organizations defend black cops accused of violating departmental regulations.

One of the more publicized defendants is 28-year-old Renault Robinson who until the spring of 1968 was what policemen call a "Cinderella cop." Never once suspended during four years of service, he had achieved an efficiency rating of 97 per cent and had won more than 50 departmental citations for outstanding police work. Then he and several other policemen boldly formed the Afro-American Patrolmen's League. Months later it had grown noticeably and Robinson's supervisor called him in, demanding: "What are you trying to start? A black Mafia?" Ironically, the supervisor was himself the president of an all-Irish police association. But he told Robinson he was opposed to an all-black group, that he felt it would be racist. Then he warned Robinson not to continue his involvement. But the black patrolman and his partners pressed on.

They spoke out against police brutality. They asked that the responsibility for policing the police be taken out of the hands of the police themselves and transferred to an independent investigation bureau. They asked that police training be improved, with a less military and more socially oriented, humanistic emphasis. They launched a campaign to get shotguns removed from the front seats of all marked police cars. The weapons had been placed in plain view to deter would be rioters. They proposed that there be more civilian involvement at all levels of police work, and especially at policy-making levels. They began building programs that included such community services as legal aid, free investigation into charges of police brutality and general advice to the public on police-related questions both in person and through a highly informative column in the Chicago Daily Defender.

It was too much. From the moment Robinson began spear-heading the reform thrust of his League, he was harassed by his fellow police. He was suspended several times without pay for a total of approximately 70 days between May 1968 and May 1, 1970. One of these suspensions came after he served on a police detail at a high school disturbance. During a calm that day, the detail sergeant gave his men permission to remove their riot helmets. Some took them off, while others kept them on. Robinson took his off. A captain came along and spotted him. "Write him up," he told the sergeant. "He doesn't have his helmet on." The sergeant tried to explain that he had given the men permission to take off the helmets. "I didn't ask you anything," the captain snapped. "I gave you an order."

Robinson was subjected to other harassments. Anonymous telephone callers repeatedly threatened his life and those of his wife and three children. Then last Novmber, the five-man Chicago Police Board slapped a one-year suspension on him for eight charges ranging from bringing "discredit upon the (police) department" to showing disrespect to a superior officer by calling him "crazy" and "a Nazi." Meanwhile, Robinson had filed a $110,000, federal court suit charging that Police Supt. James B. Conlisk Jr. and other white department officials had violated the civil rights of black policemen in the Afro-American Patrolman's League.

Though the butt of the harshest treatment himself, Robinson continues to encourage blacks to join the Chicago Police Department to boost the black police ratio from 16.5 per cent in a city which is nearly one-third black, for neither Chicago nor any other major city has a black police representation proportionate to the black population. In fact, the ratio of blacks in law enforcement has not increased appreciably during the past 20 to 30 years, according to policeman-law student Grimes, "Far worse, in terms of proportions," he adds, "are the number of black officers in supervisory positions. There are many departments where black officers have never advanced beyond their entrance rank."

Since the urban rebellions of the 1960s, the black community has pressured police administrators for more black officers. During the 1964 Harlem rebellion, reports Grimes, Congressman Adam Clayton Powell and other black leaders called for more black officers in Harlem and a black captain to command one of its police precincts. Similarly, Cleveland's black community was granted the substitution of black for white policemen during an outburst in August 1968. And in New York's Ocean-Hill Brownsville District, where pitched battles were fought over community control of the schools, local leaders were granted the replacement of white with black police officers to ease tensions generated between the community and the police.

Still, the estimated 30,000 black police in the nation's 420,000-man police force are not enough to service all of the black communities. At the same time, recruitment campaigns generally have been dismal failures. The most aggressive drive was conducted in Washington, D. C., according to New York Times reporter Paul Delaney. While blacks were only 17 per cent of the capital's force of 3,100 men four years ago, by August 1970, they totaled 1,797 of 4,994 or 35.9 per cent. Delaney explained: "Washington did it by setting up recruit-mobiles in black sections, where written exams were given; recruiting on military bases; changing physical standards, such as lowering the height requirements and modifying the eye requirement, and changing the requirements on certain illnesses, such as asthma and hay fever; conducting a 'recruit-in-moviethon,' where applicants and their dates attend free showings of Jim Brown and John Wayne movies, and a 'radiothon' in which applicants were solicited over the radio and taxicabs were sent to pick them up and bring them to the station to take their tests."

As imaginative as were these techniques, the Washington black police recruitment campaign succeeded largely because the city is an untypical 71.1 per cent black. Efforts to beef up police departments with more blacks elsewhere have been hindered by the absorption of the best qualified blacks into better-paying fields, by the heavy induction of blacks into the Army and by the general disenchantment of the black community with the police, according to New York's Deputy Police Inspector Arthur B. Hill. He explains that many blacks feel that joining the police would be like "joining the army that keeps them down." Thus, before police departments can recruit blacks successfully, police officials must first build a favorable police image in the black community, according to Grimes. He and other police experts have recommended a variety of reforms to improve police-minority relations. Among them, sociologist Nicholas Alex includes:

1) Extending human-relations trainings of recruits and officers.

2) Creating or enlarging police-community relations units within police departments.

3) Starting precinct and city-wide citizen advisory committees, including minority leaders to meet with the police.

4) Developing programs to educate the public about the police, such as visits of school children to precinct stations, lectures by police officers to adults or youth groups, and school courses in police work.

5) Running recruitment campaigns aimed at members of minority groups.

6) Ending discrimination within police departments, such as those relating to promotions, and integration of patrols.

7) Issuing orders banning use of abusive words or excessive force by police officers.

8) Developing procedures to handle citizen complaints within the police department which are fair and designed to impose real discipline.

"Many of these ideas are being adopted in different urban police departments with a fair degree of rapidity," Alex reports. "Nonetheless, there seems to be little, if any, improvement in police-minority relations; instead, relations between the police and Negroes may be worse than they have ever been before."

Such a crisis poses a challenge for black police since they are potentially the black community's first line of defense. To meet that challenge, blacks should not ignore the possibility of legislative reform, argues William Strickland, a senior research fellow at the Atlanta-based Institute of the Black World. He cites a bill proposed last year by ACTION, a veteran St. Louis human rights council, which would have required the police department to investigate all shootings of unarmed fleeing suspects (those shot were usually black), created a new position of black Co-Chief of Police and aimed for a 50 per cent black presence in all ranks of the police department. Predictably, the bill was "filed in the City Council's circular file," laments Percy Greene who heads ACTION.

Indeed, the nation's blacks have long had to live with white America's indifference to their well-being. Although the black community needs more protection than whites, it receives less. Thus, for example, police are permissive toward pimps, prostitutes, numbers racketeers and dope traffickers as long as they restrict themselves to black turf—and as long as they pay off.

Hence, the reform role of black policemen is crucial because of double standards of law enforcement and because of the wave of repression that has swept the nation in recent years. From brutal attacks on the Black Panther Party, to "no-knock" search and seizure police policies in the District of Columbia, to U.S. Atty. Gen. John Mitchell's proposal for "preventive detention" of suspects for as long as 60 days without being charged, from all of these provocative trends have emerged the beginnings of a police state. Whether it prevails, on the one hand, or whether, on the other, the black community survives, may finally be determined by the courageous effort and tenacious will of aroused black policemen around the nation.

SHOULD CHIROPRACTORS BE PAID WITH YOUR TAX DOLLARS?

by Albert Q. Maisel

from Reader's Digest, *July 1971*

The battle lines are firmly drawn between the chiropractors and their foes. In lobbying for federal payment for their services, chiropractors argue that they are members of a recognized health profession, licensed by all states except Louisiana and Mississippi. As such, they contend that they should be granted the same status that Medicare has accorded to doctors of medicine and osteopathy.

Critics of chiropractic, including the American Medical Association, maintain that it is a form of quackery, and that those who practice it are no more entitled to recognition than snake-oil peddlers. Because chiropractors lack both the training and the background to diagnose or treat diseases, critics claim, underwriting their "services" would actually endanger the lives of countless Medicare patients by delaying accurate diagnosis of major ailments.

Given these diametrically opposed viewpoints, let us try to discover where the truth and the public interest really lie.

The Palmer Method. Chiropractic owes its existence to a single man, David Daniel Palmer, a grocer-turned-"magnetic healer" who, in 1895, "cured" one patient of deafness, another of heart trouble, by manual adjustments of their vertebrae. On the basis of these two cases, Palmer concluded: "If diseases so dissimilar as deafness and heart trouble came from pressure on nerves," then "a subluxated [partly dislocated] vertebra is the cause of 95 percent of all diseases."* Since then, chiropractors have adhered basically to Palmer's single-cause theory of disease and to his method of treating all illness by adjustment of the spine.

Today, the estimated 15,000 to 17,000 active chiropractors are divided into two, often bitterly contending, groups. Representing the so-called "straights" is the International Chiropractors As-

---

*Palmer decided that the remaining five percent, including bunions and corns, were the result of "displaced bones" in the feet.

sociation, which regards any form of treatment other than spinal adjustment as a heretical deviation from the doctrines laid down by the founder. The "mixers," represented by the American Chiropractic Association, augment their spinal adjustments with nutritional supplements and with some forms of physiotherapy. Both groups, however, renounce the use of all forms of medication, vaccination and surgery.

Schools for Salesmanship. After making his discovery, Palmer opened a chiropractic school to teach others how to adjust spines. The course ran for several months, and the only admission requirement was a $500 fee. His son, B. J. Palmer, put the school on its feet with advertising that effectively promoted a cheap way to acquire quickly both a good income and prestige. "Our school," he explained, "is on a business, not a professional, basis. We manufacture chiropractors."

Soon, however, many of Palmer's newly manufactured "doctors" discovered that teaching was even more lucrative than practicing. Hundreds of colleges of chiropractic sprang up all over the country, many offering correspondence courses complete with mail-order degrees. By the late 1920s, state legislators had become alarmed that such inadequately schooled people, claiming to be "doctors," were treating hundreds of thousands of gullible people for real or imaginary ills. Thus, in state after state, "Basic Science Laws" were passed, requiring that all who thereafter sought to practice healing—medical doctors, osteopaths* *and* chiropractors —must first pass examinations in such sciences as anatomy, bacteriology, chemistry and pathology.

Unequipped to teach these sciences, the vast majority of chiropractic diploma mills soon closed down. Today, only 11 chiropractic colleges are still operating in the United States. Like medical schools, they offer a four-year course. But here the resemblance to colleges of medicine ends. With under-manned faculties instructing poorly qualified students, the education they provide is inevitably of poor quality. (This has been demonstrated in those states in which the same Basic Science examinations are given to medical and chiropractic students, and the examinations are uniformly graded by the same board. Eighty-four percent of the chiropractic students fail the exam the first time around, while an average 81 percent of medical students pass.)

Many chiropractors, however, do take a special type of postgraduate course, variously labeled "Success Motivation Seminar,"

---

*Osteopathy is a system of medicine which places particular emphasis upon the importance of the musculo-skeletal system; its practitioners receive extensive training in detecting and treating disturbances affecting bones and muscles. Like M.D.s, osteopaths must complete at least three years of pre-professional college training and four years of professional education, which is almost invariably followed by internship and residency training. They are fully licensed physicians in 40 states and the District of Columbia.

"Chiropractic Economics" or "Practice Building." In 1970 alone, for instance, more than 4000 chiropractors and their wives or receptionists attended seminars sponsored by the Parker School for Professional Success in Fort Worth, Texas.

Here, for a $250 fee, they are taught the intricacies of chiropractic salesmanship: from how to check a patient's address for income status to the "Yet" method of convincing a patient that his illness may be more severe than he thinks it is. (If the patient has a pain in his left shoulder, for example, students are instructed to ask, "Has the pain started in your right shoulder yet?") They also learn how to win the confidence of skeptical patients by placing a Bible in the reception room, and how to get patients to return by advising them to come in for a monthly adjustment "so you will stay in good health."

The Qualified License. Until late in the 19th century, most states permitted anyone who claimed to be a physician to practice medicine, without regard to training or education. By 1895, however, all existing states had passed Medical Practice Acts defining what constituted the practice of medicine, prescribing standards of education for the licensing of physicians and prohibiting the practice of medicine to all those unqualified for such licenses. So, in the early years of chiropractic, many graduates of chiropractic schools found themselves prosecuted—and frequently jailed—for violation of the Medical Practice Acts.

But chiropractors fought back, lobbying for laws that would legalize their status through licensing. They were bitterly opposed by the medical profession which—then, as now—regarded chiropractors as uneducated and dangerous charlatans. Caught between these contending lobbies, most state legislatures finally devised a compromise form of licensing which provided that chiropractors already practicing would be licensed either without examination or after passing a simple test. In many states, however, new chiropractors were required to pass more difficult tests. And in most states chiropractors were limited to spinal adjustment, and were denied the right to use most other forms of treatment such as drugs or surgery.

In lobbying for recognition under Medicare and other federal health programs, chiropractors stridently emphasize the fact that they are licensed—but studiously avoid mentioning that such licenses have been carefully hedged with restrictions intended to protect the public.

Diagnosis by "Spinograph." Unlike doctors of medicine, chiropractors maintain that it is of little or no importance to reach a diagnosis in terms of a specific disease. What they seek to determine is the misalignment of a vertebra or vertebrae, which they believe to be the basic cause of their patients' symptoms. In the early days of chiropractic, they sought such misalignments by manual examination of the spine. Today the overwhelming majority of chiropractors utilize a large X-ray film, which is likely to impress patients. Medical specialists in radiology maintain, however, that the taking of such giant (36-by-14-inch) films needlessly exposes the body to dangerous amounts of radiation and that both the poor quality of such oversize films and their distorting effect make them of little or no diagnostic use.

A dramatic demonstration of the low diagnostic value of chiropractic "spinographs" took place a few years ago as part of an investigation (by the Health Benefits Plan of the National Association of Letter Carriers) of chiropractic abuses. Representatives of both the American Chiropractic Association and the International Chiropractors Association were invited to view 20 sets of X rays which had been submitted—with bills—to the Health Benefits Plan. According to the chiropractors who had taken them, each showed at least one misalignment, and in several instances more. Invited to point out the misalignments, the chiropractic representatives were unable to identify a single one.

Tip of the Iceberg. Most people who turn to chiropractors do so because they have been experiencing backaches. Many have previously been treated by doctors of medicine or osteopaths, only to have their pains recur. In many cases, back troubles do diminish under spinal manipulation. But physicians maintain that this happens, not because of chiropractic treatment, but because some backaches (from muscular strains, for instance) tend to diminish with time.

Physicians also contend that many back pains are symptoms of more serious disorders, including coronary thrombosis, duodenal ulcer and cancer of the stomach. Diseases of the uterus and ovaries, of the liver, the kidneys, the prostate and the intestines may also manifest themselves through pain in the lower back. Since chiropractors are not trained to diagnose such severe conditions, their spinal adjustments may serve to delay proper medical care while the underlying disease worsens.

Physicians say, too, that chiropractic manipulation of the spine can be particularly dangerous for elderly patients, many of whom have previously developed osteoporosis, an extreme bone fragility resulting from loss of calcium with advancing age. In such cases, doctors assert, spinal adjustments by chiropractors can produce fractures of one or more vertebrae.

But chiropractors do not limit their ministrations to the treatment of backaches. According to a survey conducted by the American Chiropractic Association, more than 60 percent of the chiropractors reporting use their back-pressing techniques in the treatment of diarrhea, tonsillitis, hives, dermatitis, mental and emotional conditions, ulcers, deficiency anemia and even chronic heart diseases. A substantial number do not hestitate to treat sufferers from diabetes, pneumonia, appendicitis, cerebral hemorrhage, leukemia and other forms of cancer.

The more cautious chiropractors usually decline to treat such conditions when they can recognize them. But numerous court cases attest to the fact that many chiropractors have no such insights or inhibitions. In one such case, for example, a patient with tuberculosis turned to a New York chiropractor who, although advised that the man was tubercular, prescribed a vegetarian diet, alternated with fasting periods of as long as 14 days. Later, the chiropractor sent his patient to a Florida colleague, who treated him in the same manner until he had wasted away to 80 pounds. Only then was he sent to a hospital, where he died within a few days. In 1964, both chiropractors were convicted of manslaughter for having caused the death of the patient through culpable negligence.

In another case, a California chiropractor was charged with felony murder after he had induced the parents of an eight-year-old girl to remove her from medical treatment by convincing them that he could cure her of cancer. The patient died after approximately two months under his treatments. Convicted of murder in the second degree, he appealed and continued to practice for more than five years until he was again convicted, in 1968. He is serving a five-years-to-life sentence.

Chiropractors maintain that citing such court cases is unfair because they are comparatively rare and represent only the misjudgments of individuals. But physicians contend that such misjudgments, demonstrated in courts, are but the tip of an iceberg, and that only the laws of slander prevent them from citing many more.

The Battle Ahead. Before the Social Security Amendments bill comes up for passage by Congress, both the House Ways and Means Committee and the Senate Finance Committee will hold hearings on all its details, including the clause that would provide for federal payment, out of tax revenues, for chiropractic X rays and treatments.

As before, numerous chiropractic spokesmen will present their case, in the hope of winning not only their immediate goal of recognition and payment under Medicare, but also their much wider and more lucrative aim of inclusion under National Health Insurance. Once again, the American Medical Association, the American Hospital Association, the American Cancer Society and many other health organizations will make known their opposition to the chiropractic clause. So will consumer organizations, the AFL-CIO, the Consumer Federation of America and, most significantly, the National Council of Senior Citizens, which seeks to protect its 2.5 million members—all Medicare beneficiaries—from treatments it regards as "worthless and mortally dangerous."

One group, however—the millions of people whose tax dollars are at stake—will not be heard from unless the rest of us play our part by letting our Congressmen and Senators know, by letter or telegram, where we stand.

THE GREENING OF CHICAGO

by Carol Costello
from Holiday, *January–February 1973*

Say "Chicago" to a European kid, and he will mimic a machine gun and mutter knowingly, "Al Capone." Everybody knows about Chicago, Sandburg's "city of the big shoulders." It's the tough, heavy-handed Hog Butcher to the World, the vice-ridden Toddlin' Town, the gutsy City That Made Its River Run Backwards. It's the "city on the make" that keeps pulling itself up by sheer chutzpah and razzmatazz.

Chicagoans love to rail about their city's faults, but they can't leave until they see if Mayor Daley, Saul Bellow, and the Picasso sculpture in the Civic Center can get through another year together. "I should go to New York, but. . . ." They don't have to finish the sentence, whether they are sitting in a neighborhood bar or the Pump Room.

But a funny thing is happening in Chicago. It began, perhaps coincidentally, about the time the Stockyards were torn down. While no one was looking, Chicago began slouching toward Consciousness III.

Consciousness III, according to Charles Reich's *The Greening of America,* dawned with the bell-bottomed Age of Aquarius. It is a joyful, iconoclastic celebration of self that eclipses the Consciousness I jungle of pioneer America, where it was every man for himself and only the hardy survived, and the stifling corporate meritocracy of Consciousness II.

In Chicago, Consciousness III means forgetting about the Second City syndrome, taking a look around, and doing new things with old forms. Some people call it the Chicago Renaissance, but it's just the same old dynamics stalking new territory. Chicago is learning to enjoy itself. If "I will" can build skyscrapers, railroads, and steel mills, why not the finer things in life?

Artists led the greening of Chicago by staying in the city rather than scurrying off to New York moments after they sold their first painting, as had been the custom. A school of art with roots in expressionism and surrealism now often takes on an aggressively Chicagoan tone. "Its iconography can be traced to the old Chicago neighborhood candy store," writes critic Franz Schulze, "the slum funeral parlor and beauty shop, the roller rink, the sideshow freak paintings that used to doll up Riverview (Chicago's defunct amusement park) in the old days."

Chicago artists are finally begininng to talk to one another, coming together in mysterious, ephemeral groups like the Hairy Who and the Non-Plussed Some and cooperating on projects like "Blood Networks" to attract blood donors the day before Christmas. The Red Cross moves into the Museum of Contemporary Art with all their equipment while the artists display their work and writers walk around reading their stories and poems. Artists still grumble that some of the established galleries don't give them enough play, but it wouldn't be Chicago if they didn't.

Sachio Yamashita came to the city in that wonderful year, 1968, and declared Chicago "a ravine between heaven and hell." In the playful spirit of Consciousness III, he started to bridge the gap by painting the cavernous lower level of swank Michigan Avenue with bright rainbow stripes. His latest project is pure Consciousness III. He covered an old three-story corner building on the tattered edges of Old Town with a giant mural inspired by Mt. Fuji. Why? Why not?

As Old Town, Chicago's half mile of calliope entertainment and hustle, began to falter, the action moved north to Lincoln Avenue, where things are more real. There is a sense of permanence about the turn-of-the-century storefronts converted to experimental theaters, minuscule shops, bars, and restaurants. There is a fierce, contagious pride in the area and an only-in-Chicago conspiracy among funkier types—guys who've owned the corner bar for thirty years, young professionals, and older German residents—to keep Lincoln Avenue from becoming a carnival.

This kind of droll coalition is what makes Chicago "the only real American city," according to Louis Szathmáry. Louis is owner and chef of The Bakery, a Lincoln Avenue pioneer restaurant and one of the best in the city. He says in his thick Hungarian accent, "Chicago is the kind of place where a guy is sitting home with a broken leg and fascinated by cracking open almonds, so he starts an almond company. It is not the center of the U.S.A. geographically; it is the center because it *wants* to be."

A block away from Louis' is The Cafe Equinox, opened by silent film comedian Fatty Arbuckle's father in 1893 and the scene of Charlie Chaplin's *The Ice Cream Parlor*. Homemade ice cream, sauces, and soups are staples, and the huge cash register and ceiling fans are original. The Equinox stands in the heart of the old gangland arena. The St. Valentine's Day Massacre took place a few blocks away, and John Dillinger was killed across the street at the Biograph Theater.

A different kind of energy sparks the off-off-Broadway theater that now distinguishes the street. Philip Armour and George Pullman would never have believed it, but "I will" has run the gamut and is now lodged firmly in Lincoln Avenue's experimental theater district. The new companies—New Chicago Players, Café Topa, Old Town Players, Free Theater—didn't see why Chicago shouldn't be able to support more theater; and, besides, there were a lot of ideas not being presented in the Loop and a lot of talented people who wanted to try acting.

Few of the actors are full-time professionals, and they move easily from company to company. With admission usually less than a movie, the idea is for everyone to have fun. But the audiences are big and growing—for everything from The Godzilla Rainbow Troupe's Warholesque *Whores of Babylon* and the straighter *Tobacco Road* to Organic, and Dream Theater at the Body Politic, a storefront that used to house a slicing-machine company and a bowling alley.

Lincoln Avenue theater blossomed when the Kingston Mines presented *Grease,* a put-on "original rock and roll musical of the 50's" set in Chicago. It's a rare member of the Pepsi generation who hasn't sat on the floor of the old trolley barn eating red licorice whips and reveling in his personal past. Foster Beach! Yeah, remember?

The Lincoln Avenue bars have spawned so much rock, folk, and blues talent that even Mayor Daley, who has never been known to rush home and put on his stereo headset, took time in an election year to proclaim December "Chicago Songwriters' Month."

Chicago first learned about popular music when jazz came up the Mississippi River from New Orleans, and now the city is writing its own song. Steve Goodman, Bonnie Koloc, and John Prine drift between the Earl of Old Town, The 5th Peg, Wise Fools, and The Quiet Knight.

Just as other generations took it upon themselves to start almond companies and meat-packing empires, people like Magic Frank, of Magic Frank's Health Food Emporium, are leaving their advertising jobs and setting up shops east of Lincoln Avenue in what is known as New Town. They sell American Indian wares (First People); plants (Green); clothes (Sir Real, Geneva Convention, Paul B., Apple); records (Ears and Gramophone); and whatever else comes to mind. You can stop for pastry, cider, and sundry variations on espresso under a colorful patchwork gazebo at the Tivoli Gardens design shop.

"Twenty years ago, this neighborhood was nothing but rotten," says one of Magic Frank's older lady customers, "but now we come down from Evanston just to shop and talk to people." The area is a revered Chicago institution. Even young people from Peoria and Moline will usually give "Near North" or "Lakeview" instead of an address. Consciousness III, with its penchant for ethnicity and individuality, has aroused a new interest in the ethnic neighborhoods that grew up between 1900 and 1920, when one million immigrants poured into the city. In *Boss,* Mike Royko says you used to be able to tell which section you were in "by the odors of the food stores and the open kitchen windows, the sound of foreign or familiar language, and by whether a stranger hit you in the head with a rock."

Chicago's Lithuanian community of 150,000 is the largest in the country, but no one ever thought much about it. There were miles of identical Chicago Cottages along California Avenue, and the greatest density of parochial school uniforms in the city.

Then Stanley Balzekas opened the Museum of Lithuanian Culture across from his used-car lot. The little building, with its stained-glass windows and collections of coins, amber, dolls, crafts, and wayside crosses brought the neighborhood to life, and people started arriving by the busload for classes in genealogy, folk art, Easter egg decorating, heraldry, and the personal lives of American presidents. When the classes exceed 400, as they often do, Stanley simply moves them into his showroom.

In addition to excellent restaurants and musty little shops that sell whole ducks and squid, ginger root, *bak-toy*, and (under the counter) jars of leeches and ground rhinoceros horn, Chinatown has a community center that presents Chinese opera and boasts the country's first automatic fortune-cookie-making machine. The kids you see roller-skating in the parking lots around 22nd and Wentworth spend ten hours a week in special schools studying Chinese language and culture.

Little remains of the old Greektown except a long strip of restaurants, each piping its own *bazouki* band music into Halsted Street through loudspeakers. At Diana's, you walk through a grocery store to the dining room where, at some point in the evening, a waiter named Petros will turn up the jukebox and whirl around the room with a glass of wine balanced on his head. When the Greeks were urban renewaled out of their territory, they moved their homes, delis, and gift shops north to the Lawrence and Western area. They wouldn't leave the city because, as one restaurant owner put it, "Chicago is always hitting you in the face with something unbelievable, and it's exciting."

Hyde Park prides itself on *not* being ethnic. It shrugs philosophically at the incongruities of urban life, and allows the history of the city to be written on its sheets. Living next door to each other, on one of the many blocks of rambling Queen Anne mansions built in 1860's, are the Dean of the University of Chicago Law School, cartoonist Bill Mauldin, an order of priests, and Elijah Muhammad of the Black Muslims.

And now, integration. Blacks and whites mix comfortably in the leviathan Jewel, the spacious old apartment buildings, and taverns which an accident ordinance decrees must have windows at eye level. "So the wives can look in," smirks a morning beer drinker.

An accident in Chicago's history, the Great Fire of 1871, is responsible for the Loop's having the heaviest concentration of pre-eminent modern architecture in the world. While flames still smoldered on the North Side, rebuilding began on South Side lots that sold for twice what they had cost three years before. Architects who would conceive the skyscraper and the strong, clean lines of the Chicago School flocked to the city.

Adler and Sullivan's Auditorium Theatre was recently restored by one woman, Mrs. Beatrice Spachner, and is said to have the best acoustics in the world. Burnham and Root built the Reliance Building, the Monadnock Building, and the Rookery (an office building, so named because Chicago's ubiquitous and overbearing pigeons began roosting in it even before the people moved in). Mies van der Rohe's glass houses dominate the lake shore, and Frank Lloyd Wright buildings dot the area.

The painful loss of a landmark, the Old Chicago Stock Exchange, brought Consciousness III to the architecture forum. When the marble and mosaics of the Chicago Public Library were threatened, the response was so loud and angry that ambitious real estate developers were nearly ridden out of town on a rail.

One reason Chicago inspires so much loyalty is that it is still the kind of place a person can make his own. Walking along the beach as the sun sets behind the skyline, a Chicagoan can say, "That's my city!" Chicago is changing, but it is being guided by its own lights, and the guy on the beach can understand why Potter Palmer and Magic Frank would have enjoyed having a beer together.

Tooth-and-nail boosterism grew out of the Columbian Exposition, which became a showcase for what the Wonderful Town had accomplished in the twenty years since the fire. But, until recently, Chicago has been more self-conscious than self-aware. When the city let down its hair and tempered the rough and tumble with a little enlightenment and élan, the result couldn't have happened anywhere else. Nobody else had the same honky-tonk to begin with.

getting the most out
of essays and articles
on abstract ideas

In the last chapter you discovered several ways that writers of short non-fiction works *signal* to the reader their introduction or reiteration of important ideas. Because the selections included there were relatively simple in idea and structure, you probably found that you could get all that you wanted out of each work in one reading, once you understood the implications of the title and interpreted the signals in the early paragraphs—the key words and phrases and the general and thesis sentences. However, it may have occurred to you then that for more complex kinds of non-fiction a good way to make the most of signals like these is to apply some of the textbook study methods you learned in Chapter Two. (See p. 16 for a quick review of SQ3R.) This chapter suggests ways you can adapt some of these methods to reading essays like those included in freshman composition anthologies and articles of the kind found on many college reading lists. Of course, you will be dealing in this chapter (as you did in the last) with a freer form of writing than a textbook chapter, and that almost certainly means that you will be using a somewhat more flexible reading style than the one you learned in Chapter Two.

As the word "essay" is used here, it refers to any short non-fiction prose work that strongly and directly expresses the point of view of the author on whatever topic he chooses to speak; it may or may not have appeared originally in a magazine and it may or may not include much specific (textbook-like) information. Some essays—usually called "personal" essays—are simply reflections on the experiences or observations of the writer. "Article" refers to a similar kind of writing, but selections labeled "articles" are usually somewhat less personal and are more information-centered. The distinction is not a particularly important one, however. What is important is that you learn an effective way of accomplishing whatever your purposes may be in reading any short prose piece, no matter how profound its idea or how subtly organized its structure. And a technique like the SQ3R textbook study approach will often prove helpful.

AN SQ3R-TYPE APPROACH

When you SQ3R a textbook chapter—unless the writer is an unusually insistent spokesman for a particular point of view—you can generally assume that you and the writer are working toward a common objective: your mastery of the material he is presenting. In fact, one of the reasons that SQ3R works as well as it does is that textbook writers apparently anticipate your use of it and design their books accordingly. An essayist, on the other hand—and possibly to a lesser extent, an article writer—is less concerned with *your* objectives than with his own. An essayist's chief purpose may be simply to share with you his way of viewing a problem or to tell you about a passionate interest. Or it may be to convince you of the correctness of a position that is opposite to one which you hold. Even if one of an article writer's main purposes is to provide you with information—about a new scientific discovery or a medieval method of warfare or an ancient form of love-making or anything else—he will focus on the information he is presenting and on his point of view concerning it rather than on your needs as a learner.

You will need, then, to work out your own approach to an essay or article, bearing in mind *your* purpose or purposes in reading the selection (which may or may not be similar to the author's purpose in writing it). If your main purpose is simply to "receive" the writer's information, then you can probably use SQ3R almost as it was presented in Chapter Two. The only important difference from your approach to a textbook chapter will be that you will question and read the work as one piece instead of treating parts separately. But if your main purpose is one of a number of other possible objectives—ranging from getting a thorough understanding of the author's main idea or point of view to analyzing the characteristics of his style—you may find the following procedure more appropriate:

STEP ONE: *QUESTION:* Ask questions about the title even before surveying the selection.

STEP TWO: *SURVEY:* Preview the essay or article, paying particular attention to the first sentence or two (possibly the whole first paragraph), any subheadings or marginal notations, italicized words and phrases, occasional topic sentences of paragraphs, and the last sentence or two.

STEP THREE: *QUESTION AGAIN:* Have in mind the basic question that, from your previewing, you have decided the writer is going to be addressing himself to throughout the work.

STEP FOUR: *READ:* Read the selection through rapidly, looking especially for the writer's main idea and the principal supporting points he makes in developing it.

STEP FIVE: *READ AGAIN:* Re-read the selection, or parts of it, as many times as you need to to accomplish your purposes.

This plan not only allows for different reading objectives; it also fits the organizational structure of most essays and articles. Short prose pieces are usually organized quite differently from textbook chapters, chiefly because they treat point of view and information differently. A single, often very complex idea is developed from the first sentence through to the last with no interruption; sub-headings are rare and summaries unheard of. In your approach to this kind of writing, then, it will be important that you regard the work as a unified whole rather than as a series of segments. That is, in all the steps you will be concerned with how the author's point of view or main idea is developed from the title through to the last sentence.

Step One: Questioning the Title

You discovered in Chapter Three that the titles of popular magazine articles are often more striking, imaginative, and rich in implications than the titles of text-book chapters. Essays and articles on abstract ideas often have eye-catching titles, too. But because selections of this kind are especially thought-provoking, it is important that you use these titles as guides to help you start thinking along with the writers. For this reason, when you read them you should make questioning the title a separate step, one that precedes previewing. Then when you preview or survey, you can test the appropriateness of your original questions by matching them with the clues you find in other parts of the work.

Step Two: Surveying

In surveying an essay or article, you can make use of some of the same signals or clues that you noted in previewing a textbook chapter, although the form or content of these clues may be somewhat different. For example, whereas the introductory sentences of a textbook chapter may be simply a warm-up for the sections that follow, an essayist or article writer often uses his *introduction* to get directly into the main idea, or at least to set the stage for it. Therefore, you will surely want to include a quick reading of at least part of the first paragraph in your survey step.

The *concluding section* of a short prose piece is also likely to be different from that of a conventional textbook. Instead of a final summarizing statement labeled "Summary" you will probably find a concluding paragraph (or possibly two or three) that re-states the main idea in another way, or states it explicitly for the first time after building up to it, or in some other sense ties together the points the writer has been making. And just as you found that surveying the summary section of a textbook helped you to see where a chapter was going, you will discover that previewing the concluding sentences of an essay or article will help you get in tune with the writer. If you feel at first that it is cheating to read the end before you have read all of the middle, remember that you are not reading a novel or a short story; you are thoughtfully reading a complex piece of non-fiction.

It isn't cheating, either, to survey the *middle portion* of an essay or article before you read it through. And there may be some value in doing this *after* you have checked the ending. That way you can look for clues that either support or modify the impression you have obtained from the more obvious clues—the title, the beginning, and the conclusion. Although there probably will be no sub-headings, you will find that with practice your eyes will pick up a few *key phrases* and *general sentences* as you skim through the pages. Look in particular for words and phrases that are in *italics* and for *topic sentences*, which are often the first sentences in paragraphs. Again, you may have to guard against the temptation to read right through rather than to do only a survey.

Step Three: Finding the Writer's Basic Question

Most of the short non-fiction works you will read in college—particularly the essays in your freshman composition anthology—answer one general question consistently from the first sentence to the last. By comparing the signal sentences you find in your surveying with the questions you thought of when you first looked at the title, you will usually be able to identify the basic question before you start to read.

Step Four: Reading

The next step is to read the selection through, keeping in mind the writer's basic question. But you will not always be able to understand all that you want to about his answer from just one reading. For one thing, it is likely that the writer will treat the question on at least three levels, providing a *general answer* (a thesis), principal *supporting ideas*, and *details* that illustrate or explain these ideas. You will often find that you cannot give complete attention to all of these treatments at the same time. Moreover, the understanding you are after in any essay or article may include more than simply knowing what the writer has said. Perhaps you are also interested in his method of development or in ways in which his thinking or feeling relates to your own. But whatever else you are concerned about in a short piece of non-fiction, you will almost certainly be examining the writer's thesis and you will very probably want to understand and remember his main supporting points. These features, then, are the ones to focus on in your first reading.

Step Five: Reading Again

How much re-reading of an essay or article you need to do depends on your reading purpose. If your purpose is only to know what the thesis is, you may be able to accomplish it in one reading (or even simply by surveying, for that matter.) But if it is to comprehend not only the writer's main idea but also his chief *reasons* for holding it, and if you feel that you miss a few of these reasons the first time through, a re-reading of certain parts to check for them will certainly be in order. Or, if your purpose includes *remembering* the writer's details (not always as important an objective in essay reading as it usually is in textbook study), you may find that these details mean more to you in a second or a third reading, after you have a framework of ideas in which to fit them.

Although reading even parts of an essay or article two or three times surely sounds like a lot of work to put into any reading project, there may occasionally be times when you will need to dig still deeper. For example, an English class assignment may call upon you to analyze a writer's style and method of development (that is, his writing technique). You can better focus on the question of *how* a writer develops his ideas after you have read his work carefully enough to understand *what* those ideas are. Or you may want to write a response to an essay or article—to answer a writer's argument or to express your own view on whatever his topic may be. This objective could require still another reading of at least parts of the work because you will want to be careful not to confuse your ideas with the writer's.

If all this sounds complicated and time-consuming, remember that you have been discovering that reading is always easier and faster when you know what you are looking for. Each time you re-read you will no doubt have a better understanding of what to look for, and in some of your re-reading you will simply be scanning (picking out specific points here and there without reading through any part) or reading carefully certain selected portions of the piece. Remember, also, that you are encouraged to develop an individual, flexible reading style rather than always to follow a suggested method regardless of whether or not it makes sense to you in a particular reading project.

AN APPROACH TO READING "NOBODY KNOWS MY NAME"

Gene Marine's short piece "Nobody Knows My Name" was originally published as an *article* in a popular magazine (*Ramparts*), but it is sometimes anthologized in collections of *essays* used in freshman composition classes. An unusual feature of this work—whatever label may be applied to it—is its organization. Although the writer develops his point of view consistently from the title through to the last sentence and although the specific information he gives is important only as it supports this point of view, he uses the textbook technique of breaking up his presentation with occasional subheadings. For this reason, it is probably an easier work to survey than most essays and articles and it is probably a good selection on which to try out the question–survey–question–read–re-read approach to short non-fiction.

Assume, then, that you have been assigned this selection in a composition class and that you will be expected to understand the writer's main idea and his principal supporting points in order to participate in a class discussion. (You might later be asked to write an analysis of the writer's argument or a reaction to it, but that is not your concern now.) Assume, also, that you have decided that a step-by-step approach to understanding an essay may be worth a try, even though it sounds elaborate. Spaces are provided for your comments as you use this method of getting at the ideas in "Nobody Knows My Name."

The first three steps are grouped together on the next page, an arrangement that emphasizes how closely related these steps can be. In fact, you will probably find that for a selection like this one—a simply organized article on a subject about which you may already know something—you can go through these pre-reading stages so quickly and easily that you are hardly aware of transitions between them. For example, in "Nobody Knows My Name," you may find an answer to the obvious question: Who is he talking about? Almost before you know you have asked it. Even so, in working with this essay it will probably be helpful to slow down a bit and to write out questions and observations that you might otherwise simply think through quickly or perhaps jot down in the margin of your book. This way you will become conscious of how the "step" approach really works, and you can later be as formal or informal in your use of it as you choose to be. (Actually, you will probably rarely be so formal as to write down all your original questions.) Again, you are encouraged to think out your own questions and find your own clues before checking the question–survey–question analysis in Chapter Supplement II (p. 135). The essay is in Chapter Supplement I (p. 126).

Steps One, Two, and Three: Question-Survey-Question

Question: Before you look at the essay, jot down the questions that the title suggests to you.

▶

Survey: As you preview this selection, remember the importance of *point of view* in most essays and articles. Look for clues that show not only *what* the writer is talking about but also what he *thinks* or how he *feels* about his subject. The subheadings will be of some help, but don't overlook the introductory and concluding sentences. Also, you may catch two or three topic sentences while you are checking subheadings.

Note below any particularly important words, phrases, or sentences you find—especially ones that answer any of your original questions. Also, note any additional questions you think of as you survey.

▶

Question again: What basic question is Marine answering in this essay? The question will probably be more specific than any you asked before you previewed, because now you will know whom he is talking about and what specific problem he is discussing.

▶

Steps Four and Five: Reading and Re-reading

After you have read Marine's essay through once with your basic question in mind, use the spaces under "Reading" below to state the writer's thesis and to list the main supporting points you remember. (Your very question may at least imply a part of the thesis; certainly the one on p. 135 does.) Then re-read as much of the essay as you need to in order to pick up any major arguments you missed and to find other information that you believe will be important for class discussion. After you have made additional comments under "Re-reading," check Chapter Supplement III (p. 135), for an analysis of some of Marine's principal reasons for believing as he does. (Your comments, of course, may be worded quite differently.)

▶   READING

   Thesis:

Reasons:

▶ RE-READING

How many of the details Marine includes to back up his major arguments do you recall from your first or second reading? For example, do you remember the names of some of the prominent people who have used pseudonyms? Or the names of sportswriters who have ridiculed Ali and the newspapers they represent? An intriguing feature of the kind of class discussion you have been preparing for is the diversity of specific information (details) recalled by different members of a group. And this is probably just as it should be. The details in an essay are certainly important; it is through them that a writer builds his case. However, no one can tell you which specific points you as a reader should remember or how many times to read a work in order to pick up the details that you want. You probably remember most readily information that somehow relates to your own experiences or previous thinking. But you will almost certainly remember more details in an article like this—one that is clearly an argument—if you concentrate first on the writer's basic position and main reasons for holding it and let the details fall into place (usually in a re-reading) than you will if you simply plod through with no focus at all.

AN APPROACH TO READING "CLEAN FUN AT RIVERHEAD"

From the time you first look at the title of the essay in Chapter Supplement IV (p. 136) you will probably realize that this selection is a bit different from "Nobody Knows My Name" and will have to be approached differently. The author, contemporary essayist Tom Wolfe, is noted for his extravagant use of language and for his "shock treatment" of commonplace, even trivial, subjects. The title of the essay is not as startling as that of the book from which it is taken—*The Kandy-Kolored Tangerine Flake Streamline Baby*. But, knowing the writer's reputation for using words in unusual ways, you will probably find some implications in the title that go beneath the surface meaning. You won't be able to know *what* the writer is talking about until you read at least the first paragraph (try to avoid doing that until later), but you may find a strong hint of his *point of view* toward his subject in his title alone.

Step One: Questioning the Title

As this is really the questioning stage of the five-step approach, try putting at least most of your thoughts about the title in the form of questions in the space below. (This time you may want to make a few comments as well.)

▶

Did you sense that Wolfe is being *ironic* in this title—that is, using words that make him appear to mean almost the exact opposite of what he really means? You may not have put it this way, but if you did ask questions like: Is it really *clean fun*? or What does Wolfe *really* think about whatever it is he is talking about? (as well as more obvious questions like: What *is* he talking about? Where is Riverhead?), you still were "with" the writer. And even if you did not ask any of these questions, but you sensed that there was "something wrong" with the phrase "clean fun," you were probably on the right track. Many people have difficulty putting into words an interpretation of a title like this because they *feel* the implications so strongly that the words somehow seem superfluous.

Step Two: Surveying

As you survey, you will find that Wolfe's signals are usually more subtle and sometimes less conspicuous than Marine's. His *introductory paragraph* does state specifically what topic he is discussing, but it gives only a hint of his point of view about the subject. The body contains no subheadings, italicized phrases, or other indications of his emphasis. (However, the first sentences of his paragraphs are usually *topic sentences*, and your eye may catch a few especially significant ones as you skim quickly through.) The *concluding paragraph* restates his subject but again only suggests his point of view. A brief previewing, though, should give you an idea of what the writer is doing in the essay. Note below any wording you think provides an especially important clue to his purpose or point of view.

▶

In your surveying did you notice the humorous effects Wolfe accomplishes and the bizarre pictures he creates through colorful wording? You will not need to think much about problems of style and development at this point. However, because the writer showed you from the beginning (from his choice of a title) that he was putting over his point of view by unusual use of language, you were probably more aware of wording than you generally are when previewing. Again, this awareness may have been more on a feeling level than on an intellectual level. For example, did you get a vivid picture of the scene he was creating in the last sentence of the first paragraph, even though you may not know exactly what "lubberly" means and it is has been a long time since you played the game of billiards?

Step Three: Questioning Again

Unless you already knew something about it, perhaps one of the first questions you thought of as you surveyed the first paragraph was: Just what is a demolition derby? (or: How does it work?) And you would be right in assuming that this is one of the questions the essay will answer. Also, the fact that Lawrence Mendelsohn's name is mentioned in both the first and last paragraphs suggests that Wolfe will explain this man's connection with demolition derbies. But because a point of view comes through so strongly in the title and in other key parts of the essay, you can be quite certain that the writer will do much more than simply answer *what* and *who* questions.

You could state the basic question in several ways, but one easy way would be to refer back to the title and ask: In what sense are demolition derbies "clean fun?" An answer suggests itself immediately. By this time you are quite sure the writer thinks they are anything but good clean fun and you are prepared to read to find out why. Another question, then, could be: What is Wolfe's overall impression of demolition derbies? You may think of other ways of wording a question that would include both *what* the author is talking about and *how he feels* about what he is talking about:

▶

Steps Four and Five: Reading and Re-reading

If you participate in demolition derbies yourself every Sunday, you can hardly be expected to read this essay the way you would read it if you had never heard of them before. And if you are intrigued by word play, you will watch the writer's use of language more closely in the first reading than you would if you did not ordinarily think much about these things. In other words, because the subject is rather unusual and the writer's way of treating it is highly individualistic, your personality and your experiences are likely to come out more strongly in your approach to this essay than they did in your reading of "Nobody Knows My Name." In fact, you may find that the reading–re-reading pattern suggested earlier will have to be stretched just a bit to fit your needs here.

Also, your purpose in reading this selection will probably be a bit more complex than it was for "Nobody Knows My Name." Again, it will be a good idea to prepare for a class discussion of the writer's point of view and his reasons for holding it. However, because this essay is an *analysis* from the writer's point of view rather than a straight argument, you will find that there is no direct listing of "reasons." Rather, the writer gets across his impression of demolition derbies by the *way* he describes them. There are, then, three things to think about as you read and re-read this essay: *what* the writer is talking about, *why* he thinks or feels as he does, and *how* he puts across his ideas (his technique). As the *what* and *why* questions are really two parts of the two-headed basic question that came out of step three, you will want to keep these in mind in your first reading. But if you find that at this time you are also partially aware of the writer's technique, don't worry about it.

After you have read the selection through once, try filling in the spaces below to check your understanding and to see what you need to re-read for. Under "Details" write just a brief statement of what happens at a demolition derby and under "Ideas" state the writer's *thesis*—his most *general* answer to the basic question—and some of the *reasons* he states or implies for holding this position. (You will probably find some sentences that state the writer's thesis quite directly, although they are not in the places where you expect to find a thesis statement—in the introductory or concluding paragraph.)

▶   DETAILS:

▶   IDEAS:
    Thesis:

    Reasons:

Did you remember more about *what happens* or about *what Wolfe thought or felt about what happens* at these events?

Re-read the essay, looking for whichever feature you paid the least attention to the first time. Use the space below to make additional comments on either the details or the ideas; then turn to Chapter Supplement V (p. 141), where you will find an outline of the essay. In Chapter Supplement VI (p. 142) there is a report of one reader's experience in reading the selection for the first and second time, which you can compare with your own experience.

▶

Nothing was said earlier about re-reading an essay simply for pleasure, but if you feel like reading the Wolfe piece again just for enjoyment, why not? Then, unless you especially want to try an analysis of Wolfe's technique on your own, turn to Chapter Supplement VII (p. 143) and check the analysis of sytle and method of development provided there.

AN APPROACH TO READING A "CLASSICAL" ESSAY, "OUR ENEMY, THE CAT"

Alan Devoe's "Our Enemy, the Cat" is probably more representative of the kinds of essays you will read in composition and literature courses than either of the other works in this chapter. Devoe's topic is not more relevant to one time and place than to another, as Marine's certainly is, and his style is not spectacular and eccentric like Wolfe's. But you should find that your experience reading the segmentally-organized Marine piece and the stylistically-experimental Wolfe selection will make it possible for you to use the Question–Survey–Question–Read–Re-read method easily and effectively on this short essay and on longer ones like it. This one is carefully organized but in a much less obvious way than "Nobody Knows My Name," and the style is distinctive but certainly not flamboyant.

If you were discussing this work in a composition class, you would want to be able to comment on both the writer's treatment of ideas and on his style. Because Devoe examines a very common subject in a way that reflects his own personality, you could hardly talk about one of these features without discussing the other. Assume that you are preparing for such a discussion as you approach "Our Enemy, the Cat," which is in Chapter Supplement VIII (p. 144).

Step One: Questioning the Title

Again, it will be a good idea to think for a minute about the title before you turn to the essay. What questions does it suggest to you off-hand?

▶

One of your questions might have been whether the writer is discussing all members of the cat family—including wild cats, lions, and tigers—or just domestic cats. It is important to get an early answer to that question since the key title word *enemy* could take on a different meaning in each of those contexts. In fact, you might have wondered in what sense a house cat could be considered an enemy at all.

Step Two: Surveying

You will discover in your previewing that the first paragraph answers both of these questions and shows you what the basic question of the essay will be. It even contains one sentence that turns out to be a thesis statement, that is, a one-sentence general answer to that question. Indicate which sentence that is in the space below. Also note any other signals you find in your survey that confirm your understanding of the main idea. By taking a minute or two to skim the body and the concluding paragraph of this essay as well as the introduction, you will not only make sure that you know what the writer's main idea is; you will also learn something about the way he develops this idea. And that knowledge will make your first reading much easier than it otherwise would be.

▶

Step Three: Questioning Again

At this point you know that the basic question is: In what sense is a house cat an enemy of man? And you know that the writer's general answer is that the "domestic" cat is really a wild creature and not the gentle pet most people hold it to be. It is reasonable, then, to assume that the writer will answer a secondary question: In what specific ways does a cat's behavior show that it is really a wild beast? And in your previewing you probably found that he does.

Step Four: Reading

In previewing, you also discovered that Devoe develops his idea by treating the life history of a typical house cat. Therefore, in your first reading look for the comments he makes about the wild behavior of cats at different stages of their development. After you have read the essay once, use the spaces below to record some of the points you remember about:

▶   THE SEX LIFE OF CATS:

▶   GIVING BIRTH AND BEING BORN:

▶   "KITTENHOOD":

▶   ADULT CAT LIFE:

▶   DYING:

You may have mentioned the primitive sexual habits of cats, the ugliness of the newborn and the mysteriousness of their relationship to their mother, the predatory instincts of kittens, the independence of adult cats and their contempt for humans, and finally the wildness and loneliness that characterizes their dying.

Step Five: Re-reading

You probably were aware in your first reading, and you may have realized even in previewing, that from the title through the last sentence, Devoe contrasts the real character of cats with the image that most people have of them. But you may not have fully realized just how he accomplishes this contrast. One way he does this is by establishing at the beginning that cats are not "as sweet and vapid as the coy name 'kitty' by which we call them would imply" and then showing how their *behavior* at different stages contrasts with this description. But another way is by using *contrasting language* throughout the essay.

As you read it a second time, underline expressions you come across that show the way most people feel about cats or treat them and others that describe cats as Devoe sees them. List these descriptions in the columns below (some examples are included to get you started):

▶   *Most people's cat*   *Devoe's cat*
      named "kitty"   aboriginal passion
      dressed in ribbons and bells intensity of lust

(See Chapter Supplement IX (p. 147).

As suggested earlier, style and content are really almost inseparable in this work. Devoe's purpose does not include giving you new information; he is interested only in providing a new perspective on a very old subject. For that reason, he chooses unconventional language to describe the behavior of cats (descriptions like the title word "enemy") and he gives hypothetical rather than specific examples of that behavior.

By previewing this selection quickly, you may have found that you could anticipate the writer's method of developing his main idea, and by reading it a second time you almost surely learned that you could add to your understanding of his ideas and your appreciation of the way they are expressed. These discoveries are important because they show you that it is possbile to adapt textbook study techniques to the reading of material that is very different from textbook chapters. The next chapter shows you how you can use one of these techniques—previewing—in a still different kind of reading project: understanding how the various parts of a non-fiction book (other than a textbook) relate to one another to develop a single idea.

CHAPTER SUPPLEMENTS

writer is supporting ali

I.

"NOBODY KNOWS MY NAME"

by Gene Marine, with Robert Avakian & Peter Collier

Whosoever flieth from his country for the sake of the true religion of Allah, shall find in the earth many forced to do the same, and plenty of provisions.—THE KORAN

Supposition

A BRAVE RESPECT

There was once a white man who beat the hell out of Muhammad Ali.

The present heavyweight champion of the world (no matter what any boxing commission says) was not yet champion, nor was he known by his chosen religious name. He was Cassius Marcellus Clay, and he still had not left Louisville, Kentucky, and he was, at the time, eight years old.

Clay's father rescued him that day in the Louisville slum where Muhammad Ali's father still lives; but we ought to remember the cracker who for no known reason was beating the boy. We ought to remember him because you don't have to be black to know that there's a straight line from that white man in Kentucky to all the white man who recoiled in horror 17 years later at the sound of Muhammad Ali saying, "No."

What he said, in full, was, "No, I'm not going ten thousand miles from here to help murder and kill and burn another poor people simply to help continue the domination of white slave-masters over the darker people the world over."

A group of intellectuals said something very similar and equally principled not long ago: "What is citizenship if, under certain circumstances, it becomes shameful submission? Are there not cases where the refusal to serve is a sacred duty, where 'treason' means a brave respect for what is true? And when, according to the will of those who use it as an instrument of racial or ideological domination, the Army declares itself in overt or covert revolt against democratic institutions, does not revolt against the Army take on another meaning?"

Unfortunately for the decency of America, those questions were asked seven years ago, they were asked about Algeria, and the intellectuals who asked them were not American but French. Muhammad Ali's refusal to take the one step forward that constitutes formal induction into the armed forces of the United States

Story written 1960's

is rife with ironies, and not the least of them is that an athlete, representing a feared and outcast group, has committed the act of leadership in the "best educated" nation in the world, while its intellectuals, far from banding together in defense of "treason"— if treason be necessary in pursuit of truth—bicker among themselves while they compete for government grants.

But perhaps the greatest irony is the almost uniform castigation of Ali for being what Americans have always professed most to admire: a man who combines courage and principle. At worst— as in a May 7th diatribe by Melvin Durslag of the Los Angeles Times (who of course calls him "Cassius Clay")—Ali is berated as a coward or a fake or both; at best, newsmen and columnists by the dozens have quoted, with sad, wise approval, a fellow inductee who said, "If I have to go, then he ought to have to go."

None of them, so far as I know, has drawn the obvious corollary: the other guy didn't have to go either. More important, none has taken the time to think out loud about the meaning of Muhammad Ali and his act.

If Ali's act in refusing to step forward for induction was treason, then it was a treason, certainly, which "means a brave respect for what is true," and in which decent men must join or face the fact that we are, morally, valve tenders at Auschwitz. This is not to say that Muhammad Ali is America's Jean-Paul Sartre, much less to say that he holds all the principles and positions that are hastily being attributed to him. He is a symbol of the failure of the rest of us—but he is a person, a human being, before he is any kind of symbol.

A SPIT IN THE FACE

Ali is, for one thing, a 25-year-old Southern black man. He is not well educated, not even particularly bright—though he is far from the dolt some sports writers made him out to be when, under earlier and more rigid standards, he failed some Selective Service verbal tests which white America and its newsmen referred to as "mental tests." They gave his I.Q. out as 78—a figure whose meaning can be measured against the fact that before he was 20, he swung himself a highly favorable financial deal in negotiations with a group of businessmen that included the chairmen of the boards of Brown-Forman Distillers and the Brown and Williamson Tobacco Company.

Still, his I.Q. probably *was* 78. The schools he went to in Kentucky probably didn't do much to prepare him for Stanford-Binet testing. But neither did they take away his pride.

After his recent fight, Ali told reporters, "I didn't go to the body because I didn't want to get hit in the face. Body punchers get bruised, cut and swelled up. I like to be able to dress up the next day." At 18, he wore his Olympic medal to bed.

And he insists on being called by his chosen name.

It is a funny thing, that name. People in any trade can call themselves anything they want to—Mark Twain, Ross MacDonald, Jack Ruby, Robert Taylor, Fabian—and nobody much gives a damn. People change their names for religious reasons all the time, and few are the Irish sports writers who would insist on referring to Sister Mary Theresa as Annie O'Houlihan. Much less would they be likely to make fun of her religious name—like syndicated buffoon Jim Murray, out of the Los Angeles Times, who has called Ali things like "Abdullah Bull Bull" and "Abou Ben Hernia."

The case of "Muhammad Ali," however, is something else again. "Cassius Clay" is certainly a euphonious enough name, and it was as "Cassius Clay" that the man became famous. But it is not ignorance or forgetfulness that leads almost every sports writer, almost every copy desk, almost every radio or television news-actor to insist, like a spit in the face, on "Cassius Clay." And this has gone on for three years.

Sports writers do not, of course, recognize the Muslims as a religious group, any more than do prison officials across the country, any more than does the Federal government (can you see Ali commissioned a lieutnant and made a chaplain?). No sports writer would poke fun at Floyd Patterson for attending Mass, or at Barney Ross for observing Passover. But all but three or four have for three years insisted on saying every day to the heavyweight champion of the world that he will damned well wear a white name and like it.

That could make a guy a little angry. It could make him think, if he didn't think so already, that he lives in a white racist country.

BROWN BOMBER, BLACK BEAUTY

The American sports page is far more influential than most press critics have noted. It was not many years ago, for instance, when the late Bill Leiser, sports editor of the San Francisco Chronicle, quietly issued an edict to print, whenever possible, the picture of a black man who won a race or hit a home run; he knew, as few intellectuals do, the subtle and far-reaching power of his medium.

The claim that Joe Louis and Jackie Robinson have done as much as any civil rights leader to force white Americans to regard black men as something more than subhuman supernumeraries is far from unfounded. Sports figures are closer to Americans, of whatever color, than virtually any other group, with the possible exception of motion picture and television stars. At the same time, our sports pages, as much as any other segment of our national life, reflect our concern with the idea that the game ought to be played by certain rules.

A professor or a poet may protest and be greeted by the general public with a shrug; but the heavyweight champion of the world makes treason or racism, or both, stand out for everyone to face and deal with. Muhammad Ali is a long way from an intellectual. But he saw, somewhere, at some time, what being a black champion in a white country was supposed to mean, what role he was supposed to play, and he refused.

"Be a credit to your race," they told him in the vocabulary of 30 years ago, "and all will be yours: adulation, Cadillacs, women, the wide-eyed admiration of the white nation." Cassius Clay not only refused to play, he bought his own Cadillac, turned down the women, surrendered the adulation (and some millions of dollars in endorsement fees), joined an unpopular religion and changed his name.

"Be Joe Louis," they told him in effect—but you can't be the affectionately tolerated Brown Bomber if you believe in black beauty. The Brown Bomber, first in the long line of black champions, had to prove himself to the white sports writers and the white fight world; by the time of Muhammad Ali things had changed, a black world had come into existence in which it is the white man's job to prove himself. The sports writers and the Broadway wise guys and the fight game hipsters are 30 years behind the times, and they still don't know it.

And so they hate this man—the entrenched, the mighty and would-be-mighty, the black *assimilados*, the wordsmiths and the image men. He was such a nice kid, and the black devil has possessed him. If it were only 1692.

"I KNOW THE TRUTH"

At 18, young, eager, Cassius Clay returned from the 1960 Olympics in triumph, and they all loved him. He was a "warm, natural young man, totally lacking in sophistication, whose personality could be a refreshing breeze in a becalmed sport"; that was Dick Schaap, writing in The Saturday Evening Post in 1961. He was "an amiable and unsophisticated young man, who loves life and people and success and fame," said Newsweek—and the whites complacently read it, "good, simple, happy nigger."

Amiable, unsophisticated Clay swung his deal with the white Louisville businessmen—they did all the investing, he got more than half the income—and deliberately manufactured his attention-getting "I am the greatest" pose. His corny "poetry" (he writes poetry only a little better than the average sports writer) and his uncanny knack for naming the round in which his opponent would fall, was offensive to a few and misleading to many, but it brought him up the ladder fast.

Clay had only 19 professional fights before he was matched with terrible "Sonny" Liston ("the King of Hip," Norman Mailer

called him, "the Ace of Spades"). The underlying racism of the
heavyweight world had been showing on the surface more than
usual, aimed for a time at Floyd Patterson, who was then thought
by the white-hope dreamers to be black. Another amateur champion, Pete Rademacher, had been elevated to a pro and matched
with Patterson in his first fight, through a financial guarantee put
up by a racist group; Patterson had demolished him. Ingemar
Johanssen had come from Scandinavia to prove the superiority of
the white man; Patterson took the title back and kept it.

Then—as so often happens—the ringmasters realized that
things hadn't been so bad after all. "Sonny" Liston had appeared
—a burly, lazy, slow, hulking ex-con, a cool killer, the absolute
stereotype of the black man in the white man's nightmares about
his sister—and had clobbered Patterson twice, both times in the
first round.

Liston could hit like a falling boulder, and he probably wasn't
afraid of any *fighter* alive—but Clay convinced Liston that he was
facing the completely unpredictable. He pulled up in front of
Liston's house at three a.m., stood on the lawn, and shouted in-
sults. At the weigh-in before the fight, Clay turned up—somehow
with a pulse rate of 120, convincing the examining physician that
Clay was hysterically frightened. The sports writers—so devoted
to the "big black buck" stereotype that they were convinced Liston
was invincible—gleefully began to predict that Clay wouldn't show
up for the fight.

He showed up—with a steady pulse rate—and he has been
champion ever since. Immediately afterward, he announced his ad-
herence to the Muslim faith, and in March 1964—after a brief
flirtation with "Cassius X" that may have risen from his friendship
with Malcolm—he announced that, as is the custom in the Nation
of Islam, Elijah Muhammad has bestowed on him a "holy name"
because he had fulfilled the requirements of his faith. He wished,
he said, to be known as Muhammad Ali.

Two days later, Ali told reporters, "I know where I'm going
and I know the truth, and I don't have to be what you want me to
be; I'm free to be what I want to be."

Roman Catholic Floyd Patterson immediately metamorphosed
from black threat to dark-skinned white hope. "I disagree with the
precepts of the black Muslims," he said, "just as I disagree with
the Ku Klux Klan—in fact so much that I am willing and
desire to fight Cassius X to take the title from the black Muslim
leadership." He offered to fight for no purse. Cassius X turned the
offer aside with a mild put-down of Patterson (mild, possibly,
because Patterson hadn't called him "Clay") and the serious remark, "I don't want no religious war."

Any non-Muslim, black or white, who has ever read Muhammad Speaks or listened to Elijah Muhammad's broadcasts is
likely to have some reservations about the Nation of Islam. Aside
from the pseudo-science, the improbable sociology and the falsified

history, it is at least disconcerting to read about the hypocritical
white man who forces the use of the hated word "Negro"— in a
newspaper you've bought from a black man who said, "Excuse
me, sir, would you buy a paper and help the Negro?"

And there can be little doubt that the Muslims get as much
out of Ali as he ever got out of them. For one thing, they get
money; for another, they get a forum that they could never buy.
Probably it is trust rather than understanding that binds Ali to
them.

"Followers of Allah," he has said, "are the sweetest people in
the world. They don't carry knives. They don't tote weapons. They
pray. The women wear dresses that come all the way to the knees
and don't commit adultery. All they want to do is live in peace
with the world. They don't hate anybody. They don't want to stir
up any kind of trouble. All the meetings are held in secret, without
any fuss or hate-mongering."

But there is more to be said about the Muslims, and their
impact on Ali, than that. "Muslims are righteous people," Elijah
Muhammad said recently (in a lengthy interview with CBS and
ABC reporters, only a small portion of which was broadcast, on
ABC). "They do not believe in making war on anybody—and
senseless aggression against people violates a Muslim's religious
belief . . . I refused to take part in the war at that time [in 1942]
against Japan and Germany, or help America to fight those wars.
I considered myself a righteous Muslim, and I teach peace. . . .
If it is fighting for truth and righteousness—yes, we go along with
that. But if it is fighting for territorial gain, or to master and rule
people in their own spheres, no. We think it is an injustice. . . ."

A Catholic bishop could as easily make those statements, in
full conformance with his dogma, for the guidance of a Floyd
Patterson—but none has. Any leader could stand and trumpet
those words—but none has (Martin Luther King is certainly more
black leader than Baptist leader). A few lonely Christian pacifists
have always resisted war—but no major Christian religion, least of
all the Roman Catholic, has dared to step so far outside the "acceptable" on moral grounds.

The irony is not only that a group of black outcasts, hated and
feared by white America, leads in taking the one position that up-
holds the rhetoric of great American ideas, and is willing to sacrifice
American material rewards. It is equally ironic that Elijah Muhammad's Muslimism is the only religion in the United States that is
willing to say unequivocally that God is higher than Caesar—
even if they call him Allah.

"WHAT'S MY NAME?"

Ali had barely become Ali when the World Boxing Association and its president, Ed Wassman, started trying to take his

newly won title away. Fewer than 60 days had gone by before Wassman was quoted in the press as saying that the behavior of "Clay" since becoming champion was "detrimental to boxing." Since his only public behavior had been to proclaim his religion and his change of name, the meaning was clear.

On a pretext, they took the title from Ali in September 1964; the importance of the action is evident from the fact that everybody but the WBA ignored it.

Ali kept up his anti-Liston tactics in preparation for a second fight, originally scheduled for Boston. He had already made famous his nickname for Liston ("the big ugly bear"), and he turned up in downtown Boston with a coat that said "Bear hunt" on the back, running up and down stately Commonwealth Avenue, stopping motorists and asking, "Have you seen the bear?" Boston ultimately unloaded the fight, and it was finally held in Lewiston, Maine. It lasted two minutes.

In fact, the fight was over so fast that the officials and a great many television watchers thought that Liston had never been hit. The sports pages came as close as they dared to yelling "fake." Joe Louis—who is trotted out whenever Ali is in the news, to show that there are still credits to the race—said scornfully, "I don't see how any man can get so much power while punching on his toes."

Slow motion films of the fight show what happened—Ali, his pivotal foot perfectly flat and planted, had thrown a right cross hard enough so that his own shoulders turned a complete 180 degrees, and the punch lifted Liston several inches off the canvas before he dropped—but the odor of words like "fiasco" has never left the fight.

When, in November of 1965, Ali finally clobbered Patterson, he infuriated sports writers—not because he won, but because he won so easily, took 12 rounds to do it in, and was quite clear about why. All the pre-fight talk proved costly to Patterson: in the ring, Ali continually taunted Patterson by calling him "Mr. White America." The white writers were outraged, but there must have been some black smiles.

In Ali's next to last fight, Ernie Terrell threw several visibly low blows and rabbit-punched and kidney-punched throughout the fight, but when it was over and he was beaten, he called Ali a "dirty fighter"—and half the writers who covered the fight echoed the charge.

That fight, more than any other, brought down on Ali not only the contempt but the righteous wrath of the sports pages. Already he had been classified 1-A; already he had said that he wasn't going to go. Already he had been barred from fighting in several states because he refused to support the war in Vietnam. Already he had made it clear that he would play no newsman's game, that he would say what he felt like saying and insist on his dignity as a man. And already he had told them, over and over, "My name is Muhammad Ali," and they had ignored him.

Ernie Terrell chose to ignore him too, and to make a public issue out of calling him "Cassius Clay." In February 1967, Ali held Terrell up for 15 rounds while he hit him; there is no more charitable description. And every so often, Ali—the fastest heavyweight who has ever been in a ring—would throw a particularly fast combination of punches, step back, and shout, "What's my name?"

How they hated that! "He showed himself to be a mean and malicious man," Arthur Daley wept in the New York Times—as though anyone could pretend that it was only Terrell to whom the question had been addressed. "I hope he's all right," Ali said of Terrell the next day. "He's a gentleman. He's still my brother. He's black like me." But the Daleys and the Murrays missed the point.

STEVE CANYON, LYNDON JOHNSON, ET AL.

The freedom of the press, these days, is the freedom to be sure that all the propaganda is on one side. Long feature stories dot the Sunday editions about the stars who entertain the troops; the gossip columnists glorify the prizefighters (black and white) who travel in the right chic circles; Steve Canyon grimly flies the comic pages; the sports pages are celebrations of publicity for local heroes. "They tell me it would be a wonderful thing if I married a white woman," Ali once sneered, "because this would be good for brotherhood." It would be good for the gossip columnists, anyway; they'd be very noble, just as the sports writers are very noble about black prizefighters so long as they are content to be brown bombers.

But Ali challenges the sports page picture of America, and for that reason, if for no other, the sports writers must feel compelled to get him. Possibly they are all liberals; possibly they would all insist that the name change is a symbol only of separatism, and that they defy it in the cause of some word-magic variant of integration. But to Ali it must look—as, indeed, it looks to many white Americans—like an attempt to deny him his dignity, his prerogatives of choice, his opportunity to be a man.

They may be liberals; but if they are, they are the same sort of liberals as those who asked actor Ossie Davis in bewilderment why he delivered an oration at the funeral of Malcolm X—the question to which Davis answered, in part, "No Negro has yet asked me that question."

"Malcolm kept snatching our lies away," Davis wrote. "He kept shouting the painful truth we whites and blacks did not want to hear from all housetops. And he wouldn't stop for love or money." And Davis wrote: "White folks do not need anybody to remind them that they are men. We do! This was his one incontrovertible benefit to his people."

Muhammad Ali, alone among athletes, fits Davis' description. "The white men want me hugging on a white woman," Ali said, "or endorsing some whiskey, or some skin bleach . . . But by my sacrificing a little wealth I'm helping so many others. Little children can come by and meet the champ. Little kids in the alleys and slums of Florida and New York, they can come and see me where they never could walk up on Patterson and Liston. Can't see them niggers when they come to town."

He said: "Jackie Gleason tried to show me why I shouldn't be a Muslim. He said, 'Champ, why don't you think about it?' He's not the onliest one. All the big whiteys are trying. . . . Take those big niggers Floyd Patterson, 'Sonny' Liston. The whites make 'em rich, and in return they brainwash the little Negroes walking around. Liston lives in a white neighborhood, Patterson lives in a white neighborhood. I can live in the Fontainebleau, anywhere I want; but I live here in a slum with my people. I could have taken money from the whites, but it would brainwash all the little black children."

But Muhammad Ali is not a "credit to his race"; according to Ring magazine, he is "not to be held up as an example to the youngsters of the United States."

"I went in one place in Louisville," Ali once said, "and asked to be served, and the waiter told the boss, 'He's the Olympic champion,' and the boss said, 'I don't give a damn who he is, get him out of here!' "

A HIGHER BANNER

From "I don't give a damn who he is" to "What's my name?" is not so far as all that. And Olympic champion Cassius Clay, now heavyweight champion Muhammad Ali, once said he wanted "some type of little mission, something to do with the freedom of the Negro in America." He's found it, it has something to do with my freedom, too, and that of a lot of other white Americans.

It started on February 17, 1966, when Muhammad Ali was reclassified 1-A. Nine days later he announced that, as a Muslim, he would not fight in Vietnam. The New York Times quoted him as saying, "I don't have no personal quarrel with those Vietcong," but he actually said it much better than that:

"I ain't got nothing against them Viet Congs."

If that be treason, it is the kind of treason that rises to a banner above the banner of Caesar: it rises to the banner of truth. Alone, young, uneducated, Ali may not be able to take it by himself; but he certainly isn't getting any help from intellectuals.

The principled act of Muhammad Ali is a tragic-ironic heroism. He stands out not only because he is right but because he is alone, in a position which might be, but isn't, shared by all the intellectuals, the religious leaders, the men and women who by profession or position or announced dedication should today be in the forefront of "treason."

It is time, I think, to call Muhammad Ali by his right name.

II. A Question-Survey-Question Approach to "Nobody Knows My Name"

Questions: The title could suggest questions like these:
1. What is the name of the person the article is about?
2. Why doesn't anyone know his name?
3. Do people really not know his name?
4. Does the writer mean that people do not call the person by his right name? (or, possibly, that they do not know what he really is like?)

Survey clues

Introduction: The names *Cassius Clay* and *Muhammad Ali* are in conspicuous positions in the first two paragraphs. If you have followed the heavyweight champion's career, you know that Clay had his name changed to Muhammad Ali some years ago for religious reasons. If you did not know this, you might have found the beginning a bit confusing; however, the phrase "chosen religious name" is a fairly clear indication of what the writer is talking about.

The knowledge that the essay is concerned with Muhammad Ali's religious conversion and name change suggests the question: What does the writer think about this name change? Does he approve?

Subheadings and topic sentences: Although the subheadings are not very specific, together they provide a hint of the author's attitude toward his subject. "A Brave Respect," "A Spit in the Face," "Brown Bomber, Black Beauty," and "I Know the Truth" suggest a sympathetic approach. And one sentence your eye might have caught seems strongly pro-Ali: "He is a symbol of the failure of the rest of us—but he is a person, a human being, before he is any kind of symbol" (p. 127).

Conclusion: Certainly the final sentence—"It is time, I think, to call Muhammad Ali by his right name"—is clear enough. What is probably not clear yet is the writer's reasons for supporting Ali.

Basic Question: It is reasonable to assume that the essay will speak to a question like this: Why should Muhammad Ali be respected for his decision to take on a Muslim name?

Thesis (general answer): Muhammad Ali should be respected for his decision because of his courage in standing up for his convictions.

III. Major Arguments in "Nobody Knows My Name"

(Answers to the question: Why should Muhammad Ali be respected for his decision to take on a Muslim name?)
1. Muhammad Ali was more courageous than most American intellectuals have been in expressing his disapproval of the war in Viet Nam; in fact, he was the first prominent American to refuse to fight there.
2. His religious conversion was a genuine one; both the new name and his attitude toward military service are expressions of his religious convictions.
3. The refusal by sports writers and other Americans to accept Muslim principles,

whereas they accept the principles of other religious groups, reflects America's white racist attitudes.

4. Muhammad Ali (Cassius Clay) was accepted as long as he played the white man's game (accepted conventional white attitudes). He should be respected just as much now that he has decided that the way he can best help his race is by practicing the Muslim faith.

5. Prominent people in other fields have changed their names. There is no reason a sports figure should not be given the same opportunity. (Instead, Ali has been ridiculed by most American sports writers.)

6. Ali has been ridiculed for his supposed low intelligence and his bizarre behavior. He probably has more intelligence than he has been given credit for, but certainly both his limitations in learning and his occasionally unusual actions can be attributed to the restricted opportunities he was given in a white man's world.

7. Muhammad Ali should be respected for the good that he has done for his fellow humans. Like Malcolm X, he has shown that black people are fully human, too.

IV.

"CLEAN FUN AT RIVERHEAD"
by Tom Wolfe

The inspiration for the demolition derby came to Lawrence Mendelsohn one night in 1958 when he was nothing but a spare-ribbed twenty-eight-year-old stock-car driver halfway through his 10th lap around the Islip, L.I., Speedway and taking a curve too wide. A lubberly young man with a Chicago boxcar haircut came up on the inside in a 1949 Ford and caromed him 12 rows up into the grandstand, but Lawrence Mendelsohn and his entire car did not hit one spectator.

"That was what got me," he said, "I remember I was hanging upside down from my seat belt like a side of Jersey bacon and wondering why no one was sitting where I hit. 'Lousy promotion,' I said to myself.

"Not only that, but everybody who *was* in the stands forgot about the race and came running over to look at me giftwrapped upside down in a fresh pile of junk."

At that moment occurred the transformation of Lawrence Mendelsohn, racing driver, into Lawrence Mendelsohn, promotor, and, a few transactions later, owner of the Islip Speedway, where he kept seeing more of this same underside of stock car racing that everyone in the industry avoids putting into words. Namely, that for every purist who comes to see the fine points of the race, such as who is going to win, there are probably five waiting for the wrecks to which stock car racing is so gloriously prone.

The pack will be going into a curve when suddenly two cars,

three cars, four cars tangle, spinning and splattering all over each
other and the retaining walls, upside down, right side up, inside
out and in pieces, with the seams bursting open and discs, rods,
wires and gasoline spewing out and yards of sheet metal shearing
off like Reynolds Wrap and crumpling into the most baroque
shapes, after which an ash-blue smoke starts seeping up from the
ruins and a thrill begins to spread over the stands like Newburg
sauce.

So why put up with the monotony between crashes?

Such, in brief, is the early history of what is culturally the
most important sport ever originated in the United States, a sport
that ranks with the gladiatorial games of Rome as a piece of
national symbolism. Lawrence Mendelsohn had a vision of an
automobile sport that would be all crashes. Not two cars, not three
cars, not four cars, but 100 cars would be out in an area doing
nothing but smashing each other into shrapnel. The car that outrammed and outdodged all the rest, the last car that could still
move amid the smoking heap, would take the prize money.

So at 8:15 at night at the Riverhead Raceway, just west of
Riverhead, L.I., on Route 25, amid the quaint tranquility of the
duck and turkey farm flatlands of eastern Long Island, Lawrence
Mendelsohn stood up on the back of a flat truck in his red neon
warmup jacket and lectured his 100 drivers on the rules and
niceties of the new game, the "demolition derby." And so at 8:30
the first 25 cars moved out onto the raceway's quarter-mile stock
car track. There was not enough room for 100 cars to mangle each
other. Lawrence Mendelsohn's dream would require four heats.
Now the 25 cars were placed at intervals all about the circum-
ference of the track, making flatulent revving noises, all headed
not around the track but toward a point in the center of the infield.

Then the entire crowd, about 4,000, started chanting a count-
down, "Ten, nine, eight, seven, six, five, four, three, two," but it
was impossible to hear the rest because right after "two" half the
crowd went into a strange whinnying wail. The starter's flag went
up, and the 25 cars took off, roaring into second gear with no
mufflers, all headed toward that same point in the center of the infield, converging nose on nose.

The effect was exactly what one expects that many simultane-
ous crashes to produce: the unmistakable tympany of automobiles
colliding and cheap-gauge sheet metal buckling; front ends folding
together at the same cockeyed angles police photographs of night-
time wreck scenes capture so well on grainy paper; smoke pouring
from under the hoods and hanging over the infield like a howitzer
cloud; a few of the surviving cars lurching eccentrically on bent
axles. At last, after four heats, there were only two cars moving
through the junk, a 1953 Chrysler and a 1958 Cadillac. In the
Chrysler a small fascia of muscles named Spider Ligon, who
smoked a cigar while he drove, had the Cadillac cornered up
against a guard rail in front of the main grandstand. He dispatched

it by swinging around and backing full throttle through the left side of its grille and radiator.

By now the crowd was quite beside itself. Spectators broke through a gate in the retaining screen. Some rushed to Spider Ligon's car, hoisted him to their shoulders and marched off the field, howling. Others clambered over the stricken cars of the defeated, enjoying the details of their ruin, and howling. The good, full cry of triumph and annihilation rose from Riverhead Raceway, and the demolition derby was over.

That was the 154th demolition derby in two years. Since Lawrence Mendelsohn staged the first one at Islip Speedway in 1961, they have been held throughout the United States at the rate of one every five days, resulting in the destruction of about 15,000 cars. The figures alone indicate a gluttonous appetite for the sport. Sports writers, of course, have managed to ignore demolition derbies even more successfully than they have ignored stock car racing and drag racing. All in all, the new automobile sports have shown that the sports pages, which on the surface appear to hum with life and earthiness, are at bottom pillars of gentility. This drag racing and demolition derbies and things, well, there are too many kids in it with sideburns, tight Levis and winkle-picker boots.

Yet the demolition derbies keep growing on word-of-mouth publicity. The "nationals" were held last month at Langhorne, Pa., with 50 cars in the finals, and demolition derby fans everywhere know that Don Tavish, of Dover, Mass., is the new world's champion. About 1,250,000 spectators have come to the 154 contests held so far. More than 75 per cent of the derbies have drawn full houses.

The nature of their appeal is clear enough. Since the onset of the Christian era, i.e., since about 500 A.D., no game has come along to fill the gap left by the abolition of the purest of all sports, gladiatorial combat. As late as 300 A.D. these bloody duels, usually between men but sometimes between women and dwarfs, were enormously popular not only in Rome but throughout the Roman Empire. Since then no game, not even boxing, has successfully acted out the underlying motifs of most sport, that is, aggression and destruction.

Boxing, of course, is an aggressive sport, but one contestant has actually destroyed the other in a relatively small percentage of matches. Other games are progressively more sublimated forms of sport. Often, as in the case of football, they are encrusted with oddments of passive theology and metaphysics to the effect that the real purpose of the game is to foster character, teamwork, stamina, physical fitness and the ability to "give-and-take."

But not even those wonderful clergymen who pray in behalf of Congress, expressway ribbon-cuttings, urban renewal projects and testimonial dinners for ethnic alderman would pray for a demolition derby. The demolition derby is, pure and simple, a form of gladiatorial combat for our times.

As hand-to-hand combat has gradually disappeared from our civilization, even in wartime, and competition has become more and more sophisticated and abstract, Americans have turned to the automobile to satisfy their love of direct aggression. The mild-mannered man who turns into a bear behind the wheel of a car— i.e., who finds in the power of the automobile a vehicle for the release of his inhibitions—is part of American folklore. Among teen-agers the automobile has become the symbol, and in part the physical means, of triumph over family and community restrictions. Seventy-five per cent of all car thefts in the United States are by teen-agers out for "joy rides."

The symbolic meaning of the automobile tones down but by no means vanishes in adulthood. Police traffic investigators have long been convinced that far more accidents are purposeful crashes by belligerent drivers than they could ever prove. One of the heroes of the era was the Middle Eastern diplomat who rammed a magazine writer's car from behind in the Kalorama embassy district of Washington two years ago. When the American bellowed out the window at him, he backed up and smashed his car again. When the fellow leaped out his car to pick a fight, he backed up and smashed his car a third time, then drove off. He was recalled home for having "gone native."

The unabashed, undisguished, quite purposeful sense of destruction of the demolition derby is its unique contribution. The aggression, the battering, the ruination are there to be enjoyed. The crowd at a demolition derby seldom gasps and often laughs. It enjoys the same full-throated participation as Romans at the Colosseum. After each trial or heat at a demolition derby, two drivers go into the finals. One is the driver whose car was still going at the end. The other is the driver the crowd selects from among the 24 vanquished on the basis of his courage, showmanship or simply the awesomeness of his crashes. The numbers of the cars are read over loudspeakers, and the crowd chooses one with its cheers. By the same token, the crowd may force a driver out of competition if he appears cowardly or merely cunning. This is the sort of driver who drifts around the edge of the battle avoiding crashes with the hope that the other cars will eliminate one another. The umpire waves a yellow flag at him and he must crash into someone within 30 seconds or run the risk of being booed off the field in dishonor and disgrace.

The frank relish of the crowd is nothing, however, compared to the kick the contestants get out of the game. It costs a man an average of $50 to retrieve a car from a junk yard and get it running for a derby. He will only get his money back—$50—for winning a heat. The chance of being smashed up in the madhouse first 30 seconds of a round are so great, even the best of drivers faces long odds in his shot at the $500 first prize. None of that matters to them.

Tommy Fox, who is nineteen, said he entered the demolition

derby because, "You know, it's fun. I like it. You know what I mean?" What was fun about it? Tommy Fox had a way of speaking that was much like the early Marlon Brando. Much of what he had to say came from the trapezii, which he rolled quite a bit, and the forehead, which he cocked, and the eyebrows, which he could bring together expressively from time to time. "Well," he said, you know, like when you hit 'em, and all that. It's fun."

Tommy Fox had a lot of fun in the first heat. Nobody was bashing around quite like he was in his old green Hudson. He did not win, chiefly because he took too many chances, but the crowd voted him into the finals as the best showman.

"I got my brother," said Tommy. "I came in from the side and he didn't even see me."

His brother is Don Fox, thirty-two, who owns the junk yard where they both got their cars. Don likes to hit them, too, only he likes it almost too much. Don drives with such abandon, smashing into the first car he can get a shot at and leaving himself wide open, he does not stand much chance of finishing the first three minutes.

For years now sociologists have been calling upon one another to undertake a serious study of America's "car culture." No small part of it is the way the automobile has, for one very large segment of the population, become the focus of the same large segment of a higher social order. Tommy Fox is unemployed, Don Fox runs a junk yard, Spider Ligon is a maintenance man for Brookhaven Naval Laboratory, but to categorize them as such is getting no closer to the truth than to have categorized William Faulkner in 1926 as a clerk at Lord & Taylor, although he was.

Tommy Fox, Don Fox and Spider Ligon are acolytes of the car culture, an often esoteric world of arts and sciences that came into its own after World War II and now has believers of two generations. Charlie Turbush, thirty-five, and his son, Buddy, seventeen, were two more contestants, and by no stretch of the imagination can they be characterized as bizarre figures or cultists of the death wish. As for the dangers of driving in a demolition derby, they are quite real by all physical laws. The drivers are protected only by crash helmets, seat belts and the fact that all glass, interior handles, knobs and fixtures have been removed. Yet Lawrence Mendelsohn claims that there have been no serious injuries in 154 demolition derbies and now gets his insurance at a rate below that of stock car racing.

The sport's future may depend in part on word getting around about its relative safety. Already it is beginning to draw contestants here and there from social levels that could give the demolition derby the cachet of respectability. In eastern derbies so far two doctors and three young men of more than passable connections in eastern society have entered under whimsical *noms de combat* and emerged neither scarred nor victorious. Bull fighting had to win the same social combat.

All of which brings to mind that fine afternoon when some

high-born Roman women were out in Nero's box at the Colosseum watching this sexy Thracian carve an ugly little Samnite up into prime cuts, and one said, darling, she had an inspiration, and Nero, needless to say, was all for it. Thus began the new vogue of Roman socialities fighting as gladiators themselves, for kicks. By the second century A.D. even the Emperor Commodus was out there with a tiger's head as a helmet hacking away at some poor dazed fall guy. He did a lot for the sport. Arenas sprang up all over the empire like shopping center bowling alleys.

The future of the demolition derby, then, stretches out over the face of America. The sport draws no lines of gender, and post-debs may reach Lawrence Mendelsohn at his office in Deer Park.

V. Thesis, Supporting Ideas, and Details in "Clean Fun At Riverhead"

Thesis (or general answer, or general statement, or point of view): In this reader's judgment, Wolfe's most general or widely inclusive statements of his point of view about demolition derbies come in the passages in which he compares them with Roman gladiator contests. In paragraphs 7 and 19 he states directly an idea that is developed at least by implication throughout the rest of the essay: the demolition derby is the most characteristically American of all sports because it is such an overt, crude expression of hostile or aggressive drives. The following two sentences together comprise a good, direct statement of thesis:

"Such, in brief, is the early history of what is culturally the most important sport ever originated in the United States, a sport that ranks with the gladiatorial games of Rome as a piece of national symbolism." [paragraph 7]

"The unabashed, undisguised, quite purposeful sense of destruction of the demolition derby is its unique contribution." [paragraph 19]

Supporting Ideas: The following ideas are all directly stated or clearly implied, and all of them give support to the thesis:
1. Unlike other sports, this one makes no pretense of being civilized or constructive; the underlying hostilities of both the participants and the spectators are almost completely undisguised.
2. The contestants are primarily concerned with destruction rather than with demonstrating skill.
3. The crowds also are chiefly interested in the damage that is done to vehicles and in the bravado demonstrated by the drivers.
4. Automobiles are symbols of aggression for Americans; this sport is simply an especially crude example of the way Americans treat these vehicles.

Illustrative Details: This essay has three rather distinct sections, or at least three parts that are organized quite differently. The first part (paragraphs 1 to 7) is an account of the early history of demolition derbies; the second (paragraphs 8 to

11) is a narrative treatment of a typical demolition event; and the last section is an analysis of the features of these derbies from Wolfe's viewpoint. Most of the specific details about what happens at a derby are in the first two sections and most of the generalizations about them are in the last part. But details and generalizations can be quite easily matched. Consider what happens when we look in the first two sections for details that support the reasons listed above. The passages underlined here (the underlining is always added) together comprise a description of a demolition derby:

1. Demolition derbies do not disguise hostilities as other sports do—"Not two cars, not three cars, not four cars, but <u>100 cars would be out in an area doing nothing but smashing each other into shrapnel. The car that outrammed and outdodged all the rest, the last car that could still move amid the smoking heap, would take the prize money.</u>"—(paragraph 7) (Comments on the way hostilities are handled in other sports are in paragraph 15.)

2. Contestants are primarily concerned with destruction—"The starter's flag went up, and the 25 cars took off, roaring into second gear with no mufflers, all <u>headed toward that same point in the center of the infield converging nose on nose.</u>" (paragraph 9)

3. Spectators also are destruction-seekers—"Half the crowd went into a strange whinnying wail." (paragraph 9) And (when Spider Logan smashed his own car after destroying all the others) "By now the crowd was quite beside itself. Spectators broke through a gate in the retaining screen. Some rushed to Spider Logan's car, hoisted him to their shoulders and marched off the field, howling. . . . The good, full cry of triumph and annihilation rose from Riverhead Raceway. . . ." (paragraph 11)

(The fourth point, which compares demolition derbies with other uses of the automobile, is illustrated in the section in which it is brought up—paragraphs 17 and 18. See, for example, Wolfe's comment that many highway accidents are probably "purposeful crashes," paragraph 18.)

VI. One Reader's View of "Clean Fun At Riverhead": Impressions from Three Readings

First Reading: Because he is accustomed to reading for point of view and because he is interested in the unusual twists that Wolfe gives to commonplace subjects, this reader found that in the first reading he was particularly aware of Wolfe's attitude toward demolition derbies (his *point of view* concerning them). In fact, the reader concentrated so much on viewpoint he discovered he had missed some of the details. Specifically, he was not clear about how the cars are arranged on the track at the beginning, where they go, or exactly how the winner is determined. He was conscious of some of Wolfe's stylistic techniques—for example the sarcasm of his comment that sports like football are "encrusted with oddments of passive theology and metaphysics to the effect that the real purpose of the game is to foster character, teamwork, stamina," etc.—but he did not consciously discover nearly as many of Wolfe's special effects with language as he found in a later, analytical reading. What he noted most of all was the writer's insistence that demolition derbies are characteristically American because they are such overt, crude expressions of hostility (and the implied criticism of contemporary American attitudes that goes with this observation).

Second Reading: The focus in the second reading was on the way the derbies are set up and carried out. The reader scanned for the paragraphs that described these events. (They turned out to be paragraphs 8 and 9.) He discovered that in the first reading he had made the false assumption that these contests were a kind of race—even though the name of the sport makes clear what its real purpose is and even though Wolfe's description of these contests is quite explicit. (It is not at all unusual for a reader to find it difficult to get beyond his conception of the way things are "supposed to be," especially in the first reading.) The discovery that the drivers in these contests do not compete in any ordinary sense—that, instead, they all head for the center of the ring simultaneously, smashing into one another as they go—of course gave support to Wolfe's thesis that a demolition derby is an unusually brutal event.

Third Reading: The third reading was the most pleasurable of all. This time the reader went through the whole essay again, savoring the writer's sarcasm and soaking in the impression of senseless, wasteful outpouring of hostility. In this reading he was particularly struck by the way Wolfe sums up the spirit of these events succinctly by having Tommy Fox comment: "I got my brother. I came in from the side and he didn't even see me." Although the reader was not convinced that these derbies are as significant as the writer seems to think they are (or that he really thinks they are that important either, beneath what is often tongue-in-cheek commentary) he was amused by Wolfe's frequent flamboyance and impressed with the sharpness of his insights.

VII. A Fourth Reading: Style and Method of Development In "Clean Fun At Riverhead"

Having understood and enjoyed the essay, the reader settled down to the very different project of analyzing the writer's technique. This time he was aware of the basic method of development—the three part organization outlined in Chapter Supplement V—and of many stylistic features that he had not pinpointed in earlier readings simply because he had not been looking for them. Some of the techniques he found Wolfe using are outlined below. With this much of a start, you could undoubtedly find many others (and repeated uses of these) if you were to analyze the rest of the selection.

1. The word "lubberly" is not commonly used today. Derived from "lubber" as in "land-lubber," it means "awkwardly." (A land-lubber is a sailor who is awkward on land.) It is the first of a number of *slightly negative* and *humorous-sounding* words Wolfe uses to describe the participants in demolition derbies. "Carom" is a term used in billiards to mean a ball hitting one ball and rebounding to another. Although it is used here to describe the action of a stock-car race rather than that of a demolition derby, it introduces the mood of the piece by showing how dangerously men sometimes "play" with cars.

2–3. Wolfe's main character uses a couple of interesting and appropriate-sounding *metaphors*. The second one—"gift-wrapped upside down in a pile of junk"—is a colorful expression that vividly creates a picture and sounds like something Mendelsohn might actually have said. The first—"hanging upside down from my seat belt like a side of Jersey bacon"—gives the writer something to come back to in the next paragraph.

4. When Wolfe refers to the "underside of stock racing that everyone in the industry avoids putting into words" he is playing with Mendelsohn's metaphor and creating from it another one that makes a judgment of stock racing. (Mendelsohn was simply creating a picture.) There is a low-key *sarcasm* in his statement that for every "purist" who is interested in seeing who wins these races there are five others who are just waiting for the wrecks.

5. This paragraph contains some highly *vivid descriptive language*. Note the *strong, specific action verbs*—"tangle," "spin," "splatter," "spewing"—and the *down-to-earth figure of speech* (a simile): "yards of sheet metal shearing off like Reynolds Wrap and crumpling" etc.

6. The one sentence in this paragraph is highly sarcastic. Mendelsohn has thought of a way of making money by eliminating the "monotony" between crashes—he'll provide more crashes.

7. This is the paragraph that introduces Wolfe's thesis (see Chapter Supplement V). It contains an *analogy*—the comparison of demolition derbies with Roman gladiatorial contests—that is characteristically Wolfian in its grotesqueness, its vividness, and its tone of truth-through-exaggeration.

VIII.

OUR ENEMY, THE CAT

by Alan Devoe

We tie bright ribbons around their necks, and occasionally little tinkling bells, and we affect to think that they are as sweet and vapid as the coy name "kitty" by which we call them would imply. It is a curious illusion. For, purring beside our fireplaces and pattering along our back fences, we have got a wild beast as uncowed and uncorrupted as any under heaven.

It is five millenniums since we snared the wild horse and broke his spirit to our whim, and for centuries beyond counting we have been able to persuade the once-free dog to fawn and cringe and lick our hands. But a man must be singularly blind with vanity to fancy that in the three—ten?—thousand years during which we have harbored cats beneath our roof-trees, we have succeeded in reducing them to any such insipid estate. It is not a "pet" (that most degraded of creatures) that we have got in our house, whatever we may like to think. It is a wild beast; and there adheres to its sleek fur no smallest hint of the odor of humanity.

It would be a salutary thing if those who write our simpering verses and tales about "tabby-sit-by-the-fire" could bring themselves to see her honestly, to look into her life with eyes unblurred by

wishful sentiment. It would be a good thing—to start at the beginning—to follow her abroad into the moonlight on one of those raw
Spring evening when the first skunk-cabbages are thrusting their
veined tips through the melting snow and when the loins of catdom
are hot with lust.

The love-play of domestic creatures is mostly a rather comic
thing, and loud are the superior guffaws of rustic humans to see the
clumsy fumbling antics that take place in the kennels and the
stockpen. But the man had better not laugh who sees cats in their
rut. He is looking upon something very like aboriginal passion, un-
tainted by any of the overlaid refinements, suppressions, and modifications that have been acquired by most of mankind's beasts. The
mating of cats has neither the bathetic clumsiness of dogs' nor the
lumbering ponderousness of cattle's, but—conducted in a lonely
secret place, away from human view—is marked by a quick concentrated intensity of lust that lies not far from the border-line of
agony. The female, in the tense moment of the prelude, tears with
her teeth at her mate's throat, and, as the climax of the creatures'
frenzy comes, the lean silky-furred flanks quiver vibrantly as a taut
wire. Then quietly, in the Spring night, the two beasts go their
ways.

It will be usually May before the kittens come; and that
episode, too, will take place secretly, in its ancient feline fashion,
where no maudlin human eye may see. Great is the pique in many
a house when "pussy", with dragging belly and distended dugs,
disappears one night—scorning the cushioned maternity-bed that
has been prepared for her—and creeps on silent feet to the darkest
cranny of the cellar, there in decent aloneness to void her blood
and babies. She does not care, any more than a lynx does, or a
puma, to be pried upon while she licks the birth-hoods from her
squirming progeny and cleans away the membrane with her rough
pink tongue.

A kitten is not a pretty thing at birth. For many days it is a
wriggling mite of lumpy flesh and sinew, blind and unaware, making soft sucking noises with its wet, toothless mouth, and smelling
of milk. Daily, hourly the rough tongue of the tabby ministers to it
in its helplessness, glossing the baby-fur with viscid spittle, lick-
ing away the uncontrolled dung, cleaning away the crumbly pellets
of dried blood from its pointed ears. By that tenth or fourteenth
day when its eyes wholly unseal, blue and weak in their newness,
the infant cat is clean to immaculateness, and an inalienable fastidiousness is deep-lodged in its spirit.

It is now—when the kitten makes its first rushes and sallies
from its birthplace, and, with extraordinary gymnastics of its
chubby body, encounters chair-legs and human feet and other curious phenomena—that it elicits from man those particular expressions of gurgling delight which we reserve for very tiny fluffy
creatures who act very comically. But the infant cat has no coy
intent to be amusing. If he is comic, it is only because of the

incongruity of so demure a look and so wild a heart. For in that furry head of his, grim and ancient urges are already dictating.

Hardly larger than a powderpuff, he crouches on the rug and watches a fleck of lint. His little blue eyes are bright, and presently his haunches tense and tremble. The tiny body shivers in an ague of excitement. He pounces, a little clumsily perhaps, and pinions the fleeting lint-fleck with his paws. In the fractional second of that lunge, the ten small needles of his claws have shot from their sheaths of flesh and muscle. It is a good game; but it is not an idle one. It is the kitten's introduction into the ancient ritual of the kill. Those queer little stiff-legged rushes and prancings are the heritage of an old death-dance, and those jerkings of his hind legs, as he rolls on his back, are the preparation for that day when—in desperate conflict with a bigger beast than himself—he will win the fight by the time-old feline technique of disembowelment. Even now, in his early infancy, he is wholly and inalienably a cat.

While he is still young he has already formulated his attitude toward the human race into whose midst he has been born. It is an attitude not easily described, but compounded of a great pride, a great reserve, a towering integrity. It is even to be fancied that there is something in it of a sort of bleak contempt. Solemnly the cat watches these great hulking two-legged creatures into whose strange tribe he has unaccountably been born—and who are so clumsy, so noisy, so vexing to his quiet spirit—and in his feline heart is neither love nor gratitude. He learns to take the food which they give him, to relish the warmth and the comfort and the caresses which they can offer, but these profferments do not persuade his wild mistrustful heart to surrender itself. He will not sell himself, as a dog will, for a scrap of meat; he will not enter into an allegiance. He is unchangeably and incorruptibly a cat, and he will accommodate himself to the ways and spirit of mankind no more than the stern necessity of his unnatural environment requires.

Quietly he dozes by the fire or on a lap, and purrs in his happiness because he loves the heat. But let him choose to move, and if any human hand tries to restrain him for more than a moment he will struggle and unsheath his claws and lash out with a furious hate. Let a whip touch him and he will slink off in a sullen fury, uncowed and outraged and unrepenting. For the things which man gives to him are not so precious or essential that he will trade them for his birthright, which is the right to be himself —a furred four-footed being of ancient lineage, loving silence and aloneness and the night, and esteeming the smell of rat's blood above any possible human excellence.

He may live for perhaps ten years; occasionally even for twenty. Year after year he drinks the daily milk that is put faithfully before him, dozes in laps whose contours please him, accepts with casual pleasure the rubbing of human fingers under his chin—

and withdraws, in every significant hour of his life, as far away from human society as he is able. Far from the house, in a meadow or a woods if he can find one, he crouches immobile for hours, his lithe body flattened concealingly in the grass or ferns, and waits for prey. With a single pounce he can break a rabbit's spine as though it were a brittle twig. When he has caught a tawny meadow-mouse or a mole, he has, too, the ancient cat-ecstasy of toying and playing with it, letting it die slowly, in a long agony, for his amusement. Sometimes, in a dim remembrance from the remote past of his race, he may bring home his kill; but mostly he returns to the house as neat and demure as when he left, with his chops licked clean of blood.

Immaculate, unobtrusive, deep withdrawn into himself, he passes through the long years of his enforced companionship with humanity. He takes from his masters (how absurd a word it is) however much they may care to give him; of himself he surrenders nothing. However often he be decked with ribbons and cuddled and petted and made much over, his cold pride never grows less, and his grave calm gaze—tinged perhaps with a gentle distaste— is never lighted by adoration. To the end he adores only his own gods, the gods of mating, of hunting, and of the lonely darkness.

One day, often with no forewarning whatever, he is gone from the house and never returns. He has felt the presaging shadow of death, and he goes to meet it in the old unchanging way of the wild—alone. A cat does not want to die with the smell of humanity in his nostrils and the noise of humanity in his delicate peaked ears. Unless death strikes very quickly and suddenly, he creeps away to where it is proper that a proud wild beast should die—not on one man's rugs or cushions, but in a lonely quiet place, with his muzzle pressed against the cold earth.

IX. Contrasting Expressions in "Our Enemy, the Cat"

Most people's cat	Devoe's cat
named "kitty"	"aboriginal passion"
dressed in ribbons and bells	"intensity of lust"
"pet"	"frenzy"
"tabby sit-by-the-fire"	"rough pink tongue"
"pussy"	"inalienable fastidiousness"
amusing	"aloneness"
	"wild at heart"
	"inalienably a cat"
	"wild mistrustful heart"
	"unchangeably and incorruptibly a cat"
	"right to be himself"
	"uncowed and outraged and unrepenting"
	"adores only his own gods"
	"proud wild beast"

how to preview a non-fiction book

The reading approach that the last three chapters have stressed most consistently —previewing, or surveying, a book before reading it through—is one that you will find particularly adaptable to your purposes as you get into non-fiction books other than textbooks. In fact, you will be able to use it almost exactly as you did with essays, articles, and chapters of textbooks. Although you will be looking for different features as you preview, your purpose and basic approach will be the same. And you may be surprised to find how easily and quickly you can determine where a writer is going in a long non-fiction work and decide whether you want to go with him all or part of the way.

Certainly, you will often want to read the book all the way through, following the writer's complete development of his idea. Sometimes, though, you will be interested only in chapters or sections concerning a topic you are investigating—for example, one on which you are doing a research paper. For either reading purpose, you can learn much about what a book has to offer you by spending a few minutes thoughtfully skimming the pages, with particular attention to certain pages.

WHAT TO LOOK FOR IN PREVIEWING

In this previewing, you will be looking especially for *introductory* features be-cause full-length non-fiction books often have more of these than essays, articles, and textbook chapters do. For example, in addition to a *title* (and often an important *subtitle*), a book of this kind may have *acknowledgments*, a *foreword* or *preface*, a *book jacket*, and an *introduction*. And it will almost certainly have a *title page*, a *table of contents*, and (in the first chapter) *introductory paragraphs* giving you some idea of the ground to be covered later.

Of course, other portions of the book are also worth noting as you preview. By skimming through a few pages in each of two or three chapters, you can tell something about the writer's approach to his subject—whether he expresses strong personal feelings or remains relatively detached, whether his tone is seri-ous or light-hearted, whether he is presenting a narrative account of someone's experiences or an exposition of facts and ideas. And the *concluding paragraph* (or paragraphs) of the last chapter may be as helpful to you in your previewing as the final paragraph of a shorter selection usually is. For here the writer often sums up not only the main idea of the chapter but also a major point he has been developing throughout the book. Finally, there may be an *appendix*, a *bibliogra-phy*, or a section of *notes*; a quick look at any or all of these can help you get an idea of the kind of research the writer has done in the preparation of his manuscript.

WHAT'S IN A TITLE

You will find that titles of non-fiction books, like the titles of the popular maga-zine articles in Chapter Three, generally emphasize either *information* or *point of view*. However, it is probably impossible for anyone to write a full-length book on any subject without including some of his own opinions and feelings. (Chapter Three pointed out that "emotive language" is commonplace in written communication. Could anyone write three hundred pages without including any?) Therefore, when you preview non-fiction books with titles that sound strictly informative—titles like *On Aggression* (Konrad Lorenz), *The Ages of Life* (Lorus and Margery Milne), *The Origins of Totalitarianism* (Hannah Arendt)—you will probably want to look for other signals that suggest points of view. These viewpoints may not be stated obviously or directly, but they will still be there.

Some non-fiction titles do contain words that suggest specific points of view, although they may not make clear exactly what those points of view will be. For example, after checking their titles alone, you would probably know that the books *How to Survive Education* (Richard M. Gummere), *Prisoners of Psy-chiatry* (Bruce Ennis), and *Mississippi: A Closed Society* (James W. Silver) are critical of the institutions they concern, even though you would need additional clues in order to be sure of the kind of criticism they contain. The words "survive," "prisoners," and "closed" would lead you to expect fairly direct statements of opinion and of feeling.

Occasionally, a non-fiction book title will strike you as completely ambiguous—perhaps one like *Bring Me A Unicorn* (Anne Morrow Lindbergh) or *The Chickenbone Special* (Dwayne E. Walls). When this happens, unless you have missed some obvious clues, you have probably found a title that is *symbolic*; that is, one in which a concrete object represents an idea (and therefore a point of view) developed in the book. Titles of this kind are selected primarily to arouse your curiosity, not to provide information or establish a point of view. However, as you preview a book with a symbolic title, you will usually find clues pointing to the idea the title implies.

Each of these different kinds of titles will suggest different sorts of questions to you as you begin your previewing. For *symbolic* titles your first question is likely to be: What is this book going to be about, anyway? (Often, you will find an answer before you have had time to become conscious of asking the question. The sub-title of *Bring Me A Unicorn*, for example, is *The Diaries and Letters of Anne Morrow Lindbergh, 1922–28*. For information titles like *On Aggression* you are likely to have *what* questions, questions about subject matter:

What kind of aggression is Lorenz writing about?

Does he apply the term to humans or to lower animals?

Are human aggression and lower animal aggression similar? (Lorenz' answer to that one, incidentally, provides the point of view that makes the book more controversial than the title might suggest it would be.)

And for "point of view" titles like *How to Survive Education*, you will probably think of *why* questions:

Why does the writer choose the word "survive" for the title?

Why does he think that education is so bad that the word "survive" is appropriate?

Doesn't nearly everyone go through formal education (at least in America)? ("Point of view" titles can suggest *what* questions also, but sometimes a subtitle will answer one of these. For example the subtitle of *How to Survive Education* partially answers the question "What kind?" by the phrase: *Before, During and After College*.)

SOME TITLES TO WORK WITH

For each of the titles in the list below, ask yourself which of the three categories —information, point of view, or symbolic—seems most appropriate, and then see what questions come to your mind as you think about the title. Your questions may be about the author's purpose in choosing the words in his title or they may be about the content of the book. You should understand, though, that as you become accustomed to this questioning approach, your responses will become so quick and habitual that you will probably not be conscious of asking specific questions. Also, when you have the book in hand, you will have other signals to respond to almost as soon as you think about the title. The point

now is simply to understand how important titles can be to you in helping you
begin thinking along with a writer. When you have worked out your questions,
turn to Chapter Supplement I (p. 187) and compare your responses with those
you find there. Some possible questions are provided below for the first three
titles; however, you may want to add some of your own.

▶ TITLE	KIND OF TITLE	QUESTIONS
1. *Prisoners of Psychiatry*	Point of view	Who are these "prisoners?" Are they literal prisoners? (probably not) How can the writer justify the use of such a strong term? (This sounds like a serious condemnation of the psychiatric profession, doesn't it?) In what sense are the people that the writer is talking about "victims" of psychiatric approaches?
2. *Aspects of Language*	Informative	What kind of information about language does the book provide? (What does the writer mean by "aspects?") Does the writer treat "language" in a general sense or is he concerned only with the English language? Is the book written for people who have a special background in language study or for the general reader? Does the writer have a special point of view about language that is hidden behind the objective word "aspects?"
3. *The Chickenbone Special*	Symbolic	What *is* the "chickenbone special?"

▶ TITLE   KIND OF TITLE   QUESTIONS

This phrase sounds like the name of a restaurant dinner, but is it? If it is, what idea does it suggest? (If you have had experiences like the ones the writer treats in this book, you may be able to do more with this title. But otherwise you won't have much to go by.)

4. *Punishment: The Supposed Justification*

5. *The Ages of Life*

6. *Mississippi: The Closed Society*

7. *The Tyranny of Words*

8. *The Origins of Totalitarianism*

9. *Justice Denied: The Black Man In White America*

10. *The Unexpected Universe*

FINDING CLUES IN INTRODUCTORY
AND CONCLUDING PORTIONS

In the next section you will have an opportunity to match the questions some of the above titles suggest to you with other clues you find in excerpts from the corresponding books, taken from the introductory and concluding parts. (The only way you can discover what you can get out of the "body" in a quick skimming is by practicing on complete books.) First, though, here is a brief explanation of what you can expect to find in the preliminary and supplementary sections of non-fiction books and in introductory and concluding paragraphs:

1. *Subtitles:* Some non-fiction books have subtitles that are printed in relatively small type under the main title on the front cover (and on the front of the book jacket) and on the half-title and title pages. Some "subtitles" are really basic parts of the main title. One way you can tell how important the publishers consider the second part of a title to be is by noting whether the phrase is on the spine of the book (the part that shows on the library shelf) as well as on the front. If it is, you should probably regard it as a part of the main title. In that case, there will ordinarily be a colon (:) between the two parts. For example, *Justice Denied: The Black Man in White America* is the full main title whereas, in *Prisoners of Psychiatry*, the subtitle *Mental Patients, Psychiatrists and the law* is clearly subordinate. It is always a good idea, however, to note all parts of a title. Often the second part, or subtitle, will state the main idea of the book more directly than the preceding phrase does.

2. *Book jackets:* The paper covers on most new hard-cover books in bookstore racks and on recent hard-backs on the shelves of many libraries often contain comments about the books and the authors. Although you should realize that these comments are there for the purpose of selling books, you will usually find that they are worth skimming as you preview; they can help you begin to understand the emphasis and tone of the book.

3. *Title page:* The first page that will catch your attention as you preview will probably be the title page. (It is sometimes preceded by an almost blank sheet called a half-title page; this page contains only the title and the subtitle of the book.) The front side of the title page ordinarily includes—in addition to the title, the subtitle, and the author's name—the names of the publisher and of any people who made major contributions to the book (illustrators, writers of introductions, and so on). Some of this information may not be particularly important to you in your surveying, but on the back side of the title page you will usually find one very important detail: the date of publication.

4. *Acknowledgments:* Somewhere in the early part of the book—often right after the title page—many writers place a section in which they acknowledge their indebtedness to people who have worked with them or who have helped them in the preparation of the manuscript. Although you may not want to spend much time on acknowledgments, a quick skim-

ming of this section may give you an idea of the kind of information and treatment you are likely to find in the book.

5. *Preface or Foreword:* These terms are interchangeable; writers do not ordinarily use both in the same book. In a preface or foreword, the author explains his purpose, provides background information that will help the reader understand his thesis, or in other ways prepares the reader for the experience of reading the book.

6. *Introduction:* Customarily, although not always, a section labeled "Introduction" is written by someone other than the author of the book, usually a person with special knowledge about the subject of the book and the writer's career. Sometimes, however, the term is used synonymously with preface or foreword. Introductions often provide valuable background information that will help you understand the purpose and scope of the book.

7. *Table of Contents:* The introductory section that can provide you with the most information in the least amount of time as you preview is the table of contents. Here the writer outlines the book for you, showing you the organization and the emphases.

8. *Introductory and concluding paragraphs:* A quick look at the first paragraph or two (or possibly three) in the first chapter and at the last and maybe the next to the last paragraph in the final chapter (often called an "epilogue") should certainly be included in your previewing. A skimming or quick reading of these can usually give you a good idea of where the writer is taking you. Look especially for *key words*; that is, for words used in the title or for those that reinforce ideas implied by the title.

9. *Supplementary materials:* Following the last chapter of a non-fiction book you may find some pages on which the writer provides aids to the reader: a *bibliography*, listing all the sources that influenced him—even indirectly—as he prepared the manuscript; a *notes* section, giving specific sources for ideas or information footnoted in the chapters; or an *appendix*, providing the interested reader with information beyond the scope of the main part of the book. Since these are all fairly formal research devices, simply finding that they are there will tell you something about the way the writer has approached his subject. (You should not, of course, assume that all carefully written non-fiction books will make use of these devices nor that those that do cannot at the same time be entertaining.)

PRACTICING PREVIEWING

As you go through each of the following sets of extracted material, imagine that you are previewing the actual book, preparing to read it or discovering whether you want to read it. First, review the questions you asked as you thought about the title. Then, survey each of the parts of the book included here, looking for phrases and sentences that provide *general answers* to these questions or that suggest additional *related questions*. After you have completed your previewing, have in mind a *basic question* you expect the writers to answer throughout the book (although it may be a more general and complex one than the principal questions answered by the writers whose articles you have read in the last two chapters).

In the selections from the first book, *Prisoners of Psychiatry*, certain key phrases and sentences are underlined and occasional comments are inserted. These features are to help you discover ways of using a writer's signals as you preview. Then when you turn to the excerpts from the other two books you will be able to work out your own previewing style.

After you have surveyed the excerpts from *Prisoners of Psychiatry* and filled in the blank spaces following them, check your answers with those in Chapter Supplement II (p. 189) before going to the selections from the other two books. For each group of materials, set yourself a time limit of a few minutes. Of course, in that time you will not be able to read every word in all of the selections included. But remember, that is not what previewing means. It means, rather, looking for key words and phrases that will help you understand the purpose and scope of the work.

Prisoners of Psychiatry

A. Book jacket

FRONT FLAP

PRISONERS OF PSYCHIATRY
MENTAL PATIENTS,
PSYCHIATRISTS,
AND THE LAW

Bruce Ennis

Introduction by Thomas S. Szasz, M.D.

Myra Lee Glassman was Phi Beta Kappa at college and in the top 1 per cent in scientific and quantitative ability on the nationwide Medical College Admission Test. Yet thirteen medical schools rejected her application because two years earlier, under the strain of family troubles, she had voluntarily spent nine months in a private mental institution. She appealed for help to the New York Civil Liberties Union, where the author, a young lawyer, had just begun an ambitious project to ease the plight of mental patients.

Henry Mercer's mother died when he was thirteen, leaving

him in the hands of a brutal, alcoholic father. Soon Henry became disruptive in school, and the authorities, not knowing what else to do, placed him in Rockland State Hospital, a mental institution thirty miles north of New York City. There he stayed for four years, until his brother, just released from the Marines, took custody of him. No one ever claimed that Henry was mentally ill. Sixteen years later, married, a father, and having worked for eleven

BACK FLAP

years at a Bronx hospital, Mercer was denied a license to drive a cab because of his prior record of "mental illness." Bruce Ennis took the case.

In 1951, Alfred Curt von Wolfersdorf was indicted for murder in Poughkeepsie, New York—an indictment based solely on the testimony of another man, who later confessed and was electrocuted for the crime. Wolfersdorf was adjudged incompetent to stand trial and sent to Matteawan, a state institution for the criminally insane, where he still is. Ennis has been fighting three years for the release of Wolfersdorf, who is now eighty-eight years old.

These dramatic stories—and others—are told here by a man who has been intensely involved with our mental institutions and the legal and psychiatric apparatus that sustains them.

More than 750,000 Americans are housed in these institutions, and almost 3 million a year are treated in them. Some commit themselves voluntarily. Many more are incarcerated against their will not because of something they did, but because of what they told a psychiatrist. When accused of a crime, some are found "incompetent" and may languish for ten or twenty or thirty years, without a trial and without treatment. And, as these cases show, even those who are released often bear the stigma for life.

But the people in this book were more fortunate than others. Representing them were a courageous young lawyer and his staff who challenged and continue to challenge a system of judicial neglect and psychiatric injustice that is the shame of America.

OUTSIDE COVER—BACK

BRUCE ENNIS

Bruce Ennis was born in Knoxville, Tennessee, in 1941, and graduated from Dartmouth College and the University of Chicago Law School. After several years as a clerk to Federal Judge William Miller, he joined the New York Civil Liberties Union in 1968 to direct its Civil Liberties and Mental Illness Litigation Project. Since then, he has been the only lawyer in the United States to devote his full time to bringing test-case litigation on behalf of mental patients. Mr. Ennis is also the author of *The Rights of Mental Patients.*

B. Title page-front

Prisoners of Psychiatry

Mental Patients, Psychiatrists, and the Law

BRUCE J. ENNIS

Introduction by
Thomas S. Szasz, M.D.

Harcourt Brace Jovanovich, Inc.
New York

C. Title page-back

First edition

ISBN 0-15-173084-9

Library of Congress Catalog Card Number: 72-79923

Printed in the United States of America

D. Preface

This is a book about men and women whose lives were changed —and often destroyed—by the label "mental illness." It is also a book about the law, about judges who care and judges who care not at all what happens behind the locked doors of a mental hospital.

There are, right now, nearly three-quarters of a million patients in this nation's mental hospitals. Approximately 400,000 of them reside in state and county mental hospitals, the remainder in V. A. hospitals, private hospitals, and general hospitals with psychiatric wards. Many of them will be physically abused, a few will be raped or killed, but most of them will simply be ignored, left to fend for themselves in the cheerless corridors and barren back wards of the massive steel and concrete warehouses we— but not they—call hospitals. Each day thousands will die (the death rate by age group is much higher in mental hospitals than outside) or be discharged, and other thousands will take their place.

During the coming year, one and a half million Americans will find themselves patients in a mental hospital, most against their wills. At the current admission rate, one out of every ten of us will someday be hospitalized for mental illness; admissions have doubled in the last fifteen years and are steadily rising. Already there are more patients in mental hospitals than in general hospitals, and three times as many mental patients as there are prisoners.

So vast an enterprise will occasionally harbor a sadistic psychiatrist or a brutal attendant, condemned even by his colleagues when discovered. But that is not the central problem. The problem, rather, is the enterprise itself.

The most important function of mental hospitals is to provide custodial welfare. They used to be called insane asylums, but before that they were called, more accurately, poorhouses. Almost all mental patients are poor, or black, or both, and most of them are old.

Less than 5 per cent of those patients are dangerous to themselves or to others. Indeed, the incarceration of mental patients cannot be justified by their threat to the community at large. Studies have shown that they are less dangerous than the "average" citizen. They are put away not because they are, in fact, dangerous, but because they are useless, unproductive, "odd," or "different." We ask psychiatrists to treat them and make them well, but how can we expect psychiatrists to find friends for the friendless, to make the poor rich and the old young? It should not be surprising that they do not even try.

For three years I represented mental patients, trying, as a lawyer, to change the laws that strip them of their liberty and dignity. This is a book about those years.

E. Table of Contents

(These titles are figurative and do not in themselves tell you much. However, words used here are consistent with the tone of severe criticism you found in the underlined passages in the Preface.)

F. Introduction   *(This one is long; be sure to skim here.)*

I

The coercion and restraint of the mental patient by the psychiatrist is coeval with the origin and development of psychiatry. As an organized discipline, American psychiatry began in the early nineteenth century, with the construction of mental hospitals. In 1844, thirteen superintendents of mental hospitals joined to form the Association of Medical Superintendents of American Institutions for the Insane, the organization that became, in 1921, the American Psychiatric Association.

The original name of this first American psychiatric organization is revealing; and so is its first official resolution. The group's name articulated its character: it was an organization of "medical superintendents," that is, of physicians who were in charge of incarcerated individuals considered and called insane. The organization's first official proposition was: "Resolved, that it is the unanimous sense of this convention that the attempt to abandon entirely the use of all means of personal restraint is not sanctioned by the true interests of the insane."[1]

Ever since, this paternalistic justification of psychiatric coercion has been a prominent theme in psychiatry, not only in America but throughout the civilized world. In 1967—123 years after the drafting of its first resolution—the American Psychiatric Association again reaffirmed its support of psychiatric coercion and restraint. In a "Position Statement on the Question of the Adequacy of Treatment," the association declared that "restraints may be imposed [on the patient] from within by pharmacologic means or by locking the door of a ward. Either imposition may be a legitimate component of a treatment program."[2]

These resolutions must be placed in their proper historical context. In the early days of American psychiatry, alienists justified involuntary psychiatric interventions by appeals to the "true interests of the insane." At the same time, they apparently readily reconciled themselves to the fact that it was not necessary to be, or to be declared, insane to justify incarceration in an insane asylum. In one jurisdiction, it was enough to be a married woman: the 1851 Illinois commitment law states that "married women . . . may be entered or detained in the hospital [the state asylum at Jacksonville, Illinois] at the request of the husband of the woman . . . without evidence of insanity required in other cases."[3]

Nowadays, psychiatrists justify involuntary psychiatric interventions by appeals to the requirements of a "legitimate . . . treatment program" for the mentally sick patient. This justification must be viewed in the light of the fact that many psychiatrists are now ready to classify anyone and everyone as mentally sick, and anything and everything as psychiatric treatment.

The result was, and is, an apparently irrefutable justification of psychiatric force and fraud—a justification based on ostensibly altruistic motives and considerations: the "true interests" of the insane, 130 years ago; the "therapeutic needs" of the mental patient, today.

Similar justifications for involuntary psychiatric interventions of all kinds, and especially involuntary mental hospitalization,

[1] Quoted in Nina Ridenour, *Mental Health in the United States: A Fifty Year History* (Cambridge: Harvard University Press, 1961), p. 76.

[2] Council of the American Psychiatric Association, "Position Statement on the Question of Adequacy of Treatment," *American Journal of Psychiatry*, 123:1458–1460 (May), 1967, p. 1459.

[3] Quoted in Albert Deutsch, *The Mentally Ill in America: A History of Their Care and Treatment from Colonial Times,* 2nd ed. (New York: Columbia University Press, 1952), p. 424.

have, of course, been advanced, and continue to be advanced, in other countries.

In short, just as, for millennia, involuntary servitude has been accepted as a proper economic and social arrangement, so, for centuries, involuntary psychiatry has been accepted as a proper medical and therapeutic arrangement.[4]

II

There are some signs that now point to a shift in this long-established popular and professional position on involuntary mental hospitalization. For example, only ten years ago, St. Elizabeths Hospital, the American government's model mental hospital in Washington, D.C., was generally regarded as a fine, "progressive" mental hospital. No one—the best authorities assured us—was confined within its walls who did not belong there. Dr. Winfred Overholser—who was then the superintendent of St. Elizabeths, who had been a president of the American Psychiatric Association, and who was a widely respected, indeed, a revered, psychiatrist —viewed himself, and tried to make others view him, as a protector of the mental patient's civil rights. At the 1961 hearings of the Senate Subcommittee on Constitutional Rights, Dr. Overholser testified that "unfounded fears have been created regarding possible unlawful deprivation of liberty of the patient. . . . After 45 years in mental hospitals and their administration, I am convinced that the basis for the belief that persons are improperly sent to mental hospitals is, for practical purposes, entirely without foundation."[5]

In contrast to this assertion, consider a series of recent articles in the Washington newspapers. In one, titled "Who Really Needs to Be at St. Elizabeths?" we read: "A recent survey at St. Elizabeths Hospital found that 68 per cent of the patients had 'no behavior problem' requiring them to stay in the hospital. Doctors reported that 2,451 inpatients, representing two-thirds of the total, in effect did not have to live in a mental institution. 'None of these patients could be considered dangerous to themselves or others by any definition of the terms,' the report said. . . . The hospital's findings are contained in a confidential preliminary report of a patient inventory conducted by the staff in June, 1970, the first of its kind at St. Elizabeths."[6]

How are we to account for this difference at St. Elizabeths in the decade between 1961 and 1971? Is it that as long as Dr. Over-

[4] Thomas S. Szasz, *Ideology and Insanity: Essays on the Psychiatric Dehumanization of Man* (Garden City, N.Y.: Doubleday Anchor, 1970), pp. 113–139.

[5] Winfred Overholser, Statement, in *Constitutional Rights of the Mentally Ill* (Washington, D.C.: U.S. Government Printing Office, 1961), pp. 19–40; p. 21.

[6] Robert Pear, "Who Really Needs to Be at St. Elizabeths?" *Washington Star*, August 9, 1971, p. A-1.

holser was alive and at the head of this hospital only those needing confinement were committed, but that since his death, under the regime of his successors, two out of every three persons were falsely committed? That is one possibility. I think it's a very remote one.

Another possibility is that the patient population at St. Elizabeths has not changed significantly during the past decade, but that Dr. Overholser was sincerely mistaken or cravenly mendacious in his judgment of who should and who should not be confined at his hospital. I think this is a more likely explanation.

Of special significance in these reports is the attitude of the press toward this procedure. Until recently, in exposés of mental hospitals (of which there was never a shortage), the emphasis was invariably on the inadequacy of the treatment received by the "patients." In the press, the idea that the people confined in mental hospitals were sick and needed treatment was never questioned. This assumption is apparently no longer held quite so blindly. For example, an editorial in the *Washington Evening Star* entitled "People Storage" begins as follows: "What does it take these days to qualify people for lodgment in a mental institution? For many people, not much in the way of mental instability."[7]

III

Another sign of a fundamental change in the United States toward involuntary mental hospitalization, and perhaps the most important and most hopeful one, is the new position on this subject by civil libertarians—in particular by members of the American Civil Liberties Union. One result of this change is the pioneering project of the New York Civil Liberties Union on behalf of persons accused of mental illness, reported by Bruce Ennis in his moving chronology of medical abuses committed by psychiatrists under the auspices of the New York State Department of Mental Hygiene and other authorities. To appreciate the full significance of *Prisoners of Psychiatry*, this work, too, must be seen in the context of its historical development.

Until a few years ago, the New York Civil Liberties Union, as well as its parent organization, the American Civil Liberties Union, saw psychiatric problems through the lens formed by the imagery and rhetoric of psychiatry. In this view, what the involuntarily hospitalized mental patient needs is not liberty, but treatment. In its "Position Statement on Involuntary Mental Hospitalization," issued in March, 1972, the American Psychiatric Association reiterated this stand in the following words: "The American Psychiatric Association is convinced that most persons who need hospitalization for mental illness can be and should be informally and voluntarily admitted to hospitals in the same manner

7 Editorial, "People Storage," *Washington Evening Star*, August 11, 1971, p. A-18.

that is afforded for any other illness. . . . Unfortunately, a small percentage of patients who need hospitalization are unable, because of their mental illness, to make a free and informed decision to hospitalize themselves. Their need for and right to treatment in a hospital cannot be ignored. In addition, public policy demands that some form of involuntary hospitalization be available for those mentally ill patients who constitute a danger either to themselves or to others. In such cases, it is a public responsibility to guarantee the right to treatment. . . ."[8]

The American Civil Liberties Union has long supported this position. In his account of the history of the ACLU, Charles Markmann notes that toward the end of World War II, "the Union . . . began to draft model statutes for the commitment of the insane. . . . Twenty years after the first Union draft of a model bill for commitments to mental hospitals, Congress enacted for the District of Columbia a law closely following the Union's proposal."[9]

Thus, as recently as 1965, model commitment laws sponsored by the ACLU were hailed with pride by a civil liberation historian of the Union. Furthermore, although, in 1969, the New York Civil Liberties Union passed a resolution rejecting involuntary mental hospitalization as incompatible with the principles of a free society,[10] the American Civil Liberties Union has, to this date, not followed suit. Its continued support of commitment—now more tacit than explicit—is consistent with the fact that one of the vice-chairmen of its National Committee has been, and continues to be, Karl Menninger, one of the staunchest and most influential psychiatric supporters of involuntary mental hospitalization.

IV
In short, then, Prisoners of Psychiatry must be seen as a manifestation of the growing rejection of the viciously mendacious psychiatric rhetoric about "mental illness"; and of the corresponding recognition that individuals incriminated as mentally ill do not need guarantees of "treatment," but protection against their enemies—the legislators, judges, and psychiatrists who persecute them in the name of mental health.

Inasmuch as this frontal attack on the abuses of psychiatry—an attack that seeks to abolish involuntary psychiatric interventions rather than, as did former criticisms, to reform the existing psychiatric institutions—rests, in part, on my critical analyses of psychiatric principles and practices published over the past fifteen

[8] American Psychiatric Association, "Position Statement on Involuntary Mental Hospitalizaion," *American Journal of Psychiatry,* 128: 1480.

[9] Charles L. Markmann, *The Noblest Cry: A History of the American Civil Liberties Union* (New York: St. Martin's Press, 165), pp. 400–401.

[10] Resolution of the Board of Directors, January 13, 1969, Minutes, p. 3.

years,[11] it may be useful to summarize those of my views that support Mr. Ennis's presentation and conclusions, and are in turn supported by them.

1. The term "mental illness" is a metaphor. More particularly, as this term is used in mental hygiene legislation, "mental illness" is not the name of a medical disease or disorder, but is a quasi-medical label whose purpose is to conceal conflict as illness and to justify coercion as treatment.

2. If "mental illness" is an illness "like any other illness"—as official medical, psychiatric, and mental health organizations, such as the American Medical Association, the Americn Psychiatric Association, and the National Association for Mental Health, maintain—then it follows, logically and semantically, that it must be treated like any other illness. Hence, mental hygiene laws must be repealed. There are no special laws for patients with peptic ulcer or pneumonia; why, then, should there be special laws for patients with depression or schizophrenia?

3. If, on the other hand, "mental illness" is, as I contend, a metaphor and a myth, then, also, it follows that mental hygiene laws should be repealed.

4. If there were no mental hygiene laws—which alone have the legal power to create a category of individuals who, though officially labeled as "mentally ill," would prefer not to be subjected to involuntary psychiatric interventions—then the misdeeds now committed by those who "care" for "mental patients" could not come into being.

5. In short, all those who draft and administer laws pertaining to involuntary psychiatric interventions should be regarded as the adversaries, not the allies, of the so-called mental patient. Civil libertarians, and, indeed, all men and women who believe that no one should be deprived of liberty except upon conviction for a crime, should oppose all forms of involuntary psychiatric intervention.

V

Although *Prisoners of Psychiatry* is an unsettling book, I hope it will be widely read and seriously thought about. And I particularly hope that Americans in increasing numbers will begin to discriminate between two types of physicians: those who heal, not so much because they are saints, but because *that is their job;* and those who harm, not so much because they are sinners, but because *that is their job.* And if some doctors harm—torture rather than treat, murder the soul rather than minister to the body—that is,

11 See especially Thomas S. Szasz, *The Myth of Mental Illness: Foundations of a Theory of Personal Conduct* (New York: Hoeber-Harper, 1961); *Law, Liberty, and Psychiatry: An Inquiry into the Social Uses of Mental Health Practices* (New York: Macmillan, 1963); *and Psychiatric Justice* (New York: Macmillan, 1965).

in part, because society, the state, asks them, and pays them, to do so.

We saw it happen in Nazi Germany, and we hanged many of the doctors.

We see it happen in the Soviet Union, and we denounce the doctors with righteous indignation.

But when will we see the same things happening in the United States? When will we recognize—and publicly identify—the medical criminals among us? Or is the very possibility of perceiving many of our leading psychiatrists and psychiatric institutions in this way precluded by the fact that they represent the officially "correct" views and practices? By the fact that they have the ears of our legislators and judges? And by the fact that they control the vast funds, collected by the state through taxing the citizens, which finance an enterprise whose basic moral legitimacy is here called into question?

THOMAS S. SZASZ, M.D.

G. Writer's Introduction to Part I   (an unusual feature)

PART I
THE CRIMINAL AND THE KING

Mental illness is mental illness, whether it afflicts the criminal or the king.

—THE HONORABLE IRVING R. KAUFMAN
United States Circuit Judge

Most of the patients in mental hospitals are civil patients, people who have not committed any crime or broken any law. There are, however, a few mental hospitals for the "criminally insane." The label is misleading because only a few of the "criminal" patients have been convicted of a crime. Most "criminal" patients are persons who have been accused of crime, but who have not yet been convicted. Instead of being brought to trial, to establish their innocence or guilt, they are judged to be mentally "incompetent" to stand trial and are committed to a mental hospital, where they will remain until, in the opinion of the authorities, they regain competence. Then, and only then, will they have a chance to prove their innocence.

These four chapters are about people who have been labeled criminally insane. The stories are true, and they are not at all unusual. During my three years as director of the New York Civil Liberties Union's Civil Liberties and Mental Illness Litigation Project, I represented dozens of persons in Matteawan and Dannemora, New York's hospitals for the "criminally insane." I include these four stories, rather than others, only because these were the first to reach my attention.

I started working on Jerome Wright's case on my first day at the Civil Liberties Union. Within one month, I was representing Charlie Youngblood and Theodore Neely, Jr., and, a month later, Alfred Curt von Wolfersdorf.

These stories are not the cream of the crop; they are not carefully selected for their shock value from a mass of humdrum cases. If they are disturbing, it is precisely because they are so common.

H. Opening paragraphs (Chapter One)

January 18, 1969, started like any other day, with a telephone call: "Mr. Ennis, my name is Charlie Youngblood. I'm crazy but competent."

"What?"

"I can elucidate and I don't hallucinate."

"What are you talking about?"

"The United States attorney is trying to murder me."

"I don't understand."

"He says I'm not competent to stand trial for a violation of Title 18 United States Code, section 875."

I. Closing paragraphs (Epilogue)

What does all this mean? It means that the mental hospital system depends for its existence on the premise that mental patients are second-class citizens entitled to fewer protections than persons accused of crime. Under the guise of not treating patients like criminals, the system has treated patients *worse* than criminals.

It is time to change that. The goal should be nothing less than the abolition of involuntary hospitalization. That will not come soon, but it will come. (England, for example, plans to shut down all its large public mental hospitals within twenty years.) Short of that, there is still much we could do. We could insist that patients in mental hospitals be given the same rights and privileges as patients in general hospitals. We could demand that legislators spend our tax dollars for community-based outpatient treatment facilities, rather than for custodial warehouses.

Of course, we could have done these things last year or the year before. But no one bothered.

▶ ORIGINAL QUESTIONS

GENERAL ANSWERS
PROVIDED THROUGH PREVIEWING

1. Who are these prisoners?

2. Are they literal prisoners?

3. How does the author justify the term?

4. In what sense are people "victims" of psychiatric approaches?

▶ NEW QUESTIONS

▶ PROBABLE BASIC QUESTION

After you have compared your answers and questions with the ones in Chapter Supplement II (p. 189), proceed to the selections from the other two books. Before you begin previewing, it will probably be a good idea to write your original questions for the title of each book in the space following the excerpts from that book.

The Chickenbone Special

A. Book jacket

FRONT FLAP

THE CHICKENBONE SPECIAL

Dwayne E. Walls

Introduction by Robert Coles

When Donnie Gibson told his parents he was "taking a ride" the next Saturday, they well knew what he meant; no one had to tell them that the "ride" was North, for Donnie was about to repeat a pattern that has become tragically common in twentieth-century America. Every year, at graduation time in late June, thousands of people—most of them young and poor and black—bid good-by to their loved ones and head for the cities of the North. Boarding buses and trains (such as the "Chickenbone Special") in places like Kingstree, South Carolina, and Sanford, Florida, they are part of the largest movement of human beings in history, a migratory flood that began in the 1920s and has since poured upwards of a million people a year into the city ghettos.

This is their story.

It is told in the words, thoughts, and feelings of Donnie

Gibson, the Alston family, the "Fantastic Four," and Georgia Mae Perry—who all opened their hearts and homes to Dwayne Walls in the months he lived and traveled with them. Their courageous stories are in essence the experiences of millions.

People do not willingly uproot themselves from a homeland centuries old and deeply loved. But having made a decision to flee failing agricultural economies, discrimination, and grinding poverty, they bring North with them a faith in America that is often shattered in the ghetto, which proves to be no promised land at all.

This is a deeply dramatic and moving book about the failure of America to provide either a decent living on the land or a safe and secure passage into urban life.

BACK FLAP

DWAYNE E. WALLS, one of the South's brightest young journalists, has been a reporter for the Charlotte Observer since 1962. His work has earned him fourteen journalism awards, including the George Polk Memorial Award, the Sidney Hillman Foundation Award, and the American Political Science Association Award. He has three times been nominated for a Pulitzer Prize.

Born in Mogantown, North Carolina, in 1932, the son of a Baptist preacher, Mr. Walls left home at the age of fifteen. Since then he has earned a living at a variety of callings, including ambulance driver, embalmer's assistant, iceman, waiter, bellhop, short-order cook, and salesman. He worked his way through high school and college, attended Lenoir Rhyne College and the University of North Carolina at Chapel Hill.

Mr. Walls, his wife and two children live in Charlotte, North Carolina.

B. Title page-front

DWAYNE E. WALLS

The
Chickenbone
Special

[HBJ]

Harcourt Brace Jovanovich, Inc.   New York

C. Title page-back

Copyright © 1970, 1971 by Dwayne E. Walls

First edition

ISBN 0-15-117160-2

Library of Congress Catalog Card Number: 70-142099

Printed in the United States of America

D. Table of Contents

E. Preface

Although the nation's rural-to-urban migration has been written about extensively during the past two or three decades, the subject remains largely unfamiliar to most Americans. One reason for this, in my judgment, is that the countless books on the subject have been produced mainly by sociologists, anthropologists and demographers for the benefit of other sociologists, anthropologists and demographers. This is not to say, or even to imply, that those books do not have merit. Many are excellent, and almost all of them represent a great deal of hard work. If they have no appeal to readers outside the professional and academic spheres, the reason no doubt is because they never were intended to appeal to non-professional, nonacademic audiences.

I began this book keenly aware of my own limitations and more than a little doubtful that I could offer any worthwhile contribution to the body of knowledge already existing on the subject. I knew that I was not equipped by training or inclination to produce a scholarly work. I had no desire to write a book merely to be able then to say that I had written a book. Nonetheless, I *did* want to write a book—not any book, but this particular book.

My interest in migration goes back to 1962 when, with another reporter, I wrote a series of articles for the Charlotte *Observer* on election fraud in the mountains of North Carolina. We were able to prove conclusively that mountain politicians were routinely stealing elections with the use of absentee ballots. In the course of the investigation, I was appalled to discover the number of legitimate absentee ballots that were cast every year in mountain countries because of the heavy out-migration that had begun years earlier. (In a sense, my interest had already been kindled because I am one product of out-migration. My parents left the mountains as newlyweds and wandered throughout the Piedmont section of North Carolina for years before settling down.) After the election-fraud series had run, I reorganized my file to build a new one on migration. Later, I did occasional stories on migration and, in 1968, collaborated with another reporter—James K. Batten, who was then in the *Observer's* Washington bureau—to produce a series of articles on rural poverty and migration. This series coincided with the publication of a report by the President's National Advisory Commission on Rural Poverty, which dealt exhaustively with the problems of migration.

After publication of that series, Batten and I discussed expanding it into a book. We were not able to write the book, but the editors at the *Observer* agreed that migration was a story worth sticking to. So I began attending conferences and seminars on the subject, meanwhile writing some follow-up stories. One of those stories led me by accident to the discovery of the "Chickenbone Special." I rode the train North in June of 1968, and it was then that I knew I had to write the book.

Several weeks before I first rode the train, I had heard Dr. C. E. Bishop (now chancellor of the University of Maryland) describe the nation's rural-to-urban migration as the greatest movement of human beings in history. Aboard the train, I realized fully for the first time, I think, that the migrants were significant beyond the fact of their numbers. These people were not moving solely to find greater opportunity, as my parents had; as hundreds of thousands have done, and as tens of thousands continue doing every year in this country. The important thing about this migration, I determined, was that it was an *unwilling* migration. Human beings were moving not because they *wanted* to move but because they *had* to move.

I wanted to write about these people in human terms that other people would understand and appreciate. I wanted to popularize the subject of migration, and I knew that the book would have to be readable, above all else, if it were to be worth the effort. Yet it also had to be believable; and to be believable, it had to be absolutely factual.

I decided that to keep the work manageable, I would try to dramatize the migration of the many in a simple, narrative account of a few. Carrying a tape recorder and several dozen tapes, I moved into the little black community of Mayflower in May of 1969 to begin the search for the few. I wanted to live as closely as possible to the people I intended to write about, and so I accepted the hospitality of Mr. and Mrs. Ernest Turner, the one family in the community that had room for me without upsetting the family life. I lived with the Turners for a month, meantime traveling back and forth between Warren County, North Carolina, and Williamsburg County, South Carolina, interviewing potential outmigrants. Those finally selected for intensive work and inclusion in the book (out of several dozen initial interviews) were selected for a number of reasons. They had to be willing subjects first of all —willing to allow me to intrude into their lives, to ask questions that seemed at times to be unending and sometimes very personal; willing to allow me to travel with them and badger them again and again in follow-up interviews. They had to be fairly representative of one or another group in the reasons for their leaving. Partly, too, it was a matter of convenience and scheduling for me.

My one salute to scientific method was a self-imposed restriction. I insisted on talking only with those persons who already had made a decision to migrate, because I did not want my presence to influence them. I also tried not to influence them during travel and on arrival in the urban areas, but I cannot say with any certainty whether I succeeded or failed.

Some readers might wonder how I came to know the conversations and states of mind attributed to persons in the narrative. The answer is that I was present in many cases. In others, I reconstructed events and thoughts with detailed, sometimes painful questioning. The success of this technique is attributable less to the questioner than to the continued willingness of the questioned to respond. I did not actually hear Donnie Gibson say his prayer two nights before he left home. He told me about it and reconstructed it for me on the train headed North, during a long talk about his religious beliefs. Follow-up interviews with all of the principal subjects in the book continued into December of 1969. One can learn a great deal about almost anything or anyone in seven months of constant questioning.

The fruit of all the questions might be called a nonfiction

novel. But I must emphasize here that nothing in the manuscript is conjecture. The words, the thoughts, the feelings ascribed to all individuals mentioned in the book are *their* words, *their* thoughts, *their* feelings. They exist on my tapes and, in some cases of description and detail, in my note pads.

The names are real names, with the exceptions of Donnie Gibson's three sisters in Brooklyn, who asked to remain anonymous.

I have tried in this book to use simple language to tell a simple story about a national problem that is anything but simple. I hope the work has some merit.

DWAYNE E. WALLS
Charlotte, N.C.

F. Acknowledgments

This book is the product of more than the one man who did the writing. It was conceived in the spring of 1968, when I collaborated with James K. Batten, on a series of articles on rural poverty and migration. Jim Batten could not join me in producing the book. But I must acknowledge that the idea was as much his as mine, and I do so gladly and gratefully.

I am indebted also to a number of other people and organizations who contributed measurably to the year's work: Dr. Raymond M. Wheeler and Paul Anthony of the Southern Regional Council; Carey McWilliams of the *Nation* magazine; George H. Esser, Jr., of the Ford Foundation; Dr. Norman W. Schul of the University of North Carolina at Charlotte; Donald G. Tacheron, Dr. Evron M. Kirkpatrick and Dr. Howard R. Penniman of the American Political Science Association.

Grants to support the research, travel and writing were provided by the American Political Science Association, the Ford Foundation, the Louis M. Rabinowitz Foundation, the Southern Regional Council and my employer, the Charlotte *Observer*. I am indebted to each of these organizations. But I am especially grateful for the encouragement of those persons who pleaded my cause with the organizations and for their faith in my ability to produce a worthwhile book.

To Paul Anthony, who functioned throughout as a kind of gifted midwife; to Mrs. Diana Lee, who volunteered as secretary and typist and sometimes fretted as if it were *her* book; and to my wife, Judy, who felt at times as if she were living with a caged animal—to these a simple "thank you" somehow does not seem enough.

Finally, I must publicly acknowledge the greatest contribution of all—that of the people whose experiences are related in the book. Their contribution was their willingness to allow me to intrude into their lives and their minds; to live with them, to travel with them, to share in their most prvate fears and hopes. The story is their story. The words and the thoughts are their words and their thoughts, given generously and in simple faith that the gift would be used justly and that it might have some meaning.

To them I dedicate this book.

G. Introduction

I don't suppose the author of this book is in line for any professorships. No universities are knocking on his door in an effort to obtain his time and energy. No sociologists or anthropologists or psychologists are asking for his help. He has not been made a professor of journalism. Nor can I imagine the great and wise federal government seeking Mr. Walls as a "consultant." For that matter the foundations, presumably more "flexible" or "imaginative," would also be unlikely candidates for the man's services. In an age of experts, he is a mere reporter. In an age preoccupied with statistics, he offers only the literate sentence composed by the sensible mind. And at a moment when just about everyone is taking up a "position," asserting a particular side of some argument, Mr. Walls offers us only life's sadness and humor, so mixed together that any self-respecting ideologue can only shudder at the devilish naïveté yet another Southern "small-town boy" has come up with—and has the nerve to think the rest of us might want to read and find significant.

I do not believe I have just belabored some unnecessary points. Nor am I being coy—though bitter, yes, and maybe a touch envious. For well over a decade I have worked with people very much like the ones Mr. Walls brings alive (that is what he does) in the following pages. For well over a decade I have done as he has done; I have gone to the cabins, sat and listened, felt embarrassed, felt like a damn fool, tried to get talk going, tried to learn things—grab on them, sort them out, put them down on paper. But I have come to those Southern cabins, gone with families on those buses and trains that pull out of Atlanta or Memphis or Birmingham, as a New Englander and a doctor—and also as a psychiatrist trained far too long at making diagnoses, taking note of "problems," fitting people into various categories, labeling them with an array of words. So equipped, I have done my work; "cultural disadvantage" certainly has not been *my* problem. In fact, if the particular men, women and children I now meet "out in the field" defy my wish to pin them down; if they undo my cool, reserved, clinical "face"; and if they make me stop and wonder, make me confused, make me a little envious of them as well as of Mr. Walls—then clearly I know enough to realize that I have been getting myself into a lot of trouble, and had best seek "help" of some kind, maybe from a social scientist who knows his "methodology," and maybe also from a good, tough psychiatrist who can spot in a flash someone "overinvolved" and "overidentified" and all the rest.

Again I must insist that I am not beating a dead horse. If only some of the murky-minded, evasive and even deceitful words that pass for "scholarship" were more obviously suspect or discredited. If only the universities really were less subject to the arbitrary and snobbish dictates of what some call "academic tradition." If only government officials (including legislators) and foundation executives did have the will and the courage to face the blunt and aching truths that a book like this presents—rather than hiding behind the smog of words and numbers that various "authorities" provide (at a substantial price). If only our newspapers and schools of journalism saw a reporter's job as something more than that of an accountant of sorts, who tabulates events as if they were sums to be accepted at face value and listed and added up. And if only all of us who go to college and then one or another professional school were encouraged to feel at home with the heart's reasons, the world's ceaseless ambiguities and, not the least, the mind's capacity (given a choice) to say what is obvious and important and right. For the fact is that we are systematically taught to trick ourselves, as well as others; we lose our candor and openness and forthrightness of speech in response to the demands that powerful, if virtually incomprehensible educators make upon us—in their lectures, through the books and articles they assign and the kinds of examinations they insist we take. So it was natural that I would find myself confused and at a loss years after I first met certain migrant farm workers or sharecroppers or Appalachian yeomen. All I had were my theories, my costly and intimidating "training," my wordiness developed in school after school. What I lacked was what I most needed, a photographer's eye, a novelist's ear, a poet's responsiveness to sights and sounds.

We cannot, most of us, take good pictures or write good stories or summon words in ways that illuminate and entrance; but as men or women who once were children, we most certainly can look and listen and admit to amusement or anger or surprise. And we can speak our minds, let others know how we feel, what we feel—unless, that is, we happen to take stock of the "situation" around us and decide that it is dangerous to do just that, in which case we stop seeing things and shut up, or learn to speak the double talk that threatens no one and leaves us "secure," if virtually scared of our own shadows. Thus do children "grow up" and learn to surrender and stop living—and become safely (so far as our society is concerned) "mature" and "adult." So, I will say that in this book Dwayne Walls shows himself to be still a certain kind of child, an alive, questioning child; and I hope he will not mind that way of putting things.

Not far from the country in North Carolina that he knows so well and describes so vividly in the pages ahead, I came to know a poor black family whose son left the South for reasons quite other than those that prompt travelers on the Chickenbone Special. The young man was "found" by a "scout" and enabled to attend Harvard College, where I met him. I went back with him one spring (a special kind of journey, no doubt about that), and later, when both of us were safely back in Cambridge, Massachusetts, he could allow himself at least a brief tirade, and not the politically indignant one that, I fear, I assumed and expected: "I hate what poverty has done to my people, to my own parents. I hate what the white man has done to the black man in the South—and the North. But every time I go home, I get all mixed up. I see the misery, but I see my father's intelligence and his cleverness and his 'psychological acuity,' as those professors of mine call it. I see my mother's humor, her kindness, her toughness. And then I don't know what to think. On the way North I try to understand them; that's what we're taught to do in college—understand, understand. But what do college professors know about the spirit my mother has, or my father? Professors know facts, and they come up with a lot of theories. Even anthropologists are like that: they describe towns and houses and 'customs,' and then they come up with a dozen or so 'conclusions'; but they don't tell the people who read their books what goes on inside people—in their souls, I mean, not their 'minds.'

"I've been reading Flannery O'Connor in my English course. She was a white lady from down in Georgia, a maiden lady, I gather, who died very young. What does she knew about the black man, I wondered. Well, she knows about everyone who's living in the rural South, I know that since I've read her. In fact, she knows about everyone who's alive and trying to stay alive; I could say that, too. When I read a story of hers about some weird Georgia cracker, I begin to forget they are what I just said, weird Georgia crackers. They're my aunt, who laughs with tears in her eyes; and my grandfather, who got drunk every weekend and talked about 'fighting patience'—as what the nigger needs; and my cousin who's old enough to be my uncle, and all his tricks and clever sayings—'smark-aleck remarks,' the bossman used to call them, but he missed them when he didn't hear them for a while, because he used to tease my cousin. He used to say: 'When are we going to get another smart-aleck remark out of you?' Sometimes I remember all that, my family and how they lived down South and what they said and did—and then I'll decide I knew more about my 'people,' my 'race,' when I was a child than I'll ever learn from reading all these 'black studies' books I push my way through."

The young Southern emigree has never really been tempted by the social sciences, has instead developed an interest in something called "history and literature"; and so perhaps he can be considered "prejudiced" in favor of writers like Miss O'Connor and Ralph Ellison, or historians like C. Vann Woodward or T. Harry Williams. Maybe, too, he is giving up some of his angry political concerns for those more "literary" (if not obscure) preoccupations that some social critics and political ideologues find to be treacherous signs of a "sellout," a "brainwashing," a surrender to a "power structure." Yet that man has developed no loss of social indignation, no progressive indifference to the political and economic injustices he knew for years and years—and still knows, as a son does rather than a proud book reader and occasional member of this or that "cause." I think he simply senses in the South's moral complexities and racial tragedies something utterly worthy of the mind's capacity for dedicated portrayal—which is to say, he believes it is no accident that the South has produced such intense, formidable, ambitious novelists and storytellers and playwrights and journalists and historians.

Out of that tradition, and worthy of it, comes Dwayne Walls, another such writer, observer, essayist. He tells us about poor rural blacks who reluctantly head for ghettos that are no Promised Land at all; but even more, he brings alive particular human beings who share with all other human beings the knowledge of fear, the experience of dread, the surge that hope can bring, and the confusion that the mind's various maneuvers can also bring. One must continually get angrily "defensive" (as, I suppose, some psychiatrists would interpret the "reaction") about writers like Mr. Walls—because they are not the people that other people, eager, swinging, clever, wordy, self-consciously "aware" and proudly "educated," rush to for explanations, ideas, programs, solutions and, that words of words these days, "insights." Nor is it likely that this book will shock inert consciences, surprise bored and worldly experts, inflame even further already outraged activists. There is a quietness to the effort Mr. Walls makes, a slowness to his manner of approach. He wants drama to emerge from the ways of others, rather than to be of his own doing. He wants us to grow by feeling others grow on us. And I presume that, good writer and sensitive man that he is, he wants us to become once again not knowing and smart and informed, but uncertain, embarrassed, amused, and at a certain loss about various things—"states of mind" that one can only be grateful for and, these days, almost relieved to find still possible.

H. Opening paragraphs (Chapter One)

Otis Gibson sat on the cool side of the porch, looking across the little cotton patch to the cornfield beyond. Watching the corn, he could tell when the next breeze was coming by following the ripples as the wind rolled across the corn rows toward the house.

Otis was not a tall man, and the way he slumped in the wheelchair made him look much like a young boy lolling away a lazy afternoon. His bare feet were stretched out nearly to the edge of the little porch. His trousers were pulled up over his loins and left unfastened for his and his family's convenience. His shirt was only partially buttoned across the chest. His body, which he could not control entirely, was canted to one side, so that he had to twist his neck to keep his head in an upright position. Still, half of his nut-brown face seemed to sag to the right as his body did, and tiny rivulets of sweat rolled naturally toward his right chin, where they were joined by a barely perceptible overflow of saliva at the lower corner of his mouth. Small particles of food stuck to his lips because he had insisted on using the napkin himself after his noon meal, instead of allowing his wife to brush off his chin.

I. Concluding paragraphs (Chapter Fifteen)

I never saw Georgia Mae Perry again after she left Warren County. Immediately after the graduation exercises at her high school, I left for Williamsburg County, S.C., planning to return to Warren County to travel North with her. She already had left when I got back, and her family did not know where she was. On subsequent visits North that summer and into the fall, I tried to find her in Brooklyn, Harlem, Washington and Baltimore. Once, I thought I had located her. I found a Georgia M. Perry who worked in a gift shop in a Baltimore suburb; I walked into the shop about closing time one night, feeling the way some ancient quester might if he were about to touch the Holy Grail. When Miss Perry at the gift shop turned out to be an elderly lady who had lived in Baltimore for forty years, I gave up the search.

Wherever she is, I hope that Georgia Mae—like the others in this story—has found a productive place in society for herself.

| | GENERAL ANSWERS |
| ▶ ORIGINAL QUESTIONS | PROVIDED THROUGH PREVIEWING |

1. What is the "Chickenbone Special?"

2. Whatever it is, what idea does it represent for the writer?

▶ NEW QUESTIONS

▶ PROBABLE BASIC QUESTION

Compare your responses with those given in Chapter Supplement III (p. 190) before going on to the next selection.

Aspects of Language

A. Book jacket

FRONT FLAP

ASPECTS OF LANGUAGE
Dwight Bolinger

"We do not need to travel abroad nor back in time to discover the facts of language," says Professor Dwight Bolinger. "They lie all about us, in the tablets of our handwriting and the potsherds of our own speech. Almost nothing of interest to the linguist goes on anywhere that does not go on in our communication here and now. This book is an invitation to the reader to see within him and around him the objects of a science, and to glimpse how the scientist interprets them. It is not intended to teach linguistics but to help ordinary people divine themselves as the creators and perpetuators of the most wonderful invention of all time."

In this stimulating book, Professor Bolinger discusses the structure of language and how it evolves, as well as the way language shapes culture and the various modern linguistic theories.

Among the chapters are "Born to Speak" (language beginnings, not in history but in the life of the individual); "Some Traits of Language" (the "universals" that languages share); "The Phonetic Elements" (sounds, syllables, intonations); "Structure in Language: The Units of Sound" (sounds within their system: phonemes); "Structure in Language: The Higher

BACK FLAP

Levels" (morphology and syntax: morphemes, words, sentences); "The Evolution of Language: Courses, Forces, Sounds, and Spellings" (the causes and directions of linguistic change as a mechanical process); "The Evolution of Language: Meanings, Interpretations, and Adjustments" (how the message, and the hearer's view of it, affects the form); "The Evolution of Languages: Views and Measurements" (the questions of whether change has a goal, and can be measured); "Dialect" (regional and social variations); "Writing" (its relation to speech and a résumé of its history); "The Evolving Approaches to Language" (a sketch of linguistic theories); "Meaning" (how language segments reality); "Mind in the Grip of Language" (the extent to which we are controlled by language) ; "Some Practical Matters" (authority in language, the dictionary, language-learning, and language as a medium of empathy and understanding) .

DWIGHT BOLLINGER

is Professor of Romance Languages and Literature at Harvard University. He received his B.A. from Washburn University, his M.A. from the University of Kansas, and his Ph.D. from the University of Wisconsin. He has taught at Washburn University, the University of Southern California, and the University of Colorado, and was Sterling Fellow in Linguistics at Yale University and Research Fellow in Speech at Haskins Laboratories. He is the author of many books and articles.

OUTSIDE COVER—BACK

ASPECTS OF LANGUAGE

"The uses of money have their robber barons and philanthropists, capitalists and day laborers, conservatives and socialists. . . . Language also has its ethic, though for some reason we seldom pose it to ourselves in the ordinary terms of power and prestige or of good conduct and bad . . . like money [language] was created by and for society. And like money it is subject to abuse."

"The only laws against the misuse of language have to do with the content of messages: obscenity, perjury, sedition, and defamation in its various forms of libel and slander. There are no laws against the unfair exploitation of language as language, in its essence. The individual may carry as many concealed verbal weapons as he likes and strike with them as he pleases—far from being censured for it, he will be admired and applauded as a clever fellow."

"With the disappearance of the less visible tokens of birth and breeding, language has in some areas taken over their function of opening or closing the doors to membership in a ruling caste."

"Language is the most public of all public domains, to be kept free at all costs of claims that would turn any part of it into the property of some exclusive club, whether of scientists, artisans, or the socially elect. The virtue of language is in being ordinary."

B. Title page-front

Aspects
of
Language

DWIGHT BOLINGER

Harvard University

HARCOURT BRACE JOVANOVICH, INC.
New York/Chicago/San Francisco/Atlanta

C. Title page-back

LIBRARY OF CONGRESS CATALOG CARD NUMBER: 68-15946

PRINTED IN THE UNITED STATES OF AMERICA

D. Foreword

Linguists have long complained that the Wonder of Words approach to language has been almost their only contact with the outside world, but to date they have done very little about it. A number of good books have been issued or reissued in low-priced editions in the past few years: some are general outlines by scholars of a generation or two ago, but most are technical or semi-technical works on specialized topics: origins of writing, development of speech, linguistics in the nineteenth century, anthropological linguistics, and the like. One looks in vain for the book that will maintain a proper balance of readability, informativeness, and fidelity to the interests, goals, and trials of linguists as linguists see them, to give the average reader an appreciation of what modern linguistics is about. Other sciences have been able to describe themselves to the general public and to the unspecialized student. The same should be possible for linguistics. At least it is time to try.

What makes the attempt all the more imperative is that the reader of the typical book on the wonderful world of words sees in the spectacle no particular relevance to himself. Yet there is no science that is closer to the humanness of humanity than linguistics, for its field is the means by which our personalities are defined to others and by which our thoughts are formed and gain continuity and acceptance. Until linguists can bring their point of view clearly and palatably before the reader at large and the student in the language classroom, they will have only themselves to blame for what one linguist has called the towering failure of the schools to inform ordinary citizens about language. Of no other scientific field is so much fervently believed that isn't so. And not only believed but taught.

We do not need to travel abroad nor back in time to discover the facts of language. They lie all about us, in the tablets of our handwriting and the potsherds of our own speech. Almost nothing of interest to the linguist goes on anywhere that does not go in our communication here and now. This book is an invitation to the reader to see within him and around him the objects of a science, and to glimpse how the scientist interprets them. It is not intended to teach linguistics but to help ordinary people divine themselves as the creators and perpetuators of the most wonderful invention of all time.

There are no directions for reading this book beyond one mild word of caution. To follow the plays in a game one must first learn the rules. This demands a willingness to submit to certain initiatory rites. The beginning chapters, in particular Chapters 4 and 5, carry the heaviest burden of terms and concepts. They ask a measure of patience from the reader. After that he should find the going fairly easy.

To recognize individually all those whose scholarship was drawn upon in this volume would be impossible, and to settle on a few is to risk unintentionally slighting others to whom the debt may be just as great. I can only thank my intellectual mentors and creditors in a general way and assure them that the gratitude is not less for not being more specific.

Nevertheless a few must indeed be singled out—those who have criticized the manuscript in whole or in part: John Algeo, Fred W. Householder, Jr., George Lakoff, William G. Moulton, Thomas Pyles, John R. Ross, and James Sledd. Without their help this book could not have kept true to its aim, and if even so it has fallen short, the author is all the more to be blamed.

E. Table of Contents

F. Opening paragraphs (Chapter One)

FIRST STEPS

Thomas A. Edison is supposed to have parried the question of a skeptic who wanted to know what one of his fledgling inventions was good for by asking "What good is a baby?" Appearances suggest that a baby is good for very little, least of all to itself. Completely helpless, absolutely dependent on the adults around it, seemingly unable to do much more than kick and crawl for the greater part of nine or ten months, it would seem better off in the womb a little longer until ready to make a respectable debut and scratch for itself.

Yet if the premature birth of human young is an accident, it is a fortunate one. No other living form has so much to learn about the external world and so little chance of preparing for it in advance. An eaglet has the pattern of its life laid out before it hatches from the egg. Its long evolution has equipped it to contend with definite foes, search for definite foods, mate, and rear its young according to a definite ritual. The environment is predictable enough to make the responses predictable too, and they are built into the genetic design. With human beings this is impossible. The main reason for its impossibility is language.

G. Concluding paragraphs (Chapter Fourteen)

Society recognizes the problem of equal access only through the unequal efforts of the schools. They are unequal because alongside of schools striving for an ethic of equality there are others striving for an ethic of chivalry that, for all its good intentions, only deepens class lines. The *public* effort for equal access must be toward the elimination of every sort of verbal snobbery. There is nothing intrinsically bad about words as such, and by excluding another man's forms of speech we exclude him. The task of democratizing a society includes far more than speech forms, of course, but headway will be that much more difficult if we overlook the intricate ties of speech with everything else that spells privilege.

Public cures may be long in coming, but meanwhile some of the ills of unequal access can be avoided if we recognize our personal responsibility toward the sharing of experience through language. We can discharge it by trying as hard to meet our neighbor on his dialectal terms as we would try to meet a foreigner on the terms of his language. This means never using our superior verbal skill, if we have it, or our inheritance of a prestige dialect for which we never worked a day, to browbeat or establish a difference in status between our neighbor and us. It means remembering that language is the most public of all public domains, to be kept free at all costs of claims that would turn any part of it into the property of some exclusive club, whether of scientists, artisans, or the socially elect. The virtue of language is in being ordinary.

H. Additional Remarks and Applications (an unusual feature)

1. Discuss laughter as a weapon of conformity. It is no longer considered good taste to laugh at racial jokes, and it long since ceased to be good taste to laugh at the behavior of the crippled and feeble-minded. Consider to what extent we still laugh at linguistic nonconformity, for instance as the basis for stage humor.

2. Linguistic nonconformity in adult speakers usually takes one of two forms: the lapse or accidental slip of the tongue and the use of nonstandard dialectal forms. An instance of the former is the spoonerism, for example *Is the beam dizzy?* for *Is the dean busy?* Does our tendency to laugh at them make any distinction between the two?

3. A study of *shall* and *will*[22] showed that *will* has always predominated in sentences of the *I will go* type, with *shall* only in recent times gaining a special favor in England. The effort to impose *shall* when the subject is *I* or *we* is now seen as a classic instance of pedantry. See if you can describe your own uses of *shall* and *will*, and compare them with the recommendations of any reference grammar or handbook that you can readily consult.

4. One scapegoat achieved fame in the slogan for a brand of cigarette: *Winston tastes good like a cigarette should.* This way of using *like* has long been common among English writers, including Shakespeare, but nowadays stirs feelings of guilt in many speakers. For those who would also feel uncomfortably formal if they replaced *Do it like I do it* with *Do it as I do it*, what is the two-word substitute for *like?*

5. Would you regard the following as mistakes? *Tell him to kindly leave; a more perfect union; I'll explain whatever you ask about; Whenever Mary or John is at home, they answer the phone.* Decide how you would express any that you would reject.

6. In 1966 the United States Supreme Court validated a New York law permitting the literacy test for voting to be given in Spanish as well as English. Was this law a step in the right direction? (The "low IQ's" that have condemned many children of minority groups to second-rate educations have often turned out to be the result of a compulsory use of an unfamiliar language. In Mexico one of the first steps toward the

[22] C. C. Fries, "The Periphrastic Uses of *Shall* and *Will* in Modern English," *Language Learning* 7: 1–2: 38–99 (1956–57).

acculturation of Indians has been to teach them to read and write in their own language, then in the national language.)

7. Government intervention in the teaching of language to civilians was rare in the United States until 1958, when the National Defense Education Act made funds available for training teachers in foreign languages. It was extended in 1963 to cover teachers of English, and more and more support has been given in various forms, especially to the teaching of English in other countries. What economic reasons prompted this? Though the government supports the teaching of language it makes no rules for what shall be taught such as a national academy might make. Is this as it should be?

8. If it is assumed that the function of the dictionary is to constitute a record but not to rate acceptability, does there nevertheless remain a place for the guide to usage? Consider such a book as H. W. Fowler's *A Dictionary of Modern English Usage* (revised by Ernest Gowers [New York: Oxford University Press, 1965]). Is there also a place for the debunking book, such as H. L. Mencken's *American Language* (Fourth Edition, New York: Alfred A. Knopf, 1955)?

9. One pernicious fallacy about foreign language learning is that it ought to be possible to find word-for-word equivalents between one language and another. How does a grammar that gives word lists to be memorized with their meanings encourage this notion?

10. How do you react to a person who says *He don't, I won't go there no more. Who did they see? Me. I wouldnt do it?* If you react unfavorably, what is the basis for your dislike? How does one strike a balance between the opposing demands of uniformity in language and the equal right of each dialect to consideration?

▶ ORIGINAL QUESTIONS	GENERAL ANSWERS PROVIDED THROUGH PREVIEWING
1. What kind of information about language does the book provide? (What does the writer mean by "Aspects?")	
2. Does the writer treat "language" in a general sense or is he concerned only with the English language?	

3. Is the book written for people who have a background in the study of language (linguistics) or for the lay reader?

4. Does the writer have a special point of view about language that is hidden behind the objective word "aspects?"

▶ NEW QUESTIONS

▶ PROBABLE BASIC QUESTION

Compare your responses with those given in Chapter Supplement IV (p. 191).

Of course, when you survey books in libraries and bookstores, you surely will not take time to write down lists of questions taken from the titles and answers found in introductory and concluding sections of the books. But you will understand how rich in implications a non-fiction book title can be and you will know what parts of the book usually provide obvious supporting signals. You will probably work out your own adaptation of the method you have used in this chapter. Then sometime you may discover that you have learned to respond to a non-fiction writer's signals so quickly and easily as you preview that you are not consciously following any set procedure at all.

CHAPTER SUPPLEMENTS

I. Classifications and Questions for Titles

TITLE	KIND OF TITLE	QUESTIONS
4. Punishment: The Supposed Justification	Point of view	What sorts of punishment does the writer treat? He probably considers the punishment of criminals, but does he discuss other forms of punishment as well?

TITLE	KIND OF TITLE	QUESTIONS
		The use of "supposed" in the title suggests that from the writer's point of view punishment is not justified. If this is his point of view, how does he support it? Is he concerned only with other people's views on punishment or is he developing a position of his own? If we don't punish criminals, what will we do with them?
5. *The Ages of Life*	Informative	What kind of life is the book concerned with—human life or all kinds of life? If it is about the aging process in all kinds of life, does it show relationships between the aging process in humankind and in other forms of life? (If so, there may be an underlying point of view or argument here, but the basic approach will probably be informative.)
6. *Mississippi: The Closed Society*	Point of view	In what sense is Mississippi society closed? (You can be quite sure that he will treat the problem of race relations, but does he go beyond this topic?) If Mississippi is a closed society, who is on the inside? How does the writer support his point of view about Mississippi society?
7. *The Tyranny of Words*	Point of view	In what sense can words be considered to be tyrannical? (The word "tyranny" certainly implies a very definite point of view about language.) The writer apparently thinks that certain words or words used in certain ways can be harmful. What kinds of uses of language is he talking about?

TITLE	KIND OF TITLE	QUESTIONS
8. *The Origins of Totalitarianism*	Informative	What does the writer mean by "totalitarianism?" What roots or sources does she find for what she considers to be the totalitarian practices of modern governments?
9. *Justice Denied: The Black Man In White America*	Point of view	In what ways has the black man been denied justice in this country? (You will surely anticipate some of the book's answers as soon as you ask this question.) Are the writers concerned with the entire country or do they focus on the problems of one region? Do they treat just problems of the present time or historical problems as well?
10. *The Unexpected Universe*	Point of view	What is the writer concerned with? Does he mean literally the whole universe? If so, what is "unexpected" about it?

II. Preview of Prisoners of Psychiatry

ORIGINAL QUESTIONS	GENERAL ANSWERS
1. Who are these prisoners?	People who are or have been in mental hospitals.
2. Are they literal prisoners?	Yes and no—None of them are kept in places called prisons, but many are retained forcibly in mental institutions that the writer thinks are like prisons.
3. How does he justify the term?	People are kept involuntarily in mental hospitals or denied jobs after they are released. (You might not be able to tell that second point from your previewing.)
4. In what sense are people "victims" of psychiatric approaches?	They are admitted to hospitals presumably for treatment, but they are almost always given only custodial care.

NEW QUESTIONS

1. What does the writer think should happen to our present mental hospitals? (Does he think they should be eliminated?)

2. If they are eliminated, what kind of treatment should be provided for people who have serious mental or emotional problems?

PROBABLE BASIC QUESTIONS

What is wrong with our society's methods of treating people who are considered "mentally ill?"

III. Preview of The Chickenbone Special

ORIGINAL QUESTIONS	GENERAL ANSWERS
1. What is "The Chickenbone Special?"	It is the name (probably the nickname) of a train frequently taken North by poor Southern black people who are seeking a better life. See, for example, the following passages: a) Book jacket, first paragraph, line 8. b) Preface, page 171, next to last paragraph. c) Preface, page 171, paragraph beginning with "Several weeks." d) Chapter titles (by implication): "Taking a Ride," "The Station," "Window Seat."
2. What idea does it represent?	Your previewing may not have made the answer to this question entirely clear. You can probably tell, though, that it has something to do with tragedy in the lives of the people the book concerns. See, for example: a) The last sentence in the comments on the book jacket: "This is a . . . book about the failure of America to provide either a decent living on the land or a safe and secure passage into urban life." b) Preface, page 172: "Human beings were moving not because they wanted to move but because they *had* to move."

NEW QUESTIONS

1. Why did these people *have* to move? (From your previous experiences or from your reading, you may have a general idea, but you will read to find the information the writer gives about the lives of the *specific* people he deals with.)

2. Does the book treat the lives of these people before or after they migrate? (It appears that it will do both, but you cannot be sure until you read more.)

PROBABLE BASIC QUESTIONS

One or all of these: What kinds of lives do these people live? What makes their lives that way? What can society do to improve their lot?

IV. *Preview of* Aspects of Language

ORIGINAL QUESTIONS	GENERAL ANSWERS
1. What kind of information about language does the book provide? (What does he mean by "aspects"?)	Apparently it will provide the kind of information from the field of linguistics that the writer (a linguist) feels will be most helpful to the general reader in his daily uses of language. It will cover the "aspects" the writer thinks the reader should understand. See book jacket, first paragraph; Foreword, first three paragraphs.
2. Does the writer treat "language" in a general sense or is he concerned only with the English language?	He will be concerned with language in a general sense. (None of the chapter titles even mention English.) However, as he is writing for an English-speaking audience, most of his examples will probably be drawn from English. Note, for example, the attention in the "Additional Remarks" section to problems of usage in contemporary English.
3. Is the book written for specialists or for the lay reader?	It is written for the lay leader. (See Foreword.)
4. Does the writer have a special point of view about language?	You may feel that the attitude that seems to be implied in the comments on "verbal snobbery" in the concluding paragraphs and about "linguistic nonconformity" in the "Additional Remarks" section is a "special point of view."

NEW QUESTIONS

1. Is the writer saying that any speech form that a fairly large group of people uses is "right?" (See answer to 4 above.) If so, how does he justify this position?

PROBABLE BASIC QUESTION

What characteristics (aspects) of language have linguists discovered that can be of interest to the average citizen and helpful to him in his daily use of language?

recognizing main ideas and organizational patterns in non-fiction

In order to quickly and easily follow a writer's signals as you preview and read (or just preview) non-fiction works, you should be familiar with various organizational patterns. That is, you should understand the ways non-fiction writers arrange their materials, be able to recognize these patterns of arrangement, and know what signals of main and subordinate ideas to expect when each is used. In this chapter you will learn how to recognize these patterns and find these signals (including thesis statements and sentences implying main ideas). As you do so, you will note that the skillful non-fiction writer usually signals a question early in the work and then proceeds to answer it in the clearest and most effective way he can.

Because short pieces are usually much more tightly organized than full-length books and because some of the signals commonly found in essays and articles (thesis sentences, for example) are unusual in longer works, this chapter uses complete short works as examples of organizational patterns. But in your own private reading you will find that writers of non-fiction books use some of the same patterns; therefore it will make sense to add organizational structure to the points you look for when you preview this kind of a book. In your college studies, however, the most direct use you will make of your knowledge of organization will be in analytical reading of essays and "idea" articles for composition and literature courses.

RELATING TITLES TO STRUCTURAL SIGNALS

As you know, the title of an essay or article often suggests the basic question that the work will answer—a question that can be reduced to *Why?* or *How?* (or How do you?) or *What?* (or as this chapter will show, What happened?) When you have discovered a writer's basic question, you can often predict his organizational pattern. And when you have anticipated that pattern, you can usually preview efficiently because you know whether to expect a treatment of *information* (answering *how* or *what*) or of *point of view* (answering *why*). If you expect a point of view, you will look for either a *thesis sentence* directly stating it or a sentence or phrase implying it. Then you will read to discover the *reasons* given for the viewpoint (as you did with the essays in Chapter Four). But if the question is *How?* or *What?*, you will look for a different kind of organization and approach the article differently.

THE CHRONOLOGICAL PATTERN FOR "HOW-TO" ARTICLES

One of the simplest patterns to predict and to follow is the one a writer usually chooses in a "process" article, one in which the question is: How do you do it? or How is it done? When you started "How to Grow Asparagus . . . from Seeds" in Chapter Three did you have any difficulty following the flow of information and ideas? Probably not, because by the writer's choice of a title he had led you to expect a *step-by-step* treatment. And you probably were not thrown off course when you found that he introduced this time-order or chronological explanation by showing you why he thinks you would enjoy growing asparagus in your own back yard.

"How to do it" selections do not ordinarily have main ideas or thesis sentences. Neither do "how it is done" articles or chapters, material of a kind you are more likely to be asked to read in college. But in works of either type you can usually find in the first or second paragraph a *signal sentence* that supports the title and suggests *step-by-step organization*.

For example, note the way the following short "process" article is developed. After you have checked the title, read the first two paragraphs and underline the sentence that signals the organization of the rest of the article.

CHARTING FOR SPACE TRAVEL

from Science Digest, *September 1973*

Whenever you go on a long car trip, you usually take along a map, right? Well, when NASA sends astronauts off to the moon, they give them maps to take along, perhaps so they won't make a wrong turn and end up in a wrong crater. At a time when NASA sends an unmanned spacecraft to Mars, it will need maps to help guide the craft.

The task of making these space charts is being handled by two organizations: The Air Force Aeronautical Chart and Information Center (ACIC) is mapping the moon and the U.S. Geological Survey (Dept. of the Interior) is mapping Mars.

As you probably observed, the long sentence in the second paragraph shows you that the article will explain the way maps are prepared for moon travel and for the first expedition to Mars. It implies a treatment of *how it is done.* Now skim the rest of the article, noting only the sentences that have to do with steps in the process and (if you can find it quickly) the one sentence that divides the article by introducing the second part.

Neither of these jobs has been an easy one. The ACIC's moon mapping project began in 1959. At that time the most accurate moon map in existence was designed by German astronomer Julius Schmidt . . . in 1874!

The ACIC cartographers began making moon maps by studying photographs of various areas of the moon supplied to them by NASA. Although earlier photographs were taken through telescopes, the pictures used today come from lunar orbiter missions and Apollo moon landings.

Accompanying the photographs is supporting data telling how the pictures were taken, the time, height, locations and other information.

Groups of pictures are stripped together in jigsaw juzzle form to make one large photograph, which is then rephotographed to compensate for distortions caused by the pitch, yaw and inclination of the spacecraft and the curvature of the lunar surface.

An airbrush is used on the mosaic of photographs to show the proper shadow the astronauts will see as they approach the moon on a mission.

Once all the photographs are corrected and compiled into one long chart, an overlay is prepared containing all the necessary flight information. The overlay shows the spacecraft flight path, the landing target, time notations along the path, landmark names and other pertinent data, similar to the things you can find on a map of a section of earth.

Both the chart and the overlay are photographed separately by large industrial cameras. The negatives are used to print the map, using as many as five different colors.

After the maps are printed, they must be trimmed, folded and packaged for distribution to the users around the world—ground crews, technicians, trackers and astronauts.

The charts are put into a booklet for the astronauts to use on board the spacecraft. This is done by splicing the charts into a continuous strip showing about 1600 nautical miles of longitudinal coverage, and folding the sheets into a book.

It takes about six weeks to produce a set of charts for a NASA moon mission at the St. Louis ACIC center. For Apollo 11, man's first landing, more than 60 different maps were produced, including earth orbit, lunar orbit, lunar landing, lunar ascent, recovery and weather charts.

The U.S. Geological Survey is also having its problems mapping Mars. The survey is attempting to map the entire planet to help select landing sites for two Viking spacecraft scheduled to touch down in 1976. The problem is that the flood of spectacular photos returned by Mariner spacecraft have made previous maps obsolete already. Everytime a new photo or new information comes in it's as if the cartographers have a completely new planet to contend with.

"Just keeping up with each day's new influx of information," says Dr. Hal Masursky of the Survey, "is keeping many of us working almost around the clock."

Eventually, an atlas of Mars maps will be published and made available to the general public.

Did you discover that the first sentences of many of the paragraphs in the first section of the article summarize the steps in the preparation of moon maps and that the sentence "The U.S. Geological Survey is also having its problems mapping Mars" (third from the last paragraph) introduces a short second section? Your awareness of the structure of the article, then, helped you acquire the most important information in a minute or so. You might, of course, want to read it more carefully for details.

THE ANALYSIS PATTERN
FOR ARTICLES ANSWERING WHAT? OR HOW?

The following titles are for articles published in magazines that specialize in treating scientific subjects in ways laymen can understand. What *basic question* does each of these titles suggest to you?

▶   TITLE   QUESTION

"The Cry of the Human Infant"

"Science's Answer to Better Nutrition"

"Trees that Live in Glass Houses"

"The Unlikely Planet"

"Folk Art in the Barrios"

You probably asked some *what* and *how* questions—*What* is science's answer to better nutrition? (or *How* does science provide an answer to better nutrition?). *What* is unusual (or important or interesting) about the cry of the human infant? *What* planet is the article concerned with? But you may have had some difficulty thinking of basic questions at all. For all that a title like one of these can do is to let the reader know that the work *provides information* on a subject about which he presumably knows very little. The question such a title suggests can readily be reduced to: What about it? or What should I know about it? The pattern most writers use when they answer this question is the *analysis*.

A written analysis is simply a work that breaks a subject down into parts or divisions. Unless its title suggests an emphasis on point of view (as Tom Wolfe's "Clean Fun at Riverhead" does), the purpose of a selection of this kind will be informative. However, in an introductory paragraph there will probably be a *thesis sentence* making a generalization and a limited kind of judgment about the subject. And this sentence or another early sentence will indicate the *way* the subject will be divided.

Find the thesis sentence and the organizing or "dividing" sentence in the following introductory paragraphs of "Folk Art in the Barrios." (It is somewhat unusual to find an article that makes use of the analysis form and keeps point of view language to a minimum when the topic concerns human relationships. Writing of this kind is more often on scientific or technical subjects. Note, though, that this selection is from *Natural History* magazine.)

FOLK ART IN THE BARRIOS

by Eric Kroll

from Natural History, *May 1973*

Man's need to communicate can take many forms other than the written or spoken word. Today, with innumerable factions trying to make themselves heard, the trend is toward instant communication and immediate impact. Consequently, many people are turning to music, art, cinema, and television to get their message across.

In Santa Fe, New Mexico, a group of folk artists, Los Artes Guadalupanos de Aztlan, are creating bright murals on the walls of the barrios—murals that express the sentiments of the radical Chicano youth of the community. The dazzling colors and exaggerated figures of these wall paintings portray the past glory of the Aztec ancestors of the Chicanos, the repression and discrimination of the present, and the hopes for the future. Whereas words can be easily ignored, murals painted outdoors on walls are not easily dismissed or overlooked.

Did you label the first sentence in the second paragraph as the thesis statement? That sentence *limits* the subject (to folk art in Santa Fe) and makes a *generalization* about it (it expresses "the sentiments of the radical Chicano youth of the community"). If you marked any sentence in the first paragraph as the thesis, you were looking for a more general idea than the title signaled. The organizing sentence is the second sentence in the second paragraph. It indicates that the folk art treated here reflects three interests of young Chicanos: their cultural heritage, their community problems, and their future hopes.

As you read the complete article, watch for the evidence the writer gives to show that the art he talks about reflects these three interests. Also, because this is an *informative* article, you should look for answers to the usual information questions: Who? What? When? and Where? When you have finished, you will be asked to recall information the article provides, including examples of ways the three interests are expressed.

Los Artes discovered their medium of communicataion in 1970, when 12-year-old George Leyba died of a drug overdose. Shortly after, his three older brothers, Carlo, Albert, and Sammy, painted a memorial mural on one wall of a Santa Fe playground. It is a child's idealized view of Africa, reminiscent of Walt Disney. In a Garden of Eden setting, lions laze beneath a tree from which monkeys swing. In the distance, elephants amble and an impala gazes majestically about. But this pastoral mural lacks the elements of protest that dominate those that followed.

This first mural was received with enthusiasm by the Chicano community; its popularity encouraged the Leyba brothers to paint other murals that expressed their frustration and anger at a society that they felt had contributed to the death of their younger brother and had subjugated millions of Chicanos.

Under the auspices of a local methadone maintenance center, and aided by a grant from the Office of Economic Opportunity, the Leybas, joined by two other youths, Geronimo Gardunio and Gilberto Guzman, participated in a six-week experiment in mural painting. The six-week period is now long past, but the members of Los Artes continue to paint murals, supporting themselves through odd jobs and contributions.

On ten Santa Fe walls, the history of the Chicanos, both mythical and actual, is depicted in brilliant colors and disproportionate figures. Aztec medicine figures dance and gods protect peasants, all for the glory of the Chicano in the present. On some walls, the chains of bondage are being broken and the Lady of Justice, depicted as an Indian maiden, watches over both Indians and Chicanos. On others, Pancho Villa and Father Hidalgo lead the Mexican peasants to freedom. But the clenched fist at the end of grotesquely muscled arms is the most predominant image. It symbolizes unity, determination, ambition, and pride, all traits that Los Artes believe should be a part of Chicano psychology. The figures they paint are bold, upright, strong, and grasping, far from the stereotype of the Mexican-American with drooping moustache and floppy sombrero lying in the shade of a stucco building.

Members of Los Artes, as do many others, refer to themselves as "Chicanos" rather than as Mexican-Americans or Spanish-Americans, terms they feel are removed and condescending. Through the medium of their large, brightly colored murals, these folk artists are trying to express the anguish felt by the Chicanos after hundreds of years of repression and degradation. The viewer can see the chains of bondage being broken, a stake being driven through the heart of a prone Indian, or marching skeletons dressed in army fatigues throwing hand grenades. In the huge figures with their exaggerated movements, he can see spots of humor. And he can also see the quiet determination, the unbroken spirit, and the sometimes youthful naïveté of the murals' creators. However the viewer interprets them, the murals serve as reminders of the past and as hopeful portents of the future.

Obvious to all is the effect of the murals on the barrios where most of them have been painted. The outskirts of Santa Fe consist of a patchwork of square, one- or two-story buildings, all of the same red-brown color. Blank walls are numerous; the streets are narrow and dusty. Under the hot midday sun, the proximity of the Sangre de Christo Mountains to the northeast offers little solace; and the dry plains to the west are only a huge emptiness that exaggerates the fragility of the small adobe buildings. In this setting, the brightness of the murals strongly offsets the sameness of the angular buildings, and gives the surrounding area an air of hope and expectation.

For the Chicanos and Indians who live in the barrios, however, the murals do more. They reflect the antagonism many Chicanos feel toward a society that has not offered them education, that discriminates against them in employment, and that does not give them equal rights. The determination seen in the murals stems from years of harassment, the influx of drugs, the stares of tourists, and the sneers of bureaucrats.

Like other creators of folk art, and unlike most professional artists, members of Los Artes do not sign their work and will not divulge who painted specific murals. Of the five members of the group, only Sammy Leyba and Geronimo Gardunio have had any formal training. Both attended art classes for a short time, but dropped out because they did not agree with the structured routine.

Instead of entering the highly competitive art world, they have chosen, for the present, to be the voices of the radical elements of the Chicano community. They have painted on the walls of Chicano-owned buildings in the Santa Fe slum area, as well as on the walls of a high school and a health clinic. Soon after paint-their first outdoor mural, Los Artes received numerous requests to paint murals in private homes and in private institutions, requests which they refused, insisting that art should not be only the property of the rich.

In their antagonism toward private art and art galleries, Los Artes upset the traditional and well-populated Santa Fe art community early in 1972 when they were permitted to paint a mural on the walls of a tool shed on Canyon Road, in the heart of the tourist-filled art gallery district. It was a symbolic mural showing the Lady of Justice as an Indian maiden breaking the chains of bondage from an enslaved and well-muscled Chicano. To the business community it was an embarrassment; to the art galleries it was a threat; but for the Chicanos, it was their way of showing not only their innate creativity but also their attitude toward private art. The disputes that followed only highlighted the cause of Los Artes, and the flow of tourists did not diminish. On the contrary they found the mural attractive. In time, the issue simmered down and the complaints died.

To set an example for other Chicanos is another aim of Los Artes, Murals are painted on walls of the Chicano neighborhoods in the hope that latent Chicano creativity, especially in children, will surface. Los Artes believe that the potential for both creativity and freedom lies behind the adobe walls. They wish the murals to be an empirical way for children to realize that they too, can learn to express themselves. The group plans to hold art classes for the neighborhood children, and already some children have begun to paint their own murals.

The style of Los Artes flows from the work of such famous twentieth-century Mexican muralists as Diego Rivera, José Clemente Orozco, and David Alfaro Siqueiros, artists who concentrated on the turmoil between men, the resultant social injustices, and the hope of eventual harmony. Their emphasis, however, was on the universal, while the work of Los Artes is limited to what pertains to Chicanos.

The murals of Los Artes can be interpreted as a type of graffiti, but unlike most graffiti, they are not quickly administered in the quiet of night with a spray can of paint or a magic marker. The artists are not apologizing for their means of communication; rather, the details, the colors, and the symbolism reflect their pride and conviction. They chose this medium as their manner of protest: they show the Chicano not only as he was and is, but also as he can be. And in their format and setting, the murals and the message are unavoidable, they must be seen; the viewer can turn away from them, but he cannot turn them off.

▶ QUESTIONS:

1. Who are the "folk artists" the article is about? (Be as specific as you can be.)

2. Where do they live?

3. What is their group called?

4. How is their work financed?

5. Where is their painting done?

6. State two practices of these people that are different from the practices of most professional artists.

7. Mention two points the writer made that showed that these people are greatly interested in their cultural past.

8. Give one example of how their art reflects their concern with the mistreatment of their people.

9. What evidence does the writer give that these artists do have hope that their people can live happier lives in the future?

In Chapter Supplement I (p. 230), you will find some answers to compare with yours.

Regardless of whether you remembered all the details about "Folk Art" given in the answers in the supplement, you probably understood and remembered more than you would have if you had not paid some attention to the writer's purpose and developing organization as you began.

FINDING PATTERNS IN NARRATIVES

When a non-fiction title suggests a *how* or *what* question, the organizational pattern will often be one you half-consciously expected in the first place. In fact, you can usually anticipate a pattern, even when the question raised by the title or another early signal is not just "What?" but "What happened?" When a writer signals that question, however, he may have any one of several purposes in mind. And his purpose will affect his treatment of the narrative pattern you expect.

He may tell a non-fiction narrative or story (that is, tell "what happened") simply to entertain or inform; he may tell that story to develop an implied idea; or he may use it to illustrate a stated thesis. If his only purpose is to entertain or inform, he will use report language and a time-order (chronological) approach throughout. But if his basic purpose is to develop an implied or a stated idea, you may expect to find thesis and general sentences or emotive language before, during, or after his account of *what happened.*

Although you may need to preview or read a non-fiction narrative before you can be certain of the writer's purpose, you can often make an intelligent guess by noting the wording of the title. Consider the following titles, for example:

"I Discover My Father"
"Bicycle Tour Through Baja del Sur"
"The Dying Girl That No One Helped"

Put a check mark by the title of the work you think is least likely to develop an idea or thesis.

What criteria did you use in making your decision? Did you mark "Bicycle Tour," realizing that, because this title contains no obviously emotive language, it probably represents a basically factual report? If so, you may also have had the right impression of the purpose of each of the other two selections.

A quick preview will make you much surer of what each writer is doing. The three works appear on the following pages. Before you read each one, preview, or survey, it, using the Question–Survey–Question approach that you learned in Chapter Four. Note especially the underlined sentences (the underlining has been added). After each preview, write either the basic question you expect the writer to answer or comments on the *purpose* you anticipate for the work. Then read the selection through to see whether your expectations are confirmed. When you have finished reading, note your comments on the writer's purpose and the way it is carried out, and compare your reactions with those given in Chapter Supplement II (p. 231).

I DISCOVER MY FATHER

by Sherwood Anderson

from Memoirs of Sherwood Anderson

You hear it said that fathers want their sons to be what they feel they cannot themselves be, but I tell you it also works the other way. A boy wants something very special from his father. I know that as a small boy I wanted my father to be a certain thing he was not. I wanted him to be a proud, silent, dignified father. When I was with other boys and he passed along the street, I wanted to feel a flow of pride. "There he is. That is my father."

But he wasn't such a one. He couldn't be. It seemed to me then that he was always showing off. Let's say someone in our town had got up a show. They were always doing it. The druggist would be in it, the shoe-store clerk, the horse doctor, and a lot of women and girls. My father would manage to get the chief comedy part. It was, let's say, a Civil War play and he was a comic Irish soldier. He had to do the most absurd things. They thought he was funny, but I didn't.

I thought he was terrible. I didn't see how mother could stand it. She even laughed with the others. Maybe I would have laughed if it hadn't been my father.

Or there was a parade, the Fourth of July or Decoration Day. He'd be in that, too, right at the front of it, as Grand Marshal or something, on a white horse hired from a livery stable.

He couldn't ride for shucks. He fell off the horse and everyone hooted with laughter, but he didn't care. He even seemed to like it. I remember once when he had done something ridiculous, and right out on Main Street, too. I was with some other boys and they were laughing and shouting at him and he was shouting back and having as good a time as they were. I ran down an alley back of some stores and there in the Presbyterian Church sheds I had a good long cry.

Or I would be in bed at night and father would come home a little lit up and bring some men with him. He was a man who was never alone. Before he went broke, running a harness shop, there were always a lot of men loafing in the shop. He went broke, of course, because he gave too much credit. He couldn't refuse it and I thought he was a fool. I had got to hating him.

There'd be men I didn't think would want to be fooling around with him. There might even be the superintendent of our schools and a quiet man who ran the hardware store. Once I remember there was a white-haired man who was a cashier of the bank. It was a wonder to me they'd want to be seen with such a windbag. That's what I thought he was. I know now what it was that attracted them. It was because life in our town, as in all small towns, was at times pretty dull and he livened it up. He made them laugh. He could tell stories. He'd even get them to singing.

If they didn't come to our house they'd go off, say at night, to where there was a grassy place by a creek. They'd cook food there and drink beer and sit about listening to his stories.

He was always telling stories about himself. He'd say this or that wonderful thing had happened to him. It might be something that made him look like a fool. He didn't care.

If an Irishman came to our house, right away father would say he was Irish. He'd tell what county in Ireland he was born in. He'd tell things that happened there when he was a boy. He'd make it seem so real that, if I hadn't known he was born in southern Ohio, I'd have believed him myself.

If it was a Scotchman the same thing happened. He'd get a burr into his speech. Or he was a German or a Swede. He'd be anything the other man was. I think they all knew he was lying, but they seemed to like him just the same. As a boy that was what I couldn't understand.

And there was mother. How could she stand it? I wanted to ask but never did. She was not the kind you asked such questions.

I'd be upstairs in my bed, in my room above the porch, and father would be telling some of his tales. A lot of father's stories were about the Civil War. To hear him tell it he'd been in about every battle. He'd known Grant, Sherman, Sheridan and I don't know how many others. He'd been particularly intimate with General Grant so that when Grant went East to take charge of all the armies, he took father along.

"I was an orderly at headquarters and Sim Grant said to me, 'Irve,' he said, 'I'm going to take you along with me.' "

It seems he and Grant used to slip off sometimes and have a quiet drink together. That's what my father said. He'd tell about the day Lee surrendered and how, when the great moment came, they couldn't find Grant.

"You know," my father said, "about General Grant's book, his memoirs. You've read of how he said he had a headache and how, when he got word that Lee was ready to call it quits, he was suddenly and miraculously cured.

"Huh," said father. "He was in the woods with me.

"I was in there with my back against a tree. I was pretty well corned. I had got hold of a bottle of pretty good stuff.

"They were looking for Grant. He had got off his horse and come into the woods. He found me. He was covered with mud.

"I had the bottle in my hand. What'd I care? The war was over. I knew we had them licked."

My father said that he was the one who told Grant about Lee. An orderly riding by had told him, because the orderly knew how thick he was with Grant. Grant was embarrassed.

"But, Irve, look at me. I'm all covered with mud," he said to father.

And then, my father said, he and Grant decided to have a drink together. They took a couple of shots and then, because he didn't want Grant to show up potted before the immaculate Lee, he smashed the bottle against the tree.

"Sim Grant's dead now and I wouldn't want it to get out on him," my father said.

That's just one of the kind of things he'd tell. Of course the men knew he was lying, but they seemed to like it just the same.

When we got broke, down and out, do you think he ever brought anything home? Not he. If there wasn't anything to eat in the house, he'd go off visiting around at farmhouses. They all wanted him. Sometimes he'd stay away for weeks, mother working to keep us fed, and then home he'd come bringing, let's say, a ham. He'd got it from some farmer friend. He'd slap it on the table in the kitchen. "You bet I'm going to see that my kids have something to eat," he'd say, and mother would just stand smiling at him. She'd never say a word about all the weeks and months he'd been away, not leaving us a cent for food. Once I heard her speaking to a woman in our street. Maybe the woman had dared to sympathize with her. "Oh," she said, "it's all right. He isn't ever dull like most of the men in this street. Life is never dull when my man is about."

But often I was filled with bitterness, and sometimes I wished he wasn't my father. I'd even invent another man as my father. To protect my mother I'd make up stories of a secret marriage that for some strange reason never got known. As though some man, say the president of a railroad company or maybe a Congressman, had married my mother, thinking his wife was dead and then it turned out she wasn't.

So they had to hush it up but I got born just the same. I wasn't really the son of my father. Somewhere in the world there was a very dignified, quite wonderful man who was really my father. I even made myself half believe these fancies.

And then there came a certain night. He'd been off somewhere for two or three weeks. He found me alone in the house, reading by the kitchen table.

It had been raining and he was very wet. He sat and looked at me for a long time, not saying a word. I was startled, for there was on his face the saddest look I had ever seen. He sat for a time, his clothes dripping. Then he got up.

"Come on with me," he said.

I got up and went with him out of the house. I was filled with wonder but I wasn't afraid. We went along a dirt road that led down into a valley, about a mile out of town, where there was a pond. We walked in silence. The man who was always talking had stopped his talking.

I didn't know what was up and had the queer feeling that I was with a stranger. I don't know whether my father intended it so. I don't think he did.

The pond was quite large. It was still raining hard and there were flashes of lightning followed by thunder. We were on a grassy bank at the pond's edge when my father spoke, and in the darkness and rain his voice sounded strange.

"Take off your clothes," he said. Still filled with wonder, I began to undress. There was a flash of lightening and I saw that he was already naked.

Naked, we went into the pond. Taking my hand he pulled me in. It may be that I was too frightened, too full of a feeling of strangeness, to speak. Before that night my father had never seemed to pay any attention to me.

"And what is he up to now?" I kept asking myself. I did not swim very well, but he put my hand on his shoulder and struck out into the darkness.

He was a man with big shoulders, a powerful swimmer. In the darkness I could feel the movement of his muscles. We swam to the far edge of the pond and then back to where we had left our clothes. The rain continued and the wind blew. Sometimes my father swam on his back and when he did he took my hand in his large powerful one and moved it over so that it rested always on his shoulder. Sometimes there would be a flash of lightning and I could see his face quite clearly.

It was as it was earlier, in the kitchen, a face filled with sadness. There would be the momentary glimpse of his face and then again the darkness, the wind and the rain. In me there was a feeling I had never known before.

It was a feeling of closeness. It was something strange. It was as though there were only we two in the world. It was as though I had been jerked suddenly out of myself, out of my world of the schoolboy, out of a world in which I was ashamed of my father.

He had become blood of my blood; he the strong swimmer and I the boy clinging to him in the darkness. We swam in silence and in silence we dressed in our wet clothes, and went home.

There was a lamp lighted in the kitchen and when we came in, the water dripping from us, there was my mother. She smiled at us. I remember that she called us "boys."

"What have you boys been up to," she asked, but my father did not answer. As he had begun the evening's experience with me in silence, so he ended it. He turned and looked at me. Then he went, I thought, with a new and strange dignity out of the room.

I climbed the stairs to my own room, undressed in the darkness and got into bed. I couldn't sleep and did not want to sleep. For the first time I knew that I was the son of my father. He was a story teller as I was to be. It may be that I even laughed a little softly there in the darkness. If I did, I laughed knowing that I would never again be wanting another father.

▶ PREVIEW REACTIONS (BASIC QUESTION OR COMMENTS ON PURPOSE):

▶ REACTIONS AFTER READING:

BICYCLE TOUR
THROUGH BAJA DEL SUR

by Judy and Don Davis
from Westways, *January 1974*

Our bicycles fit snugly in the back aisle of the eighteen-passenger plane. The two Mexican pilots look back through the cockpit entrance and laugh and wave. They think we're loco, as do all our friends back in the states, but anyone who wants to see Baja del Sur badly enough to consider *bicycling* through it has to be a good guy, and so they've let us aboard with our bikes. And, when the slim Aeronaves Alimentadoras plane lands at the hilltop airport outside of Santa Rosalia, the pilots formally shake our hands and wish us luck on our journey.

Stretching off beyond the airport is a sandy, mouse-colored desert, dotted with the muted green of desert foliage. At one end of the landing field lies a cemetery; below the airport, Santa Rosalia sprawls haphazardly across an arroyo and up the side of the next hill.

Airport personnel and passengers waiting to board the plane

for points south stare as we carefully lift our bicycles off the plane and out into the sun of Baja. Baja del Sur, southern half of the Mexican peninsula, is famous for the remoteness and ruggedness of its terrain. Until recently, cars passing through were advised to travel in pairs and to always carry spare tires and parts. Many natives of Baja have never even seen ten-speed bicycles and a small crowd gathers as we fasten bright blue saddlebags bulging with food, water and camping supplies onto ours.

"Where are you going?" the boldest in the group finally asks.

We grin, and say, "Cabo San Lucas." His mouth falls open, he stares at us, then whistles. It is the reaction we will constantly get on our 500-mile journey through Baja.

"Don't you have a car?" gasps a boy about eighteen. We explain that we left our car in Guaymas, at the airport, where the watchman will look after it. Don checks the slim tires on the bikes one last time, I take a quick look at the odometer fastened to my front wheel and we head on down the dusty dirt road into Santa Rosalia, which combines the charm of Mexico at her best with the picturesqueness of an old French mining town.

Our next real town will be the date palm oasis of Mulege, famous for her deep-sea fishing, and a two-day ride over cactus-dotted hills to the south. We have chosen the time of year for our trip with great care. It is the last day of November when we cycle along the beach out of Santa Rosalia and, though the sun is still ferocious and we need hats to protect us from sunstroke, the snakes are asleep for the winter, and the heat isn't so bad we can't cycle through it.

The brand-new road seems our private highway. It stretches ahead, as far as the eye can see, empty except for an occasional truck bringing supplies back and forth from La Paz, Baja del Sur's largest city, and one of our southern destinations. The sky is a bleached blue and we are amused and, secretly, a little worried, by the two vultures who come within stone-throwing distance and, as we hit open country, stay with us for over forty miles.

This is a country of scorpions and tarantulas, of settlements so spread apart that ranches are named on the maps, just as though they were towns. We have planned carefully for the trip and don't consider ourselves fool-hardy, but the vultures seem to think we're worthwhile candidates for dinner. And, after all, this is their country. Maybe they know more about it than we do. This is not only our first trip to Baja, but our first bicycling trip. And we are both in our mid-thirties, two unlikely cyclists with a Spanish-English dictionary tucked in our back pockets.

The first couple of days are rough, but we survive and soon the vultures lose interest in us. Baja is a bicyclist's dream. It's a land of volcanic hills, humped like resting dinosaurs; sprawling ocotillo and huge relatives of saguaro cactus called cardons; vast deserted beaches and clear warm water, perfect for swimming. There is always something to see, some breathtaking vista or oddity of nature, some remnant of history hanging on in the form of petroglyphs or crumbling mission walls.

And Baja, of course, is a land of churches. The sheet metal church in Santa Rosalia which was shipped, piece by piece, across from France in the heyday of copper mining in Santa Rosalia . . . the rebuilt mission at Mulege, which some claim is one of the three best-preserved of all the mission churches . . . Loreto's church, topped with a tower rebuilt by money won by its priest in the national lottery . . . the crumbling wall, still standing guard over a graveyard, which is all that is left of an early mission chapel at San Juan Londo.

But mostly Baja is a land of space. There are no fences and wild horses, cattle and burros roam freely. The horses ignore us, the cattle are suspicious, but the burros are terrified and run or crowd together when we ride by. We feel badly about it and try to murmur words of reassurance, but it isn't until Don stops to take pictures, and I ride on ahead, that I see why the burros are so frightened. From a distance he looks exactly like a rider astride a nightmarish, science-fiction burro, its body formed by his sagging blue saddlebags—something a burro might have bad dreams about after eating too much wild grass.

Finding camping spots is no problem. The first four or five nights we pitch our tent along the Sea of Cortez—the Gulf of California—on beautiful palm-lined beaches. We clam, swim and watch playful dolphins splashing in the sunrise as we break camp in the mornings. As we swing away from the gulf, over the Sierra de la Giganta Range and down the Magdalena Plain, we camp in the desert, under giant cardons, mesquite trees and graceful palo blancos and paloverdes.

Baja is famous for its fabulous resort hotels and we stop at a few of these for a shower and a change from the desert floor as a bed.

We spend time, also, at Loreto, famed not only for being the first capital of Baja and a former Jesuit capital but also as a fishing resort; and at the bleak, raw-looking town of Villa Insurgente, we buy blankets because the nights are getting chilly.

Whenever we stop at or near a settlement, men and boys materialize from nowhere to stare at the bikes. "Ahhh," they say, shy smiles on their faces, hands shoved in their back pockets as they stare. The odometer on my bike always attracts special notice. One fellow, either familiar with odometers or more mechanically adept than the others, will squat, point to it, and explain how it works. But never are our bicycles or gear even touched and I am ashamed to remember worrying about theft.

The people we run into on our trip are warm and helpful, possessing a natural courtesy. Only in La Paz, a bustling free port city which sees many tourists due to its first-class airport and ferry service from both Mazatlan and Topolobampo on the mainland, do we run into "double prices"; one for the native, and another, twice as high, for the tourist. Several times, when we eat at ranches along the road, we run into the charming old Mexican custom of "Pay whatever you feel the meal is worth."

Food turns out to be our biggest problem bicycling through Mexico. We carry some, of course: dehydrated mixes, powdered eggs, fruit and date bars which we eat by the side of the road for quick energy. But we don't have enough and most markets outside of La Paz, which has a supermarket to rival any in the U.S., can do little to help us with lightweight, easily prepared food.

Our lifesaver is the ranches. Some make a regular practice of selling food to travelers. The "Fresca" sign nailed to an outside . wall identifies these. It's a cigarette ad and is invariably found on restaurant walls. Often, unless you see a gasoline-powered refrigerator sitting outside, it is the only indication that meals are sold at a particular spot. Our mode of travel, however, plus the novelty of having an American senora as a guest, assure us meals at other ranches, too.

Once, when Don cycles down a sandy road a quarter of a mile to a goat ranch nestled among the cardons, we are refused food. But as he starts to turn around to come back to the road, it dawns on the senora that he has said, "por me (sic) esposa y me" and she calls him back. His wife is with him? Where? On a bicycle, too? Of course, she will feed us!

The kitchen she ushers us into is a board lean-to tacked onto the side of her house. A soap opera plays on the ever-present battery-powered radio. We try not to stare at the businesslike rifle poked into the rafters. Rounds of goat cheese are drying on shelves along one wall. The young senora, all alone here except for her baby, pokes mesquite branches into her oil-drum stove and begins making tortillas by hand. In Baja, you accept what is offered, and she fixes us eggs, frijoles, tortillas and coffee. The food is terrific. The tortillas make us realize the wisdom of the old Mexican custom of sampling a senorita's tortillas before proposing marriage —our senora would have nothing to fear in such an arrangement —and two of the freshly gathered eggs would make six of our puny, sterile supermarket eggs.

Our speed is determined mainly by the steepness and frequency of the hills. "This whole peninsula is nothing but hills," one burly truck driver laughs when we wistfully ask about the terrain ahead. He is just about right. Except for a hundred miles or so between Villa Insurgente and La Paz, we are either slowly struggling up a hill or else speeding downhill, hunched over our handlebars like racing cyclists. Maybe the downhill stretches help; at any rate, we average thirty-two miles a day, and go fifteen miles on our slowest day, fifty on our fastest.

With each hilltop the landscape changes, and often the sheer richness of view is more than our eyes can take in. There is so much to study: the twisted shapes of the elephant trees, the noisy life in a tide pool fed by a hot mineral spring, the laboriously slow progress of a hairy tarantula as he crosses the road, seemingly oblivious of us bent over staring at him. We stop often and prop our bicycles by the side of the road to explore a fascinating bit of cacti or wildflower or simply to ease our weary bodies into the cement storm drains that line the road. They are contoured just right for our backs, and make excellent chairs to relax in while we nibble a fruit bar and take a drink of water.

The last leg of our trip, from La Paz south to Cabo San Lucas, takes a full week. The weather has been delightful, in the seventies, ever since Mulege, but once we leave La Paz we run into hot weather again, for a day, and then two days of a light drizzle. Until the road cuts back to the coast and the land of fishing resorts, we are in mining country. We spend several hours prowling around the rust-colored adobe and brick ruins at El Triunfo, where once 10,000 people thrived and where 500 now live. Farther down the road, we cycle off to take a look at San Antonio, a mining town 100 years older than El Triunfo but not nearly so beautiful.

Our favorite of the towns south of La Paz is Miraflores, where craftsmen make finely carved leather goods by hand. As we cycle along the side road that leads to Miraflores from the highway, we see newly whitewashed houses, surrounded by tin cans full of blooming flowers, and hear the unexpected sound of someone playing a violin in one of the adobe huts. Miraflores is one of the towns in Baja which boasts a restaurant (not all do) and after a fine meal of *machaca,* a national dish made of dried beef or venison, vegetables and seasonings, we visit Alcides Verduzco, a leather worker. Alcides, we have been told, knows all about Indian sites in the area. He is a small man with a big moustache who has taught himself English at night from a book. He shows us fossils and arrowheads he has collected, then takes us fifteen or twenty miles back into the hills, where he shows us rock paintings and hand prints made by extinct Indians who once populated Baja.

By the time we reach Cabo San Lucas, the twenty-five pounds of extra weight on my bike and the forty-five on Don's seem very heavy. The trip has been rough at times. We have been a little cold, a little hot, and sometimes very sore as we dismounted for the day. But we have made it. We have had an adventure we'll never forget.

And, back at the airport at La Paz, as we prepare to board a plane for the mainland of Mexico, so that we can get back to Guaymas and our camper, a bearded American of about twenty hurries up to us. "I beg your pardon," he says in astonishment, "but what are you doing with those bikes *in Baja?*"

We explain the trip we've just made and, as we answer his excited questions, we know that we may have been the first to see southern Baja from the seat of a bicycle, but we won't be the last.

▶ PREVIEW REACTIONS (BASIC QUESTION OR COMMENTS ON PURPOSE):

▶ REACTIONS AFTER READING:

THE DYING GIRL
THAT NO ONE HELPED

by Loudon Wainwright

from Life, *April 10, 1964*

To judge from the recent, bitter example given us by the good
folks of a respectable New York residential area, Samaritans are
very scarce these days. In fact, if the reactions of the 38 heedless
witnesses to the murder of Catherine Genovese provide any true
reflection of a national attitude toward our neighbors, we are
becoming a callous, chicken-hearted and immoral people. Psychiatrists, poking around in the ruins of character at the scene of the
crime, have already come up with some generous, culture-blaming
excuses for this grotesque piece of bad fellowship. But the matter
calls for something more than sheer indignation. An examination
of the pitiful facts of Miss Genovese's terminal experience makes
very necessary the ugly personal question each of must ask:
What would *I* have done?

The story is simple and brutal. As she arrived home in the
early morning darkness, Kitty Genovese, a decent, pretty young
woman of 28, was stalked through the streets close to her Kew
Gardens apartment and stabbed again and again by a man who
had followed her home and who took almost a half hour to kill
her. During that bloody little eternity, according to an extraordinary account published in the New York *Times*, Kitty
screamed and cried repeatedly for help. Her entreaties were un-
equivocal. "Oh, my God!" she cried out at one point. "He stabbed
me! Please help me! Someone help me!" Minutes later, before the
murderer came back and attacked her for the final time, she
screamed, "I'm dying! I'm dying!"

The reason the murderer's actions and his victim's calls are so documented is that police were able to find 38 of Kitty's neighbors who admitted they witnessed the awful event. They heard the screams and most understood her cry for help. Peeking out their windows, many saw enough of the killer to provide a good description of his appearance and clothing. A few saw him strike Kitty, and more saw her staggering down the sidewalk after she had been stabbed twice and was looking for a place to hide. One especially sharp-eyed person was able to report that the murderer was sucking his finger as he left the scene; he had cut himself during the attack. Another witness has the awful distinction of being the only person Kitty Genovese recognized in the audience taking in her final moments. She looked at him and called to him by name. He did not reply.

No one really helped Kitty at all. Only one person shouted at the killer ("Let that girl alone!"), and the one phone call that was finally made to the police was placed after the murderer had got in his car and driven off. For the most part the witnesses, crouching in darkened windows like watchers of a Late Show, looked on until the play had passed beyond their view. Then they went back to bed.

Not all of these people, it must be said, understood they were watching a murder. Some thought they were looking on at a lovers' quarrel; others saw or heard so very little that they could not have reached any conclusion about the disturbance. Even if one of her neighbors had called the police promptly, it cannot be definitely stated that Kitty would have survived. But that is quite beside the point. The fact is that no one, even those who were sure something was terribly wrong, felt moved enough to act. There is, of course, no law against not being helpful.

On the scene a few days after the killer had been caught and had confessed, Police Lieutenant Bernard Jacobs discussed the investigation. "The word we kept hearing from the witnesses later was 'involved,' " Jacobs said. A dark-haired, thoughtful man, he was standing on the sidewalk next to two fist-sized, dark-gray blotches on the cement. These were Kitty's bloodstains and it was there that the killer first stabbed her. "People told us they just didn't want to get involved," Jacobs said to me. "They don't want to be questioned or have to go to court." He pointed to an apartment house directly across the quiet street. "They looked down at this thing," he went on, "from four different floors of that building." Jacobs indicated the long, two-story building immediately next to him. A row of stores took up the ground floor; there were apartments on the upper floor. "Kitty lived in one of them," Jacobs said. "People up there were sitting right on top of the crime." He moved his arm in a gesture that included all the buildings. "It's a nice neighborhood, isn't it?" he went on. "Doesn't look like a jungle. Good, solid people. We don't expect anybody to come out into the street and fight this kind of bum. All we want is a phone call. We don't even need to know who's making it.

"You know what this man told us after we caught him?" Jacobs asked. "He said he figured nobody would do anything to help. He heard the windows go up and saw the lights go on. He just retreated for a while and when things quieted down, he came back to finish the job."

Later, in one of the apartment houses, a witness to part of Kitty Genovese's murder talked. His comments—agonized, contradictory, guilt-ridden, self-excusing—indicate the price in bad conscience he and his neighbors are now paying. "I feel terrible about it," he said. "The thing keeps coming back in my mind. You just don't want to get involved. They might have picked me up as a suspect if I'd bounced right out there. I was getting ready, but my wife stopped me. She didn't want to be a hero's widow. I woke up about the third scream. I pulled the blind so hard it came off the window. The girl was on her knees struggling to get up. I didn't know if she was drunk or what. I never saw the man. She staggered a little when she walked, like she had a few drinks in her. I forgot the screen was there and I almost put my head through it trying to get a better look. I could see people with their heads out and hear windows going up and down all along the street."

The man walked to the window and looked down at the sidewalk. He was plainly depressed and disappointed at his own failure. "Every time I look out here now," he said, "it's like looking out at a nightmare. How could so many of us have had the same idea that we didn't need to do anything? But that's not all that's wrong." Now he sounded betrayed and he told what was really eating him. Those 38 witnesses had, at least, talked to the police after the murder. The man pointed to a nearby building. "There are people over there who saw everything," he said. "And there hasn't been a peep out of them yet. Not one peep."

▶   PREVIEW REACTIONS (BASIC QUESTION OR COMMENTS ON PURPOSE):

▶   REACTIONS AFTER READING:

Did previewing narratives make you feel uncomfortable? If so, the reason may be that you have learned from experience that you often spoil the fun of reading a *fictitious narrative* when you read the ending before finding out what events lead up to it. This book does not recommend the previewing approach for fiction (see Chapter 8). Of course, you cannot always tell when you have found a work of fiction just by glancing at a title or by skimming a selection. (Sometimes you can tell by knowing something about the publication it appears in or about the reputation of the author.) Therefore, you will need to decide for yourself whether or not to use the previewing method when you run across a work that you think might be imaginative rather than factual. But for selections you have reason to think are non-fiction narratives, the previewing method can be a very useful way of getting started. There is one exception—the news story.

A Special Kind of Non-fiction Narrative: The News Story

Writers of conventional news stories make use of a pattern that has been specially designed to make previewing unnecessary. Although this pattern is basically chronological, it includes an opening paragraph providing *general* answers to many questions a reader might ask—not only *What* happened? but *Who* did it? *When, how,* and *where* did it happen? and perhaps *Why* did it happen? or *Why* is it important? Even the headline (the "title") of a news story often answers some of these questions. By noting the headline and the first paragraph, then, a hurried newspaper reader can get the most important information in a story and decide whether he has the time and interest to read on for details.

Even if you take this method of reading a news story for granted (and many readers do), it will be helpful to find out how much information you do get from the "head" and "lead" of a typical news story and how much you miss if you stop there.

Read the following news story headline and first paragraph, noting the ways they answer these questions: Who? and How? and Why did it happen? (When? and Where? are covered in the date line, as is customary.) Then list specific questions these portions of the story bring to mind, questions you think the remainder of the story will answer.

AFTER 30 YEARS, WORLD WAR II ENDS FOR A JAPANESE STRAGGLER

from The Washington Post, *March 11, 1974*

LUBANG ISLAND, Philippines, March 10—World War II officially ended for a Japanese straggler today, his 52nd birthday, when he formally surrendered, concluding a 30-year obedience to his commander's order to stay put "even when their units have been destroyed."

▶   SPECIFIC QUESTIONS:

The headline of this story is written in the attention-getting and metaphorical way that many newspaper headlines are. It plants the question: How could World War II have "ended" for one Japanese soldier thirty years after his country was defeated? And the answer the lead paragraph gives is a very general one: This soldier surrendered in the Philippines after following his commander's order to the letter for thirty years.

The paragraph does *not* tell you what the man's name is, where he has been all this time, why he did not surrender when almost all the other soldiers eventually did, how he became convinced that he should give up now, or how the news of his belated surrender was received in Japan. You may have listed some of these questions, all of which are answered in the completed story that follows.

> Lt. Hiroo Onoda came out of the jungle after his wartime commander, ex-maj. Yoshimi Taniguehi, showed him a copy of Emperor Hirohito's 1945 surrender order and finally convinced him the war was over.
>
> An Information Department spokesman said Onoda was given permission to retrieve his sword and other military equipment he had concealed on the island 75 miles southwest of Manila.
>
> In Tokyo the parents of the lost soldier burst into tears when they heard he was safe and apparently well.
>
> They had been formally notified long ago that he was dead. Onoda's 86-year-old father said today he would now show his son his tombstone near Tokyo. It reads, "Hiroo Onoda died on the island of Lubang on May 8, 1954."
>
> The beginning of the end of Onoda's war came last month when he met a camping Japanese student, Norio Suzuki, 24. The soldier confided that he would come out of hiding only if ordered personally by his commanding officer.
>
> Maj. Taniguchi had ordered Onoda to stay on the island and spy on the enemy in 1944.
>
> The soldier's 88-year-old mother said that training she gave her son made him obey that order for three decades.
>
> Maj. Taniguchi, 63, and Suzuki had camped in the jungle since Monday, waiting for Onoda to emerge.
>
> A Japanese embassy spokesman said Onoda spent last night at their camp, and this morning a Japanese flag was hoisted to signal to a nearby observation post that Onoda was ready to give up.
>
> This morning the three men walked out of the jungle to Lubang Air Force Base where they were met by Onoda's 62-year-

old brother Toshiro, a physician. An embassy spokesman said he would give the soldier a preliminary examination before he flew to Manila for another medical.

Onoda, with his arms on Toshiro's shoulder, said, "I am sorry I disturbed you all for such a long time."

Two years ago Onoda and another World War II Japanese soldier, Kinshichi Kozuka were involved in a gun fight with a police patrol. Kozuka was killed, but Onoda, reportedly wounded, fled back into the jungle. Since then the Japanese government mounted a search for him which cost $32,000 before the current expedition began.

As far as is known, Onoda is the last Japanese World War II straggler on Lubang.

Writers of news stories, then, modify the *narrative* pattern in a way that is appropriate for the material they handle and the readers they serve.

FINDING PATTERNS IN ARTICLES ANSWERING WHY?

When you find yourself asking "Why?" in response to a title or another early signal, you are recognizing the writer's intention to express his *point of view* on his subject. And when you discover that a work answering that question is written in a form other than narrative, you know that the writer's organization will be based on his *reasons* for thinking as he does. But until you have carefully previewed the selection, using a technique like that suggested in Chapter Four, you can have no way of knowing what pattern the writer will use in presenting those reasons. You can assume, though, that it will turn out to be a variation of one of two basic patterns: development by *contrast* or development by *direct support of thesis*.

The Contrast Pattern

If the development is by contrast, the writer's purpose is probably to show how his view of his subject differs from the view most people have or how his subject differs from something most people know well. In key portions of the essay or article he will probably signal not only his subject and his point of view but his specific purpose as well.

Preview the following essay, using the question–survey–question method. After you have completed the survey, state the writer's basic question in the most specific way you can. You may find that your question implies an answer making use of the contrast the writer intends to develop. (Note: The introduction to this essay is especially long, and the concluding paragraph is an unusually complete summary of the writer's position.)

THE LANGUAGE OF SOUL

by Claude Brown

from Esquire, *April 1968*

Perhaps the most soulful word in the world is "nigger." Despite its very definite fundamental meaning (the Negro man), and disregarding the deprecatory connotation of the term, "nigger" has a multiplicity of nuances when used by soul people. Dictionaries define the term as being synonymous with Negro, and they generally point out that it is regarded as a vulgar expression. Nevertheless, to those of chitlins-and-neck-bones background the word nigger is neither a synonym for Negro nor an obscene expression.

"Nigger" has virtually as many shades of meaning in Colored English as the demonstrative pronoun "that," prior to application to a noun. To some Americans of African ancestry (I avoid using the term Negro whenever feasible, for fear of offending the Brothers X, a pressure group to be reckoned with), nigger seems preferable to Negro and has a unique kind of sentiment attached to it. This is exemplified in the frequent—and perhaps even excessive—usage of the term to denote either fondness or hostility.

It is probable that numerous transitional niggers and even established ex-soul brothers can—with pangs of nostalgia—reflect upon a day in the lollipop epoch of lives when an adorable lady named Mama bemoaned her spouse's fastidiousness with the strictly secular utterance: "Lord, how can one nigger be so hard to please?" Others are likely to recall a time when that drastically lovable colored woman, who was forever wiping our noses and darning our clothing, bellowed in a moment of exasperation: "Nigger, you gonna be the death o' me." And some of the brethren who have had the precarious fortune to be raised up, wised up, thrown up or simply left alone to get up as best they could, on one of the nation's South Streets or Lenox Avenues, might remember having affectionately referred to a best friend as "My nigger."

The vast majority of "back-door Americans" are apt to agree with Webster—a nigger is simply a Negro or black man. But the really profound contemporary thinkers of this distinguished ethnic group—Dick Gregory, Redd Foxx, Moms Mabley, Slappy White, etc.—are likely to differ with Mr. Webster and define nigger as "something else"—a soulful "something else." The major difference between the nigger and the Negro, who have many traits in common, is that the nigger is the more soulful.

Certain foods, customs and artistic expressions are associated almost solely with the nigger: collard greens, neck bones, hog maws, black-eyed peas, pigs' feet, etc. A nigger has no desire to conceal or disavow any of these favorite dishes or restrain other behavioral practices such as bobbing his head, patting his feet to funky jazz, and shouting and jumping in church. This is not to be construed that all niggers eat chitlins and shout in church, nor that only niggers eat the aforementioned dishes and exhibit this type of behavior. It is to say, however, that the soulful usage of the term nigger implies all of the foregoing and considerably more.

The Language of Soul—or, as it might also be called, Spoken Soul or Colored English—is simply an honest vocal portrayal of black America. The roots of it are more than three hundred years old.

Before the Civil War there were numerous restrictions placed on the speech of slaves. The newly arrived Africans had the problem of learning to speak a new language, but also there were inhibitions placed on the topics of the slaves' conversation by slave masters and overseers. The slaves made up songs to inform one another of, say, the underground railroads' activity. When they sang *Steal Away* they were planning to steal away to the North, not to heaven. Slaves who dared to speak of rebellion or even freedom usually were severely punished. Consequently, Negro slaves were compelled to create a semi-clandestine vernacular in the way that the criminal underworld has historically created words to confound law-enforcement agents. It is said that numerous Negro spirituals were inspired by the hardships of slavery, and that what later became songs were initially moanings and coded cotton-field lyrics. To hear these songs sung today by a talented soul brother or sister or by a group is to be reminded of an historical spiritual bond that cannot be satisfactorily described by the mere spoken word.

The American Negro, for virtually all of his history, has constituted a vastly disproportionate number of the country's illiterates. Illiteracy has a way of showing itself in all attempts at vocal expression by the uneducated. With the aid of colloquialisms, malapropisms, battered and fractured grammar, and a considerable amount of creativity, Colored English, the sound of soul, evolved.

The progress has been cyclical. Often terms that have been discarded from the soul people's vocabulary for one reason or another are reaccepted years later, but usually with completely different meaning. In the Thirties and Forties "stuff" was used to mean vagina. In the middle Fifties it was revived and used to refer to heroin. Why certain expressions are thus reactivated is practically an indeterminable question. But it is not difficult to see why certain terms are dropped from the soul language. Whenever a soul term becomes popular with whites it is common practice for the soul folks to relinquish it. The reasoning is that "if white people can use it, it isn't hip enough for me." To many soul brothers there is just no such creature as a genuinely hip white person. And there is nothing more detrimental to anything hip than to have it fall into the square hands of the hopelessly unhip.

White Americans wrecked the expression "something else." It was bad enough that they couldn't say "sump'n else," but they weren't even able to get out "somethin' else." They had to go around saying *something else* with perfect or nearly perfect enuciation. The white folks invariably fail to perceive the soul in soulful terms. They get hung up in diction and grammar, and when they vocalize the expression it's no longer a soulful thing. In fact, it can be asserted that spoken soul is more of a sound than a language. It generally possesses a pronounced lyrical quality which is frequently incompatible to any music other than that ceaseless and relentlessly driving rhythm that flows from poignantly spent lives. Spoken soul has a way of coming out metered without the intention of the speaker to invoke it. There are specific phonetic traits. To the soulless ear the vast majority of these sounds are dismissed as incorrect usage of the English language and, not infrequently, as speech impediments. To those so blessed as to have had bestowed upon them at birth the lifetime gift of soul, these are the most communicative and meaningful sounds ever to fall upon human ears: the familiar "mah" instead of "my," "gonna" for "going to," "yo' for "your." "Ain't" is pronounced "ain"; "bread" and "bed," "bray-ud" and "bay-ud"; "baby" is never "bay-bee" but "bay-buh"; Sammy Davis, Jr., is not "Sammee" but a kind of "Sam-eh"; the same goes for "Eddeh" Jefferson. No matter how many "man's" you put into your talk, it isn't soulful unless the word has the proper plaintive, nasal "maee-yun."

Spoken soul is distinguished from slang primarily by the fact that the former lends itself easily to conventional English, and the latter is diametrically opposed to adaptations within the realm of conventional English. Police (pronounced pō'lice) is a soul term, whereas "The Man" is merely slang for the same thing. Negroes seldom adopt slang terms from the white world and when they do the terms are usually given a different meaning. Such was the case with the term "bag." White racketeers used it in the Thirties to refer to the graft that was paid to the police. For the past five years soul people have used it when referring to a person's vocation, hobby, fancy, etc. And once the appropriate term is given the treatment (soul vocalization) it becomes soulful.

However, borrowings from spoken soul by white men's slang —particularly teen-age slang—are plentiful. Perhaps because soul is probably the most graphic language of modern times, everybody who is excluded from Soulville wants to usurp it, ignoring the formidable fettering to the soul folks that has brought the language about. Consider "uptight," "strung-out," "cop," "boss," "kill 'em," all now widely used outside Soulville. Soul people never question the origin of a slang term; they either dig it and make it a part of their vocabulary or don't and forget it. The expression "uptight," which meant being in financial straits, appeared on the soul scene in the general vicinity of 1953. Junkies were very fond of the word and used it literally to describe what was a perpetual condition with them. The word was pictorial and pointed; therefore it caught on quickly in Soulville across the country. In the early Sixties when "uptight" was on the move, a younger generation of soul people in the black urban communities along the Eastern Seaboard regenerated it with a new meaning: "everything is cool, under control, going my way." At present the term has the former meaning for the older generation and the latter construction for those under thirty years of age.

It is difficult to ascertain if the term "strung-out" was coined by junkies or just applied to them and accepted without protest. Like the term "uptight" in its initial interpretation, "strung-out" aptly described the constant plight of the junkie. "Strung-out" had a connotation of hopeless finality about it. "Uptight" implied a temporary situation and lacked the overwhelming despair of "strung-out."

The term "cop," (meaning "to get"), is an abbreviation of the word "copulation." "Cop," as originally used by soulful teen-agers in the early Fifties, was deciphered to mean sexual coition, nothing more. By 1955 "cop" was being uttered throughout national Soulville as a synonym for the verb "to get," especially in reference to illegal purchases, drugs, pot, hot goods, pistols, etc. ("Man, where can I cop now?") But by 1955 the meaning was all-encompassing. Anything that could be obtained could be "copped."

The word "boss," denoting something extraordinarily good or great, was a redefined term that had been popular in Soulville during the Forties and Fifties as a complimentary remark from one soul brother to another. Later it was replaced by several terms such as "groovy," "tough," "beautiful" and, most recently, "out of sight." This last expression is an outgrowth of the former term "way out," the meaning of which was equivocal. "Way out" had an ad hoc hickish ring to it which made it intolerably unsoulful and consequently it was soon replaced by "out of sight," which is also likely to experience a relatively brief period of popular usage. "Out of sight" is better than "way out," but it has some of the same negative, childish taint of its predecessor.

The expression, "kill 'em," has neither a violent nor a malicious interpretation. It means "good luck," "give 'em hell," or "I'm pulling for you," and originated in Harlem from six to nine years ago.

There are certain classic soul terms which, no matter how often borrowed, remain in the canon and are reactivated every so often, just as standard jazz tunes are continuously experiencing renaissances. Among the classical expressions are: "solid," "cool," "jive" (generally as a noun) "stuff," "thing," "swing" (or "swinging"), "pimp," "dirt," "freak," "heat," "larceny," "busted," "okee doke," "piece," "sheet" (a jail record), "squat," "square," "stash," "lay," "sting," "mire," "gone," "smooth," "joint," "blow," "play," "shot," and there are many more.

Soul language can be heard in practically all communities throughout the country, but for pure, undiluted spoken soul one must go to Soul Street. There are several. Soul is located at Seventh and "T" in Washington, D.C.; on One Two Five Street in New York City; on Springfield Avenue in Newark; on South Street in

Philadelphia; on Tremont Street in Boston; on Forty-seventh Street in Chicago; on Fillmore in San Francisco; and dozens of similar locations in dozens of other cities.

As increasingly more Negroes desert Soulville for honorary membership in the Establishment clique, they experience a metamorphosis, the repercussions of which have a marked influence on the young and impressionable citizens of Soulville. The expatriates of Soulville are often greatly admired by the youth of Soulville, who emulate the behavior of such expatriates as Nancy Wilson, Ella Fitzgerald, Eartha Kit, Lena Horne, Diahann Carroll, Billy Daniels, or Leslie Uggams. The result—more often than not—is a trend away from spoken soul among the young soul folks. This abandoment of the soul language is facilitated by the fact that more Negro youngsters than ever are acquiring college educations (which, incidentally, is not the best treatment for the continued good health and growth of soul); integration and television, too, are contributing significantly to the gradual demise of spoken soul.

Perhaps colleges in America should commence to teach a course in spoken soul. It could be entitled the Vocal History of Black America, or simply Spoken Soul. Undoubtedly there would be no difficulty finding teachers. There are literally thousands of these experts throughout the country whose talents lie idle while they await the call to duty.

Meanwhile the picture looks dark for soul. The two extremities in the Negro spectrum—the conservative and the militant— are both trying diligently to relinquish and repudiate whatever vestige they may still possess of soul. The semi-Negro—the soul brother intent on gaining admission to the Establishment even on an honorary basis— is anxiously embracing and assuming conventional English. The other extremity, the Ultra-Blacks, are frantically adopting everything from a Western version of Islam that would shock the Caliph right out of his snugly fitting shintiyan to anything that vaguely hints of that big, beautiful, bountiful black bitch lying in the arms of the Indian and Atlantic Oceans and crowned by the majestic Mediterranean Sea. Whatever the Ultra-Black is after, it's anything but soulful.

▶ BASIC QUESTION:

Of course, the obvious question this title suggests is: What is the language of soul? That may well have been the first question you asked before you previewed. But the highly abstract and emotion-charged word "soul" may have raised some why questions too, questions like: Why does the writer call the speech of black people "soul" language? and Why is the term "language" justified at all? (Don't black people speak English?) In your previewing you found that these questions are answered in the essay. Your basic question, then, may have been something like: Why is "the language of soul" a better way for black people to talk than any other form of speech? Or simply: How does "soul talk" differ from "conventional" English?

Now read the article through, looking for an answer to your question (or to one of the above questions). When you have finished, use the space below to list in your own words the main points the writer makes in support of his thesis. (His thesis statement, as you may have noted, is the first sentence in the sixth paragraph: "The Language of Soul—or, as it might also be called, Spoken Soul or Colored English—is simply an honest vocal portrayal of black America.") As you make your list, keep in mind Brown's emphasis on contrasting "soul" with non-soul English. After you have made your responses, check them with the list in Chapter Supplement III (p. 231).

▶   MAIN SUPPORTING IDEAS:

The writer's purpose in this essay is to show that what he calls "soul language" is not just a casual, misshapen form of standard English but a separate speech system with deep and important roots in the culture of black America. Although Brown does not specify at the beginning that he is using the contrast pattern, this organization is at least hinted at in the title and is clearly implied in the concluding paragraph. If you did not fully anticipate the pattern when you previewed the selection, at least you probably had no difficulty following it once you got beyond the long introduction.

The Thesis-Support Pattern

Sometimes a writer answers the question Why? in an even more direct way. Using the thesis-support pattern, he begins either with a thesis statement or with an example leading up to one. Next he provides at least a hint of the ground he is going to cover, of the kind of supporting evidence he will use. Then, in the main part of the work, he takes up his principal supporting points one by one, giving examples for each.

In the following essay, for example, the writer makes no reference to any viewpoint other than his own. He begins with a direct statement of his position and continues by offering supporting reasons and examples. Yet you may discover that the ideas he expresses are very different from any you have thought or heard or read. If that happens, you could be faced with the problem of resisting what communications specialists call psychological interference or "noise." That is, you might want to "listen" to your own ideas on the subject rather than to the writer's—to read what you would have written instead of what he wrote. Or, if you recognized that you were not on familiar ground, you might be tempted to dismiss the writer as "crazy" or to assign to him a more extreme position than the one he holds.

In any kind of reading, the way to avoid being distracted by "noise" is to follow the writer's signals thoughtfully from his title through his last word. It is especially important that you learn to do this when you read a work like this one—a selection straightforwardly presenting arguments for a position (support for a thesis) you may never have been exposed to.

When you finish reading the essay, you will have an opportunity to write a brief summary of the writer's ideas in your own words and to compare your summary with one in the chapter supplement. There is no better way to find out whether you have understood a writer's opinions than to try to summarize them in your own words. One caution: Despite the perhaps casual-sounding title, you may find the vocabulary of this work more abstract than that of any other selection in this chapter. Before you write your summary, take time to determine the meanings of words by noting contextual clues or by checking a dictionary. Again, it will be a good idea to use the Question–Survey–Question–Read–Re-Read approach.

THE TYRANNY
OF DEMOCRATIC MANNERS

by Morton Cronin

from The New Republic, *January 20, 1958*

I maintain that democratic manners—typified by the practice of calling the boss by his first name—have reached the point in our country where they conduce not to the preservation of personal dignity but to the abject submission of one man to another. These manners, gradually developed in colonial and post-revolutionary days, worked well in a society largely of self-sufficient farmers. But circumstances have changed, with the usual ironical result.

What happens on the job at the present time? An employee greets the boss by his first name, sits down in his presence, wears the same kind of clothes the boss wears, avoids the use of *sir*, and ostensibly comports himself in general as if he and the boss were as equal as two farmers. But he and the boss are not equal, and this inequality must be signalized. It must be signalized, first, because the employee is anxious to please the boss, who can advance or impede his fortunes; and, secondly, because the boss is anxious that his authority receive recognition, without which he cannot function with any confidence.

In the absence of overt and conventional methods of expressing deference, how then does the American employee acknowledge the boss's superior status? He does so by perfecting a subtle repertoire of body movements and vocal expressions. This repertoire includes the boyish grin, the deprecatory cough, the unfinished sentence, the appreciative giggle, the drooping shoulders, the head-scratch and the bottom-waggle. But there are employees, the truly gifted ones—as actors, they would adorn the Stanislavski school—who can dispense with these definable maneuvers and simply *live* the part, their whole being radiating a kind of sweet eloquence of submission.

Now this body language, in both its definable and indefinable forms, is almost impossible to fake successfully, at least in any long-continued relationship. If it is not accompanied quite genuinely by the emotions appropriate to it, it will be contradicted and rendered sinister by involuntary movements and expressions which accord with the individual's true feelings. It is easy to execute a military salute, regardless of one's private thoughts, but the deprecatory cough—to say nothing of the Stanislavski method—requires great sincerity, else they appear villainous.

American manners, in short, decree egalitarian behavior in a hierarchical society. The result is that a subordinate, compelled to behave formally and superficially in a democratic way, is forced in making his adjustments to the facts of life to behave informally and profoundly in a hierarchical way. It should be just the opposite —the system of etiquette ought to furnish him with formal gestures of respect for his superiors and let his informal self work out its own salvation. It should be easier to render the boss what is the boss's without throwing in one's soul too.

Out of a doctrinaire devotion to palsy-walsy manners has sprung that misshapen, anomalous growth, the despotism of the nice guy. It is a truism that success on the job depends less on competence in performing one's duties than it does on ability to Get Along With People. But what is left out of this statement—it is not sporting to mention it—is that the word *People* refers to just one person—the boss. And the boss, barred from receiving any obvious obeisance, is commonly in a chronic state of insecurity—what he craves most of all is the assurance that he is really and truly the boss. The nice guy, with his fine talent for the right body language, provides this assurance better than he man who is merely efficient, is rewarded accordingly, and thus sets the pace for his clumsy fellows.

But the despotism of the nice guy reaches its fully convoluted luxuriance when, as happens, he himself is made the boss. He has not been soft-spoken, unassertive, accommodating and eager to please out of sheer masochism. However various the motives which explain his personality, ambition is one of them. Good Old Charlie likes the idea of being a boss. And if his underlings could give him a snappy salaam every day, all might be well. But Charlie would recoil from anything so Oriental in its disrespect for human dignity. All that he expects is that his subordinates will make the same sensitive, informal adjustments to his person which he used to make for the boss, a process which practically requires that they exchange their personalities for his. Only a few of them are capable of such virtuosity—Charlie's word for it is *loyalty*—but most of them do well enough to demonstrate that it is really the nice guy in authority, more than the rambunctious one, who has made America the natural habitat of the yes-man. Of course the situation is complicated by the fact that Charlie soon becomes pitifully dependent on his loyal supporters, one of whom usually emerges as a split-personality and, like a skillful wife, sweetly dominates Charlie in all things.

Everybody complains that life is too competitive, but our national imagination is so limited that the principal remedies proposed for this or any other social disease are economic remedies—better jobs, better houses, and more social security. However justified on other grounds, these remedies, beyond a certain point, just hot up this particular fire, for life becomes not less competitive but decidedly more so as one moves up the ladder. Naturally. There is more to compete for. But still the fever could be brought down a few points by a modification of manners. Once men acquire everything they need—a condition soon reached in this country—they struggle primarily for recognition. But with manners as frustratingly egalitarian as they are, who knows when he has it made? Under present circumstances the ambitious can discern no resting place short of a crushing superiority of popular fame or material wealth. Hence, the devotion of many originally fine minds to Hollywood, Broadway and the medical profession.

Consider, for instance, the folly of our disparagement of honorific titles. If a mayor were regularly addressed as *Your Honor,* and could count on this distinction after leaving office, he would be heartened in his efforts to remain honest. As it is, he must play it democratic, pooh-pooh his title, and prepare against the day when, defeated for re-election, he must face the indifference of the public at large. Mayors are commonly corrupt, judges rarely. But judges are unfailingly objects of formal homage in office, and keep their titles for life.

The sobriquets which used to attach to politicians—*Old Hickory, Tennessee Johnson, The Little Giant, The Plumed Knight*—conferred distinction. They were titles of a sort and reflected a popular disposition to honor character, individuality and superior force in public men. But now the popular taste, encouraged by gee-whiz politicians who tutoyer one another in public, is for first names and demure diminutives—*Ike, Dick, Stu, Bob, Estes* and *Foster.* What makes these familiarities characteristic of our time is precisely that they ignore what is distinctive in either the personalities or the duties of the men they designate and thus suggest that government is best which is managed by Good Joes recently graduated from a basketball team. If Woodrow Wilson were in politics today, he would probably have to submit to *Woody* —if not *Willie*—and wipe that purposeful and responsible look off his face.

But the avoidance of titles of respect is equally the fashion among highbrows. Professors in famous universities, for instance, make fun of their fellows in teachers' colleges because the latter often call one another *professor* or *doctor*, instead of plain *mister*, and are notorious for responding benignly when their students use these terms. But on this point it is the prominent professors whose perception is defective, for an examination of their total behavior reveals that they are much less democratic than those they smile at for putting on airs. Occupying positions in institutions of outstanding prestige—positions for which they have scrambled ferociously—they can afford to underemphasize their status, like wealthy men who insist that their limousines be inconspicuously black. The fact is that they maintain great distance between town and gown and also between their students and themselves.

Many of them deplore their remoteness, but without an improvement of manners there is little they can do about it. Since they discourage formal acknowledgements of their status, any meeting between them and townfolk, or even between them and their own students, imposes on both sides such a strain on their respective capacities for the appropriate body language that it is almost unbearable. The man at Lower South Central Normal suffers his students to call him professor—doctor—sir—but he can often be observed chatting loftily and genially among them, snapping his suspenders the while, undisturbed by their politely impudent questions.

But the deprecation of titles and of formal manners in general characterizes all sorts of highbrows, not just those in universities. Yet no group in America complains so clamorously that it is not sufficiently respected and appreciated. And those among them who complain most bitterly are the ones who embrace the mucker pose passionately, not only in their speech and manners but even in their dress. This furious contradiction necessitates a furious resolution. Men who will not permit their attainments to be recognized conventionally and symbolically will seek such recognition radically and violently.

But democratic manners have not promoted unnatural relations among men in their economic and professional careers. They have also corrupted relations between men and women in their romantic and domestic lives. Here, however, the democratization of manners has been one-sided. Many suitable formalities still govern the man's behavior— he follows a woman through a door, sashays around to the gutter-side of the street, etc., etc., in all of which he pays decorous tribute to her as a woman. But our culture has relieved her almost entirely of any reciprocal gestures of conventional tribute to him as a man. She does not curtsy, nor use respectful forms of address, nor stand at his shoulder when he has his picture taken. Her grandmother practiced a sweet, conventional smile. She grins, laughs uproariously, and talks in a loud voice.

For her the emphasis is now completely on body language—but, unlike that used by men with their bosses, hers is *challenging* rather than deferential.

Since he does not receive from women any standard courtesies, courtesies which, besides telling him that just being a man is a thing of some consequence, would remind him of his responsibilities, the Amercan male gravitates in his dealings with women toward one of two roles—that of a little boy or that of a predator. Frequently he ricochets between the two. In the first role he simply abandons the effort to command respect as a male and, oddly enough, often becomes an abstract enthusiast for women, like a dull student whose every humiliation in class somehow increases his school spirit. In the role of predator he compels specific respect for himself as a man in the one decisive way that is still open. And, fortunately or unfortunately, such consolation has grown steadily more available. Women as well as men are symbolic creatures, and the radical elimination of ceremony reduces the human element in them and increases the animal part. Frustrated in her naturally human desire to express her feelings formally and stylistically, the American woman must express them directly and elementally.

But the inhuman effects of democratic manners afflict another fundamental relationship, that between parents and children. They spawn the ultimate in absurdity in those instances where parents, assuming the character of domestic politicians, encourage their youngsters to abjure the use of *mother* and *father* in favor of their parent's first names. The trouble with *mother* and *father* of course is that they suggest authority (as well as love), and thus strike an undemocratic note in the family. Often the parents' real motives, like those of tail-wagging politicians, are more complicated, for people who shun authoritative titles commonly shrink from responsibility too. But they could not persevere in this self-deception if our dedication to democratic manners did not furnish them with an exalted rationale.

Fortunately, this first-name business for parents is as yet limited. But manners generally are primitive enough in American homes, as anyone knows who accepts invitations from his friends to dine *en famille*. It is undemocratic to set up a children's table. It is also undemocratic to encourage children to listen to adult conversation. Parents and guests, consequently, listen to children's conversation. During intervals—when little mouths happen simultaneously to be stuffed up with food, for instance—the parents inevitably discuss the subject of children. Children, they tell you, are *people*. The children express themselves. The parents preen themselves. The only person who does not get a piece of this democracy is the guest. This lopsided egalitarianism even favors dogs and cats, with whom a guest must often cope with no assistance whatever from his host. They too, it seems, are *people*.

I have nearly finished. But I know that some fool—most likely, one with a Ph.D.—will read this article and forever after assert as a well-known fact that I yearn for a restoration of Tsardom, for a reinvigoration of the Hindu caste system and for a truly Chinese subjugation of women and children. So let me recapitulate, in the course of which I shall add one or two points that I forgot to mention earlier.

A sensible system of manners, sensibly formal, performs various services. Besides acting as a constant reminder of some important facts of life, it affords human beings the distinctly human satisfactions of symbolic expression. Besides making collective living possible, it provides a person, thanks to its formalities, with protective armor against collective pressures. For these formalities allow the individual to acquiesce in the social order while reserving his final judgment of it. They enable him to pledge his loyalty to men in authority without making those fine adjustments whose long-term results are the same as those of brainwashing.

Democratic manners in America are eating the heart out of American democracy. With no impressive way of saluting the system, and the position which a given official occupies in it, one must prostrate himself before the man. There is a country where such prostration is even more prostrate than in America. There the humblest citizen calls his mighty ruler *comrade*.

I suggest a prudent reform in American manners, not a revolution. If the only alternative to egalitarian manners is a nerveless society exhausted by protocol and ceremony, then this discussion is futile. But that is not the only alternative, except in the minds of latter-day Jacobins for whom the stratifications of the *ancien regime* are more real than the proletarianizations of their own time. There are in-between solutions, attuned to reality, however they resist simple and consistent formulation, as the English know, and as America, in her own fashion, can discover. Pedantic democrats presume to speak for wisdom, creative ability and service, as against mere money in the bank. But without a rectification of manners most men would rather achieve a Cadillac than such virtues, for these virtues, unacknowledged in any regular way, do not show on a man, at least not conspicuously, whereas a Cadillac shows on anyone, conspicuously.

▶ SUMMARY:

(See summary in Chapter Supplement IV, p. 232.)

If you covered most of the points treated in the chapter supplement summary and if you included a sentence or sentences stating the thesis of the essay, your summary is probably satisfactory. If you did not, try re-reading the essay, noting especially the first paragraph and the last two, where you will find the writer's main ideas stated.

You have discovered, then, that before you get very far into a non-fiction selection it is helpful to find out what organizing principle the writer has used in putting the work together. Sometimes, especially when you are reading works covering subject matter that is not highly abstract, the organizing principle is implied so clearly in the title or in other early signals that you hardly need to look for it at all. But when you approach more abstract writing, it is helpful to use the Question–Survey–Question method you learned in Chapter Four, adding a look for the writer's *pattern of organization* to the techniques that were covered there.

The patterns that are treated in this chapter are commonly used by writers of the kinds of short non-fiction you will be reading in college. (Some other patterns, most of which are variations of these, probably have been covered or will be covered in your freshman composition course.)

As you preview, it will be a good idea for a while to consciously practice identifying patterns that are not completely obvious at first glance. Soon you will get to the point where you can almost unconsciously (or at least without much conscious effort) discover patterns as well as main ideas and points of view in your previewing. And probably the more quickly you can understand the organizational pattern of a non-fiction piece, the more time you will have to concentrate on other important features of the work—like those that will be discussed in the next chapter.

CHAPTER SUPPLEMENTS

I. Answer to Questions on "Folk Art in the Barrios"

1. They are young Chicanos from the barrios (Mexican-American sections) of Santa Fe, New Mexico. Some names that are mentioned are Carlo, Albert, and Sammy Leyba, and Geronimo Gardunio; but do not be concerned if you did not remember names. For most of the purposes you could have in reading an article like this, names would be unimportant.
2. See 1 above.
3. The name of the group is Los Artes Guadalupanos de Aztlan, shortened to Los Artes. (If you do not know Spanish, you could not be expected to remember the full name.)
4. It was financed originally by a local methadone center and by a grant from the Office of Economic Opportunity. However, now the artists receive no financial aid for their work; they support themselves through other jobs.
5. They paint murals on the outside walls of Chicano-owned buildings and on those of some municipal buildings (a high school and a health clinic).

6. They do not sign their work, and they do not accept assignments painting for private (and presumably wealthy) citizens for pay.
7. One painting proudly displays Aztec gods and medicine men protecting peasants; others show the Mexican leaders Pancho Villa and Father Hidalgo leading the peasants to freedom.
8. These paintings show Chicano people suffering—in chains or in army uniforms, for example. (You might also have mentioned that the writer shows that these artists are indebted to modern Mexican painters like Diego Rivera and Jose Orozco, artists who have depicted the struggles of repressed Mexican people.)
9. The article points out that these artists are very interested in the artistic development of young people in the Chicano community. (They plan to offer art classes for children.) This concern certainly shows hope for the future. Also, many of their paintings show people breaking away from the bonds that have held them.

II. Purpose and Development in Narratives

1. "I Discover My Father": It may have been difficult to think of a specific basic question for this one (although the title could have suggested something to you like: In what sense did he "discover" his father? or Why was it necessary to "discover" his father?) What is important is that you realized, through previewing, that as Anderson is telling his story he develops an important idea in a subtle and light-hearted way. He prefaces his story with a paragraph explaining his early dissatisfaction with his father and concludes with one *implying* that he learned to appreciate his father's individuality. But he does not state this idea in so many words; in other words, he *develops an implied idea.*
2. "Bicycle Tour Through Baja del Sur": The Davises stick to the details of their trip almost all the way through their article. Although the underlined last sentence implies the judgment that the trip was fun, the narrative has little opinion or personal feeling in it. The article is about as "straight" a report of "what happened" as anything you are likely to read.
3. "The Dying Girl That No One Helped": The author states his thesis specifically in the first paragraph and then illustrates it with the narrative that follows. The underlined phrase in the first sentence is a somewhat sarcastic understatement. The second sentence, particularly the last part of it, is a thesis statement worded in highly emotive language. And the last sentence of the last paragraph repeats the thesis, this time put in the words of a participant (or a non-participant) in the events the story concerns.

III. Main Supporting Ideas in "The Language Of Soul"

Your list should have included some of these ideas:
1. Black English has a long history that separates it from "standard" English. It has origins in the feelings and the problems of the black people of slavery times, a people with whom today's black speakers can readily identify.

2. The "sound of soul" has a special quality that reflects the illiterate background of its people. Throughout the years, "soul language" has kept a distance from standard English by dropping an expression whenever the white world has begun to use it widely; in this way the language has remained "hip."
3. Standard English frequently makes room for slang expressions that are borrowed from "soul" speech, but the meanings of these expressions usually change as they move over.
4. "Pure soul" is becoming rare because of two trends Brown deplores: Conservative black people are adopting the language habits of the white establishment, and militant blacks are turning to Africa and the Middle East for models.

IV. A Summary of "The Tyranny Of Democratic Manners"

Cronin is concerned about a trend he finds in American society today—the tendency of people in positions of authority to encourage their subordinates to avoid language forms and other symbols that communicate respect. Many employers, for example, like to have their employees call them by their first names; public figures spurn old-fashioned designations like "your Honor"; many college professors discourage people from calling them "doctor" or "professor." Some parents encourage their children to call them by their first names; and husbands, although they sometimes still open the door for their wives, do not expect any kind of show of respect in return. The effect of this kind of behavior is to make people uneasy in their relationships with one another. Hierarchies exist in American society as in all societies, and they should be given symbolic recognition. What happens when they are not is that the person in authority who does not get easy, superficial, ritualistic recognition for his position and accomplishments seeks this recognition in other ways—the boss by expecting his employees to be "yes men," the business man (whatever his place in his company's hierarchy) by becoming materialistic; the professor by being remote and stuffy in his relationships with students and with townspeople; and parents by boring guests with defensive tales about how wonderful their children are. Much of this socially undesirable behavior could be avoided if Americans would only be willing to return to some of the old-fashioned symbols (especially words and phrases) that indicate respect for authority and position.

Note: The underlined sentences together are a statement of the writer's thesis.

reading
beneath the lines—
for tone, inferences,
and assumptions

This chapter examines some kinds of signals that can lead you "beneath the lines" of non-fiction and shows you how far down into the writer's thinking they can take you if you are not distracted by "noise." It includes some complete short works and some passages from non-fiction books. All these selections illustrate devices and methods you should be familiar with if you want to be able to recognize a writer's implications—not just his directly-stated ideas.

TYPES OF LANGUAGE

Emotive Language and Tone

You already know what an effective signal *emotive language* can be. In earlier chapters you have seen that by using this kind of expression in a title, a thesis sentence, or a phrase signaling a main idea, a writer can often suggest more about his *point of view* than he ever tells you directly. And in Chapter Two, through analyzing a chapter in a psychology textbook, you found that writers occasionally use emotive expressions that reveal their points of view even in "objectively" prepared material. In this chapter you will find that a writer sometimes uses emotive language as a basic method of development throughout a passage or a work.

When he does this, he creates a distinctive *tone* (an impression of an underlying attitude or feeling). And you do have to do some reading beneath the lines to understand this tone and the attitude or feeling it represents. An angry writer does not tell you he is angry, nor does a cheerful one say: "Notice how good I feel about all of this." He simply signals his feelings with eye-catching language.

Consider, for example, the following passage from *Soul On Ice* by Eldridge Cleaver. From the time you read the first few words, you will be aware that the writer is developing an idea about which he has very strong feelings. And whether or not you agree with that point of view or share those feelings, the language of the paragraph will almost certainly attract your attention at least as much as its content. To find out whether this is true, try marking especially striking emotive expressions as you read the paragraph (some of these have been underlined for you). Then write a one-sentence summary of the paragraph, being as objective (unemotional) in your wording as you can be. You will probably find an interesting contrast between your version and the original.

By <u>crushing</u> black leaders, while <u>inflating</u> the <u>images</u> of <u>Uncle Toms</u> and celebrities from the apolitical world of sport and play, the mass media were able to <u>channel</u> and <u>control</u> the aspirations and goals of the black masses. The effect was to take the "problem" out of a political and economic and philosophical context and place it on the misty level of "goodwill," "charitable and harmonious race relations," and "good sportsmanlike conduct." This technique of "Negro control" has been so effective that the best-known Negroes in America have always been—and still are—the entertainers and athletes (this is true also of white America). The tradition is that whenever a crisis with racial overtones arises, an entertainer or athlete is trotted out and allowed to expound a predictable, conciliatory interpretation of what's happening. The mass media rush forward with grinding cameras and extended microphones as though some great oracle were about to lay down a new covenant from God; when in reality, all that has happened is that the blacks have been sold out and cooled out again—*"One more time, boom! One more time, boom!"*

(From *Soul On Ice* by Eldridge Cleaver, underlining added)

▶ Summary

(Compare your responses with those in Chapter Supplement I, p. 274.)

The summary sentence in the supplement is written in relatively objective language. Does yours make use of the same kind of restrained wording? If it does, it may get across the basic idea of the original (as the sentence in the chapter supplement does), but it certainly cannot convey Cleaver's feelings. The emotive expressions you underlined and found substitutes for in your summary do that. It is a feeling of anger that lies "beneath the lines" and that is responsible for the *tone* of the paragraph.

If your summary sentence makes use of words and phrases more like Cleaver's, that may be because you either share his feelings or have strong opposing feelings. Like any other writer, you can justify using emotive language if you are prepared to support your emotional appeal with specific evidence. If you expressed strong disagreement with Cleaver, think about the specific reasons you would give if you were asked to explain your position. And if you shared his anger, consider whether you could justify it as effectively as he does his in the passage that follows the quoted paragraph:

> When the question of segregation in the armed services arose during the '40s, the then heavyweight champion of the world, Joe Louis and Louis Satchmo Armstrong, who was also noted for blowing a trumpet, were more likely to be quoted on the subject than A. Philip Randolph or W. E. B. DuBois. And more recently, at the peak of a nationwide epidemic of sit-ins and demonstrations, Attorney General Robert Kennedy called together a group of "influential" Negro entertainers and athletes to meet with him in secret, to get the message from The Man and carry the gospel back to the restless natives.

The last part of this paragraph contains words and phrases that are just as emotive as those you underlined in the first passage—expressions like "the Man" and "gospel" and "restless natives." But remember that the writer's purpose is to express strong feelings. It is certainly appropriate for him to accomplish it by creating an angry *tone* through the use of emotive words and phrases in combination with *factual* or *report* language (names of people and dates of events, for example).

Report Language

This book uses the terms "factual" and "report" to apply to language that *points to* or *counts* specific objects or kinds of objects or places or events. In Chapter Three you found some examples of this kind of wording in the titles of magazine articles. In the following paragraph, taken from a book about the habits and living conditions of whales, you will find many more. Some have been underlined for you; mark any others you become aware of as you read.

Early in the present century a great zoologist began to wonder about the movements of whales. Eventually he learned a great deal about the places where they live though little about the clues that guide them to these places. He was Charles Haskins Townsend, director for thirty-five years of the New York Aquarium. On a visit to the public library in New Bedford, Massachusetts, he found, to his delight, hundreds of logbooks from Yankee whaling ships of bygone years. In the daily journals of life at sea the captains had dutifully entered the date, the bearings, and the species of whales killed.

Townsend realized that by plotting on charts the positions where large numbers of whales had been taken, much could be learned of their distribution and something of their migrations. So he drafted beautiful charts of the world ocean, showing by colored dots the month and the location of whale ships on days when whales were killed. In his labor of love he sifted the records of one hundred and sixty years of whaling, and the capture of more than thirty thousand whales.

(From *The Year of the Whale* by Victor Scheffer)

These words from the passage (in addition to those that are underlined) clearly fit into the above-mentioned categories of factual, or report, language:

thirty-five years	journals
New Bedford, Massachusetts	charts
logbooks	dots
ocean	records
one hundred and sixty years of whaling	whaling ships (whale ship)
thirty thousand whales	captain

If you included terms like "position" and "capture" and "distribution," you were extending the definition of "report" somewhat. Words of .this kind are taken up in the next section under interpretive language. What is more important now, though, is that you realize the difference between the words that are listed above and expressions like "beautiful" and "great" and "dutifully" and "labor of love." Did you sense that these emotive words add a tone of appreciation and respect to what would otherwise be a straight report of Townsend's work?

Interpretive Language

Factual, or report, language is probably more common in scientific writing than in any other kind. But even in the prize-winning scientific book from which the above passage was taken, few paragraphs have as many factual terms as those paragraphs have. The following passage from the book is more typical. As you read it, mark any words or phrases that seem to be quite different from both the emotive expressions you marked in the Cleaver paragraph and the report terms you found in the last passage.

"The swimming speed of whales is impossible," the scientists were wont to say. "By all the laws of physics their energy cannot be sustained." The men pushed wooden models through water courses and clocked the forces entertained. The movement of the whales was still beyond belief. So they made a rubber-plastic whale, a simulated whale with rippling skin—a warm, vibrating counterpart of life. That worked. The motion of its outer surface was the clue: a soft accommodating to the waves, a lack of turbulence; efficiency at peak.

And the sperm whales continue to move at speeds unrealized by man. Through a strong sculling motion of their flukes and a total, compensating motion of their trunks they surge ahead—at twenty knots in panic, under six at ease. Their spouts of air emerge as geysers from the placid sea. They glide along in solitary dignity, then join in lines like cavalry horses of old. They leap, descend, rise, and spout together in joyous mood, easy, regular, majestic. How wonderful are these beasts akin to man.

Did you mark any of the following underlined words and phrases?

"The swimming speed of whales is <u>impossible</u>"
"The movement of the whales was <u>still beyond belief</u>"
"a simulated whale with <u>rippling skin</u>"
"a <u>warm, vibrant counterpart</u> of life"
"a <u>soft accommodating</u> to the waves"
"a lack of <u>turbulence</u>"
"<u>efficiency at peak</u>"
"a <u>strong sculling motion</u>"
"twenty knots in <u>panic</u>"
"under six at <u>ease</u>"

This book labels words and phrases like these *interpretive* expressions. When Scheffer says that whales swim at an "impossible" speed, he means that the speed seems impossible to anyone who knows the laws of physics. When he describes their skin as "rippling," he means that the shape of the skin reminds him of other objects he knows that have ripples. And when he uses the words "turbulence" and "efficiency" to describe the way they move, he reveals how he perceives their motions. With all these expressions, then, he *interprets* his experiences with whales. But, as you have seen, he has been able to pack the passage with specific information, even though not all of the wording is "factual."

Sentences Illustrating the Three Kinds of Language

In both conversation and writing, you will find interpretive language is the most common of the three kinds. Consider, for example, the underlined phrases in the list of sentences below. A few of these are emotive or factual, but most are interpretive. Put "F" beside the ones you consider factual, "E" by the ones you think are emotive, and "I" beside those that seem to interpret the writer or speaker's experiences in ways that are not particularly emotional. Then turn to Chapter Supplement II (p. 275) and compare your classifications with the ones you find there. (The first three are worked out for you below.)

▶ EXPRESSION   CLASSIFICATION

1. My bedroom is exactly <u>16'8" long</u> and   F
   <u>14'3" wide</u>.
2. My zoology professor is the <u>world's lead-</u>   I
   <u>ing authority</u> on the phylum porifera.
3. Suzie Spitzhammer is the prettiest and most   E
   <u>seductive-looking</u> girl in class.
4. If any rock music could be considered
   <u>sweet</u>, it would probably be the music of
   Van Morrison.
5. The difference between a <u>liar</u> and a <u>pre-</u>
   <u>varicator</u> is a difference in <u>social status</u>.
6. Sinclair Lewis, the author of Arrowsmith,
   the <u>greatest American novel ever written</u>
   <u>about a medical doctor</u>, was born in <u>Sauk</u>
   <u>Centre</u>, Minnesota, in <u>1885</u>.
7. A long-distance runner must have plenty of
   <u>strength</u>, <u>endurance</u>, and <u>determination</u>.
8. The senator was well-known for his en-
   dorsement of <u>educational opportunities for</u>
   <u>the culturally disadvantaged</u>.
9. Some people think Marshall McLuhan is an
   <u>oracle</u>; others think his ideas are <u>dangerous</u>.
10. The teacher said that a current <u>fad</u> of young
    people is organic gardening.

Language and Idea Analysis

It is through reading larger units than a sentence or even a paragraph that you can best discover the different ways non-fiction writers use language and begin to understand what happens when you read beneath their lines. Therefore, in this section you are asked to think about the wording as well as about the ideas of three longer pieces—one complete magazine article and two passages from non-fiction books.

Two of the writers have positions or points of view that they try to persuade you to accept; the third is excited about a discovery he has made (a conclusion he has come to) that he wants to share with you. How does each writer's choice of language fit his purpose? Are you conscious of a particular tone in any of the works? Does your awareness of the way the writer uses language affect your acceptance of his idea? When you have finished reading each selection, you will have an opportunity to write your reactions.

FREE THEM ALL:
POW'S AND OTHER CRIMINALS

by Howard Zinn

from Women: A Journal of Liberation, Vol. 3, No. 3

It is good that the American POW's are coming home. They are human beings and they deserve to be free.

And now, why not open the gates of our county and city jails, our state and federal penitentiaries, and liberate those people who are cooped up there, humiliated, separated from the ones they love? Aren't they human beings too, and don't they deserve to be free?

True, these people robbed, or sold drugs, or committed vicious crimes against others. But their acts of violence are small compared with those of the Air Force crewmen who blew up houses, schools, hospitals, kindergartens, city streets, and left men, women, children dead in the rubble, or without arms or legs or eyes. If we can let bygones be bygones with the bombardiers, why not with the thieves and muggers?

We know why.

Because organized society, which deals harshly with certain individual crimes, has always had a soft spot in its heart for war.

Because we care more about law than about life. Acts of assault and murder, done by individuals and mobs outside the law, horrify us. Similar acts, done by uniformed men inside the law, are okay.

Because the fliers are almost all clean-cut, white, educated, middle-class Americans. While the people in jails are white and black and brown and mostly come from the city slums, and don't have much education.

Because the fliers attacked other people, far away, while the men in our jails have assaulted, or robbed, us right here.

Maybe also because we assume fliers have no choice but to follow orders, while ordinary criminals do their bad deeds deliberately, of their own free will. But is there so much difference between them? Don't fliers have at least a bit of free will, and shouldn't we expect of them that they have moral courage to match their physical courage, that they refuse to commit atrocities, as Captain Michael Heck did during the Christmas bombing of Hanoi?

And what about ordinary criminals—aren't they also part of a powerful machine, of money-worship and poverty and slums, which grinds them down and drives them to desperate acts? Sure, we should expect them also to show some moral responsibility. But then, they are not that much different from the fliers. Both surrender, in different ways, to the system.

Well, then, let's punish them all, some might say. The petty criminals of our jails, and the big ones in the war. We can't get the really big ones, the presidents and their advisors who gave the orders to drop bombs on cities, the monopolizers of wealth who create the conditions for petty crimes. We have to put the finger on whomever we can grab in the long chain of guilt. So let's hold war crimes trials for airmen, to match the trials we hold for the felons.

But is revenge justice? Is an eye for an eye justice? Or is that adding one injustice to another? Isn't punishment itself—locking someone up like an animal in a cage, depriving that person of human companionship—one of the worst of crimes? Karl Menninger wrote, in his book "The Crime of Punishment": "I suspect that all the crimes committed by all the jailed criminals do not equal in total social damage that of the crimes committed against them."

And if we have such compassion for the bombers, we must have it for the felons. Free them from slavery. For they are slaves as surely as were the Blacks of American history—and where are their abolitionists? The old arguments used to keep Blacks in chains are used to keep these people where they are: They are sub-human; they must be controlled; they are dangerous if free.

Isn't that true? Aren't those people in our prisons dangerous? Well, some of them probably are. But most of them never hurt anyone; they were desperate for money and they stole, as Rockefeller and the other robber barons of America have always done without spending a day in jail. Yes, they might steal again.

But the fliers are dangerous too. They are back in the military, ready to fly Phantom jets and B-52s again, ready to bomb the next cities declared enemy targets by the man in the White House. They are dangerous to the women and children, and the men, of any miserable part of the world that decides to rebel— as the Vietnamese did—against tyranny.

Dangerous as the fliers are, they should still be free. Because keeping them in prison will not stop the war crimes; the Pentagon can train fliers as fast as they can be shot down. The only way the children of the world can be safe from bombing is to do away with the political and economic systems that cause war, do away with nationalist hatred and all its symbols and institutions: the flags, uniforms, medals, armies, pledges of allegiance.

The same goes for the muggers and thieves and drug addicts, the murderers, who inhabit our prisons. Keeping them in jail does not make us more safe, because our culture of money and violence creates criminals faster than judges can lock them up. In fact, it makes us less safe, because it deceives us into thinking we are solving the problem of crime. It keeps us from facing a hard truth: people will rob and kill for money as long as we have a system like this, where life is a fierce battle for money, where some end up with most of it, and others with very little, where successful crooks are invited to the White House, and unsuccessful ones go to jail.

If we got rid of our prisons, we would be forced to begin the transformation of society, so that we could finally be safe from criminals, small and big. A society that has greedy corporations must have petty thieves. A society that engages in the violence of war abroad must endure assault and murder at home.

We could start by freeing all prisoners who (by decision of some citizens' committee of doctors and social workers) are not immediate and present dangers to other people. The only ones to be kept under guard would be those very few prisoners who are psychotically violent. The others are like the rest of us who are not in prison: if they get desperate, they may steal, or hurt someone. Our job is to prevent that desperation.

This is a rich country. We could take the billions we spend for planes and bombs—plus the billions we spend on prisons— and create job-training and jobs for the freed persons. That one act would make both governments and individuals less dangerous.

One final thought: Why were the bombers of villages and city street released, and why are the muggers and thieves still in jail? The POWs were freed because freeing them was politically useful, and this was because a number of Americans did care about them, and because the United States had the power to demand their freedom.

When will the men and women in America's jails be freed? When the compassion of their fellow Americans is joined to the power of social movements, to demand their freedom, as one of the great changes we must have to make this decent society.

It is good to see the POWs reunited with their families. It will be good to see the other prisoners released, to watch them too on television as they cross the line to freedom, to see their wives and children, their fathers and mothers, embrace them and take them home.

▶ QUESTIONS:

1. What is the main idea of the selection? (Write a one- or two-sentence summary.)

2. What is your reaction to that idea? (Do you agree, disagree, or have some reservations? Why?)

3. What convinces you or dissuades you? (Is it the information the writer gives or the language he uses? Give examples of particularly convincing or disturbing information or language.)

4. Which type of language use are you most aware of—emotive, factual, or interpretive? (Give some examples.)

5. Are you aware of a specific tone here? What is it?

(Compare your responses with those in Chapter Supplement III, p. 275.)

CHEMICAL WAR IS NOT HEALTHY FOR PEOPLE...

by Ruth Mulvey Harmer

from Unfit for Human Consumption

In the trade they are known as *economic poisons*—the more than 45,000 registered synthetic commercial killers of weeds, bugs, funguses, rats, and other organisms considered pests. Scientists are now calling them *biocides* because of their destructiveness to the web of life. A blunter, but perhaps more meaningful label for them, is *people poisons.*

That is what has been overlooked or minimized in the debate that rages over the uncontrolled use of pesticides. The lines of battle were clearly drawn two decades ago between those who advocated unlimited use until "facts" proved them harmful and those who would restrict them until "facts" proved them safe.

During the Delaney Subcommittee hearings an exchange between chief counsel Vincent A. Kleinfield and a professor of entomology revealed the opposing attitudes. Asked about the advisability of using pesticides without full knowledge of their effects on humans, Professor William M. Hoskins said he believed in animal studies, but considered them "only preliminary to use on human beings . . . there is no substitute for that." Then:

MR. KLEINFELD: I see. . . . Couldn't that be fairly called the human guinea pig approach?
DR. HOSKINS: I presume so.
MR. KLEINFELD: How do you think these human guinea pigs feel about it?
DR. HOSKINS: Why, I believe they would object. . . .

It is the human guinea pig approach that has prevailed—with relatively few objections, since most of the experimental subjects have no notion of what is happening to them. Neither do their doctors, if they have doctors. Experts say that only a small percentage of acute pesticide poisonings are reported, or even identified. Chronic and more subtle types of poisonings are frequently misdiagnosed or totally ignored: yet in some parts of the country they have already reached near epidemic proportions.

The assault begins in the womb. Scientists have found pesticide residues in the tissues of unborn babies as early as the twenty-second week of development, residues of the persistent pesticides like DDT, aldrin, and dieldrin almost as high in embryos as in adults. The under-5 population has even higher levels, particularly breast-fed babies. A Swedish toxicologist testified recently that their intake of DDT compounds, about twice the amount recommended by the World Health Organization, comes in the range of exposure in which laboratory animals began to show biochemical changes.

The assault that begins in the womb continues for a lifetime, with all of us absorbing appreciable quantities from a thousand different sources—air, water, the surfaces we touch, the garments we wear, every bite we eat. It is wishful thinking to imagine that laws and regulations preclude our absorbing unsafe amounts. Even foods and beverages, which are regulated, may contain dangerously unsafe residues. "Tolerances" for residues considered harmless are set by the Food and Drug Administration, generally at 1/100th of the smallest amount known to cause effects in the most sensitive test animals. For any compound considered too toxic to be allowed in any amount, FDA sets a zero tolerance.

While that sounds reassuring enough, protection is actually very sketchy. Zero, it seems, is a stretchable term. Further, no controls have been provided to insure that tolerances are not exceeded; the FDA's staff is so small that it checks only about one percent of the food shipments over which it has authority, and

many states are unconcerned about foods not under Federal jurisdiction. Moreover, United States tolerances have been set according
to overly optimistic estimates of damage; and they have even been
set for compounds like aldrin, dieldrin, heptachlor (epoxide),
and chlordane, although a "no effect" level in animals has never
been determined.

Regulatory agencies in Western Europe have been far more
wary in setting tolerances. Just consider a few of the differences in
the amounts of residue of various pesticides allowed on United
States citrus fruits in 1968 and those held permissible for them in
Common Market nations:

	Europe (p.p.m.)	U.S. (p.p.m.)
Captan	15.0	100.0
Lindane	2.0	10.0
Parathion	.5	1.0
Toxaphene	.4	7.0

The systematic poisoning of the country's food supply, along
with the air, water, and other unregulated sources, has continued
chiefly because people were not dropping dead after a pesticide-
laden meal. Studies showing damage have been impressive; but
they have been overshadowed, out-shouted, by industry-approved
studies that bear out the claim of "harmless to humans."

▶ QUESTIONS:

1. What is the main idea of the selection?

2. What is your reaction to that idea?

3. What is most convincing? Least convincing?

4. What types of language are used? (Give some examples.)

5. Is there a specific tone? What is it?

(Compare your responses with those in Chapter Supplement III, p. 275.)

I BECOME A STUDENT

from The Autobiography of Lincoln Steffens

It is possible to get an education at a university. It has been done; not often, but the fact that a proportion, however small, of college students do get a start in interested, methodical study, proves my thesis, and the two personal experiences I have to offer illustrate it and show how to circumvent the faculty, the other students, and the whole college system of mind-fixing. My method might lose a boy his degree, but a degree is not worth so much as the capacity and the drive to learn, and the undergraduate desire for an empty baccalaureate is one of the holds the educational system has on students. Wise students some day will refuse to take degrees, as the best men (in England, for instance) give, but do not themselves accept, titles.

My method was hit on by accident and some instinct. I specialized. With several courses prescribed, I concentrated on the one or two that interested me most, and letting the others go, I worked intensively on my favorites. In my first two years, for example, I worked at English and political economy and read philosophy. At the beginning of my junior year I had several cinches in history. Now I liked history; I had neglected it partly because I rebelled at the way it was taught, as positive knowledge unrelated to politics, art, life, or anything else. The professors gave us chapters out of a few books to read, con, and be quizzed on. Blessed as I was with a "bad memory," I could not commit to it anything that I did not understand and intellectually need. The bare record of the story of man, with names, dates, and irrelative events, bored me. But I had discovered in my readings of literature, philosophy, and political economy that history had light to throw upon unhistorical questions. So I proposed in my junior and senior years to specialize in history, taking all the courses required and those also that I had flunked in. With this in mind I listened attentively to the first introductory talk of Professor William Cary Jones on American constitutional history. He was a dull lecturer, but I noticed that, after telling us what pages of what books we must be prepared in, he mumbled off some other references "for those that may care to dig deeper."

When the rest of the class rushed out into the sunshine, I went up to the professor and, to his surprise, asked for this memorandum. He gave it to me. Up in the library I ran through the required chapters in the two different books, and they differed on several points. Turning to the other authorities, I saw that they disagreed on the same facts and also on others. The librarian, appealed to, helped me search the book-shelves till the library closed, and then I called on Professor Jones for more references. He was astonished, invited me in, and began to approve my industry, which astonished me. I was not trying to be a good boy; I was better than that: I was a curious boy. He lent me a couple of his books, and I went off to my club to read them. They only deepened the mystery, clearing up the historical question, but leaving the answer to be dug for and written.

The historians did not know! History was not a science, but a field for research, a field for me, for any young man, to explore, to make discoveries in and write a scientific report about. I was fascinated. As I went on from chapter to chapter, day after day, finding frequently essential differences of opinion and of fact, I saw more and more work to do. In this course, American constitutional history, I hunted far enough to suspect that the Fathers of the Republic who wrote our sacred Constitution of the United States not only did not, but did not want to, establish a democratic government, and I dreamed for a while—as I used as a child to play I was Napoleon or a trapper—I promised myself to write a true history of the making of the American Constitution. I did not do it; that chapter has been done or well begun since by two men: Smith of the University of Washington and Beard (then) of Columbia (afterward forced out, perhaps for this very work). I found other events, men, and epochs waiting for students. In all my other courses, in ancient, in European, and in modern history, the disagreeing authorities carried me back to the need of a fresh search for (or of) the original documents or other clinching testimony. Of course I did well in my classes. The history professors soon knew me as a student and seldom put a question to me except when the class had flunked it. Then Professor Jones would say, "Well, Steffens, tell them about it."

Fine. But vanity wasn't my ruling passion then. What I had was a quickening sense that I was learning a method of studying history and that every chapter of it, from the beginning of the world to the end, is crying out to be rewritten. There was something for Youth to do; these superior old men had not done anything, finally.

Years afterward I came out of the graft prosecution office in San Francisco with Rudolph Spreckels, the banker and backer of the investigation. We were to go somewhere, quick, in his car, and we couldn't. The chauffeur was trying to repair something wrong. Mr. Spreckels smiled; he looked closely at the defective part, and to my silent, wondering inquiry he answered: "Always, when I see something badly done or not done at all, I see an opportunity to make a fortune. I never kick at bad work by my class: there's lots of it and we suffer from it. But our failures and neglects are chances for the young fellows coming along and looking for work."

Nothing is done. Everything in the world remains to be done or done over. "The greatest picture is not yet painted, the greatest play isn't written (not even by Shakespeare), the greatest poem is unsung. There isn't in all the world a perfect railroad, nor a good government, nor a sound law." Physics, mathematics, and especially the most advanced and exact of the sciences, are being fundamentally revised. Chemistry is just becoming a science; psychology, economics, and sociology are awaiting a Darwin, whose work in turn is awaiting an Einstein. If the rah-rah boys in our colleges could be told this, they might not all be such specialists in football, petting parties, and unearned degrees. They are not told it, however; they are told to learn what is known. This is nothing, philosophically speaking.

Somehow or other in my later years at Berkeley, two professors, Moses and Howison, representing opposite schools of thought, got into a controversy, probably about their classes. They brought together in the house of one of them a few of their picked students, with the evident intention of letting us show in conversation how much or how little we had understood of their respective teachings. I don't remember just what the subject was that they threw into the ring, but we wrestled with it till the professors could stand it no longer. Then they broke in, and while we sat silent and highly entertained, they went at each other hard and fast and long. It was after midnight when, the debate over, we went home. I asked the other fellows what they had got out of it, and their answers showed that they had seen nothing but a fine, fair fight. When I laughed, they asked me what I, the D.S., had seen that was so much more profound.

I said that I had seen two highly-trained, well-educated Masters of Arts and Doctors of Philosophy disagreeing upon every essential point of thought and knowledge. They had all there was of the sciences; and yet they could not find any knowledge upon which they could base an acceptable conclusion. They had no test of knowledge; they didn't know what is and what is not. And they have no test of right and wrong; they have no basis for even an ethics.

Well, and what of it? They asked me that, and that I did not answer. I was stunned by the discovery that it was philosophically true, in a most literal sense, that nothing is known; that it is precisely the foundation that is lacking for science; that all we call knowledge rested upon assumptions which the scientists did not all accept; and that, likewise, there is no scientific reason for saying, for example, that stealing is wrong. In brief: there was no scientific basis for an ethics. No wonder men said one thing and did another; no wonder they could settle nothing either in life or in the academies.

I could hardly believe this. Maybe these professors, whom I greatly respected, did not know it all. I read the books over again with a fresh eye, with a real interest, and I could see that, as in history, so in other branches of knowledge, everything was in the air. And I was glad of it. Rebel though I was, I had got the religion of scholarship and science; I was in awe of the authorities in the academic world. It was a release to feel my worship cool and pass. But I could not be sure. I must go elsewhere, see and hear other professors, men these California professors quoted and looked up to as their high priests. I decided to go as a student to Europe when I was through Berkeley, and I would start with the German universities.

My father listened to my plan, and he was disappointed. He had hoped I would succeed him in his business; it was for that that he was staying in it. When I said that, whatever I might do, I would never go into business, he said, rather sadly, that he would sell out his interest and retire. And he did soon after our talk. But he wanted me to stay home and, to keep me, offered to buy an interest in a certain San Francisco daily paper. He had evidently had this in mind for some time. I had always done some writing, verse at the poetical age of puberty, then a novel which my mother alone treasured. Journalism was the business for a boy who liked to write, he thought, and he said I had often spoken of a newspaper as my ambition. No doubt I had in the intervals between my campaigns as Napoleon. But no more. I was now going to be a scientist, a philosopher. He sighed; he thought it over, and with the approval of my mother, who was for every sort of education, he gave his consent.

▶ QUESTIONS:

1. What is the main idea?

2. What is your reaction to that idea?

3. What is most convincing? Least convincing?

4. What types of language are used? (Give some examples.)

5. Is there a specific tone? What is it?

(Compare your responses with those in Chapter Supplement III, p. 275.)

IMPLICATIONS AND ASSUMPTIONS

Drawing Inferences

The ability to read beneath the lines of non-fiction means, in part, the ability to sense what the writer means to convey by specific interpretive and emotive words and phrases. But it means more than that. It means also the skill of *finding implied ideas* in the way a writer has put words together within a sentence or throughout a paragraph—that is, the skill of *drawing inferences.*

Look again, for example, at a paragraph you just read in the selection from Lincoln Steffens' autobiography.

The historians did not know! History was not a science, but a field for research, a field for me, for any young man, to explore, to make discoveries in and write a scientific report about. I was fascinated. As I went on from chapter to chapter, day after day, finding frequently essential differences of opinion and of fact, I saw more and more work to do. In this course, American constitutional history, I hunted far enough to suspect that the Fathers of the Republic who wrote our sacred Constitution of the United States not only did not, but did not want to, establish a democratic government, and I dreamed for a while—as I used as a child to play I was Napoleon or a trapper—I promised myself to write a true history of the making of the American constitution. I did not do it; that chapter has been done or well begun since by two men: Smith of the University of Washington and Beard (then) of Columbia (afterward forced out, perhaps for this very work). I found other events, men, and epochs waiting for students. In all my other courses, in ancient, in European, and in modern history, the disagreeing authorities carried me back to the need of a fresh search for (or of) the original documents or other clinching testimony. Of course I did well in my classes. The history professors soon knew me as a student and seldom put a question to me except when the class had flunked it. Then Professor Jones would say, "Well, Steffens, tell them about it."

In this paragraph Steffens states some ideas directly—for example, that he found the study of history exciting when he was in college, that he was a good history student, that he dreamed of some day writing an accurate history of the making of the United States Constitution. But other ideas he only implies or suggests. For example, he doesn't *say* that when he was a student he believed that history should be studied scientifically, but he *implies* this idea (gives you reason to *infer* it) when he says he found much in history "to explore, and to make discoveries in and write a scientific report about." And he does not *tell* you that by "science" he means a study based on factual evidence, but he *implies* this meaning by saying: "The historians did not know! History was not a science. . . ." What additional inferences can you draw from the paragraph, and what sentences or parts of sentences elicit these inferences most specifically? Also, what is the main idea of the paragraph? Is it stated directly in a topic sentence or simply implied?

▶ YOUR INFERENCE   SENTENCE ELICITING YOUR
                                      INFERENCE

▶ MAIN IDEA   (WHERE IS IT STATED? OR IS IT
                                      IMPLIED?)

(Compare your responses with those in Chapter Supplement IV, p. 277.)

In the next passage, a section from John Holt's *How Children Learn*, there are implications of a different sort. Holt, one of the most outspoken critics of current practices in American public schools, speculates about what would happen if children in elementary school classrooms had to be taught to speak their native language. At first, the suggestion seems absurd. It soon becomes clear, however, that Holt is implying a contrast between the complicated learning process he describes and the natural way that most children learn to speak their language. But on a deeper level he is implying something else. He is speaking to elementary teachers about a kind of teaching they do. What do you think he is "really" talking about here? Where do you find this meaning signaled in the passage?

Bill Hull once said to me, "If we taught children to speak, they'd never learn." I thought at first he was joking. By now I realize that it was a very important truth. Suppose we decided that we had to "teach" children to speak. How would we go about it? First, some committee of experts would analyze speech and break it down into a number of separate "speech skills." We would probably say that, since speech is made up of sounds, a child must be taught to make all the sounds of his language before he can be taught to speak the language itself. Doubtless we would list these sounds, easiest and commonest ones first, harder and rarer ones next. Then we would begin to teach infants these sounds, working our way down the list. Perhaps, in order not to "confuse" the child —"confuse" is an evil word to many educators—we would not let the child hear much ordinary speech, but would only expose him to the sounds we were trying to teach.

Along with our sound list, we would have a syllable list and a word list.

When the child had learned to make all the sounds on the sound list, we would begin to teach him to combine the sounds into syllables. When he could say all the syllables on the syllable list, we would begin to teach him the words on our word list. At the same time, we would teach him the rules of grammar, by means of which he could combine these newly-learned words into sentences. Everything would be planned with nothing left to chance; there would be plenty of drill, review, and tests, to make sure that he had not forgotten anything.

Suppose we tried to do this; what would happen? What would happen, quite simply, is that most children, before they got very far, would become baffled, discouraged, humiliated, and fearful, and would quit trying to do what we asked them. If, outside of our classes, they lived a normal infant's life, many of them would probably ignore our "teaching" and learn to speak on their own.

(From *How Children Learn* by John Holt)

▶   INFERENCE   SENTENCE ELICITING INFERENCE

Now that you have had a chance to think about this writer's implications, it is only fair to point out that the last paragraph, as it appears in the book, contains this additional sentence:

> If not, if our control of their lives was complete (the dream of too many educators), they would take refuge in deliberate failure and silence, as so many of them do when the subject is reading. [underlining added]

When Holt spoke of teachers teaching sounds before syllables, syllables before words, and words before sentences, did it occur to you that he was implying a criticism of the way some teachers teach reading? You may not have drawn this inference if you have not thought much about the current controversy over the way elementary children are taught to read. But if you understood his larger implication—that teachers tend to over-teach, to make learning unnecessarily difficult for students—you certainly were doing some effective reading beneath the lines.

Finding Basic Assumptions

It is not unusual for a writer to imply an idea throughout a paragraph or through several paragraphs and then finally to state it directly (for the benefit of the reader who has not been following as thoughtfully as you are learning to do). However, one kind of idea you will never find "in the lines." That is an idea that is so much a part of a writer's basic value system that he takes it for granted—and probably assumes that you take it for granted, too. This book calls that kind of idea a *basic assumption*.

Often a writer's specific implications will lead you to his basic assumptions. For example, in the passage that you read from Lincoln Steffens' account of his college experiences, the writer implies that Professor Beard may have been "forced out" of Columbia because he wrote about events in American history in ways that did not please the administration. He further implies that he thinks it is unfortunate that this happened—if it happened. But Steffens does not give any specific signal showing his basic assumption that a university should support freedom of inquiry for both faculty and students. He doesn't need to do this; he takes the idea for granted. But not everyone makes this assumption. Do you know anyone who has a conflicting assumption about the purpose of a university?

The Holt selection is also based on a buried assumption. Review that passage and use the space below to record the assumption you find. Then check the response given in Chapter Supplement V (p. 277).

▶

Many people who read "idea" non-fiction allow their own basic assumptions to interfere with their understanding of the statements and implications that identify the writer's basic assumptions. To make sure that this kind of "noise" (see Chapter Six, p. 223 does not distort your reception of the writer's "message" and your recognition of his values, you will need to approach everything you read with as open a mind as possible (nobody's mind is completely "open"). That is, you will need to convince yourself not to have any preconceptions about a writer's ideas or his underlying attitudes until you find signals that lead you to them, and not to judge what a writer has said until you have fully understood what he has stated, what he has implied, and what he has assumed.

You should also watch out for three common kinds of "assumption interference." You could be tempted to assume that a writer must have meant what you would have meant (because all reasonable people believe as you do). Or unaware, or only vaguely aware, that a writer's assumptions are different from yours, you could label everything he says as "strange" or "crazy." Or—and this is probably the most dangerous interference of all—you could conclude that a writer is "on your side" simply because he makes some points that support your basic assumptions. When you mis-read in this way, you risk being lured into accepting more of the writer's thinking than you want to because you are likely to overlook or misunderstand implications based on assumptions very different from your own.

To practice finding ideas and assumptions that probably contrast with your expectations, you will find on the following pages a passage that develops a thesis rejected by nearly all contemporary scientists and social scientists. Read it carefully, looking for stated thesis, for implications, and for basic assumptions. Consider also whether what the writer says and implies is in conflict in any way with your own basic assumptions or beliefs. The author's name is omitted here, but you will probably know who he is before you have read very far.

NATION AND RACE

There are some truths which are so obvious that for this very reason they are not seen or at least not recognized by ordinary people. They sometimes pass by such truisms as though blind and are most astonished when someone suddenly discovers what everyone really ought to know. Columbus's eggs lie around by the

hundreds of thousands, but Columbuses are met with less frequently.

Thus men without exception wander about in the garden of
Nature; they imagine that they know practically everything and
yet with few exceptions pass blindly by one of the most patent
principles of Nature's rule: the inner segregation of the species of
all living beings on this earth.

Even the most superficial observation shows that Nature's
restricted form of propagation and increase is an almost rigid basic
law of all the innumerable forms of expression of her vital urge.
Every animal mates only with a member of the same species. The
titmouse seeks the titmouse, the finch the finch, the stork the
stork, the field mouse the field mouse, the dormouse the dormouse,
the wolf the she-wolf, etc.

Only unusual circumstances can change this, primarily the
compulsion of captivity or any other cause that makes it impossible to mate within the same species. But then Nature begins to
resist this with all possible means, and her most visible protest
consists either in refusing further capacity for propagation to
bastards or in limiting the fertility of later offspring; in most cases,
however, she takes away the power of resistance to disease or
hostile attacks.

This is only too natural.

Any crossing of two beings not at exactly the same level produces a medium between the level of the two parents. This means:
the offspring will probably stand higher than the racially lower
parent, but not as high as the higher one. Consequently, it will later
succumb in the struggle against the higher level. Such mating is
contrary to the will of Nature for a higher breeding of all life.
The precondition for this does not lie in associating superior and
inferior, but in the total victory of the former. The stronger must
dominate and not blend with the weaker, thus sacrificing his own
greatness. Only the born weakling can view this as cruel, but he
after all is only a weak and limited man; for if this law did not
prevail, any conceivable higher development of organic living
beings would be unthinkable.

The consequence of this racial purity,[1] universally valid in
Nature, is not only the sharp outward delimitation of the various
races, but their uniform character in themselves. The fox is always
a fox, the goose a goose, the tiger a tiger, etc., and the difference
can lie at most in the varying measure of force, strength, intelligence, dexterity, endurance, etc., of the individual specimens.
But you will never find a fox who in his inner attitude might,
for example, show humanitarian tendencies toward geese, as
similarly there is no cat with a friendly inclination toward mice.

Therefore, here, too, the struggle among themselves arises
less from inner aversion than from hunger and love. In both cases,
Nature looks on calmly, with satisfaction, in fact. In the struggle
for daily bread all those who are weak and sickly or less deter-

mined succumb, while the struggle of the males for the female grants the right or opportunity to propagate only to the healthiest. And struggle is always a means for improving a species' health and power of resistance and, therefore, a cause of its higher development.

If the process were different, all further and higher development would cease and the opposite would occur. For, since the inferior always predominates numerically over the best, if both had the same possibility of preserving life and propagating, the inferior would multiply so much more rapidly that in the end the best would inevitably be driven into the background, unless a correction of this state of affairs were undertaken. Nature does just this by subjecting the weaker part to such severe living conditions that by them alone the number is limited, and by not permitting the remainder to increase promiscuously, but making a new and ruthless choice according to strength and health.

No more than Nature desires the mating of weaker with stronger individuals, even less does she desire the blending of a higher with a lower race, since, if she did, her whole work of higher breeding, over perhaps hundreds of thousands of years, might be ruined with one blow.

Historical experience offers countless proofs of this. It shows with terrifying clarity that in every mingling of Aryan blood with that of lower peoples the result was the end of the cultured people. North America, whose population consists in by far the largest part of Germanic elements who mixed but little with the lower colored peoples, shows a different humanity and culture from Central and South America, where the predominantly Latin immigrants often mixed with the aborigines on a large scale. By this one example, we can clearly and distinctly recognize the effect of racial mixture. The Germanic inhabitant of the American continent, who has remained racially pure and unmixed, rose to be master of the continent; he will remain the master as long as he does not fall a victim to defilement of the blood.

(From *Mein Kampf* by Adolph Hitler, translated by Ralph Manheim)

▶ MAIN IDEA:

▶ IMPLIED IDEAS:

▶ ASSUMPTIONS:

▶ YOUR ASSUMPTIONS OR BELIEFS:

(Compare your responses with those in Chapter Supplement VI, p. 278.)

As the Hitler selection demonstrates, not only can a writer's implications lead you to his basic assumptions, but his assumptions, once you find them, can tell you something about the *conclusions* he probably would come to on matters that go beyond the scope of the work. This kind of reasoning is, of course, based on inferences you make that are not signaled by the writer; and therefore it is not, strictly speaking, a reading skill. But it requires a reading skill—one that you have been developing throughout this chapter. Consider, for example, how different world history might have been if most readers of *Mein Kampf* had been able to infer from Hitler's comments about Jews in this book the possibility of the crimes that later occurred in concentration camps at Auschwitz and Dachau.

Future world history would also be affected if many people read and understood the following selection and agreed to carry out the suggestions it implies. Although the style of this piece is descriptive, the purpose is argumentative—just as Hitler's was. What ideas does the writer imply here? (There are no directly stated ideas.) What assumptions underlie these implied ideas and what conclusions can you draw from these about the writer's thinking on matters indirectly related to this work? Finally, do you accept any of the implications the writer makes here? Are there any that you do not accept?

THE POOL

by Allen Planz

from Ecostatics, the Sierra Club Handbook for Activists

On the west bank of brown river there is a place where the wildness of nature mingles savagely with the wildness of civilization. Bare rocks have shouldered the rain into a sunken meadow, and more than a dozen autobodies create a ring of metallic resonance around the small pond, from which all life, even the mosquito wriggler, has been choked by chemical stasis. Sunlight sickens on rust and purpled alloys, glints on the black water and shimmers on oilstained sand. This was a watering place once, a ford, a concourse, and one of many thousands of departure points. Buffalo rested by the rocks, heads to the wind, and geese held back the encroaching swamp for centuries, until guns killed off the geese and later gasoline killed the weeds. The erosion gulley was a stream when lush grasses upcountry sifted the rain through their roots. Now every drizzle means sudden flood. Here Indians made camp near the bank, and watched the fire shape and shadow the waters. The pioneer paused to collect his forces for the plunge farther into the west on the trail which, under moonlight, stirred faintly above the dark. A family settled here, and built a homestead, of which only a few rectangular depressions remain. This land was overgrazed, overfarmed, and abandoned, then assumed a civilized function as a dumping-ground for vandalized carwrecks from the highway a mile off. Though doubtless title to it is jealously guarded, nobody possesses it now, nobody watches over it, and it is nameless. One can come across it hiking and descend the rocks to the black pond and rest among the junked cars and among slaughtered beasts. Locusts skid in the sand or sing, entombed, in the sticky sludge spilled from crankcases. The river with its machined flow scours the pocked bank. The shadows inside and under the cars are bruises of blue air. Dustdevils snake in the fine grit, and whirl flakes of rusted metal. One may calculate and possess again all the miles he has traveled, all the cities and towns that he called home and that irresistibly erupted him back on the road. One may calculate all those whom money had bought, or killed. One may do nothing, wish nothing. If the hot breeze stirs, it brings only the hands of buried men, and bears no witness to the riposte of osprey and eagle above terraces of clear water. And the night comes on, upside down, gaining on the earth a darkness it never has in the sky. The air smells of heated iron, rancid oils, and of water thickened with sewage. Voices in the blood begin talking of the blood's cessation. One picks up a theme, then, of the splendor of empire weighted against the dust of the people who built it.

And gives it to the heaviness of the night through which one has lived each night, getting drunk under stars arranged in patterns long since prefigured in the fears of men. And with the geophysics of the night in one hand, a bottle in the other, invokes that theme, so that, when the dawn splays the broken figure of man or beast on a hilltop, the wind may come again, if ever it comes again, singing not requiem but revolution.

▶ IMPLIED IDEAS:

▶ ASSUMPTIONS:

▶ CONCLUSIONS:

▶ YOUR REACTIONS TO IMPLIED IDEAS:

(Compare your responses with those in Chapter Supplement VII, p. 278.)

SOME SPECIAL EFFECTS WITH TONE

So far you have discovered that non-fiction writers sometimes express less than their full meanings in order to get you to think along with them by following their implications. In this section you will find that certain writers sometimes avoid even clearly implying what they really mean; instead they use language in ways that give their works *apparent meanings* that are different from their *intended meanings*. Whenever a writer uses purposeful "doubletalk"—whether it is in the form of *exaggeration* or of *irony*—his objective also is to get you to think. But the method he has chosen is a "shock" approach, and if you read without full attention to his signals you are likely to think he is crazy.

Finding Irony

The signals of the ironist are usually subtle. When a writer or speaker uses irony, his words appear to have exactly the opposite meaning from the meaning he intends. When you listen to someone who is speaking ironically, his tone of voice often serves as a signal of his meanings. ("My, but you are a sharp looking group this morning.") But when you read ironic writing, about all you can rely on is a sense that he "couldn't really mean that." And you can probably best develop that sense by analyzing the techniques and the intentions of the writers of some typical ironic pieces. Three selections are included here for your practice.

Art Buchwald, a humorist who writes a column of political satire for a newspaper syndicate, frequently uses irony as a basic method of developing an idea. As you begin reading the following selection, some very early signals will tell you that the writer is going to be saying the opposite of what he means all the way through. Once you have found one of these signals, you will have no difficulty reading the article or getting the point that Buchwald is humorously making. What is the first signal of irony that you note?

After you have finished reading the piece, try writing a direct statement of the main idea in a sentence or two. This way you will be able to compare Buchwald's ironic treatment with your straight version of the same topic.

FRESH AIR WILL KILL YOU

by Art Buchwald

from Have I Ever Lied To You?

Smog, which was once the big attraction of Los Angeles, can now be found all over the country from Butte, Montana, to New York City, and people are getting so used to polluted air that it's very difficult for them to breathe anything else.

I was lecturing recently, and one of my stops was Flagstaff, Arizona, which is about 7,000 miles above sea level.

As soon as I got out of the plane, I smelled something peculiar.

"What's that smell?" I asked the man who met me at the plane.

"I don't smell anything," he replied.

"There's a definite odor that I'm not familiar with," I said.

"Oh, you must be talking about the fresh air. A lot of people come out here who have never smelled fresh air before."

"What's it supposed to do?" I asked suspiciously.

"Nothing. You just breathe it like any other kind of air. It's supposed to be good for your lungs."

"I've heard that story before," I said. "How come if it's air, my eyes aren't watering?"

"Your eyes don't water with fresh air. That's the advantage of it. Saves you a lot in paper tissues."

I looked around and everything appeared crystal clear. It was a strange sensation and made me feel very uncomfortable.

My host, sensing this, tried to be reassuring. "Please don't worry about it. Tests have proved that you can breathe fresh air day and night without its doing any harm to the body."

"You're just saying that because you don't want me to leave," I said. "Nobody who has lived in a major city can stand fresh air for a very long time. He has no tolerance for it."

"Well, if the fresh air bothers you, why don't you put a

handkerchief over your nose and breathe through your mouth?"

"Okay, I'll try it. If I'd known I was coming to a place that had nothing but fresh air, I would have brought a surgical mask."

We drove in silence. About fifteen minutes later he asked, "How do you feel now?"

"Okay, I guess, but I sure miss sneezing."

"We don't sneeze too much here," the man admitted. "Do they sneeze a lot where you come from?"

"All the time. There are some days when that's all you do."

"Do you enjoy it?"

"Not necessarily, but if you don't sneeze, you'll die. Let me ask you something. How come there's no air pollution around here?"

"Flagstaff can't seem to attract industry. I guess we're really behind the times. The only smoke we get is when the Indians start signaling each other. But the wind seems to blow it away."

The fresh air was making me feel dizzy. "Isn't there a diesel bus around here that I could breathe into for a couple of hours?"

"Not at this time of day. I might be able to find a truck for you."

We found a truck driver, and slipped him a five-dollar bill, and he let me put my head near his exhaust pipe for a half hour. I was immediately revived and able to give my speech.

Nobody was as happy to leave Flagstaff as I was. My next stop was Los Angeles, and when I got off the plane, I took one big deep breath of the smog-filled air, my eyes started to water, I began to sneeze, and I felt like a new man again.

▶ FIRST SIGNAL OF IRONY:

▶ MAIN IDEA (IN YOUR OWN WORDS):

The first signal, of course, is the title. Another early signal is the phrase big attraction in the first sentence. The main idea is simply that smog is ruining Los Angeles. However, as Buchwald's approach is completely lighthearted, that wording or any other wording you came up with may seem inappropriate. In fact, irony is really almost untranslatable. When you take away the "double-talk," you take away the writer's purpose, which is to ridicule whatever he is discussing.

Notice how the writer of the following ironic letter ridicules the organization he is writing to in such a gentle way that it looks at first as if he is poking as much fun at himself as at anyone or anything else. By the time you finish reading this letter-essay, however, you will find that bureaucracy bears the brunt of his humorous criticism. The first sentence of this one is "straight," but the second sentence has so many wild irrelevancies in it that it becomes clear the writer does not literally mean what he says there or in what follows. Read the selection just to appreciate White's ironic style. Then write a sentence or two of the letter you would have written if you had been in White's circumstances and had decided to take a "mad as hell" approach. (Don't exaggerate the feelings you think you would have had; just state them directly.)

New York, N.Y.
12 April 1951

Collector of Internal Revenue
Divisional Office
Bangor, Maine

Dear Sir:

I have your notice about a payment of two hundred and some-odd dollars that you say is owing on my 1948 income tax. You say a warrant has been issued for the seizure and sale of my place in Maine, but I don't know as you realize how awkward that would be right at this time, because in the same mail I also received a notice from the Society for the Prevention of Cruelty to Animals here in New York taking me to task for harboring an unlicensed dog in my apartment, and I have written them saying that Minnie is licensed in Maine, but if you seize and sell my place, it is going to make me look pretty silly with the Society, isn't it? Why would I license a dog in Maine, they will say, if I don't live there? I think it is a fair question. I have written the Society, but purposely did not mention the warrant of seizure and sale. I didn't want to mix them up, and it might have sounded like just some sort of cock and bull story. I have always paid my taxes promptly, and the Society would think I was kidding, or something.

Anyway, the way the situation shapes up is this: I am being accused in New York State of dodging my dog tax, and accused in Maine of being behind in my federal tax, and I believe I'm going to have to rearrange my life somehow or other so that everything can be brought together, all in one state, maybe Delaware or some state like that, as it is too confusing for everybody this way. Minnie, who is very sensitive to my moods, knows there is something wrong and that I feel terrible. And now *she* feels terrible. The other day it was the funniest thing, I was packing a suitcase for a trip home to Maine, and the suitcase was lying open on the floor and when I wasn't looking she went and got in and lay down. Don't you think that was cute?

If you seize the place, there are a couple of things I ought to explain. At the head of the kitchen stairs you will find an awfully queer boxlike thing. I don't want you to get a false idea about it, as it looks like a coffin, only it has a partition inside, and two small doors on one side. I don't suppose there is another box like it in the entire world. I built it myself. I made it many years ago as a dormitory for two snug-haired dachshunds, both of whom suffered from night chill. Night chill is the most prevalent dachshund disorder, if you have never had one. Both these dogs, as a matter of fact, had rheumatoid tendencies, as well as a great many other tendencies, especially Fred. He's dead, damn it. I would feel a lot better this morning if I could just see Fred's face, as he would know instantly that I was in trouble with the authorities and would be all over the place, hamming it up. He was something.

About the tax money, it was an oversight, or mixup. Your notice says that the "first notice" was sent last summer. I think that is correct, but when it arrived I didn't know what it meant as I am no mind reader. It was cryptic. So I sent it to a lawyer, fool-fashion, and asked him if *he* knew what it meant. I asked him if it was a tax bill and shouldn't I pay it, and he wrote back and said, No, no, no, no, it isn't a tax bill. He advised me to wait till I got a bill, and then pay it. Well, that was all right, but I was building a small henhouse at the time, and when I get building something with my own hands I lose all sense of time and place. I don't even show up for meals. Give me some tools and some second-handed lumber and I get completely absorbed in what I am doing. The first thing I knew, the summer was gone, and the fall was gone, and it was winter. The lawyer must have been building something, too, because I never heard another word from him.

To make a long story short, I am sorry about this nonpayment, but you've got to see the whole picture to understand it, got to see my side of it. Of course I will forward the money if you haven't seized and sold the place in the meantime. If you have, there are a couple of other things on my mind. In the barn, at the far end of the tieups, there is a goose sitting on eggs. She is a young goose and I hope you can manage everything so as not to disturb her until she has brought off her goslings. I'll give you one, if you want. Or would they belong to the federal government anyway, even though the eggs were laid before the notice was mailed? The cold frames are ready, and pretty soon you ought to transplant the young broccoli and tomato plants and my wife's petunias from the flats in the kitchen into the frames, to harden them. Fred's grave is down in the alder thicket beyond the dump. You have to go down there every once in a while and straighten the headstone, which is nothing but a couple of old bricks that came out of a chimney. Fred was restless, and his headstone is the same way—doesn't stay quiet. You have to keep at it.

I am sore about your note, which didn't seem friendly. I am a friendly taxpayer and do not think the government should take a threatening tone, at least until we have exchanged a couple of letters kicking the thing around. Then it might be all right to talk about selling the place, if I proved stubborn. I showed the lawyer your notice about the warrant of seizure and sale, and do you know what he said? He said, "Oh, that doesn't mean anything, it's just a form." What a crazy way to look at a piece of plain English. I honestly worry about lawyers. They never write plain English themselves, and when you give them a bit of plain English to read, they say, "Don't worry, it doesn't mean anything." They're hopeless, don't you think they are? To me a word is a word, and I wouldn't dream of writing anything like "I am going to get out a warrant to seize and sell your place" unless I meant it, and I can't believe that my government would either.

The best way to get into the house is through the woodshed, as there is an old crocus sack nailed on the bottom step and you can wipe the mud off on it. Also, when you go in through the woodshed, you land in the back kitchen right next to the cooky jar with Mrs. Freethy's cookies. Help yourself, they're wonderful.

Sincerely yours,
E. B. White

(*From* "Two Letters, Both Open," *in* The Second Tree From The Corner
by E. B. White)

▶ YOUR LETTER:

Again, you will probably find that what you have written is so different from the original that it is as if you are talking about a completely dissimilar event. But by comparing the two treatments, you can see what irony does. By pretending to be ready to cooperate with the authorities if they should decide to take over his house, White almost (but not quite) hides from the reader the fact that he is so disgusted with bureaucratic mismanagement and misuse of the English language that he will only go down fighting (and also the fact that he knows he won't have to).

Sometimes writers scatter ironic comments in among statements written in "straight" English. When they do this, they usually sound (and intend to sound) highly critical of the practices they are discussing, whereas writers like Buchwald and White seem only to be laughing at absurdities. A passage from *The American Way of Death*, Jessica Mitford's book analyzing and criticizing practices of American morticians, will illustrate this occasional and serious use of irony. As you read, underline phrases that you think the writer has intended the reader to interpret ironically. Also, consider what general point about the practices of morticians she is making in these remarks. She deals here with the kinds of coffins that are made available to the families of the deceased.

The latest in casket styles range from classic (that is, the "urn theme,") to colonial to French provincial to futuristic—the "Transition" casket, styled for the future—surely, something here to please everybody. The patriotic theme comes through very strong just now, finding its most eloquent expression in Boyertown Burial Casket Company's "Valley Forge." This one is "designed to reflect the rugged, strong, soldierlike qualities associated with historic Valley Forge. . . . Its charm lies in the warm beauty of the natural grain and finish of finest Maple hardwoods. A casket designed indeed for a soldier—one that symbolizes the solid, dependable, courageous American ideals so bravely tested at Valley Forge." The Valley Forge casket is pictured in a full-page color spread in the October, 1961, issue of *Casket and Sunnyside*, resting on a scarlet velvet drapery, flanked by some early American cupboards. For all its soldierlike qualities it looks most comfortable, with its nice beige linen pillow and sheets. On the wall behind it hangs a portrait of George Washington who is looking, as usual, rather displeased.

For the less rugged, the bon vivant who dreams of rubbing shoulders with the international smart set, the gay dog who would risk all on the turn of a card, there is the "Monaco," a Duraseal metal unit by the Merit Company of Chicago, "with Sea Mist Polished Finish, interior richly lined in 600 Aqua Supreme Cheney velvet, magnificiently quilted and shirred, with matching jumbo bolster and coverlet." Set against a romantic background depicting a brilliant Riviera sky, its allure heightened by suggestions of tropical ferns and a golden harp, this model can be had for not much more than the cost of a round-trip flight to Monte Carlo.

And for the homebody who is neither rugged nor daring, but is interested in solid comfort, Mr. Leslie Gruber, president of Major Casket Company, announces that their medium-priced metal caskets are now equipped with the "Beautyrama Adjustable Soft-Foam Bed. Quality mattress fabric is used and height adjustment is accomplished by patented means which eliminate cranking. Modified during a year of product development," he continues, "the bed is soft and buoyant, but will hold firm without slipping. . . . Beautyrama beds will be standard at no additional cost on the the entire Major half couch, hinge cap and 20-gauge Sealtite line." Major will continue to use Sealy innerspring mattresses (we are assured) in its quality line of 18-gauge and copper Sealtite Caskets.

Children's caskets, "specially made for boys and girls," come in blue and white or pink and gold. These can be displayed on "attractive formica-covered biers."

Well, there is a great deal more to it. The observer, confronted for the first time by the treasures and artifacts of this unfamiliar world, may well feel something akin to the astonishment of Bernal Díaz at his first glimpse of the hitherto undiscovered court of Montezuma: "We were amazed," he declared, "and some of the soldiers even asked whether the things we saw were not a dream."

(*From* The American Way of Death *by Jessica Mitford*)

▶ MAIN IDEA:

Some ironic expressions you might have underlined in the Mitford passage include her comment that one of the caskets is "styled for the future," her observation that another "looks most comfortable with its nice beige linen pillows and sheets," and her description of a third as suitable for "the bon vivant" (lover of life!). In these phrases and throughout the passage Mitford builds the impression that American morticians are very unrealistic about the needs of both the dead and their survivors.

Interpreting Exaggeration

Deliberate exaggeration is usually fairly easy to recognize. But to discover what a writer is doing with exaggeration, why he has chosen this strange form of expression, may take a bit of thought. Actually, relatively few writers try this tricky technique, and each who does uses it in distinctive ways that suit his particular personality. The two newspaper columnists whose works are represented below make frequent and purposeful use of exaggeration. By discovering how they have matched technique with purpose, you can get an idea of the possibilities of this form of writing. Also, you can learn to avoid the shock that keeps some people from enjoying and understanding deliberate exaggeration when they come across it.

Jim Murray, a sports writer for the *Los Angeles Times*, is widely known for his extravagant use of language. One of his reasons for using this style is simply to entertain his readers. However, sometimes, as in the following column, he drives home a point about a problem he finds in the sports world through the use of humorous exaggeration. What is the first signal of his main idea that you find in this article? What is that idea? How seriously concerned is Murray about the problem he discusses? How does his tone of exaggeration fit his attitude?

IN A HUFF OVER PUFF

by Jim Murray

from the Los Angeles Times, *April 4, 1974*

Despite what you read in the Reader's Digest, there are times when a man needs a cigaret. Like, after a hard day in the shot put ring.

Since Brian Oldfield was over 21, did not have emphysema or a heart-lung disorder, was not in a library or the no-smoking section of an airplane, in bed or in the midst of a dry national forest that day in 1972, he lit up.

You would have thought he got caught selling spy secrets to Russia, peeking in a convent or robbing a poor box, from the uproar that went up. Jack the Ripper didn't arouse the public indignation he did. You would have thought they'd caught the Queen Mother drinking from a bottle, an archbishop at a crap game. Brian would have done better taking his clothes off or placing obscene phone calls.

The scene was the Olympic Trials in Eugene, Ore., and Brian had just won his way onto the U.S. team for Munich. As it turned out, he was smoking on national TV, probably the only cigaret commercial that found its way on the medium that year, and the resultant newspaper picture went all over the globe. Cigarets are not normally one of the products that bear the Olympic shield. It's hardly Marlboro country.

The U.S. Olympic Committee took it personally. Brian Oldfield very nearly became the Eleanor Holm of the '72 Olympics. Eleanor, you may remember, was the girl swimmer tossed off the 1936 Olympic team for quaffing champagne on a ship.

Oldfield thought the uproar was silly. He didn't promise to quit smoking, but he did promise to quit smoking in the shot put ring. No sooner did the team get to Europe than they discovered another flaw in his character: he liked girls.

This was almost too much for the Olympic Committee. When Brian disappeared from the practice field in Oslo to fly to Sweden for a weekend at the home of a stewardess he dated, the Americans were sure they had recruited the Marquis de Sade. They just hoped Brian wouldn't appear in any X-rated movies before they got home.

Then there was the incident of the hotel chambermaid. Brian insisted it was all a misunderstanding. What he wanted the girl to do was *make* the bed. Apparently, it lost something in the translation.

Although the Olympic team was hardly made up of vicars, Oldfield was probably the only one on it who had ever been a bouncer in an Elgin, Ill., gin mill. He gave up that job when he broke the jaw of the leader of a motorcycle gang one night.

Oldfield finished sixth in the Olympics, probably the highest ever for a putter with nicotine on his fingers. His throw was less than a foot off the Olympic record and was probably a remarkable achievement for a guy who was the subject of an almost nightly meeting to decide whether to strip him of his sweatsuit and send him home on the even of his event.

The coaches even approached Randy Matson, the defending gold medalist and first alternate, to replace Oldfield. Matson didn't want to owe his presence on the team to tobacco, and declined.

Now a pro, Oldfield is a contract football player with the New York Stars of the new World Football League and as a member of the pro track tour will compete at the Sports Arena in a meet April 13.

He is now prepared to agree with the surgeon general that

smoking is bad for you. Not for your health, for your career. When you have to spend most of your time at the Olympics defending yourself instead of preparing yourself, Brian feels you would be better off chewing tobacco.

And the Olympic Committee is now free of its fear that, if Brian won a gold medal, he might try to exchange it on the victory stand for a cigaret lighter or a carton of Camels.

▶ MAIN IDEA:

▶ FIRST SIGNAL OF MAIN IDEA:

▶ WRITER'S ATTITUDE (HOW SERIOUS IS HE?):

▶ APPROPRIATENESS OF LANGUAGE:

The article's title, "In a Huff Over Puff," certainly suggests both the main idea and the writer's attitude toward his subject. Murray criticizes the Olympics Committee for making an issue of such a trivial matter as an athlete participating in a cigarette commercial. But the problem is not an earth-shaking one, and the author knows it. In a sense, Murray himself is "in a huff over puff." From the first paragraph of exaggerated remarks about the committee's behavior ("You would have thought he had got caught selling spy secrets to Russians") to the last sarcastic sentence, Murray is simply chiding the Olympics group and making the whole story sound completely ridiculous. He is certainly not trying to arouse the public to oppose the committee; if that had been his purpose he would have adopted a different tone.

Like Art Buchwald, Art Hoppe is a columnist who feels at home with both exaggeration and irony. And, like Buchwald, he uses humor as a means of attacking social and political problems. In the selection that follows, Hoppe's exaggeration takes the form of fantasy, but at the end he makes it clear that he is talking about the society he lives in. You will get more enjoyment from this piece, though, if you understand the writer's general purpose from the beginning. Where do you first find a signal that Hoppe is exaggerating (or at least that he is humorously using language in strange ways)? Where do you first get a hint that he is criticizing the practices of modern universities? (It may help to know that Damon and Pythias were Greek mythological characters who were very close friends. However, Hoppe has deviated far from the idea of the original Greek myth.) You should have no difficulty stating his idea in literal language because he comes close to doing this himself.

TEACHER SMEECHER

by Art Hoppe

from the San Francisco Chronicle, *November 27, 1966*

Once upon a time there were twin brothers named Damon and Pythias Smeecher, who shared a deep love of learning. The only difference between them was that Damon loved to acquire learning and Pythias loved to give it away.

Loving learning as they did, they naturally joined the faculty of the University of Megapolis, which was the greatest treasure trove of learning in the whole wide world.

Damon decided to become a scholar of ancient Etruscan funeral orations because he loved dead languages and things like that. Pythias decided to become a teacher of Life, because he loved life and things like that.

In hardly any time at all, Damon became the greatest scholar of ancient Etruscan funeral orations in the whole wide world. He wrote papers and books and was universally recognized as a leading authority in his field by both other authorities in his field.

The only cross he had to bear was the university regulation requiring him to lecture to students from 1 to 1:40 p.m. on alternate Wednesdays.

With a great effort, he would tear himself away from his beloved Etruscan funeral orations, scurry to the lecture hall and rattle off his lecture without once looking up from his notes. Actually, he delivered the exact same lecture every alternate Wednesday for 32 years. But as he delivered it entirely in ancient Etruscan, which nobody understood, there were few complaints.

So grants poured in to Damon from the Ford, Rockefeller and Maidenform Foundations. He was made a full professor at 27, head of his department at 31 and was always described at faculty teas as "a jewel in the diadem of this great university."

Meanwhile, his brother Pythias became the greatest teacher of Life in the whole wide world.

His students loved him. They would flock to sit at his feet as he taught them how the stars wheel in their courses, why a cowslip blooms and what goodness was. He poured out everything he knew about everything and a generation of students grew up wiser and kinder, instilled with a love of learning and a love of life.

Of course, this kind of teaching took a lot of time and Pythias never did finish his paper entitled "What Life Is All About." But, as he said to himself, "No scholarly journal would publish a paper like that anyway."

At the age of 62, Pythias was called into the Dean's office. "Look here, Smeecher," said the Dean, "I noticed your name on the faculty roster. What do you do around here anyway?"

"I guess I just teach, sir," said Pythias apologetically.

"Good heavens, Smeecher," cried the Dean, canceling his contract on the spot, "how can we go on being the greatest treasure trove of learning in the world, if you keep giving the stuff away?"

Moral: The modern university is a perfect place to get an education. If you're a member of the faculty.

▶ FIRST SIGNAL OF EXAGGERATION:

▶ FIRST HINT OF CRITICISM:

▶ MAIN IDEA:

You probably recognized the title as a clear signal that the tone is to be one of humorous exaggeration and also the first sentence as a criticism (in a gently sarcastic way) of the attitude Hoppe thinks university administrators take toward teaching. The last sentence states his main idea indirectly and facetiously. A more direct statement would be that the modern university overemphasizes research and does not sufficiently stress good teaching.

The last example of a work making use of the tone of exaggeration may strike you at first as completely "straight." But you may sense that there is something odd about the title, especially if you think about it a bit. In the space below write the probable thesis that comes to your mind first when you read the title "Let's Not Get Out the Vote."

▶

Did you say that the writer somehow disapproves of voting? The title could easily be taken that way. It certainly seems to be saying that he does not believe in encouraging other people to vote. But now read the first two paragraphs, printed below, and underline a sentence that could be considered a thesis statement. Does this sentence throw any new light on the title?

LET'S NOT GET OUT THE VOTE

by Robert E. Coulson
from Harper's, *November 1965*

Three years ago anyone who failed to vote had to face the combined scorn of both political parties, the schoolteachers, boy scouts, war veterans, chambers of commerce, and leagues of women voters. Last year bar associations, girl scouts, tavern keepers, President Eisenhower, radio and TV stations, and junior chambers of commerce joined the crusade. There is every prospect that in future elections, non-voters will face jail sentences or fines, or be called to testify before investigating committees.

Before this happens, someone should come to their defense. Non-voters are often more intelligent, more fair-minded, and just as loyal as voters. The right not to vote is as basic as the right to. If voting is made a duty, it ceases to be a privilege.

You probably underlined either the next to the last sentence or the last sentence in the second paragraph. In fact, these two sentences together could be said to state the writer's thesis. Although Coulson does say that non-voters are often superior to voters in certain respects, there is nothing here to indicate that he thinks people should not vote. The title, then, is probably a slight exaggeration. List below any other words or phrases in these paragraphs that you think are exaggerated expressions of the writer's idea.

▶

Coulson probably does not expect you to take seriously his idea that in the future people will be put in jail for not voting. And although tavern keepers and girl scouts may at one time or another have said something about voting, putting them in the same sentence with President Eisenhower and the Bar Association certainly seems to be a way of exaggerating.

Read the rest of the article and note any language you think comes close to exaggeration. (You will find some wording that is at least highly emotive.) Is the writer's argument convincing? Does his strong language help make his point? What is his principal justification for his thesis?

Let's look at the voting behavior of Mr. and Mrs. Whipcord and Mrs. Whipcord's brother Harold, on the day of the local school-board election. Mrs. Whipcord says, "I have studied the candidates and have made up my mind. I will vote for Jones." Mr. Whipcord says, "I know nothing about the candidates or the issues. I will stay home, and allow the election to be decided by the votes of those who have made a study and formed an opinion." Harold says, "I don't know anything about the candidates or the problems, but by golly, I'm going to vote. It's my duty. I'll pick the fellows with the shortest names."

If there is a bad citizen among these three, which one is it? Whose procedure is least likely to bring good government to the school district?

Non-voting, multiplied by the thousands, is said to mean voter apathy, and this is supposed to be a sin. Have we lost our sacred American right to be apathetic? Suppose Mr. Whipcord studied the candidates carefully and concluded that Candidate Jones was a boob and Candidate Smith was a thief. Is it un-American to refuse to choose between them? Or suppose he is satisfied that Jones and Smith are equally qualified, equally able, and that the school's problems are in good hands no matter which man wins. He is not apathetic; he is satisfied. Why should he be forced to choose between candidates on some esoteric basis?

The notion that "getting out the vote" makes for better election results is neither non-partisan, patriotic, nor logical. It is a device to favor the machines of both parties. It handicaps independent candidates, unfairly burdens the party in power, makes elections more expensive to conduct, greatly slows the tallying, and —worst of all—places the emphasis on the ritual of voting rather than the thought behind the vote.

If you fill in all the blank spaces on the ballot, the political machines will steal three-fourths of your vote. Let's see how this works, in a typical primary election.

Here are seven offices to be filled by nomination, with two or three candidates for each office. Citizen Stringfellow is interested in seeing Jones win for Auditor. He has no information about the candidates for Attorney General, Treasurer, Superintendent of Schools, or the others. He votes for Jones and then looks on down the list. He has been persuaded that it is his duty to vote for *somebody* for each office. So for six of the seven offices, he marks an X opposite the name best known to him, or the name on top, or the name suggested by his committeeman. These are machine candidates, and Citizen Stringfellow has given away six-sevenths of his vote.

After him, comes Citizen Stalwart, who knows the candidates for two of the seven offices. He also fills in all the blanks, letting the machine steal five-sevenths of his vote. One of his blind votes cancels out the intelligent vote cast by Citizen Stringfellow. At this rate, during a day's balloting, the candidates backed by the strongest machines with the biggest publicity budgets will win, even though not a single voter had an intelligent preference for them.

Is this what Thomas Jefferson had in mind?

"Getting out the vote" is always partisan. A calm and dignified effort benefits the party in power. An excited or hysterical effort benefits the party out of power. The Republicans were very happy to use the pressure of "neutral" groups in the 1952 elections. But they had better learn that this is a two-edged sword. Next time, the girl scouts, veterans' groups, radio stations, newspapers, and community funds may be out needling the Republicans with propaganda.

"Vote this time or your vote may be gone forever." "This may be your last chance." "Vote now or never." Anyone who is led to the polls by such arguments is going to vote against whoever brought us to the edge of this crevasse. As the pressure on the public increases, the party out of power is most likely to benefit in direct proportion to it.

All public-opinion surveys show that a certain proportion of the electorate has no opinion about many vital issues, does not know who is running for office, and does not care. A gentle campaign to bring a submissive one-third of the apathetic sheep to the polls gets out a voting majority for the candidates who have had the greatest amount of publicity—who usually belong to the party in power. A rip-snorting effort to get out all the ignoramuses tends to turn them into the rebel column, and thus benefits the outs.

In either event, the girl scouts should wash their hands of it. The job of getting out the vote is a partisan effort which belongs to the professionals.

The silliest idea of all is the notion that it is un-American or unpatriotic not to vote. "A plague on both your houses" is a fair American attitude—all too often a logical one. Stupidity does not become wisdom by being multiplied.

In every election not more than one-third of the people care very much how it comes out. A certain percentage may have some sort of belief or opinion without feeling very strongly about it; another percentage may have studied the matter a little without forming an opinion; another percentage may not even have studied it; and so on, until we come to the people who are not even aware that an election is being held. The more we urge these people to clutter up the polling place, the more delay there is in voting, the more the cost of ballots and clerks, and the slower the returns.

If Candidate Jones would normally have won by 3,000 votes to 1,000, and we corral 10,000 more people into the polling places, won't Candidate Jones still win, by 8,000 to 6,000? Mathematically the last-minute coin flippers may make the election look close, but what patriotic purpose is accomplished?

And if the coin-flippers should happen to defeat the will of the informed majority, the cause of good government would emphatically not have been served.

Our city had a referendum recently in which the people voted for a tax increase to build an incinerator and against a tax increase to operate it. Every one of your communities has probably known referendums where the voters approved the bonds for a school but disapproved the sites, or voted for the site and against the bonds. All those voters who marked in opposite directions on the same afternoon were unwisely pressured into voting.

You have also seen primary elections where the boob with the catchy name ran away from the able man whose publicity was colorless. You have seen final elections where the straight party voters and the blank fillers smothered any discriminating choices which the thoughtful voters had made. You may have noticed with distress some of the undignified didos, cruel epithets, pompous verbosities, and Shakespearean gestures with which even good men become burdened early in their campaigns. All of these are caused in large measure by "get out the vote" efforts which emphasize putting a cross in half the squares.

Instead of urging people to vote, we ought to be urging them to study and form opinions. If thought and inspection of the candidates do not create a real desire to vote, then the citizen should be encouraged to stay at home on election day. A low rate is part of the public record and itself a significant voter reaction which ought to be preserved. Maybe neither of the candidates was worth voting for.

Certainly the right to vote is important and should not be curtailed. A fool who is willing to walk all the way to the polling place should be given every freedom to record every stupid impulse he feels, for these will tend to cancel each other out. But no one should pretend that marking X in a square is any proof of patriotism or even intelligence. It is not your duty to vote, but, if you choose to, then it should be your duty to be intelligent about it.

▶ NOTES ON LANGUAGE:

▶ SUPPORT FOR THESIS:

You probably noted that some of the names are a bit unusual; in fact, some (Citizen Stringfellow, Citizen Stalwart) are even symbolic. And words like "boob," "thief," "rip-snorting," and "ignoramus" are emotive, name-calling terms, if not actual exaggerations. But these expressions are worked in with serious argumentative language. Before you had proceeded very far, you probably knew that the writer meant most of what he said. He supports his thesis with a logical explanation of the way mass, ill-considered voting contributes to the causes of political machines. The exaggerated language is window-dressing, calculated to arouse and hold your interest. Whether or not you find it effective is largely a matter of taste.

You have seen, then, that when a writer uses exaggeration that is heavy or irony that is obvious and extended, his purpose is usually to ridicule a condition or an idea. The ridicule may be gentle (as in White's letter-essay) or it may be strong (as in Buchwald), but it will probably be "pure"; that is, it will not be combined with an attempt at problem-solving. If a writer's purpose is reform of any kind (as, in a sense, Coulson's is, and as Mitford's certainly is), he is more likely to combine far-fetched expressions or ironic phrases and sentences with straightforward criticism. In other words, the skillful writer who chooses to use irony or exaggeration will match language with purpose. To find his purpose you will certainly have to read beneath his lines just as you did with the selections in the earlier portions of this chapter. Again, the signals will be subtle, but they will be there.

In Chapter Eight you will learn how the skills that have been treated so far in this book—and especially the ones that have taken you beneath the lines of subtly-developed works of non-fiction—can be applied to the reading of imaginative literature.

CHAPTER SUPPLEMENTS

I. Emotive Expressions and Main Idea in Soul on Ice

The following expressions seem to be particularly charged with feeling:

>   "black masses"
>   "misty level"
>   "problem," "Negro control," and all the other words and phrases in quotation marks

"crisis with racial overtones"
"great oracle"
"One more time, boom"
(And because the total passage has such an angry tone, you could probably justify labeling many more expressions *emotive* rather than interpretive).

Summary: Cleaver says that whenever serious racial tensions develop in America, the mass media (which are controlled by whites) persuade a few well-known black entertainers and sports figures (people who have had little to do with racial strife even though they are black) to say a few calming words to the angry blacks; in this way the media use these celebrities for their own ends.

II. Classification of Expressions

4. sweet—interpretive (possibly emotive, although the total context does not imply much of a value judgment)
5. liar, prevaricator, and social status—interpretive ("Liar" often conveys feeling, but in this context it is just a classification.)
6. greatest American novel ever written about a medical doctor—emotive (because of "greatest")
   Sauk Centre, Minnesota and 1885—factual
7. strength, endurance, and determination—interpretive
8. educational opportunities for the culturally disadvantaged—interpretive
9. oracle—emotive (in this context)
   dangerous—emotive
10. fad—interpretive or emotive (depending on the tone of voice in which the teacher spoke the word, and the sentence as written doesn't give you that information)

III. Language and Idea Analysis

A. "Free Them All: POWs and Other Criminals"
1. *Main idea:* The author believes (and he is quite serious) that nearly all prisoners should be released from American prisons and given an opportunity to lead free lives. He contrasts the way we treat prisoners of war with the way we treat domestic prisoners, claiming that both groups should be shown compassion because both have been victims of systems that made them live different lives than they wanted to live; the men in our prisons, he says, are no more dangerous than the fliers (who have bombed innocent people) and therefore they should be treated no differently.
2. *Your reaction:* Whether or not you agree with the writer will probably depend to a great extent on your acceptance or rejection of what a later part of this chapter calls his *basic assumptions.* For now, you might simply ask yourself whether you believe in the same kind of ideal social organization that he does. Obviously he thinks that our society should be re-planned to minimize the competition he says breeds both crime and war: "A society that has greedy corporations must have petty thieves. A society that engages in the violence of war abroad must endure assault and murder at home." If you do not

accept this premise, you probably will not want to accept his solution, no matter what you think of his uses of language.

3. and 4. *The language and the argument:* The "information" that is given here is all supportive of the above-mentioned view of the function of an ideal society. There are probably no facts that you did not know before you read the article. What the writer has done is to arrange information (facts about POWs and about American domestic prisoners) in ways that support his case, using emotive language to make his point. Expressions like "open the gates of our country," "we care more about law than about life," "we have to put the finger on whomever we can grab in the long chain of guilt," are certainly highly emotive as are the individual words "mugger," "slave," "free," "surrender," "revenge." This kind of language is appropriate to the writer's purpose; he does not intend to give you new information or new interpretations of old information but rather to persuade you to *feel* as he does that the old order must be changed. If you disagree, you are likely to find his language disturbing.

5. *Tone:* The tone could probably best be described as indignation (over injustice) or compassion (for mistreated people).

B. "Chemical War Is Not Healthy for People"

1. *Main idea:* Ms. Harmer's thesis is that the federal government should regulate the manufacture and use of chemical pest control products much more stringently than it does now. She says that because manufacturers continually underestimate the dangers of these products, Americans are being used as guinea pigs and their lives are being endangered without their knowledge or consent.

2. *Your reaction:* As in the last selection, your acceptance of the writer's position depended partly on your acceptance of an unstated assumption (that a government must regulate the activities of private industry when the lives of its citizens are at stake). However, as you read this passage, you were probably more aware of factual information than you were in the preceding selection, because there is much more of it here. You may have compared the facts given here with information or opinions you have heard from other sources.

3. and 4. *The Language and the argument:* The writer uses some emotive language in making key points ("Chemical War Is Not Healthy for People," "people poisons," "the assault that begins in the womb"), but much of her wording is factual. If you accept her basic assumption, and if you have no reason to believe her factual statements are incorrect, you will probably find her argument convincing.

5. *Tone:* You may not be aware of a specific tone here; the writer's approach to her subject is basically factual.

C. "I Became a Student"

1. *Main Idea:* Steffens' point is that during one period of his college career he discovered, to his excitement and astonishment, that his professors did not have the final answers he had previously thought they had; that, in fact, there seemed to be no final answers to any questions; and that there was abundant room in the world of scholarship for any answers he might be able to contribute himself.

2. *Your reaction:* Because Steffens' purpose here is to show you the significance of a personal experience rather than to convince you of the value of an idea, whether or not you react favorably to the passage is likely to depend on whether you have had similar feelings about your education. Have you ever been excited to find that there were questions for you to answer for yourself instead of only answers to be learned?
3. and 4. *The Language and the argument:* This selection is not really an argument, and that is one reason Steffens' language is quite different from that of the other two writers. Although he has used some emotive and some factual terms, the key words here are interpretive—words like "education," "student," "specialize," and "science." This kind of language is appropriate because his purpose is to *interpret* for the reader (explain the meaning he found in) his college experiences.
5. *Tone:* You could call his tone enthusiastic (although you may not be as conscious of tone in this work as you are in some of the other selections in this chapter).

IV. Inferences and Main Idea in the Steffens Paragraph

Your inference

1. Most people, including historians, have the erroneous belief that the founding fathers of the United States intended to create and did create a democratic government.

2. The accepted interpretations of American history are not challenged more often partly because our educational institutions do not want them challenged.

3. Most people depend too much on what the authorities say, rather than seeking out facts from original sources themselves.

Sentence eliciting your inference

"In this course, American constitutional history, I hunted far enough to suspect that the Fathers of the Republic who wrote our sacred Constitution of the United States not only did not, but did not want to, establish a democratic government. . . ."

". . . Beard (then) of Columbia (afterward forced out, perhaps for this very work)"

"In all my other courses . . . the disagreeing authorities carried me back to the need for (or of) the original documents or other clinching testimony."

Main idea and method of presentation: No single sentence in the paragraph states the topic. The idea Steffens implies throughout is that through his study of history he discovered that scholars are not the absolute authorities he had always thought they were and that much knowledge remained for him to discover through his own research.

V. Basic Assumption in How Children Learn

The writer assumes that most children have enough curiosity and interest in learning to develop fundamental communication skills (especially reading) on their own if they are left to their own resources and not prodded and made to feel that learning has to be hard work. (Although this is a debatable assumption, many educators accept it.)

VI. Stated Ideas, Implied Ideas, and Assumptions in Mein Kampf

Main idea: Hitler states that because racial intermarriage weakens races, the German "race," which has always been the strongest, should remain pure; that is, it should discourage or prohibit the mating of Germans with people of other "races."

Implied ideas: He implies that the biological category *species* and the anthropological category *race* are equivalent.

Assumptions: He assumes that the German people are a distinct race and that this race is superior to all others.

Your assumptions and beliefs: Whatever they are, you should know that almost all scientists and social scientists today consider both of the above assumptions to be completely false.

VII. Implied Ideas, Assumptions and Conclusions in "The Pool"

Implied ideas: By describing a once-beautiful pool or pond, now despoiled by cast-off industrial products, the writer intends to show the reader the need for drastic change of the economic system responsible for such conditions (note especially his last few words).

Assumptions: The writer clearly assumes that preserving natural resources is a more important goal for America than maintaining the economic prosperity of America's industrial and business leaders.

Conclusions: You can assume that he would favor restructuring society in a way that would encourage cooperation rather than competition.

on reading
imaginative literature

There are whole courses and complete textbooks on the subject of how to understand and appreciate each of the different kinds of imaginative literature —novels, short stories, poems, and plays. Therefore, these topics can only be touched on in a general text on college reading. But in this chapter you will at least be able to discover some important differences between the methods of developing ideas and the ways of using language that are common in non-fiction and those that are frequently found in works that critics call "imaginative." Once you understand these basic differences, you will be able to adapt to new purposes the reading techniques you learned in earlier chapters. Because short works are the easiest kind to examine in a book like this, the emphasis of the chapter is on reading poems and short stories. However, experience of this sort should help you develop effective ways of reading or studying any of the different kinds of imaginative literature.

FIGURATIVE LANGUAGE

All the uses of language that you will come across in poetry or in fiction are also found in non-fiction—or, for that matter, in everyday conversation. But one language use is so often thought of as "belonging" to imaginative literature that its treatment is probably more appropriate here than anywhere else in the book. That is *figurative language*—a kind of verbal play through which a writer (or speaker) makes clear that his words are not to be taken literally, that his meaning is quite different from the meaning the same words would have if he had used them to refer to specific objects or events.

That probably sounds like the methods used by Buchwald, Hoppe, Murray, and the other ironic and exaggerating non-fiction writers you read in the last chapter. Certainly their methods are types of figurative expression. But the sorts of figurative writing this chapter will examine—the kind most people associate with poems and with stories—are *metaphorical expressions and symbols.* When a writer makes use of exaggeration or irony, he builds up a double meaning through a tone that permeates the entire work. But when he uses symbolic or metaphorical language, he always accomplishes the "second" meaning through the use of specific words and phrases.

Metaphorical Expression

When you think of metaphorical language, you probably think of the language of poetry. And that makes sense because poets frequently do use metaphors. What you may not realize, however, is that you use them yourself almost every day—not for the purpose of being "flowery" or confusing (as many people mistakenly think poets do) but rather for the purpose of achieving quick, effective communication. For example, if you say to a friend, "Come into the garage and see the lemon I made the mistake of buying," you know that he will not be looking for a moldy citrus fruit; he will be preparing to sympathize with you for your bad choice of an automobile. And if you tell a friend that it is time to split or that Dylan turns you on, neither of you is thinking of any of the other (and, until recently, more common) uses of these terms; you are simply sharing an attitude in a way you both find completely clear and probably rather satisfying.

Slang, then—the language of very informal speech—includes many expressions comparing an object with another object (I've got to make some bread," "Look at her! What a fox!"), an action with another action ("Cool it"), or a characteristic of one kind of thing with a characteristic of another ("She wore a sharp-looking outfit"). The purpose anyone has in using these unstated comparisons (metaphors) is to communicate with someone he feels comfortable with in an easy, casual, sometimes quite emotional way.

The main difference between the metaphorical slang expressions in your speech and the metaphors you will find in poetry and in fiction is that the slang words and phrases usually convey a very *general* feeling or attitude. For many purposes these expressions serve you well, but they do not really particularize experiences. For example, when you hear someone say, "she sure is sharp-looking," you form your own mental picture; but you have no way of knowing that your picture is much like the one in the mind of the person who makes the statement. However, when Alfred Noyes, in the opening lines of the poem "The Highwayman," describes the wind as a "torrent of darkness," a road as "a ribbon of moonlight," and the moon as "a ghostly galleon tossed upon cloudy seas," he induces you to hear the wind and to see the road and the moon in the particular way he perceives them. Poets and fiction writers, then, use metaphors in precise ways to communicate observations, impressions, and feelings as accurately as they can.

Notice that Noyes' metaphors make use of words that "point" directly to things—words like "ribbon," "galleon," and "seas." But in the music of his lines they do much more than simply point to objects or refer to experiences. By creating vivid word-pictures, they communicate feeling. This use of picture or sense-impression language (which may include "pictures" of sounds and smells and tastes) is one of the basic characteristics of poetry, even of lines that are not metaphorical. When the pictures are simply straight descriptions of what the poet perceives, not phrases implying a comparison, they are called *images*. For example, when the highwayman is introduced, he is described as having

> . . . *a French cocked-hat* on his forehead, *a bunch of lace* at his chin,
> *A coat of the claret velvet* and *breeches of brown doe-skin.*

And when the picture-language compares one thing or experience with another by the use of *like,* or *as,* the figurative expression is called a *simile* rather than a metaphor. For example, later in Noyes' poem the highwayman is killed

> When they shot him down on the highway,
> Down like a dog on the highway

(The full poem is given in Chapter Supplement I, p. 308, if you want to see how it all fits together.)

The purpose of this discussion of the language of poetry is certainly not to convince you that before you can understand and enjoy a poem you need to be familiar with a lot of technical terminology. On the contrary, you may be able to share a poet's feeling without analyzing his language at all. But when you read a poem, you will probably find it helpful to know whether there is some figurative language there. Sometimes by recognizing a phrase as a metaphor or a simile and asking yourself what it could suggest, you will open up the meaning of a line, a stanza, or the whole poem.

As you read the following poem, just try to discover the poet's basic feeling about her subject and decide whether you share that feeling. (Many people do, but some do not.) You may need to read the poem more than once before you can be sure you know what the poet is talking about, but you will probably not have to analyze her uses of language. The metaphor "narrow fellow in the grass" in the first line is explained by the actions that are described throughout the poem.

A NARROW FELLOW IN THE GRASS

by Emily Dickinson

A narrow fellow in the grass
Occasionally rides;
You may have met him—did you not?
His notice sudden is.

The grass divides as with a comb,
A spotted shaft is seen;
And then it closes at your feet
And opens further on.

He likes a boggy acre,
A floor too cool for corn.
Yet when a boy, and barefoot,
I more than once, at morn,

Have passed, I thought, a whip lash
Unbraiding in the sun,—
When, stooping to secure it,
It wrinkled, and was gone.

Several of nature's people
I know, and they know me;
I feel for them a transport
Of cordiality;

But never met this fellow,
Attended or alone,
Without a tighter breathing,
And Zero at the Bone.

Does any part of the poem describe especially well a reaction to snakes or an impression of them you have had yourself—or one that is quite different from your experiences? (Don't make a problem of the fact that a woman poet, writing in the first person, speaks of having been "a boy." The "I" in a poem does not always represent a writer in a literal way.)

▶

Now read the poem again, noting in the space below some of the metaphors and similes you find. Think about ways each of these contribute to the literal meaning of the poem.

▶

These are some figurative expressions (mostly metaphors) from the four stanzas:

"occasionally rides" (a verb can be a metaphor, too)
"grass divides as with a comb" (a simile)
"floor too cool" (We do speak of the forest floor, but that is a metaphor, too. The only literal uses of floor are in references to buildings.)
"spotted shaft" (metaphor)
"It wrinkled" (metaphor)
"Tighter breathing" (metaphor)
"nature's people" (metaphor)
(And you could probably make a case for calling "It (grass) closes and opens" and "people I know, and they know me" metaphors, since these words are not used here to refer to humans, as they usually are.)

Several of these figures—"shaft," "wrinkled," and "narrow fellow"—describe a snake's thin, line-like structure. Others—"tighter breathing" and "Zero at the Bone"—suggest that whatever the snake associates with (including the narrator) becomes tight, and thin, and lacking a full, healthy expression of life. These last two figures introduce the idea of fear: the snake is frightening to the narrator because it is so unlike other living things.

The title metaphor of this poem, then, becomes a *symbol*. That is, the wording not only compares an object with another object (a snake with a person) but it suggests a relationship of that object to an abstract idea (the "narrow" snake produces the narrow, tight feeling of fear). As Laurence Perrine has pointed out in *Sound and Sense*, the difference between a metaphor and a symbol is that a metaphor "means something other than what it is" whereas a symbol "means what it is and something more, too." But there is no reason that the same expression cannot serve as both a metaphor and a symbol.

Interpreting Symbols in Poetry

Many students panic at the mention of literary symbols. And probably with good reason, because in some classrooms and in some textbooks "symbol-hunting" has been made a chore that has interfered with the reader's spontaneous and personal responses to poems and stories. But every reader of works of imaginative literature—especially poetry—must at least occasionally decide whether to take a word at face value or to interpret it metaphorically or symbolically. And when he decides to interpret it symbolically, he must have some reasons (whether he is consciously aware of them or not) for thinking that the word stands for one idea and not for another.

When you have this kind of decision to make as you read a poem, the best way to begin is to look for contextual clues within the poem. Although they may be less obvious than the clues that tell you that an expression is a metaphor or a simile, poets usually signal at least a very general intended meaning for a symbol in ways much like those you found non-fiction writers using to communicate their implied meanings. Because the implied meaning of a symbol often is so general, you usually will find that your own private, personal associations complement or expand that meaning.

But what if a word or phrase in a poem suggests to you a symbolic meaning that is not supported by any clues within the poem? This might happen in your first reading of the poem that follows—"The Eagle." Because in our society there are a number of qualities and experiences that people frequently associate with eagles, the very title of this poem will probably be rich in implications for you. Before you read the poem, note briefly in the space below any ideas, feelings, or situations you connect with eagles.

▶

Now read the poem through once to see whether your associations are similar to the poet's. This will be very much like the previewing you did for essays, articles, and non-fiction books. But you will be reading to find out whether you had the right first impression of the direction the poem was to take instead of skimming to see whether you had asked the right question.

THE EAGLE
by Alfred Lord Tennyson

He clasps the crag with crooked hands;
Close to the sun in lonely lands,
Ring'd with the azure world, he stands.

The wrinkled sea beneath him crawls;
He watches from his mountain walls,
And like a thunderbolt he falls.

Were any of your original associations with eagles on a different track from the one you found the writer was on? Which of your impressions was closest to the symbolic significance the poet finds in the eagle whose position and movements he observed?

▶

Some readers who approach this poem without "previewing" it insist that the eagle in the poem represents the United States. Was that one of your associations with the title? It might well have been, since the bald eagle is the national emblem. But is there any signal in the poem to suggest that the poet—Alfred Tennyson, an Englishman—is connecting the eagle he describes with the United States?

Of course, one of the reasons the people of this country chose an eagle for their national symbol in the first place was that the bird represented for them some qualities they regarded highly—qualities that the words "power," "energy," "strength," and "independence" describe. Did you use any of these words, or similar words, in your first comments on the title? There is much evidence in the poem that what the poet admires about the bird can be expressed by one or more of those words.

Read the poem again, looking this time for *metaphors* that compare the eagle with a strong and effective person and for others that describe the eagle's environment. Every line of this poem contains metaphorical expressions, and all of them serve one of these two purposes. (Some critics and teachers make a distinction between *metaphor* and *personification*, using personification to refer to expressions that assign human attributes to non-human things. For your purposes here, however, it will be appropriate to think of figures like "crooked hands" as metaphors.) List in the space below the other metaphors you find.

▶ METAPHORS DESCRIBING   METAPHORS DESCRIBING
    THE EAGLE   HIS SURROUNDINGS

Now think again about the symbolic meaning Tennyson's eagle takes on within the context of the poem. Which of the qualities you originally associated with eagles does the poem focus on? What "clues" show you this emphasis?

▶

(See Chapter Supplement II, p. 311, for comments on the metaphors and symbolism in "The Eagle.")

You may have some private associations with eagles that are suggested to you by your reading of this poem but for which there are no specific contextual clues. If so, list them below. Finding these private meanings is certainly an important part of the experience of reading a poem, but this part should not be confused with your understanding of the idea that is developed through specific references within the poem.

▶

FINDING IDEAS IN MODERN POETRY

The main idea of a poem will not always be a central symbol like the snake or the eagle. Modern poets, in particular, often use subtler and more complex methods to develop ideas. One of these is *contrast*—usually a contrast between the poet's experiences or observations and his ideals or desires.

The following poem tells the story of a wartime casualty that the poet regards as completely futile. It also implies some contrasts between the experience the protagonist had and experiences he might have had if he had lived in a better world. Read the poem through once, mainly to find out "what happened." Many poems tell stories, but they usually tell them in less direct ways than fiction and non-fiction narratives do. You will find here some hints about where the action takes place, what war it is, how the protagonist was killed, and what kind of person he was. But they will be only hints. (In fact, some of these comments will leave more than one interpretation open.) As you read for these story "clues," see if you can also pick up some of the contrasts the poet is making.

ULTIMA RATIO REGUM

by Stephen Spender

The guns spell money's ultimate reason
In letters of lead on the Spring hillside.
But the boy lying dead under the olive trees
Was too young and too silly
To have been notable to their important eye.
He was a better target for a kiss.

When he lived, tall factory hooters never summoned him.
Nor did restaurant plate-glass doors revolve to
        wave him in.
His name never appeared in the papers.
The world maintained its traditional wall
Round the dead with their gold sunk deep as a well,
Whilst his life, intangible as a Stock-Exchange rumour,
        drifted outside.

O too lightly he threw down his cap
One day when the breeze threw petals from the trees.
The unflowering wall sprouted with guns,
Machine-gun anger quickly scythed the grasses;
Flags and leaves fell from hands and branches;
The tweed cap rotted in the nettles.

Consider his life which was valueless
In terms of employment, hotel ledgers, news files.
Consider. One bullet in ten thousand kills a man.
Ask. Was so much expenditure justified
On the death of one so young, and so silly
Lying under the olive trees, O world, O death?

▶ STORY TOLD BY POEM:

▶ CONTRASTS USED BY POET:

Did you place the action in the Spanish Civil War of the 1930s? Don't worry if you did not, but the mention of the olive trees and the tweed cap might have indicated that time and place to you—if you happened to remember certain geographical and historical facts. Did you realize that the protagonist is a young man who has probably only recently become a soldier? (Some readers think of him as being a civilian at the time he is killed, but the phrase "too lightly he threw down his cap" suggests that he had officially joined the conflict.) He is probably very young (fifteen to eighteen?). The description of him as being "a better target for a kiss" combined with the comment that "tall factory hooters never summoned him" probably means that he was a youth almost ready for an adult life of work and love. His life, then, was ironically cut off just as he was getting ready to live. The poet contrasts the world of the "important" people who have made this war—a world of riches, bullets, and death—with the world the boy knew—a world of "Spring hillsides," kisses, and life.

Now read the poem again, this time looking for *ironic images*—that is, for picture-words that contrast the scene the poet observes with the scene he would like to have been able to see, or that contrast two aspects of the scene he does see. Actually, most of the ironic images in this poem do both of these things at the same time: for example, "letters of lead (a metaphor) on the Spring hillside" and "the unflowering wall sprouted with guns." What other examples of ironic picture-language do you find in the poem?

▶

You may have wondered about the use of the word "silly" in the first and last stanzas. (In a poem, as in an essay, the opening and closing lines are good places to look for points of emphasis.) Certainly the boy is not portrayed as silly in the usual derogatory sense of "foolish." If anyone in the poem is foolish (and the term is really too mild to be appropriate anywhere in this grim piece), it is the people who brought about the war in the first place. In earlier times, however, the word "silly" meant first "happy" and later "weak" or "frail" and "rustic" or "simple." And it is still sometimes used in all but the first of these senses. There is, then, a kind of double irony in the poet's use of this word. The boy is both silly and the opposite of silly. He is rustic and innocent and in comparison with the guns he is weak; but because he is a human being, he is important and he is worthy of respect.

In the same way, the word "important" in the fifth line takes on a double meaning, one of these being strongly ironic. The phrase "their important eye" is a direct reference to the "eye" of each of the guns that are shooting at the time the young man happens to walk by; and it is also an indirect reference to the military establishment that provided the soldiers with these guns. The guns and the military are "important" in the sense that they are able to control the lives of a lot of people, but insofar as ultimate value or worth is concerned, they are unimportant; one human life is worth much more.

You might discuss with your classmates and with your instructor the ironic senses of "as a Stock Exchange rumour" (in what ways was the boy's life *not* like a Stock Exchange rumor?), the symbol of olive trees (what do olive trees usually symbolize?), the word "valueless" in the first line of the last stanza, and the image of "flags and leaves" falling from "hands and branches."

Read the poem through one more time to get the full theme, the specific main idea. The poet is saying more than just that it was unfortunate that the young man was killed. Whom or what is he blaming for this tragic accident? A translation of the title will probably help you in this reading, although the first line alone might be a sufficient first signal of the main idea, now that you have thought about the story and some of the irony of the poem. The Latin title means in English "The Final Reason for Things."

▶ MAIN IDEA (THEME) OF THE POEM:

(See the comments in Chapter Supplement III, p. 312)

Many poems are quite different in form, in ideas, and even in language from any of the three you have just read. And you will find that many will not require the number of readings you gave the Splender poem. But through your multiple readings of these poems, you have discovered that you can approach a poem in much the same way that you approach an essay or an article. That is, you can usually find in the title or in an opening line a signal that will give you some idea of the direction the work will take. When there are no helpful early signals, you can often get at least a general understanding of the main idea by reading the poem through once, thinking mainly about the story it tells or the information it gives. Then when you have this general understanding of the main idea (the theme), you can read the work through carefully, looking for deeper implications This approach also works well with the short stories in the last part of this chapter and with the short and long works of fiction you will read while in college and afterward.

FINDING IDEAS IN SHORT STORIES

Unlike most of the non-fiction writing you read in earlier chapters, poems and stories are usually written to entertain the reader rather than primarily to inform him. But writers of imaginative literature also often imply *judgments* about the people and the conditions they write about, and critics and teachers often call these judgments *themes*. Unfortunately, many students have the idea that a "theme" is something complicated and mysterious that they can find only by looking outside the "what happens" part of the story or poem, the part in which they are usually most interested. But, as you discovered in the last section, your understanding of the theme of a poem can grow out of your understanding of what happened in it—and of the significance the writer found in the events he described.

This is also true of short stories. In your first reading of a short story, as in your first reading of a poem, it is a good idea to pay particular attention to the title and to the opening lines. If the story has a central symbol, the title will usually mention it. And either the title or an early sentence will probably suggest a point of emphasis, an important inference the writer draws from the circumstances he relates.

The following story, for example, has a very simple plot. Yet as you read it to see what happens (and *plot* is simply another word for the "what happens" part of a story) you will probably find yourself thinking about the title—"The Japanese Quince"—and about the condition of the protagonist that the first sentence describes. What is Mr. Nilson's "problem"? What does it have to do with the quince tree? Does he resolve this problem?

THE JAPANESE QUINCE
by John Galsworthy

As Mr. Nilson, well known in the City, opened the window of his dressing-room on Campden Hill, he experienced a peculiar sweetish sensation in the back of his throat, and a feeling of emptiness just under his fifth rib. Hooking the window back, he noticed that a little tree in the Square Gardens had come out in blossom, and that the thermometer stood at sixty. 'Perfect morning,' he thought; 'spring at last!'

Resuming some meditations on the price of Tintos, he took up an ivory-backed hand-glass and scrutinised his face. His firm, well-coloured cheeks, with their neat brown moustaches, and his round, well-opened, clear grey eyes, wore a reassuring appearance of good health. Putting on his black frock coat, he went downstairs.

In the dining-room his morning paper was laid out on the sideboard. Mr. Nilson had scarcely taken it in his hand when he again became aware of that queer feeling. Somewhat concerned, he went to the French window and descended the scrolled iron steps into the fresh air. A cuckoo clock struck eight.

'Half an hour to breakfast,' he thought; 'I'll take a turn in the Gardens.'

He had them to himself, and proceeded to pace the circular path with his morning paper clasped behind him. He had scarcely made two revolutions, however, when it was borne in on him that, instead of going away in the fresh air, the feeling had increased.

He drew several deep breaths, having heard deep breathing recommended by his wife's doctor; but they augmented rather than
diminished the sensation—as if some sweetish liquor in course
within him, together with a faint aching just above his heart.
Running over what he had eaten the night before, he could
recollect no unusual dish, and it occured to him that it might possibly be some smell affecting him. But he could detect nothing except a faint sweet lemony scent, rather agreeable than otherwise,
which evidently emanated from the bushes budding in the sunshine. He was on the point of resuming his promenade, when a
blackbird close by burst into song, and, looking up, Mr. Nilson saw
at a distance of perhaps five yards a little tree, in the heart of
whose branches the bird was perched. He stood staring curiously
at this tree, recognizing it for that which he had noticed from
his window. It was covered with young blossoms, pink and white,
and little bright green leaves both round and spiky; and on all
this blossom and these leaves the sunlight glistened. Mr. Nilson
smiled; the little tree was so alive and pretty! And instead of passing on, he stayed there smiling at the tree.

'Morning like this!' he thought; 'and here I am the only person in the Square who has the—to come out and—!' But he had
no sooner conceived this thought than he saw quite near him a
man with his hands behind him, who was also staring up and
smiling at the little tree. Rather taken aback, Mr. Nilson ceased to
smile, and looked furtively at the stranger. It was his next-door
neighbour, Mr. Tandram, well known in the City, who had oc-
cupied the adjoining house for some five years. Mr. Nilson per-
ceived at once the awkwardness of his position, for, being married,
they had not yet had occasion to speak to one another. Doubtful
as to his proper conduct, he decided at last to murmur: "Fine
morning!" and was passing on, when Mr. Tandram answered:
"Beautiful, for the time of year!" Detecting a slight nervousness
in his neighbour's voice, Mr. Nilson was emboldened to regard
him openly. He was of about Mr. Nilson's own height, with firm,
well-coloured cheeks, neat brown moustaches, and round,
well-opened, clear grey eyes; and he was wearing a black frock
coat. Mr. Nilson noticed that he had his morning paper clasped
behind him as he looked up at the little tree. And, visited somehow
by the feeling that he had been caught out, he said abruptly:

"Er—can you give me the name of that tree?"

Mr. Tandram answered:

"I was about to ask you that," and stepped towards it. Mr.
Nilson also approached the tree.

"Sure to have its name on, I should think," he said.

Mr. Tandram was the first to see the little label, close to
where the blackbird had been sitting. He read it out.

"Japanese quince!"

"Ah!" said Mr. Nilson, "thought so. Early flowerers."

"Very," assented Mr. Tandram, and added: "Quite a feelin'
in the air to-day."

Mr. Nilson nodded.

"It was a blackbird singin'," he said.

"Blackbirds," answered Mr. Tandram, "I prefer them to thrushes myself; more body in the note." And he looked at Mr. Nilson in an almost friendly way.

"Quite," murmured Mr. Nilson. "These exotics, they don't bear fruit. Pretty blossom!" and he again glanced up at the blossom, thinking: 'Nice fellow, this, I rather like him.'

Mr. Tandram also gazed at the blossom. And the little tree, as if appreciating their attention, quivered and glowed. From a distance the blackbird gave a loud, clear call. Mr. Nilson dropped his eyes. It struck him suddenly that Mr. Tandram looked a little foolish; and, as if he had seen himself, he said: "I must be going in. Good morning!"

A shade passed over Mr. Tandram's face, as if he, too, had suddenly noticed something about Mr. Nilson.

"Good morning," he replied, and clasping their journals to their backs they separated.

Mr. Nilson retraced his steps towards his garden window, walking slowly so as to avoid arriving at the same time as his neighbour. Having seen Mr. Tandram mount his scrolled iron steps, he ascended his own in turn. On the top step he paused.

With the slanting spring sunlight darting and quivering into it, the Japanese quince seemed more living than a tree. The blackbird had returned to it, and was chanting out his heart.

Mr. Nilson sighed; again he felt that queer sensation, that choky feeling in his throat.

The sound of a cough or sigh attracted his attention. There, in the shadow of his French window, stood Mr. Tandram, also looking forth across the Gardens at the little quince tree.

Unaccountably upset, Mr. Nilson turned abruptly into the house, and opened his morning paper.

Comment briefly on Mr. Nilson's reaction to the quince tree. Is "The Japanese Quince" an appropriate title for this story? Why?

▶

Whether or not you used the word "symbolic" or "symbol" in your answer, you probably saw that the quince tree in the garden means a great deal to Mr. Nilson on this particular spring morning. It represents to him springtime, freedom, and, above all, the expression of feeling. Its blossoms somehow induce him to let go of just a little of the emotion he has repressed while becoming "well known in the City." For example, he admits to himself that the smell of the spring blossoms is "rather agreeable than otherwise" and he manages to hold a conversation of sorts with a neighbor he hasn't spoken to in five years, even thinking: "Nice fellow, this, I rather like him."

What about that neighbor—Mr. Tandram? What obvious similarities are there between Mr. Tandram and Mr. Nilson? In what ways are their experiences and their reactions on this particular day alike? How do you account for these similarities? You will possibly need to read the story again in order to fully understand the role Mr. Tandram plays in it. If you do read it through again with particular attention to Mr. Tandram, you will get an increased understanding of what it is that is bothering Mr. Nilson (at the beginning of the story).

▶ SIMILARITIES OF MR. NILSON AND MR. TANDRAM:

▶ MR. NILSON'S "PROBLEM":

Mr. Nilson and Mr. Tandram are much alike physically, socially, and psychologically. They are of about the same height, they both have "neat brown moustaches," they both are "well known in the City," and they both—on this day— enjoy the scents and sights of the beginning of spring and try to communicate their pleasure to each other. But they are too repressed emotionally to do any more than talk stiffly and intellectually about what is really an intensely emotional experience and then walk away into their private worlds, clasping their newspapers to their backs.

The "queer" feeling that disturbs Mr. Nilson at the beginning of the story, then, is not only the physical sensation he gets from smelling the quince tree blossoms; it is also a vague awareness that he has been missing something in life. (He has "a feeling of emptiness just under his fifth rib" and "a faint aching just above his heart.") This awareness becomes stronger as he talks to Mr. Tandram in the garden by the quince tree. Then his old inhibitions return and he is ashamed of the feeling he had begun to experience. After he has admitted to himself that he likes his neighbor, whose feelings are apparently much like his own, he withdraws: "It struck him suddenly that Mr. Tandram looked a little foolish; and, as if he had seen himself, he said: "I must be going in. Good morning!"

Some readers see Mr. Tandram only as a reflection of Mr. Nilson's personality, not as an actual second person. However, because the narrator describes a conversation in the garden and ends it with the two men walking away from each other, it is reasonable to assume that a meeting takes place rather than to regard the episode as a fantasy of Mr. Nilson's. But it is true that the reader sees the second man only through Mr. Nilson's eyes. (The whole story, in fact, is told from his point of view.) And Mr. Nilson finds in Mr. Tandram the qualities he is most aware of in himself. Therefore, in one sense, Tandram is a "reflection" of Nilson. At any rate, the protagonist's morning encounter with his neighbor in the garden intensifies for him a conflict he has had since he woke up: He would like to relax and enjoy springtime and the deep feelings it brings out in him, but such attitudes do not befit a man of the "City," and he must get to work. The theme of the story is simply that a man of business has a conflict between his need to be practical and his desire to express feelings and finds that the only way he can resolve it is by denying or repressing his emotions. Whether this man is like others of his class or like anyone you know is for you to decide; but the writer does leave such an interpretation open.

One of the biggest problems you may have in understanding ideas (finding themes) in fiction is knowing how much to generalize from the particular experiences that are being recounted. For example, if a story is about a young man who drops out of college to marry a high school girl and who proceeds to get them both deeper and deeper into trouble, does that mean that the theme of the story is that young men should not leave college to get married? The answer to that one is almost certainly—No.

The idea, or theme, of a story grows out of the particular situation the writer sets up in the lives of the particular characters he creates. This theme becomes a *moral*—a lesson showing how people should live—only if the writer provides specific signals suggesting that interpretation (as in the Biblical parables and *Aesop's Fables*). But most modern story writers do not do this. Most of them, in fact, do not create characters who are symbolic to the extent that the two characters in "The Japanese Quince" are. Anyway, the symbolism in that story does not show the way successful British businessmen *should* live; it simply shows the way some such men *do* live.

The next story, "Warm River" by Erskine Caldwell, is more typical of contemporary short stories. The words of the title appear again in key places in the story—for example, in the opening and closing paragraphs—and thereby suggest that they should be interpreted symbolically. But you will find that the symbol of the warm river has a very private meaning for the protagonist, and there is no indication in the story that you should interpret it in a more general sense —that is, apply it to anyone else's life (although you probably will identify with the protagonist as you read).

Read this story any way you want and as many times as you want. Because it is the kind of story you can lose yourself in during the first reading, you may want to forget about any kind of analysis until you have read it through just to enjoy identifying with the protagonist's experiences. When you are ready, write

in the space at the end of the story some brief comments on the central symbol
and on the theme, which are closely related.

WARM RIVER
by Erskine Caldwell

The driver stopped at the suspended footbridge and pointed out
to me the house across the river. I paid him the quarter fare for
the ride from the station two miles away and stepped from the car.
After he had gone I was alone with the chill night and the star-
pointed lights twinkling in the valley and the broad green river
flowing warm below me. All around me the mountains rose like
black clouds in the night, and only by looking straight heavenward
could I see anything of the dim afterglow of sunset.

The creaking footbridge swayed with the rhythm of my stride
and the momentum of its swing soon overcame my pace. Only by
walking faster and faster could I cling to the pendulum as it swung
in its wide arc over the river. When at last I could see the other
side, where the mountain came down abruptly and slid under the
warm water, I gripped my handbag tighter and ran with all my
might.

Even then, even after my feet had crunched upon the gravel
path, I was afraid. I knew that by day I might walk the bridge
without fear; but at night, in a strange country, with dark mountains towering all around me and a broad green river flowing
beneath me, I could not keep my hands from trembling and my
heart from pounding against my chest.

I found the house easily, and laughed at myself for having
run from the river. The house was the first one to come upon after
leaving the footbridge, and even if I should have missed it,
Gretchen would have called me. She was there on the steps of the
porch waiting for me. When I heard her familiar voice calling my
my name, I was ashamed of myself for having been frightened by
the mountains and the broad river flowing below.

She ran down the gravel path to meet me.

"Did the footbridge frighten you, Richard?" she asked ex-
citedly, holding my arm with both of her hands and guiding me
up the path to the house.

"I think it did, Gretchen," I said; "but I hope I outran it."

"Everyone tries to do that at first, but after going over it once,
it's like walking a tightrope. I used to walk tightropes when I was
small—didn't you do that, too, Richard? We had a rope stretched
across the floor of our our barn to practice on."

"I did, too, but it's been so long ago I've forgotten how to do
it now."

We reached the steps and went up to the porch. Gretchen
took me to the door. Someone inside the house was bringing a

lamp into the hall, and with the coming of the light I saw
Gretchen's two sisters standing just inside the open door.

"This is my little sister, Anne," Gretchen said. "And this is
Mary."

I spoke to them in the semidarkness and we went on into the
hall. Gretchen's father was standing beside a table holding the
lamp a little to one side so that he could see my face. I had not met
him before.

"This is my father," Gretchen said. "He was afraid you
wouldn't be able to find our house in the dark."

"I wanted to bring a light down to the bridge and meet you,
but Gretchen said you would get here without any trouble. Did
you get lost? I could have brought a lantern down with no trouble
at all."

I shook hands with him and told him how easily I had found
the place.

"The hack driver pointed out to me the house from the other
side of the river, and I never once took my eyes from the light.
If I had lost sight of the light, I'd probably be stumbling around
somewhere now in the dark down there getting ready to fall into
the water."

He laughed at me for being afraid of the river.

"You wouldn't have minded it. The river is warm. Even in
winter, when there is ice and snow underfoot, the river is as warm
as a comfortable room. All of us here love the water down there."

"No, Richard, you wouldn't have fallen in," Gretchen said,
laying her hand in mine. "I saw you the moment you got out of the
hack, and if you had gone a step in the wrong direction, I was
ready to run to you."

I wished to thank Gretchen for saying that, but already she
was going to the stairs to the floor above, and calling me. I went
with her, lifting my handbag in front of me. There was a shaded
lamp, lighted but turned low, on the table at the end of the
upper hall, and she picked it up and went ahead into one of the
front rooms.

We stood for a moment looking at each other, and silent.

"There is fresh water in the pitcher, Richard. If there is anything else you would like to have, please tell me. I tried not to
overlook anything."

"Don't worry, Gretchen," I told her. "I couldn't wish for
anything more. It's enough just to be here with you, anyway.
There's nothing else I care for."

She looked at me quickly, and then she lowered her eyes. We
stood silently for several minutes, while neither of us could think
of anything to say. I wanted to tell her how glad I was to be with
her, even if it was only for one night, but I knew I could say that
to her later. Gretchen knew why I had come.

"I'll leave the lamp for you, Richard, and I'll wait downstairs
for you on the porch. Come as soon as you are ready".

She had left before I could offer to carry the light to the

stairhead for her to see the way down. By the time I had picked up the lamp, she was out of sight down the stairs.

I walked back into the room and closed the door and bathed my face and hands, scrubbing the train dust with brush and soap. There was a row of hand-embroidered towels on the rack, and I took one and dried my face and hands. After that I combed my hair, and found a fresh handkerchief in the handbag. Then I opened the door and went downstairs to find Gretchen.

Her father was on the porch with her. When I walked through the doorway, he got up and gave me a chair between them. Gretchen pulled her chair closer to mine, touching my arm with her hand.

"Is this the first time you have been up here in the mountains, Richard?" her father asked me, turning in his chair towards me.

"I've never been within a hundred miles of here before, sir. It's a different country up here, but I suppose you would think the same about the coast, wouldn't you?"

"Oh, but Father used to live in Norfolk," Gretchen said. "Didn't you, Father?"

"I lived there for nearly three years."

There was something else he would say, and both of us waited for him to continue.

"Father is a master mechanic," Gretchen whispered to me. "He works in the railroad shops."

"Yes," he said after a while, "I've lived in many places, but here is where I wish to stay."

My first thought was to ask him why he preferred the mountains to other sections, but suddenly I was aware that both he and Gretchen were strangely silent. Between them, I sat wondering about it.

After a while he spoke again, not to me and not to Gretchen, but as though he were speaking to someone else on the porch, a fourth person whom I had failed to see in the darkness. I waited, tense and excited, for him to continue.

Gretchen moved her chair a few inches closer to mine, her motions gentle and without sound. The warmth of the river came up and covered us like a blanket on a chill night.

"After Gretchen and the other two girls lost their mother," he said, almost inaudibly, bending forward over his knees and gazing out across the broad green river, "after we lost their mother, I came back to the mountains to live. I couldn't stay in Norfolk, and I couldn't stand it in Baltimore. This was the only place on earth where I could find peace. Gretchen remembers her mother, but neither of you can yet understand how it is with me. Her mother and I were born here in the mountains, and we lived here together for almost twenty years. Then after she left us, I moved away, foolishly believing that I could forget. But I was wrong. Of course I was wrong. A man can't forget the mother of his children, even though he knows he will never see her again."

Gretchen leaned closer to me, and I could not keep my eyes

from her darkly framed profile beside me. The river below us made no sound; but the warmth of its vapor would not let me forget that it was still there.

Her father had bent farther forward in his chair until his arms were resting on his knees, and he seemed to be trying to see someone on the other side of the river, high on the mountain top above it. His eyes strained and the shaft of light that came through the open doorway fell upon them and glistened there. Tears fell from his face like fragments of stars burning into his quivering hands until they were out of sight.

Presently, still in silence, he got up and moved through the doorway. His huge shadow fell upon Gretchen and me as he stood there momentarily before going inside. I turned and looked towards him but, even though he was passing from sight, I could not keep my eyes upon him.

Gretchen leaned closer against me, squeezing her fingers into the hollow of my hand and touching my shoulder with her cheeks as though she were trying to wipe something from them. Her father's footsteps grew fainter, and at last we could no longer hear him.

Somewhere below us, along the bank of the river, an express train crashed down the valley, creaking and screaming through the night. Occasionally its lights flashed through the openings in the darkness, dancing on the broad green river like polar lights in the north, and the metallic echo of its steel rumbled against the high walls of the mountains.

Gretchen clasped her hands tightly over my hand, trembling to her fingertips.

"Richard, why did you come to see me?"

"I don't know why I came, Gretchen."

Her voice was mingled with the screaming metallic echo of the train that now seemed far off.

I had expected to find her looking up into my face, but when I turned to her, I saw that she was gazing far down into the valley, down into the warm waters of the river. She knew why I had come, but she did not wish to hear me say why I had.

I do not know why I had come to see her, now. I had liked Gretchen, and I had desired her above anyone else I knew. But I could not tell her that I loved her, after having heard her father speak of love. I was sorry I had come, now after having heard him speak of Gretchen's mother as he did. I knew Gretchen would give herself to me, because she loved me; but I had nothing to give her in return. She was beautiful, very beautiful, and I had desired her. That was before. Now, I knew that I could never again think of her as I had come prepared.

"Why did you come, Richard?"

"Why?"

"Yes, Richard; why?"

My eyes closed, and what I felt was the memory of the star-pointed lights twinkling down in the valley and the warmth of the river flowing below and the caress of her fingers as she touched my arm.

"Richard, please tell me why you came."

"I don't know why I came, Gretchen."

"If you only loved me as I love you, Richard, you would know why."

Her fingers trembled in my hand. I knew she loved me. There had been no doubt in my mind from the first. Gretchen loved me.

"Perhaps I should not have come," I said. "I made a mistake, Gretchen. I should have stayed away."

"But you will be here only for tonight, Richard. You are leaving early in the morning. You aren't sorry that you came for just this short time, are you, Richard?"

"I'm not sorry that I am here, Gretchen, but I should not have come. I didn't know what I was doing. I haven't any right to come here. People who love each other are the only ones—"

"But you do love me just a little, don't you, Richard? You couldn't possibly love me nearly so much as I love you, but can't you tell me that you do love me just a little? I'll feel much happier after you have gone, Richard."

"I don't know," I said, trembling.

"Richard, please—"

With her hands in mind I held her tightly. Suddenly I felt something coming over me, a thing that stabbed my body with its quickness. It was as if the words her father had uttered were becoming clear to me. I had not realized before that there was such a love as he had spoken of. I had believed that men never loved women in the same way that a woman loved a man, but now I knew there could be no difference.

We sat silently, holding each other's hands for a long time. It was long past midnight, because the lights in the valley below were being turned out; but time did not matter.

Gretchen clung softly to me, looking up into my face and laying her cheek against my shoulder. She was as much mine as a woman ever belongs to a man, but I knew then that I could never force myself to take advantage of her love, and to go away knowing that I had not loved her as she loved me. I had not believed any such thing when I came. I had traveled all that distance to hold her in my arms for a few hours, and then to forget her, perhaps forever.

When it was time for us to go into the house, I got up and put my arms around her. She trembled when I touched her, but she clung to me as tightly as I held her, and the hammering of her heart drove into me, stroke after stroke, like an expanding wedge, the spears of her breasts.

"Richard, kiss me before you go," she said.

She ran to the door, holding it open for me. She picked up the lamp from the table and walked ahead up the stairs to the floor above.

At my door she waited until I could light her lamp, and then she handed me mine.

"Good night, Gretchen," I said.

"Good night, Richard."

I turned down the wick of her lamp to keep it from smoking, and then she went across the hall towards her room.

"I'll call you in the morning in time for you to catch your train, Richard."

"All right, Gretchen. Don't let me oversleep, because it leaves the station at seven-thirty."

"I'll wake you in plenty of time, Richard," she said.

The door was closed after her, and I turned and went into my room. I shut the door and slowly began to undress. After I had blown out the lamp and had got into bed, I lay tensely awake. I knew I could never go to sleep, and sat up in bed and smoked cigarette after cigarette, blowing the smoke through the screen at the window. The house was quiet. Occasionally, I thought I heard the sounds of muffled movements in Gretchen's room across the hall, but I was not certain.

I could not determine how long a time I had sat there on the edge of the bed, stiff and erect, thinking of Gretchen, when suddenly I found myself jumping to my feet. I opened the door and ran across the hall. Gretchen's door was closed, but I knew it would not be locked, and I turned the knob noiselessly. A slender shaft of light broke through the opening I had made. It was not necessary to open the door wider, because I saw Gretchen only a few steps away, almost within arm's reach of me. I closed my eyes tightly for a moment, thinking of her as I had during the day's ride up from the coast.

Gretchen had not heard me open her door, and she did not know I was there. Her lamp was burning brightly on the table.

I had not expected to find her awake, and I had thought surely she would be in bed. She knelt on the rug beside her bed, her head bowed over her arms and her body shaken with sobs.

Gretchen's hair was lying over her shoulders, tied over the top of her head with a pale blue ribbon. Her nightgown was white silk, hemmed with a delicate lace, and around her neck the collar of lace was thrown open.

I knew how beautiful she was when I saw her then, even though I had always thought her lovely. I had never seen a girl so beautiful as Gretchen.

She had not heard me at her door, and she still did not know I was there. She knelt beside her bed, her hands clenched before her, crying.

When I had first opened the door, I did not know what I was about to do; but now that I had seen her in her room, kneeling in prayer beside her bed, unaware that I was looking upon her and hearing her words and sobs, I was certain that I could never care for anyone else as I did her. I had not known until then, but in the revelation of a few seconds I knew that I did love her.

I closed the door softly and went back to my room. There I found a chair and placed it beside the window to wait for the coming of day. At the window I sat and looked down into the bottom of the valley where the warm river lay. As my eyes grew more accustomed to the darkness, I felt as if I were coming closer and closer to it, so close that I might have reached out and touched the warm water with my hands.

Later in the night, towards morning, I thought I heard some-one in Gretchen's room moving softly over the floor as one who would go from window to window. Once I was certain I heard someone in the hall, close to my door.

When the sun rose over the top of the mountain, I got up and dressed. Later, I heard Gretchen leave her room and go downstairs. I knew she was hurrying to prepare breakfast for me before I left to get on the train. I waited awhile, and after a quarter of an hour I heard her coming back up the stairs. She knocked softly on my door, calling my name several times.

I jerked open the door and faced her. She was so surprised at seeing me there, when she had expected to find me still asleep, that she could not say anything for a moment.

"Gretchen," I said, grasping her hands, "don't hurry to get me off—I'm not going back this morning—I don't know what was the matter with me last night—I know now that I love you—"

"But, Richard—last night you said—"

"I did say last night that I was going back early this morning, Gretchen, but I didn't know what I was talking about. I'm not going back now until you go with me. I'll tell you what I mean as soon as breakfast is over. But first of all I wish you would show me how to get down to the river. I have got to go down there right away and feel the water with my hands."

▶ SYMBOL AND THEME:

(Compare your comments with those in Chapter Supplement IV, p. 312.)

Not all short stories, of course, are based on symbols that are introduced in their titles. The themes of many stories grow out of conflicts in the lives of the central characters that are only hinted at in the titles. In John Updike's story, "A & P," for example, the title and the opening lines do not convey much except that this is a story about a young grocery store clerk who has a somewhat unusual day at work. But as you read on, you will find that this young man, the narrator of the story, reveals a lot about himself as he talks. One of the things he reveals is the way he feels about where he works. The title, then, takes on more meaning as you get deeper into the story and as you think about the boy's personality. Again, it will probably be a good idea to read the story the first time mainly to find out what happens, keeping in the back of your mind questions about the title and the boy's attitude. Do you identify with the protagonist? Would you have done what he does? After you have read the story as many times as you like, answer the questions on page 307.

A & P

by John Updike

In walks these three girls in nothing but bathing suits. I'm in the third checkout slot, with my back to the door, so I don't see them until they're over by the bread. The one that caught my eye first was the one in the plaid green two-piece. She was a chunky kid, with a good tan and a sweet broad soft-looking can with those two crescents of white just under it, where the sun never seems to hit, at the top of the backs of her legs. I stood there with my hand on a box of HiHo crackers trying to remember if I rang it up or not. I ring it up again and the customer starts giving me hell. She's one of these cash-register-watchers, a witch about fifty with rouge on her cheekbones and no eyebrows, and I know it made her day to trip me up. She'd been watching cash registers for fifty years and probably never seen a mistake before.

By the time I got her feathers smoothed and her goodies into a bag—she gives me a little snort in passing, if she'd been born at the right time they would have burned her over in Salem—by the time I get her on her way the girls had circled around the bread and were coming back, without a pushcart, back my way along the counters, in the aisle between the checkouts and the Special bins. They didn't even have shoes on. There was this chunky one, with the two-piece—it was bright green and the seams on the bra were still sharp and her belly was still pretty pale so I guessed she just got it (the suit)—there was this one, with one of those chubby berry-faces, the lips all bunched together under her nose, this one, and a tall one, with black hair that hadn't quite frizzed right, and one of these sunburns right across under the eyes, and a chin that was too long—you know, the kind of girl other girls think is very "striking" and "attractive" but never quite makes it, as they very well know, which is why they like her so much—and then the third one, that wasn't quite so tall. She was the queen. She kind of led them, the other two peeking around and making their shoulders round. She didn't look around, not this queen, she just walked straight on slowly, on these long white prima-donna legs. She came down a little hard on her heels, as if she didn't walk in her bare feet that much, putting down her heels and then letting the weight move along to her toes as if she was testing the floor with every step, putting a little deliberate extra action into it. You never know for sure how girls' minds work (do you really think it's a mind in there or just a little buzz like a bee in a glass jar?) but you got the idea she had talked the other two into coming in here with her, and now she was showing them how to do it, walk slow and hold yourself straight.

She had on a kind of dirty-pink—beige maybe, I don't know —bathing suit with a little nubble all over it and, what got me, the straps were down. They were off her shoulders looped loose around the cool tops of her arms, and I guess as a result the suit had slipped a little on her, so all around the top of the cloth there was this shining rim. If it hadn't been there you wouldn't have known there could have been anything whiter than those shoulders. With the straps pushed off, there was nothing between the top of the suit and the top of her head except just *her,* this clean bare plane of the top of her chest down from the shoulder bones like a dented sheet of metal tilted in the light. I mean, it was more than pretty.

She had sort of oaky hair that the sun and salt had bleached, done up in a bun that was unravelling, and a kind of prim face. Walking into the A & P with your straps down, I suppose it's the only kind of face you *can* have. She held her head so high her neck, coming up out of those white shoulders, looked kind of stretched, but I didn't mind. The longer her neck was, the more of her there was.

She must have felt in the corner of her eye me and over my shoulder Stokesie in the second slot watching, but she didn't tip. Not this queen. She kept her eyes moving across the racks, and stopped, and turned so slow it made my stomach rub the inside of my apron, and buzzed to the other two, who kind of huddled against her for relief, and then they all three of them went up the cat-and-dog-food-breakfast-cereal-macaroni-rice-raisins-seasonings-spreads-spaghetti-soft drinks-crackers and cookies aisle. From the third slot I look straight up this aisle to the meat counter, and I watched them all the way. The fat one with the tan sort of fumbled with the cookies, but on second thought she put the package back. The sheep pushing their carts down the aisle— the girls were walking against the usual traffic (not that we have one-way signs or anything)—were pretty hilarious. You could see them, when Queenie's white shoulders dawned on them, kind of jerk, or hop, or hiccup, but their eyes snapped back to their own baskets and on they pushed. I bet you could set off dynamite in an A & P and the people would by and large keep reaching and checking oatmeal off their lists and muttering "Let me see, there was a third thing, began with A, asparagus, no, ah, yes, apple-sauce!" or whatever it is they do mutter. But there was no doubt, this jiggled them. A few houseslaves in pin curlers even looked around after pushing their carts past to make sure what they had seen was correct.

You know, it's one thing to have a girl in a bathing suit down on the beach, where what with the glare nobody can look at each other much anyway, and another thing in the cool of the A & P, under the fluorescent lights, against all those stacked packages, with her feet paddling along naked over our checker-board green-and- cream rubber-tile floor.

"Oh Daddy," Stokesie said beside me. "I feel so faint."

"Darling," I said. "Hold me tight." Stokesie's married, with two babies chalked up on his fuselage already, but as far as I can tell that's the only difference. He's twenty-two, and I was nineteen this April.

"Is it done?" he asks, the responsible married man finding his voice. I forgot to say he thinks he's going to be manager some day, maybe in 1990 when it's called the Great Alexandrov and Petrooshki Tea Company or something.

What he meant was, our town is five miles from a beach, with a big summer colony out on the Point, but we're right in the middle of town, and the women generally put on a shirt or shorts or something before they get out of the car into the street. And anyway these are usually women with six children and varicose veins mapping their legs and nobody, including them, could care less. As I say, we're right in the middle of town, and if you stand at our front doors you can see two banks and the Congregational church and the newspaper store and three real-estate offices and about twenty-seven old freeloaders tearing up Central Street be-cause the sewer broke again. It's not as if we're on the Cape; we're north of Boston and there's people in this town haven't seen the ocean for twenty years.

The girls had reached the meat counter and were asking McMahon something. He pointed, they pointed, and they shuffled out of sight behind a pyramid of Diet Delight peaches. All that was left for us to see was old McMahon patting his mouth and looking after them sizing up their joints. Poor kids, I began to feel sorry for them, they couldn't help it.

Now here comes the sad part of the story, at least my family says it's sad, but I don't think it's so sad myself. The store's pretty empty, it being Thursday afternoon, so there was nothing much to do except lean on the register and wait for the girls to show up again. The whole store was like a pinball machine and I didn't know which tunnel they'd come out of. After a while they come around out of the far aisle, around the light bulbs, records at dis-count of the Caribbean Six or Tony Martin Sings or some such gunk you wonder they waste the wax on, sixpacks of candy bars, and plastic toys done up in cellophane that fall apart when a kid looks at them anyway. Around they come, Queenie still leading the way and holding a little gray jar in her hand. Slots Three through Seven are unmanned and I could see her wondering between Stokes and me, but Stokesie with his usual luck draws an old party in baggy gray pants who stumbles up with four giant cans of pineapple juice (what do these bums *do* with all that pineapple juice? I've often asked myself) so the girls come to me. Queenie puts down the jar and I take it into my fingers icy cold. Kingfish Fancy Herring Snacks in Pure Sour Cream: 49¢. Now her hands are empty, not a ring or bracelet, bare as God made them, and I wonder where the money's coming from. Still with that prim look she lifts a folded dollar bill out of the hollow at the center of her nubbled pink top. The jar went heavy in my hand. Really, I thought that was so cute.

Then everybody's luck begins to run out. Lengel comes in from haggling with a truck full of cabbages on the lot and is about to scuttle into that door marked MANAGER behind which he hides all day when the girls touch his eye. Lengel's pretty dreary, teaches Sunday school and the rest, but he doesn't miss that much. He comes over and says, "Girls, this isn't the beach."

Queenie blushes, though maybe it's just a brush of sunburn I was noticing for the first time, now that she was so close. "My mother asked me to pick up a jar of herring snacks." Her voice kind of startled me, the way voices do when you see the people first, coming out so flat and dumb yet kind of tony, too, the way it ticked over "pick up" and "snacks." All of a sudden I slid right down her voice into her living room. Her father and the other men were standing around in ice-cream coats and bow ties and the women were in sandals picking up herring snacks on toothpicks off a big glass plate and they were all holding drinks the color of water with olives and sprigs of mint in them. When my parents have somebody over they get lemonade and if it's a real racy affair Schlitz in tall glasses with "They'll Do It Every Time" cartoons stencilled on.

"That's all right," Lengel said. "But this isn't the beach." His repeating this struck me as funny, as if it just occurred to him, and he had been thinking all these years the A & P was a great big dune and he was the head lifeguard. He didn't like my smiling—as I say he doesn't miss much—but he concentrates on giving the girls that sad Sunday-school-superintendent stare.

Queenie's blush is no sunburn now, and the plump one in plaid, that I liked better from the back—a really sweet can—pipes up, "We weren't doing any shopping. We just came in for the one thing."

"That makes no difference," Lengel tells her, and I could see from the way his eyes went that he hadn't noticed she was wearing a two-piece before. "We want you decently dressed when you come in here."

"We *are* decent," Queenie says suddenly, her lower lip pushing, getting sore now that she remembers her place, a place from which the crowd that runs the A & P must look pretty crummy. Fancy Herring Snacks flashed in her very blue eyes.

"Girls, I don't want to argue with you. After this come in here with your shoulders covered. It's our policy." He turns his back. That's policy for you. Policy is what the kingpins want. What the others want is juvenile delinquency.

All this while, the customers had been showing up with their carts but, you know, sheep, seeing a scene, they had all bunched up on Stokesie, who shook open a paper bag as gently as peeling a peach, not wanting to miss a word. I could feel in the silence everybody getting nervous, most of all Lengel, who asks me, "Sammy, have you rung up their purchase?"

I thought and said "No" but it wasn't about that I was thinking. I go through the punches, 4, 9, GROC, TOT—it's more complicated than you think, and after you do it often enough, it begins to make a little song, that you hear words to, in my case "Hello (*bing*) there, you (*gung*) hap-py *pee*-pul (*splat*)!"—the *splat* being the drawer flying out. I uncrease the bill, tenderly as you may imagine, it just having come from between the two smoothest scoops of vanilla I had ever known were there, and pass a half and a penny into her narrow pink palm, and nestle the herrings in a bag and twist its neck and hand it over, all the time thinking.

The girls, and who'd blame them, are in a hurry to get out, so I say "I quit" to Lengel quick enough for them to hear, hoping they'll stop and watch me, their unsuspected hero. They keep right on going, into the electric eye; the door flies open and they flicker across the lot to their car, Queenie and Plaid and Big Tall Goony-Goony (not that as raw material she was so bad), leaving me with Lengel and a kink in his eyebrow.

"Did you say something, Sammy?"

"I said I quit."

I thought you did."

"You didn't have to embarrass them."

I started to say something that came out "Fiddle-de-doo." It's a saying of my grandmother's, and I know she would have been pleased.

"I don't think you know what you're saying," Lengel said.

"I know you don't," I said. "But I do." I pull the bow at the back of my apron and start shrugging it off my shoulders. A couple customers that had been heading for my slot begin to knock against each other, like scared pigs in a chute.

Lengel sighs and begins to look very patient and old and gray. He's been a friend of my parents for years. "Sammy, you don't want to do this to your Mom and Dad," he tells me. It's true, I don't. But it seems to me that once you begin a gesture it's fatal not to go through with it. I fold the apron, "Sammy" stitched in red on the pocket, and put it on the counter, and drop the bow tie on top of it. The bow tie is theirs, if you've ever wondered. "You'll feel this for the rest of your life," Lengel says, and I know that's true, too, but remembering how he made that pretty girl blush makes me so scrunchy inside I punch the No Sale tab and the machine whirs "pee-pul" and the drawer splats out. One advantage to this scene taking place in summer, I can follow this up with a clean exit, there's no fumbling around getting your coat and galoshes, I just saunter into the electric eye in my white shirt that my mother ironed the night before, and the door heaves itself open, and outside the sunshine is skating around on the asphalt.

I look around for my girls, but they're gone, of course. There wasn't anybody but some young married screaming with her children about some candy they didn't get by the door of a powder-blue Falcon station wagon. Looking back in the big windows, over the bags of peat moss and aluminum lawn furniture stacked on the pavement, I could see Lengel in my place in the slot, checking the sheep through. His face was dark gray and his back stiff, as if he'd just had an injection of iron, and my stomach kind of fell as I felt how hard the world was going to be to me hereafter.

▶ QUESTIONS:
1. Why do you think Sammy quits his job? (Note his comment that "it seems to me that once you begin a gesture it's fatal not to go through with it" and also his remark that he knows Lengel is right when he says, "You'll feel this for the rest of your life.")

2. Sometimes a good way to get at the theme of a story is to think about what a character learns or does not learn or about how he changes or does not change during the story. Try stating the theme of this story beginning with "This is a story about a young man who" and commenting on any change or self-discovery Sammy makes.

3. Is "A & P" a good title for this story? Why?

(Compare your answers with those given in Chapter Supplement V, p. 312.)

Often when you read a story, a novel, or a poem for a class project or just for your own enjoyment, you will become so absorbed in the emotion the work generates that attention to techniques like characterization and symbolism and theme will be irrelevant for you. Certainly, if you had these matters on your mind every time you read a work of imaginative literature, you would soon kill any interest you ever had in reading. But you can spare yourself that fate by doing exactly what you did when you were learning approaches to different kinds of non-fiction: you can adapt your reading style to your reading purpose. When you are reading an emotion-arousing novel, poem, or story for your own pleasure, you may not want to or need to do any conscious analysis at all. (However, some of the analytical skills you have been learning—recognizing the significance of titles, for example—will soon become such basic parts of your reading style that you will use them without knowing it.) But when you are studying a complex imaginative work—for example, when you are preparing to write a critical review of a novel or a short story—you may need to read the work through several times, each time adding a little to your understanding by asking more questions and reading to find the answers to them. The flexible reading style you have been developing since you began this book will, then, be your method of finding understanding and enjoyment in your reading of both fiction and non-fiction.

CHAPTER SUPPLEMENTS

I. ## "THE HIGHWAYMAN"
by Alfred Noyes

PART I

The wind was a torrent of darkness among the gusty trees,
The moon was a ghostly galleon tossed upon cloudy seas,
The road was a ribbon of moonlight over the purple moor,
And the highwayman came riding—
        Riding—riding—
The highwayman came riding, up to the old inn-door.

He'd a French cocked-hat on his forehead, a bunch of lace
    at his chin,
A coat of the claret velvet, and beeches of brown doe-skin;
They fitted with never a wrinkle; his boots were up to the
    thigh!
And he rode with a jeweled twinkle,
        His pistol butts a-twinkle,
His rapier hilt a-twinkle, under the jeweled sky.

Over the cobbles he clattered and clashed in the dark
    inn-yard,
And he tapped with his whip on the shutters, but all was
    locked and barred;

He whistled a tune to the window, and who should be
    waiting there
But the landlord's black-eyed daughter,
       Bess, the landlord's daughter,
Plaiting a dark red love-knot into her long black hair.

And dark in the dark old inn yard a stable wicket creaked
Where Tim the ostler° listened; his face was white
    and peaked;
His eyes were hollows of madness, his hair like moldly hay,
But he loved the landlord's daughter,
       The landlord's red-lipped daughter,
Dumb as a dog he listened, and he heard the robber say—

"One kiss, my bonny sweetheart, I'm after a prize tonight,
But I shall be back with the yellow gold before the morning
    light;
Yet, if they press me sharply, and harry me through the day,
Then look for me by moonlight,
       Watch for me by moonlight,
I'll come to thee by moonlight, though hell should bar the
    way."

He rose upright in the stirrups; he scarce could reach her
    hand,
But she loosened her hair i' the casement! His face burned
    like a brand
As the black cascade of perfume came tumbling over his
    breast;
And he kissed its waves in the moonlight,
       (Oh, sweet black waves in the moonlight!)
Then he tugged at his rein in the moonlight, and galloped
    away to the West.

PART II

He did not come in the dawning; he did not come at noon;
And out o' the tawny sunset, before the rise o' the moon,
When the road was a gipsy's ribbon, looping the purple moor,
A red-coat troop came marching—
       Marching—marching—
King George's men came marching, up to the old inn door.

They said no word to the landlord, they drank his ale instead,
But they gagged his daughter and bound her to the foot
    of her narrow bed;
Two of them knelt at her casement, with muskets at their
    side!
There was death at every window;
       And hell at one dark window;
For Bess could see, through her casement, the road that *he*
    would ride.

They had tied her up to attention, with many a sniggering jest;
They had bound a musket beside her, with the barrel beneath
   her breast;
"Now keep good watch!" and they kissed her. She heard the
   dead man say—
Look for me by moonlight;
   Watch for me by moonlight;
I'll come to thee by moonlight, though hell should bar the
   way!

She twisted her hands behind her; but all the knots held
   good!
She writhed her hands till her fingers were wet with sweat
   or blood!
They stretched and strained in the darkness, and the hours
   crawled by like years,
Till now, on the stroke of midnight,
   Cold, on the stroke of midnight,
The tip of one finger touched it! The trigger at least was hers!

The tip of one finger touched it; she strove no more for
   the rest!
Up, she stood up to attention, with the barrel beneath
   her breast,
She would not risk their hearing: she would not strive again;
For the road lay bare in the moonlight;
   Blank and bare in the moonlight;
And the blood of her veins in the moonlight throbbed to her
   love's refrain.

Tlot-tlot; tlot-tlot! Had they heard it? The horse-hoofs ringing
   clear;
Tlot-tlot, tlot-tlot, in the distance? Were they deaf that they
   did not hear?
Down the ribbon of moonlight, over the brow of the hill,
The highwayman came riding,
   Riding, riding!
The red-coats looked to their priming! She stood up,
   straight and still!

Tlot-tlot, in the frosty silence; *Tlot-tlot,* in the echoing
   night!
Nearer he came and nearer! Her face was like a light!
Her eyes grew wide for a moment; she drew one last deep
   breath,
Then her finger moved in the moonlight,
   Her musket shattered the moonlight,
Shattered her breast in the moonlight and warned him—
   with her death.

He turned; he spurred to the Westward; he did not know
who stood
Bowed, with her head o'er the musket, drenched with her
own red blood!
Not till the dawn he heard it, his face grew gray to hear
How Bess, the landlord's daughter,
The landlord's black-eyed daughter,
Had watched for her love in the moonlight, and died in
the darkness there.

Back, he spurred like a madman, shrieking a curse to the
sky,
With the white road smoking behind him, and his rapier
brandished high!
Blood-red were his spurs in the golden noon; wine-red was
his velvet coat.
When they shot him down on the highway,
Down like a dog on the highway,
And he lay in his blood on the highway, with the bunch
of lace at his throat.

And still of a winter's night, they say, when the wind is in
the trees,
When the moon is a ghostly galleon tossed upon cloudy seas,
When the road is a ribbon of moonlight over the purple
moor,
A highwayman comes riding—
Riding—riding—
A highwayman comes riding, up to the old inn-door.

Over the cobbles he clatters and clangs in the dark inn-yard;
And he taps with his whip on the shutters, but all is locked and
barred;
He whistles a tune to the window, and who should be waiting
there
But the landlord's black-eyed daughter,
Bess, the landlord's daughter,
Plaiting a dark red love-knot into her long black hair.

II. Metaphors and Symbolic Meaning in "The Eagle"

METAPHORS DESCRIBING THE EAGLE	METAPHORS DESCRIBING HIS SURROUNDINGS
"He clasps" (You could think of this as literal language, but don't we usually use the word for the grasp of a human hand?)	"lonely lands" "ring'd with" "azure world" (probably the sea and the sky together)
"he stands"	"wrinkled sea" that "crawls"
"like a thunderbolt" (a simile)	

Symbolic meaning: The eagle is alone in his world. There are no other living things near him, there is no land for him except his isolated crag, and even the sea is so far below that it looks "wrinkled." Yet he is in full control. And when he decides to leave the position in which he is "ringed" by the sky and the sea, he "falls" the way a thunderbolt falls—straight for his mark. "Power" and "independence" are two words that could describe what the poet finds in the eagle's position and behavior, but you may have thought of others, too.

III. Main Idea in "Ultima Ratio Regum"

The poem blames a society that is based on economic greed and on warfare for this young man's death (and, by implication, for the death of many others like him). The "final reason for things" in the world the poet knows is the need of the people in power to protect that power (which money has bought them) by making sure that no one else gets it. And the only way they can do this is by waging war. The ultimate irony of the poem is that the boy who was the victim of this power struggle apparently had little interest in it; he wanted only to live a simple, happy life. In a sense, then, he is a symbol of the kind of life that is being destroyed by greedy men and nations.

IV. Symbol and Theme in "Warm River"

The "warm river" symbolizes for Richard the experience of loving. At the beginning of the story he is afraid of the river and afraid of, and confused about, his feelings toward Gretchen. But during his visit with Gretchen and her father, he is much affected by the spirit of love that pervades their household; he continually associates the warmth of the river with the warmth of these people. (Gretchen's father tells him that "all of us here love the water down there" and laughs at him for being afraid of it.) He is impressed by Gretchen's deep love for him and by her father's enduring love for his dead wife. Soon he is able to admit to himself his love for Gretchen and to express his feelings to her. Then the next thing he wants to do is to go down to the river and immerse his hands in it—that is, to be under its influence.

V. Answers to Questions about "A & P"

1. As Sammy tells his story, it becomes clear that one reason he quit his job was because he had never liked it very much anyway. He found working the cash register so boring that he made up little games to amuse himself as he worked it, he thought his boss was stuffy and conservative, and he regarded the customers as sheep. The girls in bathing suits represented everything to him that the store was not: they were a bit daring (for that time and place) in contrast with the store, which was stodgy and conventional—with everything exactly in the right place.
His defense of the girls is, then, in one sense a bid for his own freedom. But in another sense it is an act of protest against what he considers the mistreatment of three "free souls." He admires their courage and decides to match it with a courageous act of his own. Whether you think he is really courageous

or simply foolish will largely depend on your own personal values. But at least you should be able to see that he has made a decision that is important for him. He will "feel it for the rest of his life" because his family and most of the people he knows will think he has acted foolishly—and also probably because his unconventional act will lead to others like it.

2. This is a story about a young man who discovers that he has to act according to his own values and his own personality, regardless of what other people may think. (You may feel, however, that he is a bit immature; and certainly the brashness with which he tells his story leaves that interpretation open.)

3. "A & P" may not be the almost inevitable title that "The Japanese Quince" and "Warm River" are. But the establishment it stands for does represent the life-style that Sammy brashly and impetuously discards. Can you think of a better title?

copyrights
and acknowledgments

For permission to use the selections reprinted in this book, the author is grateful to the following publishers and copyright holders:

THE AMERICAN MERCURY   For "Our Enemy, the Cat" by Alan Devoe from *The American Mercury* (December 1937). Reprinted by permission of *The American Mercury*, P.O. Box 1306, Torrance, California 90505.

THE ASSOCIATED PRESS   For "After 30 Years, World War II Ends for Japanese Straggler" from *The Washington Post* (March 11, 1974). Reprinted by permission of The Associated Press.

ROBERT COULSON   For "Let's Not Get Out the Vote" by Robert Coulson from *Harper's Magazine* (November 1965).

THE CURTIS PUBLISHING COMPANY   For "The Greening of Chicago" by Carol Costella from *Holiday Magazine* (January/February 1973). Reprinted with permission from *Holiday Magazine*. © 1973 The Curtis Publishing Company.

DON AND JUDY DAVIS   For "Bicycle Tour Through Baja del Sur." Reprinted from *Westways* (January 1974). Copyright 1974 Automobile Club of Southern California.

THE FAMILY HANDYMAN   For "How to Grow Asparagus from Seeds" by John McMahan from *Natural Gardening* (February 1973). Reprinted by permission.

FARRAR, STRAUS & GIROUX, INC.   For "Clean Fun at Riverhead" from *The Kandy Kolored Tangerine Flake Streamline Baby* by Tom Wolfe. Copyright © 1963, 1964, 1965 by New York Herald Tribune, Inc. Reprinted with the permission of Farrar, Straus & Giroux, Inc.

HARCOURT BRACE JOVANOVICH, INC.   For excerpts from *Aspects of Language* by Dwight Bolinger, © 1968 by Harcourt Brace Jovanovich, Inc.; for an excerpt from *Power of Words* by Stuart Chase; for an excerpt from *Memoir of a Revolutionary* by Milovan Djilas; for excerpts from *Prisoners of Psychiatry* by Bruce Ennis and for the Introduction by Thomas S. Szasz, M.D. to *Prisoners of Psychiatry*, © 1972, by Bruce J. Ennis; for an excerpt from *Language in Thought and Action*, Third Edition, by S. I. Hayakawa; for Chapter 1 from *Psychology: An Introduction* by Jerome Kagan and Ernest Havemann, © 1968, 1972 by Harcourt Brace Jovanovich; for excerpts from *On Aggression* by Konrad Lorenz; for an excerpt from Introduction to *The Consumer and Corporate Accountability*, edited by Ralph Nader, © 1973 by Harcourt Brace Jovanovich; for Chapter 17 from *The Autobiography of Lincoln Steffens*, copyright, 1931, by Harcourt Brace Jovanovich, Inc.; copyright, 1959, by Peter Steffens; for excerpts from *The Chickenbone Special*, copyright © 1970, 1971, by Dwayne E. Walls; and for the Introduction by Robert Coles to *The Chickenbone Special*, © 1971, by Dwayne E. Walls. All reprinted by permission of Harcourt Brace Jovanovich, Inc.

HARPER & ROW, PUBLISHERS, INC. For an excerpt from *Now, Barabbas* by William Jovanovich; and For "Open Letter to the Collector of Internal Revenue" (pp. 85-88) from *The Second Tree from the Corner* by E. B. White. Copyright 1951 by E. B. White. Originally appeared in *The New Yorker*. By permission of Harper & Row, Publishers, Inc.

HARVARD UNIVERSITY PRESS   For "A Narrow Fellow in the Grass" (#986) by Emily Dickinson. Reprinted by permission of the publishers and the Trustees of Amherst College from Thomas H. Johnson, Editor, *The Poems of Emily Dickinson*, Cambridge, Mass.: The Belknap Press of Harvard University Press, Copyright 1951, 1955, by The President and Fellows of Harvard College.

ARTHUR HOPPE   For "Teacher Smeecher" by Arthur Hoppe from *San Francisco Chronicle* (November 27, 1966). Copyright 1966 Chronicle Publishing Company. Reprinted by permission of the author.

HOUGHTON MIFFLIN COMPANY   For an excerpt from *Silent Spring* by Rachel Carson; and for "Nation and Race" from *Mein Kampf* by Adolf Hitler, translated by Ralph Manheim. Copyright 1943 and 1971 by Houghton Mifflin Company. Reprinted by permission of the publisher.

JOHNSON PUBLISHING COMPANY, INC.   For "The Dilemma of the Black Policeman" by Alex Poinsett from *Ebony* (May 1971). Reprinted by permission of *Ebony* Magazine, copyright, 1971 by Johnson Publishing Company, Inc.

ALFRED A. KNOPF, INC. For "A & P" by John Updike. Copyright © 1962 by John Updike. Reprinted from *Pigeon Feathers and Other Stories*, by John Updike, by permission of Alfred A. Knopf, Inc. Originally appeared in *The New Yorker*.

J. B. LIPPINCOTT COMPANY   From *Collected Poems* (In One Volume) by Alfred Noyes. Copyright 1906, renewed 1934 by Alfred Noyes. Reprinted by permission of J. B. Lippincott Company.

THE STERLING LORD AGENCY   For "The Language of Soul" by Claude Brown. Copyright © 1968 by Claude Brown. Reprinted by permission of The Sterling Lord Agency, Inc. First appeared in *Esquire*.

McGRAW-HILL BOOK COMPANY   For an excerpt from *Soul on Ice* by Eldridge Cleaver. Copyright © 1968 by Eldridge Cleaver. Used with permission of McGraw-Hill Book Company.

McINTOSH AND OTIS, INC.   For "Warm River" by Erskine Caldwell from *The Complete Stories of Erskine Caldwell*. Copyright © 1932 by Richard Johns. Copyright renewed by Erskine Caldwell. Reprinted by permission of the author and McIntosh and Otis, Inc.

JIM MURRAY   For "In a Huff Over Puff" by Jim Murray from *Los Angeles Times* (April 4, 1974).

NATURAL HISTORY   For "Plants Have a Few Tricks, Too" by Arthur W. Galston from *Natural History* Magazine (December 1972). Copyright © The American Museum of Natural History, 1972; and for "Folk Art in the Barrios" by Eric Kroll from *Natural History* Magazine (May 1973). Copyright © The American Museum of Natural History, 1973. Both reprinted with permission from *Natural History* Magazine.

THE NEW REPUBLIC   For "The Tyranny of Democratic Manners" by Morton J. Cronin from *The New Republic* (January 20, 1958). Reprinted by permission of *The New Republic*, © 1958 Harrison-Blaine of New Jersey, Inc.

PITMAN PUBLISHING CORPORATION   For an excerpt from the book, *How Children Learn* by John Holt. Copyright © 1967, 1969 Pitman Publishing Corporation. Reprinted by permission of Pitman Publishing Corporation.

PRENTICE-HALL, INC.   For an excerpt from the book, *Unfit for Human Consumption* by Ruth Mulvey Harmer. © 1971 by Ruth Mulvey Harmer. Published by Prentice-Hall, Inc., Englewood Cliffs, New Jersey.

G. P. PUTNAM'S SONS   For "Fresh Air Will Kill You" from *Have I Ever Lied to You?* by Art Buchwald. Copyright © 1966, 1967, 1968 by Art Buchwald. Reprinted by permission of G. P. Putnam's Sons.

RAMPARTS   For "Nobody Knows My Name" by Gene Marine, with Robert Avakian and Peter Collier, from *Ramparts* (June 1967). Copyright Ramparts Magazine, Inc. 1967. Reprinted by permission.

RANDOM HOUSE, INC.   For "Ultima Ratio Regum" by Stephen Spender. Copyright 1942 and renewed 1970 by Stephen Spender. Reprinted from *Selected Poems*, by Stephen Spender, by permission of Random House, Inc.

READER'S DIGEST   For "Should Chiropractors Be Paid with Your Tax Dollars?" by Albert Q. Maisel. Reprinted with permission from the July 1971 *Reader's Digest*. Copyright 1971 by The Reader's Digest Assn., Inc.; and for "The Nibbling Away of the West" by James Nathan Miller. Reprinted with permission from the December 1972 *Reader's Digest*. Copyright 1972 by The Reader's Digest Assn., Inc.

SCIENCE DIGEST   For "Charting for Space Travel." Reprinted with permission of *Science Digest*. © The Hearst Corp.; September, 1973. All Rights Reserved.

CHARLES SCRIBNER'S SONS   For "The Japanese Quince" from *Caravan* by John Galsworthy. Copyright 1925 Charles Scribner's Sons; and for excerpts from *The Year of the Whale* by Victor B. Scheffer. Copyright © 1969 Victor B. Scheffer. Both reprinted by permission of Charles Scribner's Sons.

SIMON & SCHUSTER, INC.   For excerpts from *The American Way of Death* by Jessica Mitford. Copyright © 1963, by Jessica Mitford. Reprinted by permission of Simon & Schuster; and for "The Pool" by Allen Planz from *Ecotactics: The Sierra Club Handbook for Environment Activists*. Copyright © 1970, by The Sierra Club. Reprinted by permission of Pocket Books, a division of Simon & Schuster, Inc.

TIME INC.   For "The Dying Girl That No One Helped" by Loudon Wainwright from *Life Magazine* (April 10, 1964). Copyright © 1964 Time Inc. Reprinted with permission.

THE UNIVERSITY OF NORTH CAROLINA PRESS   For "I Discover My Father" by Sherwood Anderson from *Memoirs of Sherwood Anderson*, edited by Ray Lewis White.

THE VIKING PRESS, INC.   For an excerpt from *Rockets, Missiles, and Men in Space* by Willy Ley. Copyright © 1968 by Willy Ley. All rights reserved. Reprinted by permission of The Viking Press, Inc.

WESTWAYS   For "Bicycle Tour Through Baja del Sur" by Don and Judy Davis. Reprinted from *Westways* (January 1974). Copyright 1974 Automobile Club of Southern California; and for "The Marketplace of the Unnecessary" by Jack Smith. Reprinted from *Westways* (October 1972). Copyright 1972 Automobile Club of Southern California.

WOMEN: A JOURNAL OF LIBERATION   For "Free Them All: POWs and Other Criminals" by Howard Zinn. Copyright 1972 by *Women: A Journal of Liberation*, 3028 Greenmount Ave., Baltimore, Md. 21218.